The Knopf Collectors' Guides to American Antiques

Robert Bishop & William C. Ketchum, Jr.
Series Consultants

A Chanticleer Press Edition

Pottery
&
Porcelain

William C. Ketchum, Jr.

With photographs by Schecter Me Sun Lee

Alfred A. Knopf, New York

This is a Borzoi Book
Published by Alfred A. Knopf, Inc.

All rights reserved. Copyright 1983 under the International
Union for the protection of literary and artistic works (Berne).
Published in the United States by Alfred A. Knopf, Inc., New
York, and simultaneously in Canada by Random House of
Canada Limited, Toronto. Distributed by Random House, Inc.,
New York.

Prepared and produced by
Chanticleer Press, Inc., New York.

Color reproductions by Nievergelt Repro AG, Zurich,
Switzerland. Type set in Century Expanded by Dix Type Inc.,
Syracuse, New York. Printed and bound by Dai Nippon Printing
Co., Ltd., Tokyo, Japan.

First Printing

Library of Congress Catalog Number: 82-48946
ISBN: 0-394-71494-6

Contents

Acknowledgments

Many people have helped to make this book possible. Special thanks are due to all the individuals and institutions who made their collections available to us, particularly Fran and Doug Faulkner for their stoneware and spongeware, Osna Fenner for her modern pottery, and Robert and Marie Condon, whose extensive Rockingham collection proved invaluable. I am also grateful to Samuel Herrup, George Hamell, and George E. Schoellkopf, who allowed us to photograph their redware. Glenda Galt patiently arranged for photography of ceramics from the Brooklyn Museum. Schecter Me Sun Lee, assisted by John P. Bellacosa, spent months photographing almost all of the objects in this book. Robert Bishop's encouragement was invaluable; he also read the manuscript and made many helpful suggestions. Marvin D. Schwartz carefully reviewed the manuscript and price guide. Amelia Weiss and Robert Braine copy-edited the text. I am especially grateful to Paul Steiner and the staff at Chanticleer Press: Gudrun Buettner and Susan Costello, who developed the idea for this series; Mary Beth Brewer, who, with the help of Cathy Peck, edited and coordinated the project; Carol Nehring, who supervised the art and layouts; and Helga Lose, who directed the production of the book. Finally, I want to thank Charles Elliott, Senior Editor at Alfred A. Knopf, for his encouragement and support.

About the Author, Photographer, and Consultant

William C. Ketchum, Jr.
A member of the faculty of The New School for Social Research, author William C. Ketchum, Jr., is also a guest curator at the Museum of American Folk Art in New York City and a consultant to several major auction houses. Dr. Ketchum has written 18 books, including *Early Potters and Potteries of New York State*, *The Pottery and Porcelain Collector's Handbook*, and, most recently, *Chests, Cupboards, Desks & Other Pieces* for the Knopf Collectors' Guides to American Antiques. He is an associate editor at *Antique Monthly*.

Schecter Me Sun Lee
Schecter Lee is a New York-based freelance photographer whose works have been published in national and international magazines. Among his most recent books are *American Folk Dolls*, published by Alfred A. Knopf, as well as *Dolls* and *Folk Art: Paintings, Sculpture & Country Objects*, two new volumes in the Knopf Collectors' Guides to American Antiques. Mr. Lee is currently preparing an exhibition and a book of photographs based on his recent travels in the Soviet Union.

Robert Bishop
Director of the Museum of American Folk Art in New York City, consultant Robert Bishop is author of more than 30 books, among them *American Decorative Arts, 1620–1980* and *The Knopf Collectors' Guide to Quilts, Coverlets, Rugs & Samplers*. He established the first master's degree program in folk art studies at New York University. Dr. Bishop is on the editorial boards of *Art & Antiques*, *Horizon Magazine*, and *Antique Monthly*.

Preface

For thousands of years, pottery has been produced in this country, first by Native Americans, and then later by European settlers. American craftsmen have produced wares that appeal to every taste and budget. Small wonder, then, that pottery and porcelain have been avidly collected for well over a century. Some collectors specialize in certain forms, such as bottles or jugs; others collect pieces made from a single material, such as red earthenware. Still other people focus on a type of decoration, or on products manufactured by a specific company or from a certain area.

Pottery and porcelain are rapidly becoming 2 of the most popular collecting fields. However, interest has not always been so great; it was only in the late 19th century that American ceramics began to attract the attention of collectors. The first enthusiasts sought out porcelain, which, because of the difficulties and expense involved in its manufacture, had always been produced in relatively small quantities. By the end of the 19th century, people began to collect the handsome sgraffito-decorated redware made in Pennsylvania and the sophisticated art pottery being produced in small studio workshops. Interest soon spread to yellowware adorned with the distinctive mottled Rockingham glaze or a flint-enamel finish. Although these types of ceramics are still much in demand, today's collector is just as likely to specialize in utilitarian stoneware or even in ceramics that were mass-produced within the past 50 years.

This book covers every type of American pottery and porcelain, from early hand-thrown redware and stoneware to factory-made examples from the 1960s. The pieces illustrated include such common forms as mugs and dinner plates, as well as unusual ones, such as foot warmers and funnels. To help collectors recognize and identify the objects they find, we have organized this guide by shape and function rather than by chronology, method of manufacture, or decorative style. Each illustrated entry describes a representative object and tells where and when it was made. Further, it provides historical background along with practical hints on what to look for and what to avoid. To help you determine what you can expect to pay, the price guide lists current price ranges for the types of ceramics illustrated. Many of the pieces are no more expensive than quality ceramics being produced today, and some are substantially less, indicating that collecting pottery and porcelain can be within everyone's means. Using this guide, anyone can build a distinctive collection of fine American ceramics.

A Simple Way to Identify Pottery and Porcelain

From the time of the first settlers, Americans have enjoyed the useful and beautiful products of the nation's skilled potters. The simplest of their wares are rugged and utilitarian, usually thrown by hand on a wheel; the most elaborate are painstakingly hand-decorated showpieces, meant to display the sophisticated skills of the craftsman.

This guide presents the full range of American ceramics, including the most common, inexpensive pieces available, as well as some rare, costly examples that are important for an understanding of the development of the American pottery and porcelain industry. To help you identify, date, and assess the value of the pieces you encounter, we have chosen 367 representative objects for full picture-and-text coverage. The color plates and accompanying text are organized visually, according to shape, so that beginners can find a piece quickly, without any previous knowledge of the field. Experienced collectors who may want to refer directly to a specific type can turn to the index.

The introductory essays on the history of the American ceramics industry and on how pottery and porcelain are made provide background information that will help you assess the pottery and porcelain that you encounter. For collectors who specialize in a particular type of decoration, the appendixes include a list of plates organized by decoration. The table of pottery and porcelain manufacturers offers a quick reference to many American manufacturers, their dates of operation, location, and the types of wares they made. The discussion of pottery marks makes it easier to recognize and research those you find, and the glossary defines specialized terms. Finally, the up-to-date price guide lists the current price ranges for all of the pottery and porcelain illustrated in this book; for the convenience of collectors who specialize in particular types of ceramics, the price guide is organized by material; for example, all redware objects are grouped together.

Using all these tools—photographs, descriptions, essays, illustrations, and tables—both the beginner and the connoisseur will find that this book makes collecting pottery and porcelain more enjoyable and rewarding.

History of the American Ceramics Industry

When the first settlers arrived in the New World, they found a land rich in clay. In the 1630s, an English potter, Philip Drinker, had begun work at Charlestown, Massachusetts, and by 1655, a Dutchman, Dirck Claesen, had established a shop in Manhattan. Throughout the 18th century the industry grew, and it has been estimated that by 1800 more than 300 potters had worked in New England alone. Most worked by themselves or with 1 or 2 assistants, producing a variety of useful wares such as bowls, plates, and mugs. Almost none of their pottery has survived.

English Competition

Initially, the most successful potters were probably those who worked with red earthenware, for the clay was readily available throughout most of the country and the wares made from it were in great demand. Other potters suffered from England's colonial policy, which favored the export of finished goods to the colonies and the import of raw materials from the new land. Periodically, British manufacturers "dumped" large quantities of high-quality ceramics on the American market, offering them at prices local craftsmen could not profitably match. American porcelain and white earthenware manufacturers could never succeed under these conditions, and it was not until long after the Revolutionary War that these industries became firmly established in America. To a lesser extent, makers of stoneware and yellowware were similarly affected by British imports.

The Redware Potters

The earliest redware potteries were established in New England, Pennsylvania, and along the mid-Atlantic coast. The shops were small, typically run by 1 or 2 men who threw their wares by hand on a wheel. Often they operated only periodically, serving little more than their immediate vicinity. As the frontier moved west, these shops proliferated, spreading wherever pioneers settled. Often people were totally dependent on the locally produced redware until improved transportation allowed more sophisticated ceramics to be carried inland.

Since redware is fragile and often somewhat crude, most people preferred the sturdier stoneware or white or yellow earthenware. By 1850 redware potteries had mostly disappeared from settled areas; those that remained usually confined themselves to producing flowerpots and drain tiles. In some relatively isolated areas, however, such as portions of the South and the West, redware remained in demand until the late 1800s. Most redware vessels were utilitarian—crocks, jugs, jars, plates, platters, and mugs—and were intended for everyday use. Yet some potters embellished their wares, and today these decorated pieces are among the most highly esteemed of American pottery. The most elaborately decorated redware was produced in Pennsylvania, Virginia, North Carolina, and New England. In Pennsylvania, German settlers applied complex sgraffito- and slip-decorated designs to their wares. Potters from Virginia excelled in sculptural forms, and those from New England in slip decoration. North Carolina potters were also skilled in slip decoration. In addition, they cast small pieces in molds, a technique that was very rarely used by redware workers.

Stoneware Potteries

The stoneware industry developed more slowly than redware manufacture, and it was never as widespread. Unlike redware, stoneware requires large and somewhat sophisticated kilns; further, the clays necessary for its production are not widely distributed throughout America. None, for example, are found in New England. Yet because of its strength, stoneware gradually became preferred to redware, and as transportation improved, the industry began to flourish.

As early as 1735 the Crolius and Remmey families were operating stoneware kilns in Manhattan, and in 1743 Grace Parker established a similar shop in Boston. Although the New York operations were successful, Parker soon failed, the victim of the same problem that plagued many early stoneware potteries located far from clay sources: the expense of transporting the heavy clay to Boston and the finished wares to marketplaces. Other early stoneware shops were established in Pennsylvania and quite possibly in North Carolina.

Until the 1830s, stoneware potteries were largely confined to coastal areas. When canal systems were built across the Northeast, the area was opened to potters who could obtain raw materials and ship their wares by flatboat. At about the same time, stoneware clay was found near East Liverpool, Ohio, and by the 1850s, Ohio had become a major pottery center. Later in the century, stoneware kilns were established in Missouri, Arkansas, Texas, and even in California.

Like redware, most stoneware was thrown by hand on a potter's wheel. It was usually given a simple salt glaze, although brown and white glazes were also employed. Salt-glazed pieces were often decorated with cobalt-blue slip, which might be painted or trailed onto the object before firing. Simple floral motifs were common at first, but by around 1850 elaborate scenes sometimes adorned these utilitarian pieces. By the 1880s other potteries began to decorate some stoneware vessels with spongework inspired by English examples.

As modern molding methods were introduced in the large midwestern factories, manufacturing stoneware by hand became less profitable. By 1900, most of the large northeastern stoneware potteries had gone out of business. Yet in parts of the South and Southwest, potters continued to work in the traditional way until the 1920s.

Yellowware and Rockinghamware

The fine clays from which yellowware is made are found primarily in New Jersey and Ohio, and it is in those areas that the craft flourished. Among the earliest shops were those of John Hancock, established at South Amboy, New Jersey, around 1828, and John and David Henderson, whose Jersey City Pottery opened a year later. In 1838 the Bennett family established a pottery at East Liverpool, Ohio. These fledgling industries were afflicted with high costs, technical problems, and competition from high-quality English imports and it was not until after 1850 that American yellowware factories became truly successful.

In New England, the most successful manufacturer was the United States Pottery Company in Bennington, Vermont; in Baltimore, the factory that Edwin Bennett established in 1846 was soon profitable. By 1859 there were 10 such firms in East Liverpool, Ohio, alone; in Trenton and other cities in New Jersey, yellowware potteries also flourished.

Although some of the earliest pieces of yellowware were wheel-thrown, most examples were cast in molds. Products were primarily utilitarian—bowls, rolling pins, pitchers, molds, pie plates, teapots, and coffeepots. The pieces were typically covered with a clear glaze; in the late 19th century, many pieces were decorated with bands of colored slip.

In the mid-19th century, Rockingham-glazed yellowware was also produced by most of the major factories. With its distinctive, mottled brown finish, Rockinghamware remained popular well into the 1870s. The finest examples came from Bennington, Vermont; Baltimore, Maryland; and several factories in the area of East Liverpool, Ohio. Plain yellowware was made well into the 1930s.

White Earthenware

During most of the 19th century white earthenware manufacturers in America faced stiff competition from European companies, especially those in England. Although a high-quality white earthenware body had been developed at Jersey City's American Pottery Company in the 1840s, the whiteware industry did not compete successfully with European firms until the 1880s, when tariffs were placed on imported ceramics. Since the clay needed for white earthenware is found primarily in New Jersey and Ohio, it was in those states that most factories were built.

Like yellowware, white earthenware was customarily produced in molds. Tableware was the most common product. Many large companies produced full sets that included plates, bowls, cups and saucers, and various serving pieces. By the late 19th century, some firms were manufacturing a dozen or more patterns in quantity. Much of it had a plain clear glaze, although transfer printing, hand painting, and embossed designs were also popular. In the mid-19th century, some companies began to decorate their wares with spongework as well.

Ironstone, a type of white earthenware, proved especially suitable for everyday use, since it was both durable and attractive. From 1870 until the 1920s, factories in New York, New Jersey, Ohio, and Maryland manufactured vast quantities of this tableware. Much of it resembles that produced in England. American establishments not only imitated English shapes and patterns, some of them also modeled their marks on those of English companies, hoping their products would be mistaken for the more fashionable imports.

In the 20th century, the production of ironstone continued to expand. Some manufacturers relied on traditional 19th-century models; others were inspired by the Art Deco style and other contemporary design movements.

Porcelain Production

Because porcelain is difficult and expensive to produce, early attempts to manufacture it in America were usually unsuccessful. In addition to the cost and technical problems involved, the market for porcelain was relatively small, and most customers preferred stylish imported pieces to the domestic wares. As early as 1739 Andrew Duché of Savannah, Georgia, had produced true porcelain, and in 1769 Gousse Bonnin and George Morris opened a porcelain factory in Philadelphia. The Bonnin & Morris firm failed a few years later, and it was not until 1826 that a porcelain company proved reasonably successful. In that year, William Tucker, along with several partners, established a firm that remained in operation until 1838. By the 1840s and 1850s, New York had 2 successful porcelain firms: William Boch & Brothers and Charles Cartlidge.

Boch's company eventually became the highly profitable Union

Porcelain Works, which operated into the 20th century.

By 1890, the American porcelain industry had come of age. Factories sprang up'in New York and New Jersey west to Ohio. Parian, a type of unglazed porcelain that resembles marble and that was often used for statuary and vases, was made at Bennington, Vermont, as well as at factories in New York, New Jersey, and Ohio. High-quality porcelain tableware was produced in Syracuse, New York, and fine Belleek china was made by both Ott & Brewer in Trenton, New Jersey, and by Knowles, Taylor & Knowles in East Liverpool, Ohio.

Art Pottery

The art pottery movement began in America in around 1880. In part reacting to the shoddily produced factory wares that had become common, some potters both in America and abroad began to insist on quality in manufacture and on carefully conceived hand-decoration. In their goals, the art potters were allied with the English Arts and Crafts movement. The American interpretation of art pottery is distinctive and original.

Much of the impetus for the art pottery movement can be traced to the Philadelphia Centennial Exposition of 1876. There potters were exposed to exotic Oriental forms as well as sophisticated French porcelain that relied for its effect on elaborate underglaze decoration. Among the most important of the early American companies that fostered the new movement was the Rookwood Pottery, founded in 1880 by Maria Longworth Nichols in Cincinnati. Nichols had been strongly influenced by the French examples she had seen in Philadelphia, and used similar underglaze techniques to decorate the wares her firm turned out. Other important companies that grew from small workshops include the Grueby Pottery and the Chelsea Keramic Art Works, both in Massachusetts. By 1900 the groundwork had been laid for such major industrial art potteries as Weller and Roseville in Ohio. Where the earlier firms had concentrated on one-of-a-kind, hand-decorated pieces that were usually wheel-thrown, the larger factories relied on molds. One of the principal proponents of mold-cast pottery was Artus Van Briggle, who with his wife Anna, founded the Van Briggle Pottery in Colorado in 1901. Van Briggle saw molds as a way of producing enough high-quality pottery to make the industry financially successful. Although some small studio potteries continued well into the 1930s, by then most art pottery was factory produced.

Dating Pottery by Shape

Unmarked pottery is usually difficult to date. However, certain kinds of pieces can be given approximate dates on the basis of shape.

Jugs

Before 1800 redware and stoneware jugs were elongated and ovoid, but they became squatter and almost ball-shaped by 1820. For the rest of the century, stoneware jugs continued to evolve in shape. A straight-sided form with a sloping shoulder became common around 1850, and by 1890 jugs were distinctly cylindrical with a square, ridgelike shoulder.

Bottles

Early 19th-century redware and stoneware bottles were graceful and ovoid, with a long neck and tapering shoulder. By 1840 this shape had been superseded by a cylindrical form with a straight or slightly curving shoulder and a thick, shaped rim. Stoneware examples in both shapes are much more common than redware examples, no doubt because of redware's fragility.

Crocks

Stoneware and redware crocks made in the late 18th and early 19th centuries were ovoid with a high waist and often had 2 handles protruding from the shoulder. After 1820 they became more cylindrical, and by 1850 they were made with straight sides and with handles tucked tightly against the body. This became the standard form for stoneware crocks for more than 50 years.

How Pottery and Porcelain Are Made

Fashioning a crude earthenware toy by hand is a simple process requiring only a few tools that almost anyone can follow, but making an elaborate porcelain vase is complex and can be accomplished only by skilled craftsmen using costly and sophisticated equipment. Although each ceramic medium must be handled differently, all are fundamentally similar. No matter what type of clay is used, it must first be mined and processed, then shaped, decorated, and fired at least once. The following section explains many of the common techniques used in earthenware and stoneware production and discusses those that are specific to each ceramic type.

Mining and Processing Clay

Traditional potters search for local deposits of clay by exploring stream banks, road cuts, or other areas where the deep beds have been exposed. After digging the clay out, they first break it into chunks and remove pebbles, twigs, and other debris. Then they add water to the clay and place it in a device known as a pug mill; inside the mill, heavy wooden paddles or sharp knives rotate on a shaft. As the paddles or knives move, they chop and grind the clay into a solid mass of uniform consistency. The clean, wet clay is shaped in blocks, which are covered with a wet cloth until they are ready to be used.

When the potter is ready to begin working with the clay, he slices off a portion from the block and then kneads it to remove tiny air pockets, which can cause the finished product to crack and break when it is fired.

Shaping the Clay

The most basic method used by potters is hand shaping, or modeling. Clay is pinched into shape, or formed into slabs that are then joined. Sometimes ropes of clay are coiled on top of one another and then worked into shape. Although modeling is an age-old pottery process that is still used today, most of the pieces shown in this book were produced by means of the potter's wheel or molds.

The Potter's Wheel

In its simplest form, a pottery wheel consists of 2 horizontally placed disks that are joined by a vertical shaft. Although wheels are now often powered electrically, traditionally they are driven by the potter. No matter how a wheel is powered, the potter controls the speed at which it turns. The lower shaft is attached to a treadle that, when pushed, causes the disks to rotate. The potter centers a kneaded lump of clay on the upper disk and, aided by centrifugal force as the disk spins, he shapes the clay by hand. Often the potter uses tools as he works the clay into shape; these can smooth the surface, erasing the marks made by the fingers, or they can straighten out the sides or smooth the rim. After the piece is completed, the potter cuts it from the wheel, often using a piece of wire or string.

Before removing the vessel from the wheel, the potter often decorates the soft clay. A variety of tools may be used. In one technique, a pointed tool is pressed against the soft clay to produce straight or curving lines or to incise pictorial motifs. In another, a coggle wheel—a small wooden or metal disk with a shaped edge—is rolled over the body to create patterns. Some potters use small punches that leave shaped impressions on the surface. Small molded or hand-shaped decorative elements such as flowers, leaves, and stars are sometimes attached to the surface, a technique known as sprigging. Other potters cut away portions of a piece in decorative patterns to create pierced designs similar to those found on early silver. Details such as pouring spouts may be shaped by hand, often by pulling a portion of the rim outward.

Handles and long tubular spouts are usually separately shaped and then attached to the completed object. To form handles, small balls of clay might be rolled out, then pressed into shape. In another method, coils or ropes of clay are moistened, then pulled by hand to create the desired shape. Other potters force a lump of clay through a shaped piece of wood; these extruded handles show characteristic ridged surfaces. Separately shaped elements are then attached to the damp object with slip.

Molds

Pieces like plates and platters are often shaped by means of a process called drape molding. Balls of clay are rolled flat, then cut into the desired shape and draped over wooden, clay, or plaster molds. After the clay slab has assumed the shape of the mold and has hardened, the outside is smoothed with a sponge, and the plate or platter is removed and set aside to dry. This method is especially useful in the production of large or unusually shaped pieces that could be difficult, if not impossible, to fashion on a potter's wheel.

In a similar process, a slab of clay is pressed into, rather than draped over, a mold composed of one or more pieces. Sometimes the mold itself is covered with elaborate decoration that becomes impressed into the soft clay. After the clay has hardened, the piece is removed from the mold.

In slip casting, liquid clay is poured into a plaster mold, which is often made of 2 or more pieces. As the water is absorbed by the plaster, a thin layer of clay adheres to the sides of the mold. The potter then pours the surplus slip out of the mold. After the remaining clay has stiffened, the mold is opened and the piece is removed.

As in wheel-thrown pottery, elements such as spouts and handles are usually cast separately and then applied.

Glazing

After the potter removes the wares from the wheel or mold, they are allowed to dry to a leatherlike state before they are fired or glazed. In one method of producing glaze, sand and powdered clay and water, and occasionally a coloring agent, are ground to a uniform consistency in a glaze mill, or potter's quern. A quern consists of 2 heavy stones; the upper stone is smaller and fits within the lower one. As the upper stone is turned, the materials are ground against the lower stone; the ground glazing mixture passes out of a hole in the base of the mill. The glaze is then mixed with water and clay and applied to the pottery by dipping the vessels into it, by pouring it into their interior, or by painting it on with a brush. The bottoms and sometimes the rims are left unglazed since the ware is usually stacked when it is fired; separate pieces can be bonded together if the parts that touch are glazed.

Firing the Clay

Baking or firing is a critical step in pottery production, during which all water is removed from the clay. Early 19th-century potters used what are today called groundhog kilns, which are shaped like a loaf of bread with an arched roof; there is a door at one end and a chimney at the other. The potter stacks his unfired wares in the kiln and places piles of wood about them, then ignites the wood. In a groundhog kiln, temperatures are difficult to control and the wares often fire unevenly. As early as the 18th century, some American potters employed more sophisticated kilns that were built on 2 levels. The lower level contained the burning fire, and the upper one held the ware. Today many types of kilns are used, including some that are heated by gas and electricity.

Using woodburning kilns, firing is a tedious and delicate process. It takes at least 30 to 40 hours to bake a kiln full of ware, and a week or more to cool the pottery before it can be removed. Different types of clay require different firing temperatures, and controlling the temperature is crucial. If the fire becomes too hot, the ware may melt to slag; if it does not become hot enough, the ware will not harden sufficiently. Excavations of 19th-century kilns have revealed large "waster" dumps filled with ware that was damaged in firing.

Redware Manufacture

Redware pottery is made from a number of clays found almost worldwide and throughout most of North America; although they vary in color from tan to red or even black all fire to a shade of red. Simple country redware is usually wheel-thrown then fired at a relatively low temperature.

Glazing and Decoration

Redware pieces that are meant to store liquids must be glazed to make them impervious to fluids, either on the interior or on both the interior and the exterior. One glaze often used on redware is lead based; it fires to a clear glasslike skin that is not only waterproof, but also much more attractive than the rough unglazed surface. While most 18th- and 19th-century redware was glazed with a clear lead slip, the finish could be varied by the addition of any of several metallic oxides, such as manganese, which fires dark brown or black, or copper, which fires green.

In Pennsylvania, potters enlivened their redware with sgraffito decoration, especially their pie plates and platters. The surface was covered with an opaque slip, which was usually cream-colored, and the potter would then scratch designs through the slip, disclosing the red clay body. Often the sgraffito design was enhanced by slip decoration executed in 1 or more colors. The potter poured slip into a small cup with 1 or more openings that were customarily fitted with hollow turkey quills. Moving the cup over the surface of the plate or platter, he regulated the flow of the slip by covering or uncovering the quills with his fingers. Occasionally slip was painted onto redware; this technique was more often used on stoneware.

Stoneware Techniques

Because redware is fragile, other wares, especially stoneware, quickly became preferred during the 19th century. Stoneware clays are found in parts of New Jersey, New York, and Pennsylvania along the mid-Atlantic coast, in Ohio and Texas, and elsewhere throughout North America; none are present in New England. In their natural state these clays vary from blue to white in hue; they fire to a tan or light gray color. Baked at an extremely high temperature, stoneware becomes nonporous and *18* vitreous, and as hard, though not as strong, as steel.

Shaping and Glazing

Until the late 19th century, most stoneware was wheel-thrown. By the 1880s large factories, particularly in Ohio, introduced sophisticated mechanical molding machines that could produce crocks and jugs in a fraction of the time it took a potter to form them.

Stoneware was baked in large, room-size kilns that became larger and more complex as the 19th century advanced. At first fired with vast quantities of wood, by the end of the 1800s those that were more efficient were fueled by natural gas, making it much easier to regulate temperature. In the South, many small groundhog kilns remained in use after 1900.

Although stoneware fires to a waterproof state and technically does not need to be glazed, it almost always was. The earliest and most common finish was salt glazing. Quantities of salt were thrown into the kiln when the heat was most intense; the salt vaporized and combined with the outer layer of the pottery to form a clear, vitreous finish that was characteristically pebbled, resembling an orange peel. Interiors were sometimes glazed with slip, since the salt vapor could not reach the interiors of stacked ware, especially pieces with small mouths like jugs. By the 1820s, glaze made from a rich brown clay found near Albany, New York, and known as Albany slip, was often used on the interior of stoneware vessels. By the mid-19th century, it was commonly used as an exterior glaze as well. Late in the 19th century an opaque white slip was also employed on stoneware, especially factory-molded pieces made in the Midwest and Southwest. Occasionally it was combined with Albany slip to produce the familiar brown-and-white pottery that is still made today. In the South, a distinctive glaze was produced by mixing wood ash with water to generate lye; the lye was combined with sand or powdered clay and then heavily applied, firing to a streaky brown glaze that was often locally referred to as a "tobacco spit" finish.

Decoration

Like redware, some stoneware made before 1830 had incised decoration; most often the designs were crude arrangements of leaves and flowers. More complex examples include birds, ships, and in rare cases, human figures or entire scenes. Other early pieces bear impressed decoration.

Decoration on stoneware was often executed with cobalt-blue slip. Sometimes used to highlight incised or impressed designs, more often it was painted or trailed onto a stoneware surface. Early American stoneware often bears touches of blue at the handles or a slash of it across the impressed potter's mark. In the 18th century, freehand spiral and floral designs appeared. In the early 1800s, decoration became more complex; flowers and leaves were depicted, as well as birds, and occasionally ships or portraits. By 1850 the designs had become fluid and calligraphic, and in the second half of the 19th century elaborate decoration was common. It might consist of bunches of flowers, birds, and other animals, including some exotic ones like elephants, human figures, buildings, and even entire village scenes. By 1900 decoration was usually simply stenciled onto stoneware.

Some stoneware was decorated in other ways. Certain Pennsylvania and Ohio potters used applied decoration similar to that found on redware. Some stoneware glazed with Albany slip was embellished in the sgrafitto manner by scratching through the dark brown glaze to the lighter stoneware body.

Yellowware Production

Yellowware is made from a variety of fine clays that fire to a
light to dark yellow. The clays are found primarily in New Jersey
and parts of the Midwest, particularly Ohio. Although
yellowware was manufactured in England during the 18th
century, it was not introduced in America until the late 1820s,
when its production began at South Amboy, New Jersey. Other
factories were established in the 1840s in East Liverpool, Ohio;
Baltimore, Maryland; and Bennington, Vermont. During the
second half of the 19th century, yellowware became increasingly
popular, and great quantities were still being made well after
1900.

Shaping the Clay

In a process commonly used in factory production of many types
of pottery, the raw clay was first mixed to a creamy consistency
in a steam- or water-powered churn called a blunger. Then
sifters known as bolters removed all foreign bodies, and a power-
driven wedging machine shaped the clay into blocks of
approximately the sizes of the pieces to be shaped. Although
sometimes wheel-thrown, much more frequently yellowware was
mold-cast, either in stamping presses or by slip casting. Many
molds were elaborately shaped and decorated, resulting in pieces
with highly embossed surfaces.

Glazing and Firing

Although yellowware is not porous, after firing it was,
nevertheless, customarily covered inside and out with a clear
alkaline glaze to accentuate its yellow color. Many pieces simply
received a clear glaze, but others, especially mixing bowls, were
embellished with painted bands of colored slips.

When it was first introduced to America, yellowware was
typically fired in the same type of kiln used for stoneware, but in
large, late 19th-century factories it was baked in huge, gas-fired
ovens. The usual procedure was to fire the ware twice, once to
harden it (the bisque firing), then a second time at a lower
temperature to fix the glaze that had been applied after the first
firing.

Rockingham and Flint Enamel

During the 19th century, yellowware was often covered with
Rockingham or flint-enamel finishes. The pieces chosen for these
finishes were often more elaborately embossed than those used
for plain, clear-glazed yellowware.

The Rockingham finish consists of a rich brown glaze that is
usually manganese-based. It was spattered or dripped onto a
revolving piece of pottery, causing the glaze to run, streak, and
spot. The yellow body showed through, creating a mottled
tortoiseshell appearance. The most desirable Rockinghamware
has this quality, but other pieces appear muddy and brown with
just a few areas of yellow showing through, especially those
made from 1870 to 1900.

Although flint enamel differs substantially from Rockingham, it
is sometimes considered a variety of Rockingham and the 2 types
are easily confused. To produce the flint-enamel finish, a piece of
yellowware was first covered with a clear alkaline glaze; while
the glaze was still wet, various powdered metallic oxides were
sprinkled over it. When the piece was fired, the greens, browns,
and blues from the oxides melted and fused with the glaze and
flowed across the piece, creating a spectacular finish. Probably
because of the expense of the copper and cobalt oxides that fired

green and blue, many pieces show a preponderance of the less expensive brown decoration and strongly resemble Rockinghamware.

Both Rockingham and flint-enamel pieces were fired in much the same manner as plain yellowware. Sometimes Rockingham was first fired with a clear glaze, and then fired a second time after the characteristic Rockingham finish had been applied.

White Earthenware and Ironstone Techniques

White earthenware is made from a number of highly plastic, fine-grained clays that fire to a tan or chalk-white finish. They are fired at high temperatures, and most have opaque, nonvitreous, slightly porous bodies. Ironstone, a variety of white earthenware, has a highly vitrified, nonporous body of great hardness and density. Both types are usually made from a mixture of several clays chosen for their special properties; they are almost always molded. Most are coated with a clear alkaline glaze.

Decoration

White earthenware and ironstone made in the 19th century were often transfer decorated. In this process, an impression is lifted from an engraved copper plate onto a thin piece of tissue paper. The paper is laid over the piece of pottery, and during firing the inked design is transferred to the pottery while the paper burns away. Other pieces were painted by hand or decorated with gilding or stenciling.

Most white earthenware was fired twice, first in an unglazed state, then a second time to set the glaze. If transfer decoration or hand painting was then added, the piece was fired a third time at a much lower temperature to set the decoration.

How Porcelain Is Made

True, or hard-paste, porcelain is composed principally of feldspar, silica, and kaolin, a fine clay that is virtually free of impurities. Fired at very high temperatures, true porcelain is characteristically translucent and white, and possesses great strength and hardness. Extremely difficult to shape, it is almost always cast in molds. The beauty and decorative potential of the pure white clay more than compensate, however, for the technical problems involved in its production.

Soft-paste porcelain was made in imitation of true porcelain. It differs from true porcelain in that it contains significant amounts of ground glass, which enables it to be fired at a much lower temperature. Soft-paste porcelain is vitreous and translucent. Because it has even less plasticity than true porcelain, it is even more difficult to shape and is almost always cast in molds.

Fired, unglazed porcelain is known as bisque. Parian ware, so named because of its resemblance to statuary marble, is a slightly granular type of bisque that is often used for figurines and decorative wares.

Decoration

Porcelain may be decorated at a number of stages in its production. Prior to glazing, the bisque ware is often decorated with colored underglazes or stains. The glaze is applied to bisque and fired at a much lower temperature than the clay body itself. After the ware has been glazed and fired, it is often further decorated with overglazes, metallic lusters, enamels, or decals, then fired yet again at an even lower temperature.

Parts of a Ceramic Object

Hot-water Bottle

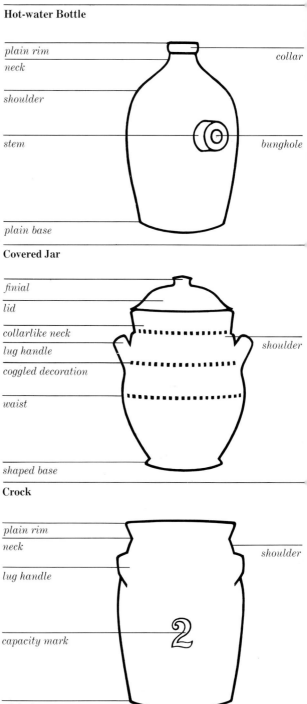

plain rim   collar

neck

shoulder

stem   bunghole

plain base

Covered Jar

finial

lid

collarlike neck

lug handle   shoulder

coggled decoration

waist

shaped base

Crock

plain rim

neck   shoulder

lug handle

capacity mark

plain base

Covered Bowl

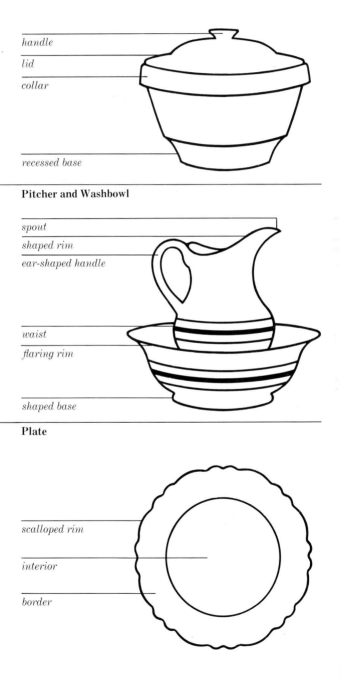

handle

lid

collar

recessed base

Pitcher and Washbowl

spout

shaped rim

ear-shaped handle

waist

flaring rim

shaped base

Plate

scalloped rim

interior

border

How to Use This Guide

Identifying and dating American pottery and porcelain requires a combination of many skills: an understanding of how ceramics are made, an appreciation of decorative techniques, an ability to research makers' marks, and an awareness of current market activity. The simple steps outlined below should help you acquire these skills and make it easy to identify, date, and evaluate the pieces you find.

Preparation

1. Turn to the Visual Key to become acquainted with how the pottery and porcelain in this book is organized. Based on shape and function, the 367 plates are divided into 12 groups; similar pieces within each division are grouped together.
2. Read the brief introduction that precedes each group, which discusses the forms illustrated.

Using the Color Plates to Identify Your Piece

1. Compare the object you have found with the drawings in the Visual Key. Find the drawing that most closely resembles your piece and then turn to the entries listed above the drawing.
2. Continue the visual comparison by narrowing your choice to a single color plate. Remember that your piece may not match it exactly; for example, your piece may be decorated, while the illustrated example is plain. The text account lists the variations you will most often encounter.
3. Read the text account to check your identification. Here you will find a detailed description of the piece as well as collecting hints.
4. After you have verified your identification, turn to the Price Guide for an estimate of the current market value of the piece. In the price guide, objects are grouped by material; the title of each text entry will indicate which group to turn to. The introduction to each group explains many of the factors that can affect price.

Developing Expertise

1. Begin by reading the brief History of the American Ceramics Industry section.
2. Familiarize yourself with the basic terminology. The Glossary explains pottery terms, and drawings on pages 22 and 23 point out the parts of typical pieces of pottery and porcelain.
3. The section on How Pottery and Porcelain Are Made will acquaint you with the techniques potters employ.
4. If you are interested in the works of a particular individual or company, consult the table of American Pottery and Porcelain Manufacturers. It is an alphabetical list that includes dates of operation, location, and the principal types of wares produced.
5. Collectors who specialize in specific types of decoration should refer to the List of Plates by Decoration.
6. Serious collectors will want to learn how to research manufacturers' marks. The section Pottery and Porcelain Marks lists several good reference books and explains what pitfalls to avoid.
7. One of the best ways to learn about ceramics is to visit museum collections. The Public Collections section lists those near you.
8. Consult the Bibliography for major books on ceramics.
9. The section Buying Pottery and Porcelain explains where you are likely to find types of objects you are looking for, and how to effectively bid at auction.

Information-at-a-Glance

Each color plate in this book is accompanied by a full text
description. At a glance, you can recognize the type of object you
are looking at and then find the information you need to identify
and date it. Whenever possible, the titles for the entries have
been taken from the catalogues and price lists published by
ceramics manufacturers.

Description
Each description covers the general shape of the object, its
decoration, and such important secondary features as handles
and lids. Inscriptions and trademarks, which may not be visible
in the photograph, are noted whenever possible. The description
usually concludes with the most common variations you are likely
to encounter. Technical terms are defined in the Glossary and
drawings on pages 22 and 23 point out the parts of typical pieces
of pottery and porcelain.

Materials and Dimensions
This section notes the materials used for each piece and describes
its method of manufacture. A dimension range is also provided
for each object, with the most conspicuous measurement given
first.

Locality and Period
This category indicates where the object was made and the dates
of its manufacture, and then goes on to tell where and when
similar examples were produced.

Comment
The history of the type of object illustrated is related here,
including its uses, popularity, and influence. Information drawn
from such contemporary sources as catalogues and price lists is
frequently provided.

Hints for Collectors
These tips point out what to look for and what to avoid, what
factors affect value, how to detect reproductions, and the most
reliable signs of age and authenticity. Hints are also given on
caring for ceramics and displaying your collection.

Visual Key

The ceramic objects included in this guide have been divided into 12 groups. For each group, a symbol appears on the left along with a brief explanation of the types of objects in that group. Drawings of representative pieces in the group are shown on the right, with the plate numbers for each indicated above. The group symbol is repeated on the opening page of the section concerning that group.

Crocks, Pots, and Related Objects (*Plates 1–28*)
These pieces are all widemouthed storage vessels. Some are cylindrical, and others have gently curving sides. Many have small, semicircular handles attached horizontally below the rim, and some were made with matching lids.

Jars, Bean Pots, and Related Objects (*Plates 29–70*)
These containers were designed to hold a variety of foodstuffs. Jars are usually tall and cylindrical, while bean pots and sugar bowls are short and squat. Most have a relatively wide mouth. Bean pots and sugar bowls often have matching lids, and some have handles. Rundlets and water coolers are barrel-shaped and have a small hole that is often located near the base.

Bottles, Jugs, and Flasks (*Plates 71–98*)
All of the objects included in this section were designed to store liquids. Bottles are usually tall, with a long neck and shaped rim. Jugs are squatter and always have a handle. Flasks are often ovoid and flattened, allowing them to fit into a pocket.

Pitchers, Teapots, Coffeepots, and Related Objects
(*Plates 99–144*)
These pieces all have a pouring spout and a handle, and some possess matching lids. In pitchers, the spout forms part of the rim. Teapots and coffeepots have a tubular spout that is usually attached toward the base. Batter jugs, which are squatter than teapots and coffeepots, also have a tubular spout. Sauceboats usually have a small, shaped pouring spout and are low, often with an oval body.

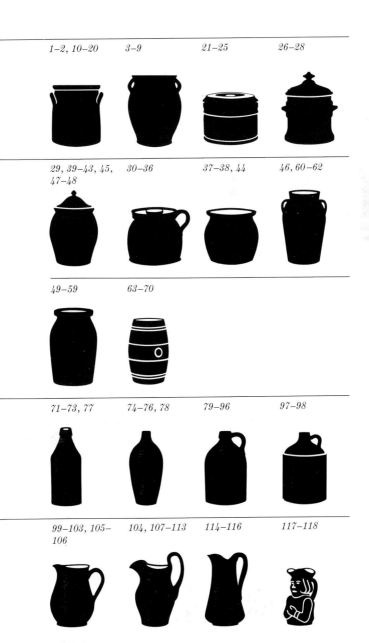

1–2, 10–20   3–9   21–25   26–28

29, 39–43, 45,   30–36   37–38, 44   46, 60–62
47–48

49–59   63–70

71–73, 77   74–76, 78   79–96   97–98

99–103, 105–   104, 107–113   114–116   117–118
106

Pitchers, Teapots, Coffeepots, and Related Objects
(*Plates 99–144*)
Continued.

Cups, Mugs, Tumblers, and Goblets (*Plates 145–168*)
These drinking vessels vary greatly in shape. Cups and mugs
both have handles, but cups are lower than mugs and usually
have curving sides, while mugs are tall and often cylindrical.
Tumblers are either cylindrical or have tapering sides,
resembling mugs without handles. Goblets have a cuplike section
that rests on a stem mounted on a broad foot.

Plates, Platters, and Serving Dishes (*Plates 169–196*)
Plates are usually circular, although some are octagonal or
square. Their sides are low and may either slope gently or angle
sharply outward to form a wide border that surrounds the
central, recessed area. Platters are larger than plates and are
usually oval or rectangular. The miscellaneous serving dishes
included here range from elaborate sweetmeat dishes to leaf-
shaped relish dishes.

Bowls and Related Objects (*Plates 197–237*)
These pieces range from large mixing bowls to small dishes
intended for salad or soup. Some rest on a plain base, others on a
shaped one. Many of the mixing bowls have a tall, thick collar
and are broad with gently sloping sides. Baking dishes, or
bakers, are generally lower than mixing bowls, often with
straight sides and a collar. Serving bowls are oval or round and
usually have low, sloping sides. Miscellaneous bowls include
broad, shallow milk pans, and batter bowls, which resemble
mixing bowls but have a large pouring spout.

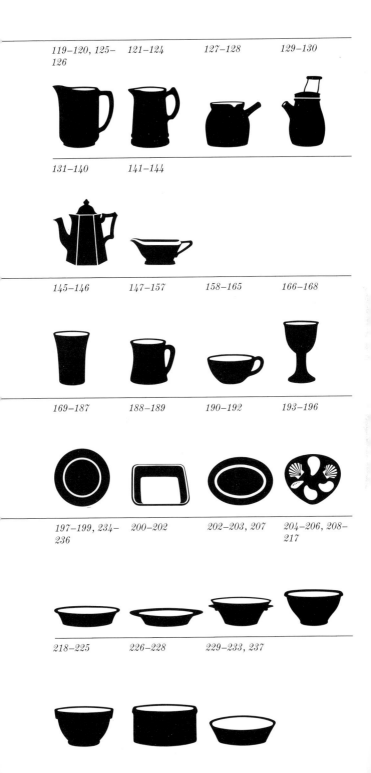

119–120, 125–126   121–124   127–128   129–130

131–140   141–144

145–146   147–157   158–165   166–168

169–187   188–189   190–192   193–196

197–199, 234–236   200–202   202–203, 207   204–206, 208–217

218–225   226–228   229–233, 237

Kitchenware (*Plates 238–259*)
All of the objects in this section were intended for use in the kitchen. Most baking molds have fluted sides or embossed decoration on the interior, while custard cups are usually less elaborate. Colanders resemble mixing bowls, but they have punchwork on the lower half of the body. Also included here are such diverse kitchen pieces as egg cups, rolling pins, salt and pepper shakers, and a water cooler.

Pitchers and Washbowls, Chamber Pots, Spittoons, and Related Objects (*Plates 260–277*)
These utilitarian items were designed for personal hygiene. The most familiar are probably pitchers and washbowls. Chamber pots resemble squat bowls, but they have a handle. Most spittoons are low and circular, with a discharge hole in the side; their interior slopes inward. Also included in this section are bedpans, a tublike footbath, and a shovel-shaped foot warmer.

Miscellaneous Objects (*Plates 278–297*)
The diverse objects included in this section range from simple pipe heads to elegant trinket boxes. Some of the most decorative are the tiles that were produced in quantity around the turn of the century. Desk accessories, including ink bottles, inkwells, sanders, and a stacking desk set are also featured, as are a variety of banks. Other miscellaneous pieces are doorknobs, flasks, and an ashtray.

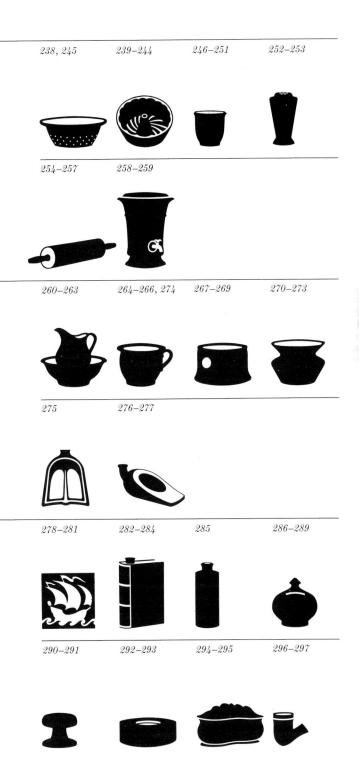

238, 245   239–244   246–251   252–253

254–257   258–259

260–263   264–266, 274   267–269   270–273

275   276–277

278–281   282–284   285   286–289

290–291   292–293   294–295   296–297

Flowerpots, Vases, and Candleholders (*Plates 298–333*)
Most of these decorative pieces were designed to hold flowers or plants. Flowerpots are commonly cone-shaped and often have an attached saucer. Vases come in a variety of shapes. Some resemble drinking goblets, with a cuplike section resting on a stem and foot. Others are urnlike or bowl-like. Wall pockets, or plant holders, often have a flattened back and a hook or hole for hanging. Planters and jardinieres are oblong or rectangular and are usually larger than vases. Most candlesticks have a tall, thin, stemlike body, often with a sloping foot; some are attached to vases.

Figurines (*Plates 334–367*)
These decorative objects are usually shaped like animals or human beings. Some are simply ornamental and were often displayed on mantels or tables, sometimes in pairs. Others are also functional, including paperweights, doorstops, flasks, and creamers.

298–306

307–309, 320, 333

310–311

312–313

314–318

319, 321, 325–327

322–324

328–332

334–337, 339

338

340–341

342–345

346–352

353–357

358–367

Crocks, Pots, and Related Objects

All of the objects in this section are widemouthed storage vessels. Most have straight sides, although in some the sides swell gently. The majority have semicircular handles, which made it easier to lift and carry the vessels when they were full. Very few originally came with matching lids; instead ceramic covers could be purchased separately or plain tin or wooden lids might seal the containers.

Today the examples with gentle swelling sides are usually called "cream pots," while the straight-sided vessels are referred to as "crocks" or "butter pots" and "cake pots." These distinctions are, for the most part, modern inventions. Price lists and catalogues from the early 19th century refer to "cream pots" and "pots" interchangeably, and call the straight-sided pieces both "crocks" and "pots." The largest crocks, which could be as tall as 3′ with a capacity of 70 gallons, were usually called "meat tubs." Crocks less than 8″ tall were called "cake pots."

Although some crocks and pots were made of red or yellow earthenware, the vast majority were made of stoneware, a material well suited for vessels that had to withstand a great deal of rough use. These stoneware pieces provided an artist with a broad surface on which to demonstrate his skill, and, as a consequence, they are among the most lavishly decorated of all American pottery.

Decoration on stoneware was typically executed with cobalt-blue slip. The decorator might either paint the design by hand or trail the slip across the surface. The earliest pieces have simple floral or abstract patterns, or feature stylized birds. Some vessels also bear impressed or incised decoration—often with touches of cobalt blue—techniques that were rarely used after the middle of the 19th century. By 1840 complex floral and figural compositions were becoming increasingly common and entire scenes might be depicted. Stenciling, an inexpensive alternative to impressed decoration, also appeared at this time.

Other types of storage vessels are also featured here. These include such diverse pieces as water coolers, tobacco jars, slop jars, often part of a toilet set and intended to hold waste water, and a few widemouthed jars that resemble crocks.

Spongeware slop jar

Description
Large vessel with sides that slope in from base to shaped shoulder. Above shoulder, sides swell out to plain rim. Beneath rim on interior, small ledge present. Band of embossed floral and geometric figures between shoulder and rim. 2 small semicircular lug handles below rim. Rimmed base. *Variations:* Handles may be absent. Some examples have lids.

Materials and Dimensions
Stoneware with yellow glaze. Decorated with green spongework; similar pieces decorated in blues, browns, and various combinations, especially blue and white, brown and yellow, and green and brown. Molded; handles separately shaped and applied. Height: 10–11″. Diameter: 9–10½″.

Locality and Period
New Jersey and Ohio. c. 1890–1920.

Comment
Slop jars were usually sold as part of matching toilet sets, which included washbowls and pitchers, soap boxes, toothbrush holders, and other items for personal hygiene. They held dirty wash water until it could be removed from the bedroom or bathroom. The small platform or ledge around the inside of the jar's mouth hints that a matching lid was once present.

Hints for Collectors
If a slop jar is missing its lid, its value is probably decreased by 10 to 20 percent, but it might still be worthwhile purchasing if it completes a toilet set. Since these pieces were made in more or less standard sizes, eventually it may be possible to find a matching top.

Spongeware water cooler

Description
Large water container with sides that slope out from base to
rounded shoulder, then in to wide neck marked by incised line
and thick, flat rim. Circular hole just above plain base. "No. 9"
stenciled just below incised line at neck. *Variations:* Some water
coolers are keg-shaped.

Materials and Dimensions
Stoneware; exterior glazed with white slip; interior glazed with
brown Albany slip. Decorated with blue spongework; similar
pieces decorated with green or brown spongework. Molded;
similar examples wheel-thrown. Height: 11–14″. Diameter:
10–12″.

Locality and Period
New Jersey and Ohio. c. 1890–1920.

Comment
Spongeware water coolers produced around the turn of the
century were made in several sizes to match sets of spongeware
bowls and other kitchenware. Like the example illustrated, many
had stenciled or impressed capacity marks. The circular hole
near the base customarily held a metal spigot. The mouth was
covered by a ceramic lid that did not necessarily match the
cooler.

Hints for Collectors
Spongeware water coolers, uncommon today, are a real find for
any collector who specializes in spongeware. By the end of the
19th century they were beginning to fall out of favor as
refrigeration became common. The absence of a lid is not a
serious flaw: Contemporary advertisements indicate that
common brown-and-white crock tops were often used as covers.

3 Redware jar

Description
Wide-mouth jar with high waist. Above waist, sides curve in to wide neck with thick, rolled rim. Below waist, sides taper to shaped base. Decorated with incised and painted bird on leafy branch. *Variations:* Incised decoration usually geometric. Base usually plain.

Materials and Dimensions
Red earthenware; exterior with clear lead glaze; interior with opaque, off-white glaze. Bird incised freehand and then filled with blue-green slip. Wheel-thrown. Height: 8–10″. Diameter: 7–8½″.

Locality and Period
Western New York. c. 1830–40. Similar pieces from New England west to Pennsylvania, south to Virginia. c. 1780–1870.

Comment
Although rather common on early stoneware, incised pictorial decoration is quite rare on redware. The bird motif on the jar illustrated resembles a motif used in the Albany-Troy area of New York State in the 1820s. The blue-green slip is probably cobalt, which typically fired to a dark shade when applied to redware. Although the shape of this jar is rather ordinary, its decoration transforms it into a lovely and rare piece.

Hints for Collectors
All incised redware is worth collecting, especially pieces decorated with birds, yet it is not necessarily costly. Collectors who specialize in slip-decorated redware are not always interested in incised pieces, which sometimes pass through auctions or sales at low prices.

Stoneware crock

Description
Tall storage vessel with sides that slope gradually out to very high shoulder marked by 2 incised lines. Shoulder curves in to wide neck and shaped rim. 2 flattened lug handles attached at shoulder level. Plain base. Incised number "8" in oval on shoulder. Front decorated with scene of deer in forest. *Variations:* Handles may be larger and more elaborate. Decoration may be floral or may depict other animals or humans.

Materials and Dimensions
Stoneware; exterior with salt glaze; interior glazed with brown Albany slip. Cobalt-blue decoration. Wheel-thrown; handles separately shaped and applied. Height: 16–22″. Diameter: 11–15″.

Locality and Period
Pennsylvania, New Jersey, and Virginia. c. 1850–80.

Comment
Pieces like that shown are characteristic of Pennsylvania, New Jersey, and to a lesser extent Virginia. The flattened handles are also found on brown- and alkaline-glazed southern stoneware but not on blue-decorated, salt-glazed stoneware produced elsewhere; they are wider and flatter than those on most northeastern and midwestern stoneware. Large crocks like this were used to store dried corn or other grains.

Hints for Collectors
The unusual, realistic decoration on this crock is much more desirable than the stylized decoration typically found on stoneware and makes this piece a pleasure to own and a wise investment. The style in which the deer and the trees are painted somewhat resembles that seen in the work of Rufus Porter and other 19th-century American folk artists.

5 Stoneware crock

Description
Large storage vessel with high shoulder and wide mouth. Shoulder tapers sharply to thin, shaped ring at base of wide, collarlike neck with plain rim. 2 lug handles attached at shoulder. Below shoulder, body tapers to shaped base. Upper portion decorated with floral motifs in blue. Number "3" impressed on neck. *Variations:* Neck may be plain, not collarlike. Decoration may be absent, figural, or less elaborate.

Materials and Dimensions
Stoneware; exterior with salt glaze; interior glazed with brown Albany slip. Cobalt-blue decoration. Wheel-thrown; handles separately shaped and applied. Height: 10–15″. Diameter: 9–12″.

Locality and Period
Probably Pennsylvania. c. 1840–80. Similar pieces from New Jersey, Maryland, and Virginia. c. 1840–90.

Comment
This crock's shape and decoration are typical of pieces made near Philadelphia, especially those from the Remmey pottery there. Many crocks made in Pennsylvania have "rolling" floral decoration covering a large part of the surface. The firm of Hamilton and Jones, active in Greensboro, Pennsylvania, from around 1866 to 1897, made such crocks in 12 sizes, from half a gallon to 20 gallons, with the larger sizes most common. The handles on this piece were not shaped by hand, as was common, but were made by pushing clay through a hollow "extruder."

Hints for Collectors
Pieces made at the Remmey factory are easiest to find in Pennsylvania. Some bear the mark "RCR" while others have a characteristic oval, dotted cartouche around an impressed capacity number.

6 Stoneware cream pot

Description
Storage vessel with high shoulder and wide mouth. Shoulder tapers slightly to wide, collarlike neck marked by 2 incised lines and with plain rim. Below waist, sides taper to slightly shaped base. 2 semicircular handles attached below neck. "C. CROLIUS/ MANUFACTURER/NEW-YORK" impressed on upper body. Touches of cobalt blue at base of handles and around potter's mark. *Variations:* Number of incised lines varies.

Materials and Dimensions
Stoneware; exterior with salt glaze; interior with ocher glaze. Rare pieces lack interior glaze. Cobalt-blue decoration. Wheel-thrown; handles separately shaped and applied. Height: 10–13". Diameter: 9–11".

Locality and Period
Clarkson Crolius, New York City. c. 1795–1820. Similar pieces from New England to Pennsylvania. c. 1790–1830.

Comment
In a price list from 1809, Clarkson Crolius, the maker of this piece, referred to such examples simply as "pots." Other manufacturers called them "open cream pots," "cream pots," and "pots without covers." They were probably used to separate milk and cream and to store cream.

Hints for Collectors
Cream pots made between 1790 and 1830 have a space between the horizontal handle and the side of the pot, as seen in this example. In later pieces the horizontal handles are flush with the side of the pot. Those made before 1790 have vertically positioned handles and are very rare.

Stoneware cream pot

Description
Storage vessel with high shoulder and wide mouth. Shoulder
slopes in slightly to flat, shaped rim. Below shoulder, sides curve
in to plain base. 2 semicircular lug handles on shoulder. Date
"1868" and simple blue decoration on front. Impressed near rim:
"HUDSON. N.Y/POTTERY" and with numeral "2." *Variations:* Curve
of sides may be more pronounced. Incised line may be present at
level of handles.

Materials and Dimensions
Stoneware; exterior with salt glaze; interior glazed with brown
Albany slip. Cobalt-blue decoration. Wheel-thrown; handles
separately shaped and applied. Height: 8–12″. Diameter: 7–11″.

Locality and Period
Hudson Pottery, Hudson, New York. 1868. Similar pieces from
New England west to Indiana, south to the Carolinas.
c. 1830–90.

Comment
Cream pots like this were popular until the end of the 19th
century. In 1865, the Hart pottery in Sherburne, New York, sold
cream pots from 1 to 5 gallons at $3.50 to $12 per dozen
wholesale. Larger and more expensive than most stoneware,
these pots were also more often decorated. The date on this pot
probably refers to the year in which the Hudson Pottery came
under new management.

Hints for Collectors
Dated pottery usually costs more than similar, undated pieces.
Determining what the date means will increase the value of your
piece. Dates may refer to a pottery's founding or important
events in the potter's or purchaser's life as well as the year when
a piece was made.

8 Stoneware cream pot

Description
Squat vessel with sides that slope in from rounded waist to neck marked by 3 incised lines. Wide, flaring rim. 2 lug handles attached to sides. Below waist, sides taper to plain base. Center of pot has incised decoration, including date "1835," deer, flowers, and a bird. "C. DILLON & CO./ALBANY." impressed on upper front. "HEINRICH DUMIG" incised on back. *Variations:* Incised decoration varies.

Materials and Dimensions
Stoneware; exterior with salt glaze; interior glazed with brown Albany slip. Wheel-thrown; handles separately shaped and applied. Height: 8–11″. Diameter: 10–13″.

Locality and Period
Charles Dillon & Company, Albany, New York. 1835. Similar pieces from New England west to Ohio, south to the Carolinas. c. 1815–50.

Comment
Cream pots provided an ideal surface on which the artist could demonstrate his skills, and consequently they are among the more lavishly decorated pieces from this period. Scenes of running deer are common on European, especially German, stoneware made in the early 19th century. The incised name on the back suggests that this piece was made either by a German potter or for a German customer.

Hints for Collectors
The incised decoration on this pot and its early date make it highly desirable and consequently expensive. Decoration outlined or touched in blue would command a still higher price, perhaps 50 percent more. Simpler designs based on leaves and flowers are most common and are less costly.

9 Redware crock

Description
Low, broad storage vessel with sides sloping out to slightly flared, shaped rim. 2 incised lines below rim mark position of 2 lug handles. Shaped base decorated with incised bands. Handles decorated with yellow lines; abstract floral pattern in yellow and brown about midsection; bands of yellow and brown about base. *Variations:* Bands on base rarely present. Handles usually undecorated.

Materials and Dimensions
Red earthenware with clear lead glaze. Decorated with yellow and brown slip. Wheel-thrown; handles separately shaped and applied. Height: 6–8″. Diameter: 9–12″.

Locality and Period
New York, New Jersey, and Pennsylvania. c. 1830–50. Similar pieces from New York south to the Carolinas. c. 1780–1870.

Comment
Often called pots, redware crocks with curved sides, like the piece shown, gave way in the mid-19th century to straight-sided pieces that resembled those then made of stoneware. They had no matching tops but were covered with cloth or oiled paper or a homemade wooden lid. Made in various sizes, they were used to store such essentials as flour, sugar, and lard.

Hints for Collectors
Redware crocks are far less common than their stoneware cousins, possibly because redware is less durable, and marked examples are extremely rare. The fragile handles often separated from the piece. Check them for cracks and signs of repair.

Redware butter pot

Description
Tall crock with sides sloping slightly outward to rolled rim.
Below rim, series of incised lines between bands of wavelike
incised decoration. 2 large lug handles attached at level of bands.
Plain base. Impressed on front "MORGANVILL." *Variations:* May
be cylindrical.

Materials and Dimensions
Red earthenware with clear lead glaze. Wheel-thrown; handles
separately shaped and then applied. Height: 5–9″. Diameter:
4–7″.

Locality and Period
Morganville Pottery, Morganville, New York. c. 1855–75.
Similar pieces from New England west to Indiana, south to the
Carolinas. c. 1840–80.

Comment
The Morganville Pottery in western New York operated from
around 1830 to 1900. Like most small, rural potteries, it
employed just 1 or 2 men and never had a yearly output of more
than $1,500 worth of wares. From 1880 to 1900 it produced
mostly flower pots. Contemporary stoneware butter pots from
the same area had straight sides and flush handles.

Hints for Collectors
Since potters rarely marked their redware, any marked piece is
valuable. Graceful shape and pleasing decoration, as in this
example, further increase value. The Morganville Pottery also
marked its preserve jars, cuspidors, pitchers, and flower pots;
these rare pieces are all real finds.

Redware butter pot

Description
Cylindrical pot with wide, flaring mouth. Sides rise to heavy, rolled ridge. Above ridge, collar with plain rim. 2 lug handles attached just beneath ridge. Plain base. Decorated with black splotches. *Variations:* Handles may be absent.

Materials and Dimensions
Red earthenware with clear lead glaze; exterior splotched with manganese black. Wheel-thrown; handles separately shaped and applied. Height: 9–12″. Diameter: 7–9″.

Locality and Period
New England and New York, particularly Connecticut.
c. 1820–70.

Comment
The terms "butter pot" and "butter crock" appear frequently in the price lists of early redware potters. In 1814 William Jackson of Lynn, Massachusetts, advertised "butter pots and covers," and in 1829 Clark and Fox of Athens, New York, offered similar items in 1-, 1½-, and 2-gallon sizes. Such pieces probably had sloping sides. With its straight sides, the crock shown here resembles those made of stoneware in the late 19th century, and most redware examples were probably made after 1850. Potteries in the Connecticut Valley, the probable source of this piece, favored the splotched decoration shown here.

Hints for Collectors
Although straight-sided redware storage crocks are far less common than similar stoneware pieces, they are also less popular with collectors and sometimes cost less than other types of multiglazed redware. Matching crock tops with touches of manganese black are rare and add greatly to the value of a piece.

Stoneware crock

Description
Cylindrical vessel with thick, shaped rim. 2 lug handles applied
below rim. Plain base. Figure of cow in profile stamped on one
side. Impressed above is number "2" and oval with mark
"GARDINER STONEWARE/MANUFACTORY/GARDINER, ME."
Variations: Decoration varies.

Materials and Dimensions
Stoneware; exterior with salt glaze; interior glazed with brown
Albany slip. Mark and impressed decoration may be touched
with cobalt-blue slip. Wheel-thrown; handles separately shaped
and applied. Height: 9–13″. Diameter: 9–12″.

Locality and Period
Gardiner Stoneware Company, Gardiner, Maine. c. 1874–87.
Similar pieces from Massachusetts, New York, and New Jersey.
c. 1800–80.

Comment
The use of a small metal or wooden stamp to decorate stoneware
pottery was introduced in New Jersey around 1800. The
technique was never very popular, probably because of the
prohibitive cost of the specially made stamps. Some stamps are
commonly found on pottery from a certain area. For example,
fish appear on some early 19th-century Boston pieces, and
eagles, serpents, and stacks of cannonballs were stamped onto
Charlestown, Massachusetts, examples from 1800 to 1825.

Hints for Collectors
With the exception of the relatively common and rather late
Gardiner examples, stoneware with impressed decoration is hard
to come by and expensive. The more valuable Gardiner pottery
will have more than one figure stamped on a single piece and
strong, blue outlines.

13 Stoneware butter pot

Description
Large, cylindrical crock with thick, shaped rim. 2 lug handles attached below rim. Plain base. On front, freehand decoration of large bird on branch with flowers and leaves. Number "6" and "WHITE'S UTICA" impressed on front below rim. *Variations:* Shape of rim varies. Size and placement of handles vary. Base may be chamfered.

Materials and Dimensions
Stoneware; exterior with salt glaze; interior glazed with brown Albany slip. Decoration cobalt blue; rarely manganese brown or combination of blue and brown. Wheel-thrown; handles separately shaped and applied. Height: 8–16″. Diameter: 9–14″.

Locality and Period
White's Pottery, Utica, New York. c. 1865–77. Similar pieces from Maine to Virginia and Texas. c. 1840–1910.

Comment
Although they were called butter pots, these large vessels stored many other foods, including pickles that were being cured. In the 1850s, a stoneware factory in Albany, New York, offered them in 9 sizes ranging from ¼ gallon to 6 gallons. The ¼-gallon size retailed for 19 cents. Butter crocks usually came equipped with tops, which were usually stoneware glazed with gray or brown and white slip.

Hints for Collectors
Because of their large size, crocks are among the most lavishly decorated of all stoneware and among the most interesting pieces to collect. Floral designs are most common, followed by birds. Rarer and more expensive are other animals, people, houses, ships, and scenes.

Stoneware butter pot

Description
Cylindrical crock with shaped rim that protrudes from body.
2 lug handles attached below rim. Plain base. Decorated in blue
with bird and capacity mark. Impressed "J. A. & C. W.
UNDERWOOD,/FORT EDWARD, N.Y." *Variations:* Most examples are
undecorated.

Materials and Dimensions
Stoneware; exterior with salt glaze; interior glazed with brown
Albany slip. Decorated with cobalt blue. Wheel-thrown; handles
separately shaped and applied. Height: 7–12″. Diameter: 7–11″.

Locality and Period
J. A. & C. W. Underwood, Fort Edward, New York. c. 1865–67.
Similar pieces from New England to Texas. c. 1840–1900.

Comment
Although most collectors refer to them simply as crocks, pottery
price lists indicate that straight-sided storage pieces like the one
illustrated were called by different names according to size.
Those with heights 6″ or less were called cake pots, while larger
pieces were butter pots. The very large 30-, 40-, and 50-gallon
examples were known as meat tubs. As a general rule, the larger
a crock, the less likely it is to be elaborately decorated.

Hints for Collectors
Crocks and jugs decorated with birds are among the most
popular of all stoneware pieces. They are sometimes referred to
as "bluebirds." Prices vary depending on the size of the bird,
rarity of the type (chickens are more desirable than robins),
quality of execution, and condition. Look for examples such as
this one with well-drawn birds that are neatly centered on the
crock.

Stoneware butter pot

Description
Large, cylindrical crock with shaped rim. 2 lug handles attached below rim. At level of handles, 2 sets of 3 incised lines. Plain base. On front, large freehand basket of flowers. "J. & E. NORTON/ BENNINGTON VT." impressed on front near rim. "6" impressed beneath mark. *Variations:* Shape of rim varies. Size and placement of handles vary. Decoration varies.

Materials and Dimensions
Stoneware; exterior with salt glaze; interior glazed with brown slip. Decoration cobalt blue. Height: 10–16″. Diameter: 9–14″.

Locality and Period
Julius & Edward Norton, Bennington, Vermont. c. 1850–59. Similar pieces from Maine to Virginia and Texas. c. 1840–1910.

Comment
The most common decorated pieces from the second half of the 19th century are butter pots with floral patterns. Few, however, are as elaborate as this example, made by Julius and Edward Norton, who controlled the Bennington stoneware pottery from 1850 to 1859. The motif seen here—a basket filled with flowers—was frequently used on silver from about 1825 to 1840. Around 1850, potters began to use it to decorate stoneware.

Hints for Collectors
Although pots made at Bennington are comparable to those from New York, Pennsylvania, Massachusetts, and Virginia, collectors are almost always willing to pay 30 to 50 percent more for a piece with the coveted Bennington mark. But artistic merit is the real test of quality. A poorly decorated pot from Bennington is still a poorly decorated pot and should be priced accordingly.

Stoneware butter pot

Description
Cylindrical crock with thick, shaped rim. 2 lug handles below rim attached close to sides. Plain base. Front with stenciled eagle. *Variations:* Handles may be larger. Decoration varies. Base may be chamfered.

Materials and Dimensions
Stoneware; exterior with salt glaze; interior glazed with brown Albany slip. Decoration cobalt blue. Wheel-thrown; handles separately shaped and applied. Height: 8–12″. Diameter: 7½–11″.

Locality and Period
New England south to Pennsylvania and West Virginia. c. 1860–1900.

Comment
Although craftsmen had used stencils earlier to decorate furniture and other products, stoneware manufacturers turned to the technique relatively late, and then only in a limited area. Several potteries in New England and at least 2 in New York used stenciling, but it was most popular in Pennsylvania and West Virginia. There, potters decorated their wares with complex compositions that frequently included patriotic symbols, as well as flowers, cows, and geometric shapes.

Hints for Collectors
The best stenciled pieces have well-balanced, interesting compositions and crisp decoration. If the design is blurry, the value of the piece will be substantially less. Some of the finest examples of stenciled stoneware are the work of Pennsylvania potters such as Hamilton and Jones and the Eagle Pottery of Greensboro.

17 Stoneware butter pot

Description
Large crock with sides rising to heavy, shaped rim. Sides angle out slightly to plain base. 2 lug handles attached below rim. Front with freehand slip decoration of chicken. *Variations:* Shape of rim varies. Size and placement of handles may vary. Base may be slightly chamfered.

Materials and Dimensions
Stoneware; exterior with salt glaze; interior glazed with brown Albany slip. Decoration cobalt blue; rarely manganese brown or combination of blue and brown. Wheel-thrown; handles separately shaped and applied. Height: 10–14″. Diameter: 10–14″.

Locality and Period
New York. c. 1850–90. Similar pieces from Vermont and Pennsylvania. c. 1850–90.

Comment
Although bird designs are common on crocks made in the second half of the 19th century, the so-called "chicken pecking corn" shown here is associated primarily with New York potteries, especially those in Poughkeepsie, West Troy, Fort Edward, and Ellenville. The basic design varies so little from piece to piece that it could be the work of one artist.

Hints for Collectors
Note that the decoration on this piece appears grayish rather than bright blue; this indicates that the crock was overfired, although not seriously. Overfiring can result in blistered or bubbled glaze, which substantially lessens the value of a piece even if the decoration is interesting. Look for bright blue slip with a rich luster.

Stoneware butter pot

Description
Storage vessel with heavy, shaped rim. 2 lug handles below rim. Lower body swells slightly above plain base. Oval stamp below rim, "J. BURGER, JR./ROCHESTER N.Y.," alongside slip-painted number "3." Slip-painted bird decorates front. *Variations:* Different birds may be shown.

Materials and Dimensions
Stoneware; exterior with salt glaze; interior glazed with brown Albany slip. Cobalt-blue decoration. Wheel-thrown; handles separately shaped and applied. Height: 7–10″. Diameter: 6½–9″.

Locality and Period
John Burger, Jr., Rochester, New York. c. 1878–90. Similar pieces from New England west to Ohio. c. 1850–1900.

Comment
Birds on crocks are usually robins or chickens, more rarely eagles, pheasants, birds of paradise, and, as on the piece shown here, partridges. Unlike birds on crocks elsewhere, those from Rochester, New York, usually have bodies decorated with a series of tiny dots in an almost pointillistic manner. The number painted on this piece indicates a 3-gallon capacity. Such numbers were more often impressed with a stamp.

Hints for Collectors
The folk-art quality of blue-decorated stoneware has attracted many collectors. Most of these pieces, however, are highly stylized; bird crocks from potteries in New York, Pennsylvania, and Vermont can look amazingly similar. Because examples from Rochester are unique in design, they are inevitably in greater demand.

19 Stoneware crock

Description
Large storage vessel with thick, shaped rim. Incised line below rim marks position of 2 lug handles. Lower body swells slightly above plain base. Front decorated with doe standing before palm tree and number "6." Impressed below rim "HUBBELL & CHESEBRO/GEDDES, N.Y." *Variations:* Decoration usually plainer.

Materials and Dimensions
Stoneware; exterior with salt glaze; interior glazed with brown Albany slip. Cobalt-blue decoration. Wheel-thrown; handles separately shaped and applied. Height: 10–16″. Diameter: 9–12″.

Locality and Period
Hubbell & Chesebro, Geddes (Syracuse), New York. c. 1867–84. Nearly identical examples from Havana (Montour Falls), New York; similar decoration on crocks from Vermont, Massachusetts, and New Jersey. c. 1860–1900.

Comment
Scenes of deer occur fairly often on elaborately decorated salt-glazed stoneware, but the distinctive deer shown here appears only on the wares of 2 roughly contemporary potteries, Hubbell and Chesebro of Geddes, New York, and Albert O. Whittemore of Havana (now Montour Falls), New York. Sophisticated decoration like this may have been done by professionals who traveled from pottery to pottery, specializing in certain designs.

Hints for Collectors
The white stains on the inside of this crock are caused by water glass, a food preservative used in the 19th century. They are extremely difficult to remove, but do not greatly affect a piece's value if they are confined to the interior. A coat of vegetable oil or shellac will make them less noticeable.

Stoneware crock

Description
Massive, cylindrical storage vessel with heavy, shaped rim. 2 lug handles below rim. Plain base. Impressed below rim "6" and "WILLIAM WARNER/WEST TROY, N.Y." Elaborate decoration of lion and trees on front. *Variations:* Handles may be placed lower. Decoration varies.

Materials and Dimensions
Stoneware; exterior with salt glaze; interior glazed with brown Albany slip. Decorated in cobalt blue. Wheel-thrown; handles separately shaped and applied. Height: 12–17″. Diameter: 10–13″.

Locality and Period
William E. Warner, West Troy (Watervliet), New York. c. 1850–59. Similar pieces from Vermont, Massachusetts, New York, and New Jersey. c. 1850–1900.

Comment
This piece carries the stamp of one of the first stoneware manufacturers to use elaborate slip decoration. Warner produced pieces embellished with animals, eagles, human figures, and even groups of buildings. Although unusual, the lion decoration is not unique. It reflects a prevalent 19th-century interest in wild animals.

Hints for Collectors
Simple floral designs were the customary blue decoration on stoneware pieces. Elaborately decorated pieces were generally made to order, and are extremely difficult to find. Most are now in public or private collections. Look for them at sales of old estates and long-held collections. If available, they will be quite expensive.

Yellowware crock

Description
Cylindrical storage vessel with shaped rim and base. 2 shield-shaped handles present. Decorated at midpoint with dark brown band between 6 thinner white bands. *Variations:* Handles may be medallion- or crescent-shaped. Decorative bands vary or may be absent.

Materials and Dimensions
Yellow earthenware with clear alkaline glaze. Decorated with dark brown slip and white slip. Molded; handles separately shaped and applied. Height: 9–11″. Diameter: 5–7″.

Locality and Period
New Jersey west to Ohio. c. 1890–1910.

Comment
Most yellowware crocks were small and not intended to be moved about. Consequently, there was no need for large utilitarian handles such as those customarily found on stoneware crocks. Since stoneware pieces were often much larger than those of yellowware, and when full might weigh as much as 10 to 20 pounds, sturdy handles were a necessity. The elaborate, decorative handles on the crock illustrated are unusual for what was basically a utilitarian piece.

Hints for Collectors
A familiarity with common yellowware forms will make it easy to spot unusual pieces like this one. The shield-shaped handles, along with the attractive slip decoration, make this crock a real find. Not only is it worth spending a bit extra to obtain extraordinary pottery, but examples like this are worth buying even if they have minor cracks or chips.

Description
Small, cylindrical storage vessel with thick, shaped rim and matching lid. Small holes in sides anchor wire bail handle; handle attached to wire clamp that secures lid. Lid has shaped rim and raised knob with cross-shaped indentation to hold clamp. Plain base. "Kaukauna Klub/Manf'd By/South Kaukauna Dairy Company/KAUKAUNA WISCONSIN" transfer-printed on front. *Variations:* Some pieces lack wire snap closure. Lid may be plain, without raised knob.

Materials and Dimensions
Stoneware glazed with white Bristol slip; rim and underside of top unglazed. Handle and clamp iron wire. Molded. Height: 2½–5″. Diameter: 3¼–7″.

Locality and Period
New England west to California, south to Texas. c. 1890–1940.

Comment
Many types of molded storage containers were mass-produced from the late 19th century well into the 20th. Some, like the Weir canning jar, were used to preserve foods. Others, like the crock illustrated here, contained cheese, butter, and other products. The customer could use the empty crock for storage. Most of these pieces were made in quantity in the Midwest after 1900.

Hints for Collectors
Mass-produced crocks are plentiful and inexpensive, but make sure that you get a complete unit with the closure intact. Often parts of the top or handle are missing. Since they are so common, look for them in secondhand shops and at yard sales.

Stoneware cake pot

Description
Cylindrical storage vessel with matching lid. Single shaped band below plain, unglazed rim. Bottom of pot slightly recessed. Lid has shaped rim and sunken center, divided by unglazed band. Central button-shaped handle. *Variations:* Some pieces lack shaped band below rim.

Materials and Dimensions
Stoneware glazed with white Bristol slip and brown Albany slip; other examples entirely white or brown. Molded. Height: 4–6". Diameter: 6–8".

Locality and Period
New Jersey west to Ohio. c. 1890–1930.

Comment
When modern casting techniques were introduced at the large New Jersey and Ohio potteries, many of the less-efficient kilns that relied on the potter's wheel were forced to close. With mass production both form and color became standardized, and the brown-and-white combination illustrated here was most often used. Such pots are common, and have only recently attracted collector attention, primarily because of their utility and the increase in price of earlier crock types. Made in many different large factories, none seem to have borne potters' marks.

Hints for Collectors
Do not confuse turn-of-the-century brown-and-white crocks with the reproductions now being made. The latter have a smoother surface, thinner walls, and a lighter brown glaze. They also lack wear on the bottom and the light chips or abrasions that are usually found on older pieces.

Yellowware crock

Description
Cylindrical storage vessel with matching lid. Straight sides topped by thick collar with plain rim. Shaped base. Lid with button-shaped handle in circular recessed area. Crock and lid with wide band of white between 2 narrow brown bands. *Variations:* Thick collar below rim usually absent. Color combinations vary.

Materials and Dimensions
Yellow earthenware with clear alkaline glaze. Decorated with brown and white slip. Molded. Height: 5–6″. Diameter: 7–8″.

Locality and Period
New Jersey and Ohio. c. 1890–1920.

Comment
The vessel illustrated here is typical of yellowware storage crocks, which were less varied in shape and usually smaller than those made of stoneware. Decorated attractively with banding or other details, they were intended for display in the kitchen, where they served as storage vessels for flour, sugar, and other foodstuffs. In fact, magazine ads from around 1910 show these crocks resting on kitchen shelves.

Hints for Collectors
Many yellowware crocks have lost their original lids. But because they were cast in molds, and came in standard sizes, it is often possible to replace a missing top. Since a complete piece is worth more, many collectors buy spare tops whenever they find them. The color combination on this crock resembles that found on some bowls and is therefore particularly desirable. Less popular though more common are crocks with 2 or 3 thin white bands.

Spongeware crock

Description
Cylindrical storage vessel with matching lid. Slight ridge present just below plain rim. Similar ridge and 2 grooves above plain base. Embossed design of peacocks and columns on body. Flat lid has recessed area with button-shaped handle. *Variations:* Embossed decoration varies and may be absent.

Materials and Dimensions
Stoneware with tan glaze. Decorated with brown sponging; color of sponging varies. Molded. Height: 5–6″. Diameter: 6–8″.

Locality and Period
New Jersey west to Ohio, south to Maryland. c. 1890–1920.

Comment
Spongeware crocks may be decorated in several color combinations, including green and brown and blue and white. A few bear the mark "USA" on the bottom, an impression also found on custard cups and mixing bowls. Although this mark is associated with certain factories in Liverpool, Ohio, it also appears on other American pottery of the early 20th century. The kind of embossed decoration that appears on the crock illustrated is found more often on spongeware than any other type of American pottery.

Hints for Collectors
Pieces decorated with brown sponging are sometimes confused with earlier Rockingham ware. However, the oblong sponge marks on the piece illustrated, particularly noticeable near the base, are typical of later spongework. In contrast, Rockingham has a "dripped look"; the glaze usually flows over the surface in a random way.

Stoneware pot

Description
Storage crock with 16 fluted sides and matching lid. Rim and base elaborately shaped. 2 handles formed of wreathlike rings suspended from brackets, all set tightly against sides. Stepped lid with buttonlike handle. Bottom stamped "EDMANDS & CO." *Variations:* Lid may be more elaborate, with acorn- or steeple-shaped handle. Number of sides varies.

Materials and Dimensions
Stoneware glazed with brown Albany slip; areas near rim and base unglazed; similar pieces with Rockingham glaze. Molded; handles separately shaped and applied. Height: 8–11″. Diameter: 7–10″.

Locality and Period
Edmands & Co., Charlestown, Massachusetts. c. 1835–50. Similar pieces from Portland, Maine, and Burlington and Bennington, Vermont. c. 1830–60.

Comment
Price lists from the United States Pottery Company in Bennington, Vermont, refer to these molded pots as tobacco jars, and other lists call them cookie jars. No matter what their original function was, they are much more elaborate than the usual cake or butter pot. Many were marked on the bottom rather than the side, probably because the pottery did not wish to mar their surfaces.

Hints for Collectors
Pots like the one illustrated are rather uncommon, since most 19th-century stoneware was thrown, not molded. Further, very few examples are shaped like this; most are circular. The interesting, decorative handles and the rich glaze also set this pot apart from run-of-the-mill pieces.

Rockingham tobacco jar

Description
Storage vessel with matching lid. Sides embossed with
alternating wide and narrow ribs. Shaped rim. 2 shaped handles.
Heavily shaped, slightly flaring base. Matching top with
embossed petal-like decoration radiating from mushroom-shaped
handle set on short neck. Bottom impressed "Lyman Fenton &
Co./Fentons/ENAMEL/PATENTED/1849/BENNINGTON, Vt."
Variations: Embossed decoration varies. Tops vary greatly.

Materials and Dimensions
Yellow earthenware with Rockingham glaze. Molded; handles
separately shaped and applied. Height: 7–12″. Diameter: 6–9″.

Locality and Period
United States Pottery Company, Bennington, Vermont.
c. 1849–58. Similar pieces from New England west to Ohio,
south to Maryland. c. 1850–80.

Comment
Because they were luxury items, tobacco jars, or humidors, were
usually somewhat more ornate than other ceramic pots. In the
19th century, they were made not only of earthenware but also
of glass, wood, leather, and metal. Despite their popularity,
relatively few of these pieces have survived. Those that have
often have broken handles.

Hints for Collectors
Without their original tops, tobacco jars may be mistaken for
rather elaborate storage jars. Ornate handles, however, are
rarely present on other storage jars. A tobacco-jar base or top is
worth keeping; if you are lucky, you may eventually find a
matching part.

Redware jar

Description
Bulbous vessel with wide mouth and matching lid. Neck marked by coggled line. Collar with slightly flared rim. 2 lug handles just below neck. Shaped base. Coggled lines at base of handles and at waist. Dome-shaped lid with small, caplike handle. *Variations:* Coggled lines vary greatly; incised lines may be present. Base may be plain.

Materials and Dimensions
Red earthenware with clear lead glaze; exterior daubed with manganese black. Wheel-thrown; handles separately shaped and applied; lid separately shaped. Height: 9–13″. Diameter: 7–9″.

Locality and Period
Connecticut. c. 1820–50. Similar pieces from New Jersey and Huntington, Long Island. c. 1800–60.

Comment
Storage jars of this sort are customarily attributed to southwestern Connecticut. They were produced in several different localities, including Norwalk and South Norwalk. Since their lids fit loosely, they were unsuitable for the storage of perishable foods, and most probably held dry goods such as flour, sugar, cornmeal, and other staples.

Hints for Collectors
The jar and lid seen here differ slightly in color and glaze. Since the 2 pieces were usually made and fired separately, these differences are common. Attractive redware jars like this, decorated with splotches of black, are fairly plentiful, and they are popular with collectors. Consequently, they often command a good price, especially in Connecticut, where many of them were produced.

Jars, Bean Pots, and Related Objects

These largely utilitarian storage vessels were designed to hold a variety of foodstuffs and beverages, ranging from preserves to whiskey. Some are tall and cylindrical, while others are short and squat. All have a relatively wide mouth.

Jars are perhaps the most familiar of these pieces. An essential part of the 19th-century kitchen, jars held preserves such as stewed fruits and vegetables, as well as staples such as flour. Although redware examples were probably once common, they are harder to find today than their sturdier stoneware counterparts, many of which were salt-glazed and decorated with cobalt-blue slip.

Churns, traditionally used to make butter, somewhat resemble jars, although they are much larger. Redware churns occasionally appear on the market, but most that have survived are stoneware. Especially popular with collectors are miniature churns, which were most likely intended as toys or novelties.

Among the other large pieces included in this section are water coolers. These barrel-shaped containers held water, cider, or wine, and were often decorated with embossed or incised bands, probably to mimic the straps on beer barrels. Rundlets, smaller versions of the water cooler, were carried to fields or workshops filled with water or whiskey. Many of these little kegs were made of red earthenware.

Bean pots are short and squat, and were usually equipped with matching lids. The earliest examples lacked handles; most were made of red earthenware and glazed only on the interior. Later examples, often of stoneware, had a handle attached near the rim and at midbody. Most frequently, these were glazed on the interior and exterior with brown or a combination of brown and white slip.

Like bean pots, most sugar bowls are short and squat. The examples seen here range from elaborate early 19th-century sgraffito- and slip-decorated pieces to those that were mass-produced in the 1900s.

A few crocks and vases that resemble jars are also included here, as well as such unusual pieces as hot-water bottles and chicken waterers.

Flint-enamel sugar bowl

Description
Gourd-shaped vessel with dome-shaped lid. Bowl has fluted sides. Neck defined by line and with shaped rim. 2 elaborate branch-form handles with scrolled ends attached at shoulder and waist. Lower body curves in to shaped base. Matching lid with mushroomlike handle. *Variations:* Body may be octagonal with wide panels. Lid and handles may be in geometric forms.

Materials and Dimensions
Yellow earthenware with clear alkaline glaze sprinkled with brown manganese and green copper oxides. Molded; handles separately shaped and applied. Height: 7–7½". Diameter: 5½–6".

Locality and Period
United States Pottery Company, Bennington, Vermont. c. 1849–58.

Comment
While sugar bowls with Rockingham glaze were made at many potteries from New Jersey to Ohio and Maryland, examples with a flint-enamel finish were only produced in Bennington, Vermont. The flint-enamel technique was patented in 1849. In this technique, powdered metallic oxides were applied to a fired pot, which was then refired. During firing, the oxides ran together, producing the characteristic finish.

Hints for Collectors
Flint-enamel tea and coffee sets usually consist of a teapot, a coffeepot, a creamer, and a covered sugar bowl. They are not easy to come by, and the cost of a matching set is quite high. It is usually more economical to assemble your own set through several purchases.

Rockingham pipkin

Description
Cooking vessel with dome-shaped lid. Sides curve in from low
waist to neck with shaped rim. S-curved handle attached just
above waist. Plain base. Matching lid with overhanging rim and
flat, buttonlike handle mounted on short stem. *Variations:*
Handle of bowl may be hollow.

Materials and Dimensions
Yellow earthenware with Rockingham glaze. Molded; handle
separately shaped and applied. Height: 6–10″. Diameter: 6–8″.

Locality and Period
Vermont, New York, New Jersey, and Ohio. c. 1845–90.

Comment
Used primarily in the baking of beans, pipkins were produced by
several large potteries in the Northeast. Examples from the
United States Pottery Company at Bennington, Vermont, may
bear the firm's 1849 mark, but most pipkins from other kilns
were not marked. Bennington pipkins were produced in 4 sizes,
ranging in price from $3.50 to $7.50 per dozen. Some of these
pieces have hollow handles, which allowed steam to escape
during cooking.

Hints for Collectors
With their long, outcurving handles, pipkins were easily broken,
and intact Rockingham examples are rare today. Always make
sure that the handle has not been reglued or replaced. The
original lids matched the bodies in both glaze and style. If the top
is missing, one from a crock, tobacco jar, or similar vessel will
make a piece more useful, but, of course, it will still be less
valuable than a pipkin with its original lid.

Art pottery sugar bowl

Description
Squat bowl with high waist and plain rim. Below waist, sides curve in slightly to plain base. Thick handle with flattened end attached at rim. Matching lid has plain edge, ring decoration, and disklike handle. *Variations:* Most bowls have semicircular handles attached at top and base.

Materials and Dimensions
Red earthenware with clear alkaline glaze. Decorated with thick green glaze dripped over upper bowl, lid, and handle. Molded; handle separately shaped and applied. Height: 3–4″. Diameter: 3½–4½″.

Locality and Period
Frankoma Pottery, Sapulpa, Oklahoma. c. 1948–60.

Comment
Regional art potteries like Frankoma often emphasize local clays and decorative motifs related to the area's history. Frankoma pieces, for instance, are sometimes decorated with wagon wheels, desert flowers, and Indian motifs, and have earth-tone glazes with names like prairie green and desert gold. The clay used to make this sugar bowl was dug in Sapulpa.

Hints for Collectors
The products of small potteries are often higher-priced in the region where they are made than they are elsewhere. Frankoma wares, for example, will cost more in Oklahoma and Arkansas than in the Northeast. Frankoma pieces are currently quite plentiful in the East and Midwest and, although gaining in popularity, they are still inexpensive.

Spongeware bean pot

Description
Rounded vessel with sides curving in to collarlike neck marked by shallow ring. Neck tapers slightly to plain rim. U-shaped handle attached just below rim and at waist. Narrow rimmed base. Lower body embossed with fluting set at angle. Matching lid with knoblike handle rests on interior ledge. *Variations:* Some pieces lack fluting or have other embossed decoration.

Materials and Dimensions
Stoneware glazed with cream-colored slip. Decorated with dark green and brown spongework; similar pieces decorated with blue or white spongework. Similar pieces sometimes in white earthenware. Molded; handle separately shaped and applied. Height: 6–7″. Diameter: 6–7″.

Locality and Period
New Jersey and Ohio. c. 1890–1920.

Comment
Spongeware bean pots are less common than examples in redware or plain stoneware. Although termed bean pots in turn-of-the-century advertisements and price lists, pieces like this may have served as sugar bowls or mustard pots. Examples that were actually used for baking beans have a dark brown cast on the bottom.

Hints for Collectors
This pot retains the original lid with its knoblike handle, which makes it a particularly choice piece. Decorated in 3 colors, it is more highly valued than those with the more common 2-color decoration. Since many dealers are not aware of these color distinctions, it is still possible to find bargains.

Redware herb pot

Description
Small, rounded pot with sides curving in from waist to pinched
neck and heavy collar. Large ear-shaped handle attached at neck
and just below waist. Sides curve in from waist to shaped base.
Disklike lid with small knoblike handle rests on interior ledge.
Variations: May have small pouring spout. Base may be plain.

Materials and Dimensions
Red earthenware with clear lead glaze; base unglazed. Decorated
with touches of manganese black; similar pieces decorated with
yellow, green, brown, or orange glaze. Wheel-thrown; handle
separately shaped and applied; lid separately shaped. Height:
5–6″. Diameter: 4½–5½″.

Locality and Period
New England and New York. c. 1820–60.

Comment
Some of these small pots held medicinal herbs for teas, and
others were used to preserve dough scraps that provided yeast
for the next batch of bread. Often used at the table, these pots
were frequently glazed in several colors. Although today
collectors usually call them herb pots, early price lists simply
refer to them as pots.

Hints for Collectors
A piece with a narrow ledge inside the neck was designed to
have a lid. If the lid is missing, the value of a pot will decrease as
much as 30 percent. Lids should match in shape, size, and
decoration, but not necessarily in the shade of clay. They were
often made from a different batch of clay than the pots and fired
separately.

Stoneware bean pot

Description
Squat, rounded vessel with sides sloping in to pinched neck and thick collar. Plain rim. Broad, shaped base. Ear-shaped handle attached at neck and high on waist. Matching lid with flat, round knoblike handle rests on interior ledge. *Variations:* Some examples lack handles, others have 2.

Materials and Dimensions
Stoneware glazed with brown Albany slip; base unglazed. Wheel-thrown; handle separately shaped and applied; lid separately shaped. Height: 6–8″. Diameter: 7–9″.

Locality and Period
New England west to Missouri and throughout much of the Southwest and South. c. 1840–1910.

Comment
Although not as common as their redware cousins, stoneware bean pots were made over a long period of time throughout much of America. In 1858 a stoneware pottery at Bennington, Vermont, was making 2 sizes, the smaller priced at $2.00 per dozen, the larger at $3.00. Nine years later they were still being produced, but the price had increased by 50 cents per dozen for each size.

Hints for Collectors
Although most of these pieces originally came with lids, many have lost them. If you pick up pots and lids whenever you can, eventually you should be able to pair them. Frequently, both were marked with the numbers of the molds they were cast in, which you can often use as a guide in matching pieces.

Stoneware bean pot

Description
Squat pot with sides that slope in from waist to wide, collarlike neck with plain rim. Ear-shaped handle attached just below rim and on shoulder. Plain base. Ledge inside rim supports matching lid with knoblike handle. Upper portion dark brown; lower portion white. "YORK/P" stamped on front with ink. *Variations:* Usually unmarked.

Materials and Dimensions
Stoneware; exterior glazed with brown Albany slip and white Bristol slip; interior glazed with brown Albany slip. Molded; handle separately shaped and applied. Height: 5–7″. Diameter: 6–7″.

Locality and Period
York, Pennsylvania. c. 1920–50. Similar pieces from New England west to Texas and throughout the South and Southwest. c. 1900–50.

Comment
Bean pots have been made for more than 150 years. Most mid- and late 20th-century examples are stoneware glazed with brown and white slip, which was also used for stoneware crocks and churns. The bulk of the pieces produced today are made in Texas and Ohio.

Hints for Collectors
Stoneware decorated with brown and white slip is inexpensive and ideal for the beginning collector. Because all pieces look much the same, it can be difficult to distinguish those that are older. They will be wheel-thrown rather than molded and will show wear on the bottom. Chips may be present on the rim and lid, and the glaze occasionally shows crazing.

Redware bean pot

Description
Tall pot with sides that taper to collarlike neck. Plain rim.
Incised ring at neck and on shoulder. Plain base. Ear-shaped
handle attached near rim and at waist. Matching lid with knob-
shaped handle. *Variations:* Some pots have 2 handles.

Materials and Dimensions
Red earthenware; exterior unglazed; lid and interior with clear
lead glaze. Some examples with clear lead or manganese-black
glaze on exterior. Wheel-thrown; handle separately shaped and
applied; lid separately shaped. Height: 5–7″. Diameter: 5½–7½″.

Locality and Period
New England west to Pennsylvania, south to Virginia and the
Carolinas. c. 1820–1900.

Comment
After 1850, bean pots with handles gradually replaced those
without them, although many potters continued to make both
types. Pieces were commonly glazed only on the inside, reflecting
the potter's economy in dealing with ordinary kitchenware.
These pots sold for just a few pennies and were usually replaced
after a few years of use. They were often referred to as "dirt
dishes," reflecting their utilitarian function.

Hints for Collectors
Bean pots, common and inexpensive, make attractive storage
containers for such things as coffee, flour, and sugar. They can,
of course, also be used for their original purpose, although
cracked pieces placed over heat or in the oven are likely to
break. Marked examples are rare and therefore more valuable.

Redware bean pot

Description
Squat container with high waist and sides that taper sharply to shaped rim. Below waist, sides slope gradually to plain base. Initials "DSB" crudely incised in side at waist level. *Variations:* Most pieces lack incised initials or decoration. Later pieces have handle.

Materials and Dimensions
Red earthenware; exterior unglazed; interior with clear lead glaze. Rare examples glazed with several colors on exterior. Wheel-thrown. Height: 4–6". Diameter: 5–7".

Locality and Period
New England west to Pennsylvania, south to the Carolinas. c. 1770–1870.

Comment
Beans were a staple of the early American diet, especially in New England, and traditionally they were baked in small pots such as the one seen here. The earliest examples lacked a handle; in the mid-19th century, versions with a single handle became the common form. Cheaply made and sold, most of these pots were undecorated because as ovenware they tended to have a short life span. They were glazed on the interior to prevent leakage of liquids; a small number had additional decoration such as a colored glaze or incised designs.

Hints for Collectors
Often pots made as gifts or to order were inscribed with initials, as on the piece illustrated. The initials are probably those of the person for whom the pot was made. Individual touches like this almost always increase the worth of a piece.

Miniature redware bean pot

Description
Small, bulbous pot with swelling sides that taper above waist to neck and shaped rim. Below waist, sides slope gradually to plain base. "BOSTON BAKED BEANS" impressed in side. *Variations:* Impressed wording varies.

Materials and Dimensions
Red earthenware, unglazed. Wheel-thrown. Height: 1¾–3". Diameter: 2–3".

Locality and Period
New England, possibly Massachusetts. c. 1890–1920.

Comment
The most common of all miniatures, containers for samples of Boston baked beans were produced around the turn of the century in New England. The impressed words clearly indicate what these pots were intended to promote. The pot shown here is the most common size; few large examples were made. Rarest of all is a set of salt and pepper shakers in this shape with pewter tops. All known examples are unglazed, and all appear to be handmade.

Hints for Collectors
An interesting collection of miniature bean pots might include examples of various sizes and with variations of the impressed lettering. Look for such pots among the wares of dealers specializing in miniatures. Minor damage will not significantly lessen value. However, since these pots are quite common and prices are reasonable, there is no need to purchase a severely chipped or cracked example.

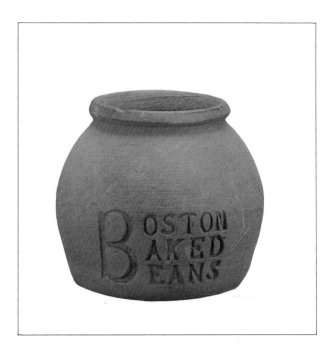

Redware herb jar

Description
Small container with matching lid. Sides slope in from waist to neck and collar. Plain rim. Below waist, sides curve in to shaped base. Matching lid with rounded knoblike handle rests on interior ledge. *Variations:* May lack collar.

Materials and Dimensions
Red earthenware with clear lead glaze; similar pieces with manganese-black glaze. Decorated with green, yellow, and manganese brown. Wheel-thrown; top separately shaped. Height: 4–7″. Diameter: 3–5″.

Locality and Period
New England west to Ohio, south to the Carolinas. c. 1800–80.

Comment
These small vessels are often referred to as herb jars, but as with many early storage pieces, their specific function is not known. Condiments might have been kept in them, and the decorative glazing suggests that they were used at the table, perhaps to hold jam or honey. They are seldom, if ever, marked, and it is extremely difficult to attribute any example to a specific pottery.

Hints for Collectors
Always examine multiglazed pieces carefully. These pieces bring high prices because of their beauty, but sometimes hard-to-spot repairs have been made on areas with chipped or flaked glaze, usually by applying paint or epoxy. Ultraviolet light is helpful in spotting such restoration, which can substantially lower the value of a piece.

Redware jar

Description
Tall vessel with matching lid. Above waist, sides slope in to neck defined by incised line. Flat rim. Below waist, sides slope in to shaped base. Decorated with incised and slip-painted floral motifs, including large tulips and date "1822" surrounded by heart; sgraffito decoration also present. Dome-shaped matching lid with buttonlike handle similarly decorated. *Variations:* Form of lid varies. Decoration varies and may include pierced areas.

Materials and Dimensions
Red earthenware with yellow lead-base glaze; areas of lower body unglazed. Decorated with manganese brown and copper green. Wheel-thrown; top separately shaped. Height: 7–9½". Diameter: 4–5½".

Locality and Period
Attributed to Pennsylvania. 1822. Similar pieces from New Jersey, Virginia, and North Carolina. c. 1780–1880.

Comment
The spectacular decoration and specific date suggest that this piece was made for a special occasion or as a gift. Showpieces of this quality are rare and extremely expensive. They required far more time and skill than most pieces, and were made primarily in Pennsylvania, where potters maintained a long tradition of such work.

Hints for Collectors
Workmanship like that seen here justifies high prices. The jar illustrated is in very good condition, but such a piece would still be quite valuable even with far greater damage. Buying such a jar broken in pieces might be worthwhile if a skilled restorer could salvage some of its beauty. Get an estimate beforehand; restoration can be costly.

Redware sugar bowl

Description
Squat vessel with tall, crown-shaped lid. Sides of bowl slope in to
wide neck with heavy, shaped rim. 2 lug handles attached just
above midpoint. Shaped base. Decorated with applied floral
motifs. Lid decorated with notching and applied balls and strips
of clay. *Variations:* May have pierced decoration. Lids often less
elaborate.

Materials and Dimensions
Red earthenware with heavy brown glaze. Decorated with
polychrome slip. Wheel-thrown; handles separately shaped and
applied; lid separately shaped; decorative details modeled and
molded. Height: 7–8″. Diameter: 5–6″.

Locality and Period
John Nase, Montgomery County, Pennsylvania. c. 1830–40.
Similar pieces from New Jersey to Virginia. c. 1790–1870.

Comment
This sugar bowl was made by one of Pennsylvania's better-
known redware potters, John Nase. Nase produced redware for
several decades at the pottery his father Johannes Neesz (1775–
1867) had established. His output included slip- and sgrafitto-
decorated pie plates, shaving basins, and platters as well as
covered bowls.

Hints for Collectors
Highly decorated redware pieces like this are among the most
expensive of American ceramics, especially those made by well-
known potters such as John Nase, David Spinner, and Samuel
Troxel. Most of this pottery is in museum collections and rarely
appears on the market, but skillful reproductions exist. Check
any prospective acquisition for wear and for the tiny glaze cracks
that come with age.

Art pottery sugar bowl

Description
Bowl and lid decorated to resemble an ear of corn. Sides of bowl slope in from low waist to neck, then flare out to plain rim. Shaped base. Matching lid cone-shaped with elongated acorn-shaped handle. Impressed "Shawnee/USA" on bottom.
Variations: Form usually less naturalistic.

Materials and Dimensions
White earthenware; exterior with green and yellow glaze; interior with yellow glaze. Molded. Height: 5½–6″. Diameter: 5–5½″.

Locality and Period
Shawnee Pottery, Zanesville, Ohio. c. 1937–55. Similar pieces from New Jersey and Ohio. c. 1930–50.

Comment
Fruit- and vegetable-shaped pottery vessels were first made in quantity in Europe in the 19th century, and their popularity continued both abroad and in America in the 20th century. The Shawnee Pottery produced an entire line of corn-shaped objects, including long, narrow dishes shaped like corn cobs. Although most potteries had their own designers, for some years the Shawnee firm produced wares to the specifications of their clients.

Hints for Collectors
Twentieth-century pottery produced by Shawnee, Frankoma, A. E. Hull, and other firms offers the collector an opportunity to purchase interesting American ceramics for modest sums. Choose only marked examples in good condition. A complete set of matching pieces is always more valuable than a mixed set.

Description
Cone-shaped vessel with matching lid. Sides angle outward to plain rim. 2 triangular handles with shaped base attached just below rim. Incised lines present at level of handles. Flaring base. Stepped lid decorated with concentric circles and with central triangular handle.

Materials and Dimensions
White earthenware with opaque, deep rose glaze; other examples in all standard Harlequin colors. Molded; handles separately shaped and applied. Height: 4–4¼". Diameter: 3–3⅕".

Locality and Period
Homer Laughlin Company, Newell, West Virginia. c. 1938–64.

Comment
A complete set of tableware and accessories was produced in the Harlequin pattern, and collectors today attempt to acquire as many matching pieces as possible. The form seen in this sugar bowl will also be found in such items as baking dishes, cups, teapots, and small soup bowls with handles, which were called cream soups.

Hints for Collectors
Like pieces in the Fiesta pattern, Harlequin pottery has found its way into antiques shops, but it can still be found—and often for much less—in flea markets and house sales. Even if a bowl has lost its lid, it is probably worth purchasing if it is in good condition; with a little luck it should be easy to find a matching one. Purchased separately, the pieces will cost less than they would together.

Redware bowl

Description
Small vessel with high waist defined by thin, incised line. Above this, sides curve in to short, collarlike neck with slightly rolled rim. Below waist, body slopes sharply to heavy, shaped base. 2 lug handles attached just above waist. *Variations:* May have matching lid and shallow ledge inside mouth. May have more elaborate handles. May be decorated with pierced work.

Materials and Dimensions
Red earthenware with clear lead glaze. Decorated with green and yellow slip. Wheel-thrown; handles separately shaped and applied. Height: 3–4″. Diameter: 2¾–3½″.

Locality and Period
New England west to Illinois, south to Virginia. c. 1780–1860.

Comment
Many potteries produced small bowls like this. Those that came with lids were probably used as sugar bowls. Others served as salt bowls. Inventories and price lists from 19th-century potteries mention both types. In the 1820s, several potteries in Maine sold bowls like this for 4 cents.

Hints for Collectors
If there is a shallow ledge present on the inside of the rim, or if the rim shows substantial wear, the bowl probably came with a cover. Since a missing lid usually devalues a piece by about 30 to 50 percent, make sure you are not paying a premium for a piece that is incomplete. The bowl illustrated lacks the interior ledge and signs of wear about the rim; it probably never had a matching lid.

Miniature redware churn

Description
Small vessel with sides that slope in gradually to wide neck defined by incised line. Flaring rim. 2 lug handles below neck. Plain base. Matching lid has raised central section with hole and rests on interior ledge. *Variations:* Neck may have 2 incised lines.

Materials and Dimensions
Red earthenware with cream-colored glaze; areas near rim and base unglazed; most examples with clear lead glaze. Decorated with green spongework. Wheel-thrown; handles separately shaped and applied; lid separately shaped. Height: 2½–3″. Diameter: 1¾–2¼″.

Locality and Period
New York and New England. c. 1820–60.

Comment
Miniature churns are very rare, unlike the common miniature jugs and crocks. The scarcest are those made of redware with a multicolored glaze, like the piece illustrated. Similar examples in stoneware were made in Bennington, Vermont; Fort Edward, New York; and in some Pennsylvania potteries. These miniature pieces were probably intended to be toys or novelties.

Hints for Collectors
A churn like this, complete with original lid, would be a real find for the collector of miniature American redware. Few early miniatures retain their lids, and the presence of one may double the value of a piece. Whenever you buy a piece missing its lid, ask if the lid is available—there is always the chance the dealer or owner may have simply misplaced it.

Redware vase

Description
Tall vase with high waist and shoulder marked by incised lines.
Above waist, sides slope in sharply to neck then out to flaring
rim. 2 spiral-shaped handles below neck. Below waist, sides slope
in to plain base. *Variations:* May have applied decoration. Some
examples have elaborate ear-shaped handles.

Materials and Dimensions
Red earthenware; exterior with green and brown glaze on cream
base; interior with cream glaze. Wheel-thrown; handles
separately shaped and applied. Height: 12–15″. Diameter: 6–7½″.

Locality and Period
Virginia. c. 1860–1900. Similar pieces from Maryland to North
Carolina. c. 1800–1900.

Comment
The shape and decoration of this piece suggest that it may be
from the well-known Bell pottery in Strasburg, Virginia, a state
noted for its richly decorated redware. Much of this pottery was
produced in the late 19th century, when financial difficulties had
closed almost all of the northeastern potteries. Virginia redware
may bear marks of Bell family members, or those of Jacob
Eberly, Anthony Baecher, or George Schweinfurt, all of whom
were active in Strasburg.

Hints for Collectors
Many of the Virginia potters were of German extraction, and
their pottery has European characteristics, such as ornate
handles and heavy modeling, that set it apart from more
conservatively decorated American examples. If a piece is not
marked and its origin is in doubt, compare it with documented
examples of southern pottery in museums or books.

Redware jar

Description
Tall vessel with egg-shaped body. Shoulder slopes in to tall neck with plain rim. Below, sides taper to slightly flaring, shaped base. Flattened, disklike lid with round, buttonlike handle. *Variations:* Later pieces have squatter or straight-sided bodies. Rare examples have tooled or incised decoration.

Materials and Dimensions
Red earthenware with clear lead glaze; similar pieces with touches of green, yellow, or black glaze. Wheel-thrown; lid separately shaped. Height: 8–11″. Diameter: 6–9″.

Locality and Period
New England. c. 1790–1820.

Comment
Early redware jars, like the vessel illustrated here, were very plain, with egg-shaped bodies. They were made in small shops, usually run by 1 or 2 men, for use in the local community. Because jars and lids were made separately, both were numbered so they could be properly matched. These jars were glazed inside and out to accommodate both moist and dry foodstuffs.

Hints for Collectors
Small chips, such as those seen here about the rim, are almost always present in examples from the late 18th and early 19th centuries. They rarely affect value because such pieces are so hard to find. A bad crack, however, would substantially reduce the jar's worth.

Redware spice jar

Description
Small container with pronounced shoulder accentuated by 2 incised lines. Sides slope sharply in to neck, then out again to wide, flaring rim. Below shoulder, sides taper to shaped base. Flat lid with buttonlike handle rests on interior ledge.
Variations: Body may have straight sides and less flaring rim.

Materials and Dimensions
Red earthenware with clear lead glaze; base and lower body unglazed. Similar pieces with black glaze and multicolored glaze, often green and yellow. Wheel-thrown; lid separately shaped. Height: 3–6″. Diameter: 2½–4″.

Locality and Period
New England west to Ohio, south to the Carolinas. c. 1800–60.

Comment
The term "spice jar" does not appear in early potters' price lists, but it has become customary among collectors to call very small, lidded vessels "spice jars" or "spice pots." Contemporary accounts confirm that herbs and spices were often stored in such containers, but it is unclear whether or not they were specifically made and sold for this purpose.

Hints for Collectors
Whatever they may have been intended for, spice jars are often lovely little pieces of redware. They are particularly valuable if found in a multihued glaze—most appear, as the example illustrated, in the more common clear lead glaze. A matching lid will also increase the value of the piece. Check the bottom for a number when searching for a replacement lid; the same incised number may mean the lid and body go together.

Redware preserve jar

Description
Tall jar with sides that slope gradually out to high shoulder and then in to neck and shaped rim. Interior of rim has ledge to hold tin or ceramic lid. Plain base. Front marked "A. WILCOX/ED PROSSER." *Variations:* Shape may differ. Interior ledge may not be present.

Materials and Dimensions
Red earthenware with clear lead glaze. Wheel-thrown. Height: 7–10″. Diameter: 5–6″.

Locality and Period
Alvin Wilcox, West Bloomfield, New York. c. 1850–55. Similar pieces from New England west to Indiana and south to the Carolinas. c. 1790–1870.

Comment
This preserve jar was made at the pottery of Alvin Wilcox, which was apparently managed from time to time by an employee named Edwin Prosser. Except for the mark, it is typical of high-shouldered preserve jars made throughout much of the eastern United States during the 19th century. Printing type, cheaper than special potters' stamps, was used to make the impression, a common practice among country potters.

Hints for Collectors
Not only potters' names were impressed on redware. Names of such merchants as grocers and liquor dealers also appeared. Redware in particular was seldom marked by the maker, and a potter's mark substantially increases the value of a piece; a merchant's name will not.

Stoneware preserve jar

Description
Vessel with high, rounded shoulder sloping in to wide neck defined by incised line. Flaring, shaped rim with interior ledge to support cover. Plain base. Stenciled around middle of jar "A. P. DONAGHHO/PARKERSBURG, W. VIRGINIA." *Variations:* Shape of neck and rim varies. Base may be chamfered.

Materials and Dimensions
Stoneware; exterior with salt glaze; interior glazed with brown Albany slip. Names stenciled on exterior in cobalt blue. Wheel-thrown. Height: 7–10″. Diameter: 5–7″.

Locality and Period
A. P. Donaghho, Parkersburg, West Virginia. c. 1866–1908. Similar pieces from New Jersey to Indiana. c. 1860–1910.

Comment
The A. P. Donaghho pottery produced a large number of stencil-decorated preserve or canning jars. Stencil decoration was inexpensive because it could be done quickly by people with little training or artistic ability. The stenciled decoration was painted onto the unfired pot, which was then salt-glazed in the kiln. This technique was used primarily in Pennsylvania and West Virginia.

Hints for Collectors
A jar with a single stenciled bird or other object is far less important and less expensive than one covered with a stenciled composition of flowers, leaves, eagles, or names. Look especially for pieces decorated with patriotic paraphernalia; these are currently the most popular and costly of all stencil work.

Stoneware preserve jars

Description
Cylindrical storage vessels. Sides rise to high, rounded shoulder
and grooved neck marked by 1 or more incised lines. Flaring
collar with plain rim. Floral decoration below shoulder.
Variations: Collar may be shorter. Collar may have wider flare.
Decoration varies.

Materials and Dimensions
Stoneware; exterior with salt glaze; interior glazed with brown
Albany slip. Decorated with cobalt blue. Wheel-thrown. Height:
6–12″. Diameter: 4–8″.

Locality and Period
Pennsylvania and West Virginia. c. 1860–90. Similar pieces from
New York west to Indiana, south to Virginia. c. 1800–1900.

Comment
Some of the most attractive preserve jars are the blue-decorated
examples produced in Pennsylvania and West Virginia.
Decoration is generally floral rather than figural, and was applied
either freehand or using stencils. The straight sides made it
easier to store the jars together. Most are fairly small; few hold
more than a quart.

Hints for Collectors
Common but well made, jars like those shown here are in great
demand and are becoming expensive, particularly if marked.
Among the most sought-after are marked examples from the
Remmey pottery in Philadelphia and the pottery owned by John
Bell in Waynesboro, Pennsylvania. Look for examples that have
good proportions and elaborate decoration, such as the piece at
right.

Description
Cylindrical storage vessels with sides tapering gradually to neck marked by heavy, incised line. Shaped rim and plain base. Jar at right swells slightly at waist; below waist, sides slope in and flare slightly out at base; interior of rim has ledge to support tin lid. Jar at left decorated with 3 irregular bands of blue slip.
Variations: Rim may be heavier or may have incised ring.

Materials and Dimensions
Stoneware. Left: exterior with salt glaze, decorated with cobalt blue. Right: exterior glazed with brown Albany slip. Both: interior glazed with brown Albany slip. Wheel-thrown. Height: 6–10″. Diameter: 3½–6″.

Locality and Period
New Jersey west to Missouri, south to Delaware. c. 1860–1900.

Comment
Stoneware preserve, canning, or fruit jars, or "jugoos" as they were popularly known in western Pennsylvania, were of 2 basic types. The form shown here at left was sealed with a bound piece of cloth or paper over a layer of hot wax. The more sophisticated form at right was a later development: a tin lid fit into the neck of the jar and was then sealed with wax. In the 1900s, glass canning jars replaced both types.

Hints for Collectors
Preserve jars in various shapes and sizes can make an interesting collection. Marked examples are fairly uncommon and command a higher price. Many of these jars cracked, often near the rim, during firing. Pieces with large cracks should be avoided, especially if the cracks run into the decoration.

Stoneware preserve jar

Description
Storage or canning vessel with sides that slope gradually in from waist to shoulder marked by 2 incised lines. Wide neck and flaring rim. Interior of rim has ledge to support lid. Lower body slopes in to base marked by incised line. *Variations:* Most preserve jars have straighter sides.

Materials and Dimensions
Stoneware glazed with brown Albany slip. Wheel-thrown. Height: 8–10″. Diameter: 5½–6½″.

Locality and Period
New York west to Indiana, south to Virginia. c. 1840–80.

Comment
Preserve jars with a pronounced ledge around the inside of the neck were often called "wax sealers," since a tin or pottery lid could rest on the ledge and be sealed into place with hot wax. Wax sealers with egg-shaped bodies like the one shown here are uncommon—most examples had straight sides. The curving form probably indicates that the piece is earlier than most wax sealers.

Hints for Collectors
The glaze on this jar is one of those happy accidents of pottery. Overheating in the kiln changed the glaze from brown to a mixture of olive green and tan, producing a remarkably beautiful piece. Many collectors fail to appreciate uncalculated variations, and such pieces are often reasonably priced. Avoid pieces that were overfired enough to burn the clay or blister the surface. Some potteries threw away badly overfired jars, while others sold them at a reduced price.

Yellowware preserve jar

Description
Small storage vessel with body that tapers gracefully from
rounded shoulder to plain base. Incised ring at shoulder beneath
an incurving neck and flaring, shaped rim. Bottom slightly
recessed. *Variations:* May have straight shoulder and rolled
rather than flaring rim.

Materials and Dimensions
Yellow earthenware with clear alkaline glaze. Wheel-thrown.
Height: 6–8″. Diameter: 4–5″.

Locality and Period
New Jersey and Ohio. c. 1860–80.

Comment
Intended to hold fruit or vegetables, these jars are both graceful
and compact. They lack, however, the durability of stoneware
preserve jars and the transparency provided by glass Mason
jars. The absence of marked pieces and references to these jars
in company price lists makes it difficult to identify exactly where
they were made, but most examples have been found in the East
and Midwest.

Hints for Collectors
Yellowware preserve jars, unlike their numerous stoneware and
redware cousins, were never made in quantity, and are therefore
hard to find. An unusual piece like the jar shown here would be
an important addition to any pottery collection. Since it is not a
popular collector's item—decorated yellowware seems to be
favored—you might be able to buy one from a dealer or flea
market vendor who does not know what it is and thus
underprices it. Any collector lucky enough to find such a piece
should acquire it regardless of condition. The chance may not
come again.

Stoneware fruit jar

Description
Tall preserve jar with high, rounded shoulder, narrow neck, and flaring collar with plain rim. Plain base. Brown floral slip decoration on front. *Variations:* Shoulders may be less rounded. Collar may be straight. Most examples lack decoration and marks.

Materials and Dimensions
Stoneware; exterior with light tan glaze; interior glazed with dark brown Albany slip. Decorated with reddish-brown manganese glaze. Wheel-thrown; some later examples molded. Height: 8–10″. Diameter: 5–6″.

Locality and Period
New York west to Missouri and throughout the Mid-Atlantic states. c. 1870–1900.

Comment
Also known as corkers, fruit jars were made to keep fruit and vegetable preserves and were produced primarily in Pennsylvania and the Midwest. Most brown-glazed examples were undecorated and unmarked. They remained popular until the end of the 19th century despite competition from the newly developed vacuum jar. Fruit jars were sealed by pouring hot wax over a tin, wooden, or pottery lid.

Hints for Collectors
Fruit jars are common and inexpensive, but decoration renders them valuable. If they are decorated in manganese brown rather than the usual cobalt blue, they are even more desirable. Unusual pieces like this are often overlooked and can sometimes be purchased inexpensively.

Redware jar

Description
Tall vessel with high shoulder defined by incised lines. Above neck, thin, flaring rim forms wide mouth. Plain base. Crude floral slip decoration on front. Side impressed "L. JOHNSON/NEWSTEAD." *Variations:* Rim may be thicker and less flared.

Materials and Dimensions
Red earthenware with clear lead glaze. Decorated with brown slip. Wheel-thrown. Height: 9–12″. Diameter: 6–8″.

Locality and Period
Lorenzo Johnson, Newstead, New York. c. 1840–60. Similar pieces from New England west to Indiana, south to the Carolinas. c. 1800–80.

Comment
Storage jars with wide mouths were used for a variety of purposes, including pickling, preserving fresh eggs, and storing dry foods such as flour and cracked wheat. Since they were primarily utilitarian, such pieces were usually not decorated, although some have simple designs like the one shown here.

Hints for Collectors
A rare mark can make an otherwise ordinary piece of redware quite important. Neither the shape nor the glaze of this piece is outstanding, but there is an impressed pottery mark—that of Lorenzo Johnson, who worked in Newstead, New York, in the second half of the 19th century. He is best known for redware covered with a thick, off-white glaze, which was designed to resemble stoneware. Any piece of marked redware is considered a rarity, and the presence of Johnson's name greatly enhances the value of this jar.

Redware jar

Description
Cylindrical storage jar has sharply angled shoulder marked by 2 incised lines. Collarlike neck with plain, slightly flaring rim. Plain base. *Variations:* Ledge may be present on interior of rim. Base may be shaped.

Materials and Dimensions
Red earthenware with clear lead glaze; base unglazed. Exterior decorated with sponging in manganese black; similar pieces with overall black glaze or sponged with brown, yellow, orange, and green. Wheel-thrown. Height: 6–12″. Diameter: 3½–6½″.

Locality and Period
New England west to Pennsylvania, south to Maryland. c. 1800–70.

Comment
Although most straight-sided storage jars have a black glaze, a substantial number have a clear glaze daubed or sponged with manganese black, such as the piece illustrated. These are generally attributed to Connecticut potteries, especially those in the Norwalk area, but similar pieces were made in Pennsylvania. Less common are jars with a multicolored glaze in various combinations of brown, green, yellow, and orange.

Hints for Collectors
These jars are extremely attractive and practical, especially in sets of various sizes. However, jars less than 7″ high are uncommon, and examples marked by a potter are almost nonexistent. Rim damage is very common on redware jars; either avoid these pieces or pay substantially less for them.

Redware jar

Description
Cylindrical vessel with incised line at sharply angled shoulder.
Pinched neck and slightly flaring rim. Interior of mouth with
small sloping ledge. 2 incised lines at base. *Variations:* Some
examples more ovoid than cylindrical. Shoulder may be
impressed with coggled line.

Materials and Dimensions
Red earthenware with shiny black manganese glaze. Wheel-
thrown. Height: 6–12″. Diameter: 3½–7″.

Locality and Period
New England west to Pennsylvania. c. 1790–1860.

Comment
Straight-sided storage jars with a shiny black glaze were made in
large numbers, especially in Pennsylvania and Connecticut. The
glaze, which includes a black manganese compound, was popular
throughout the first half of the 19th century and is found on jugs,
spittoons, and other objects. The jars were used for preserving
foods like fruits and vegetables and storage of such things as
herbs, flour, and sugar. Most of the jars were not made with
matching lids.

Hints for Collectors
An overall black glaze is not popular with most collectors today.
Consequently, these jars can be purchased quite reasonably.
They were produced in a variety of sizes, making it possible to
assemble a matching set ranging from 6″ to somewhat more than
12″. The smallest examples, probably used to store herbs, are
harder to find but particularly desirable.

Stoneware churn

Description
Tall churn with sides that taper slightly above waist to neck and flaring collar with shaped rim. 2 lug handles below neck. Plain base. Transfer-printed heart and capacity number "2" in blue just below waist. Matching lid with raised central ridge and central hole. *Variations:* Some examples have straighter sides and larger handles.

Materials and Dimensions
Stoneware; exterior glazed with white Bristol slip below waist and brown Albany slip above; interior and lid glazed with brown Albany slip; rim unglazed. Cobalt-blue decoration. Similar examples glazed entirely with white slip. Molded; handles separately shaped and applied. Height: 12–16″. Diameter: 8–10″.

Locality and Period
New England west to Texas. c. 1880–1920.

Comment
These late 19th-century mold-cast churns are not nearly as common as the brown-and-white crocks made in large quantities at the turn of the century. By then making butter at home was becoming a novelty in most areas of the country. The use of stenciled rather than impressed or freehand capacity numbers was another late 19th-century innovation. This quicker and more efficient process lowered costs.

Hints for Collectors
Of little interest to most collectors, these churns should be inexpensive despite their scarcity. They make useful planters and storage pieces and are a necessary addition for a complete collection of brown-and-white stoneware.

Stoneware churn

Description
Tall, massive vessel; sides taper above waist to neck and flaring collar and below to plain base. 2 lug handles at shoulder. Incised line at level of handles. Large floral decoration and the number "3" painted on front. Impressed below rim "N. CLARK & CO/ ROCHESTER, N.Y." Matching lid has bulbous center knob with hole. *Variations:* Early examples have straighter sides.

Materials and Dimensions
Stoneware; exterior with salt glaze; interior and lid glazed with brown Albany slip. Cobalt-blue decoration. Wheel-thrown; handles separately shaped and applied; cover separately shaped on wheel. Height: 14–17″. Diameter: 8–11″.

Locality and Period
Nathan Clark & Company, Rochester, New York. c. 1841–52. Similar pieces from New England to Ohio and south to the Carolinas. c. 1790–1890.

Comment
This churn bears the mark of a stoneware factory established in Rochester in 1841 under the management of John Burger, a skilled Alsatian potter who later took over the company under his own name. Pieces made by this firm during the 19th century are among the finest of blue-decorated stoneware. A dasher for churning cream passed through the hole in the cover.

Hints for Collectors
Some of the most interesting blue decoration is found on churns, since their large surfaces provided ample space for the artist's designs. The churn shown here has a prominent chip in the rim and brown burn marks, but if damage does not mar the design, the extensive decoration makes such pieces a worthwile investment.

Stoneware crock

Description
Tall vessel with sides sloping gently from high waist to neck defined by incised line. Collar has plain rim. Ear-shaped handle attached at shoulder and waist; opposite side with lug handle. Lower body tapers to plain base. Band of blue circles body at base of handles. Number "6" impressed on shoulder. *Variations:* Handles vary in shape and placement. Single handle may be present.

Materials and Dimensions
Stoneware with alkaline glaze; unglazed near base. Decorated with cobalt blue. Wheel-thrown; handles separately shaped and applied. Height: 11–19″. Diameter: 6–9″.

Locality and Period
North Carolina. c. 1870–90. Similar pieces from the Carolinas south to Florida. c. 1800–1920.

Comment
The type of alkaline glaze most often used on stoneware in the South is made by first mixing wood ashes with water to produce lye. The lye is then combined with either slaked lime, sand, ground glass, or clay to make a thick paste that in firing becomes green to brown. Equally characteristic of southern pieces is the combination of lug and ear-shaped handles, which was rarely used in the North.

Hints for Collectors
Southern potters seemed to have preferred crocks, jugs, and jars; other forms are uncommon and therefore especially desirable. Pieces decorated with cobalt blue are also rare. Since southern ware was seldom marked, an example bearing the stamp of a potter is a real find.

Stoneware crock

Description
Large vessel with sides that slope gently in from high waist to
short neck. Wide, flaring rim. Below waist, sides taper to plain
base. At shoulder on each side, heavy lug handle with ends
extending down body. *Variations:* Handles vary in shape or
placement. Single handle may be present.

Materials and Dimensions
Stoneware with salt glaze; similar pieces with alkaline glaze.
Wheel-thrown; handles separately shaped and applied. Height:
12–18″. Diameter: 7–9″.

Locality and Period
Attributed to J. Dorris Craven, Seagrove, North Carolina.
c. 1850–90. Similar pieces from the Carolinas south to Florida.
c. 1800–1920.

Comment
Although salt-glazed stoneware was common in North Carolina,
in other parts of the South alkaline glaze was preferred. Most
southern salt-glazed ware was undecorated or had, at most,
touches of cobalt blue at the base of handles and around marks or
capacity numbers. The crock illustrated here has the gently
sloping sides characteristic of much southern pottery; by the
second half of the 19th century, when this piece was made,
northern potters were usually producing straight-sided crocks.

Hints for Collectors
Southern stoneware is relatively unknown and unappreciated
outside of the South, yet it is an interesting part of the American
ceramic heritage. Particularly scarce are such small pieces as
inkwells and figural mantel ornaments, especially those with
cobalt-blue decoration.

63 Stoneware hot-water bottle

Description
Ovoid container with high shoulder that slopes sharply to knoblike finial with slight indentation around it. Shoulder encircled by incised band. Bunghole raised on thick stem. Back (opposite bunghole) flattened slightly. Marked "BANGOR STONEWARE CO./BANGOR MAINE" above plain base. *Variations:* Shoulder may slope more gently. Body may be rounder.

Materials and Dimensions
Stoneware with salt glaze; interior glazed with brown Albany slip; top of finial and lower body unglazed. Similar examples with shiny white Bristol glaze. Wheel-thrown; similar pieces molded. Height: 8–10″. Diameter: 5–7″.

Locality and Period
Bangor Stoneware Company, Bangor, Maine. c. 1890–1910. Similar pieces from New England to Ohio. c. 1870–1920.

Comment
Hot-water bottles became common in America in the late 19th century. Some early wheel-thrown redware vessels may have been used as hot-water bottles, but most examples are made of stoneware and were cast in molds. Wheel-thrown stoneware pieces like the one illustrated are less common. The flattened back prevented the bottle from rolling. The string and cork were probably not sold with the bottle.

Hints for Collectors
American hot-water bottles are sometimes confused with the more numerous English examples. The latter are usually marked with the name and location of an English pottery and are glazed with a rich, light brown slip. Most marked American hot-water bottles were made in Massachusetts at the Dorchester Pottery Works, which began operation in 1895.

Stoneware chicken waterer

Description
Cylindrical vessel with recessed and domed upper section
terminating in flattened finial. Round hole, partially covered by
rounded, cuplike projection with larger oblong opening near plain
base. *Variations:* In earlier examples, upper section may not be
recessed.

Materials and Dimensions
Stoneware glazed with white Bristol slip; upper section unglazed.
Molded; upper section and cuplike projection separately shaped
and applied. Height: 8–11″. Diameter: 6–8″.

Locality and Period
New England west to Missouri, south to the Carolinas.
c. 1840–1920.

Comment
Chicken waterers provided water for chickens, turkeys, and
other fowl. Water was poured through the hole into the tilted
vessel. With the vessel upright, water ran out the hole and rose
to the lower edge of the cuplike projection. As the chickens
drank, water refilled the cuplike area. Chicken waterers were
not made by most potteries, and early 19th-century examples are
rare. Late 19th-century cast models, however, such as the
example illustrated, are more common. The earlier examples
were made of red earthenware or of salt-glazed stoneware.

Hints for Collectors
A chicken waterer is an interesting addition to a stoneware
collection. The late 19th-century cast pieces are easier to find.
Look for examples that have the manufacturer's name, usually
stenciled, on them. The more color or decoration these pieces
have, the more desirable they are.

Stoneware water cooler

Description
Large, barrel-shaped vessel with sides sloping in from waist to plain rim and base. 3 embossed blue bands at top and bottom and 2 above and below waist. Large bunghole with protruding stem close to base. Top and bottom recessed. Impressed "W. SMITH/ GREENWICH/NEW YORK" below rim. *Variations:* May have drain hole in top. May have elaborate incised or slip decoration.

Materials and Dimensions
Stoneware; exterior with salt glaze; interior glazed with brown Albany slip. Cobalt-blue decoration on embossed banding. Wheel-thrown; top and bunghole stem separately shaped and applied. Height: 14–22″. Diameter: 10–13″.

Locality and Period
Washington Smith, New York City. c. 1833–61. Similar pieces from New England west to Ohio and south to the Carolinas. c. 1780–1880.

Comment
Such pieces, called water coolers or fountains, were generally made to order. Their price depended on capacity: In the 1830s the Clark and Fox pottery in Athens, New York, sold their coolers for 24 cents per gallon; in the 1850s the Norton stoneware pottery at Bennington, Vermont, was charging only a penny more per gallon. The embossed bands on the example shown simulate barrel straps, a favored decoration for such pieces.

Hints for Collectors
Water coolers are interesting forms and can be made more practical by adding a wooden spigot, which can be found in most housewares departments, to fit the bunghole.

Redware water cooler

Description
Barrel-shaped vessel with sides tapering to plain rim and base
from low waist. 6 incised bands encircle body. Top and bottom
slightly recessed. Bunghole at waist on one side; smaller hole on
top. Incised on bottom: "1854." *Variations:* Late 18th-century
kegs are taller and slimmer. Some examples have embossed,
concentric bands on sides.

Materials and Dimensions
Red earthenware with clear lead glaze; similar pieces with
multicolored or black glaze. Wheel-thrown in 2 sections, then
joined at waist; top and bottom separately shaped and applied.
Height: 9–12″. Diameter: 7–10″.

Locality and Period
New England west to Ohio, south to Virginia. c. 1780–1860.

Comment
Although apparently made in substantial numbers, few redware
water coolers have survived. They are heavy, fragile, and hard
to handle. Nearly all examples have a clear lead glaze; multicolor
or black glazes are rare. The incised bands on the piece
illustrated here mimic barrel straps, perhaps because whiskey
was stored in barrels.

Hints for Collectors
Unlike most pieces of redware, the water cooler shown here is
marked with the date of manufacture, which enhances the value
of any piece. Dates, potter's marks, and other inscriptions help
reveal the history of a pottery. This piece shows chips and
abrasions, especially on the top and bottom edges; the damage is
minimal, but it does affect value. The more noticeable the
damage, the less the piece is worth.

67 Redware rundlet

Description
Small, barrel-shaped vessel with 4 embossed ridges at top and at bottom. Bunghole at slightly swelling waist. *Variations:* Some rundlets lack decorative ridges. Others have hole in top as well as bunghole.

Materials and Dimensions
Red earthenware with black glaze. Molded in 2 pieces, then joined at waist. Height: 4–6″. Diameter: 3–4″.

Locality and Period
New England west to Pennsylvania. c. 1800–50.

Comment
Most redware rundlets have an opaque black glaze and are mold-cast rather than thrown. Since many of these pieces vary only slightly in their dimensions, the molds must have been more or less standardized. Like other small kegs, rundlets held alcoholic beverages, primarily rum, and were taken to the field or workshop. The hole sometimes present in the top made pouring or drinking easier since it allowed air in to displace the liquid pouring out.

Hints for Collectors
Rundlets are interesting and rather uncommon pieces of pottery. Since most collectors do not seem to like the black glaze, it is often possible to purchase a black-glazed example for much less than what a multicolored-glazed redware piece or a stoneware example would cost. Since black-glazed examples are relatively common, avoid those that are chipped or otherwise damaged. It should be easy to find a piece in good condition.

Stoneware rundlet

Description
Barrel-shaped vessel with 3 decorative bands at each end and 2
above and below bunghole. Circular bunghole with flaring,
shaped rim is raised on short stem. Impressed "C. CROLIUS/
STONE-WARE MANUFACTURER/MANHATTAN WELLS NEW YORK."
Variations: Later pieces slightly larger or with different
arrangements of decorative bands. Some Ohio pieces have
applied ear-shaped protrusions with drilled holes.

Materials and Dimensions
Stoneware; exterior with salt glaze; interior glazed with ocher
slip. Decorated with cobalt blue. Wheel-thrown; top, bottom, and
bunghole stem separately shaped and applied. Height: 6–7".
Diameter: 4–5".

Locality and Period
Clarkson Crolius, New York City. c. 1800–14. Similar pieces
from New England to Ohio. c. 1780–1840.

Comment
Although not common today, stoneware rundlets, or swiglers, as
they were sometimes known, were produced by most early
eastern potteries. Used to carry liquor or water, the smallest
held about a pint; those with a capacity of more than 3 pints were
generally termed "kegs" or "water coolers." Marked examples
like this one are extremely rare, but unmarked pieces appear
fairly often. Pieces with drilled holes could be carried on string.

Hints for Collectors
Rundlets are relatively obscure and not commonly sought after.
They are small enough to store and display easily, always an
advantage for the collector. Furthermore, since they stored the
whiskey that our forefathers were apparently so fond of, they
are wonderful conversation pieces.

Redware rundlet

Description
Squat, barrel-shaped vessel with 4 decorative bands at top and
bottom and 2 above and below bunghole with protruding stem.
Top and bottom slightly recessed. *Variations:* Most examples
have simpler banding. Bunghole may be flush with surface. Top
and bottom usually not recessed.

Materials and Dimensions
Red earthenware with mustard-brown and orange glaze; similar
examples with black or multicolored glaze. Wheel-thrown; top,
bottom, and bunghole stem separately shaped and applied.
Height: 4–6″. Diameter: 4–5″.

Locality and Period
New England to Pennsylvania. c. 1800–50.

Comment
This rundlet is unusual because it was thrown as a cylinder, not
made from 2 separately thrown pieces. The top and bottom were
shaped separately and attached to the body with gluelike slip.
Rundlets made in this time-consuming way were usually a special
order rather than production items. A few of these specially
made pieces have incised or slip-trailed figural decoration.

Hints for Collectors
Like all pieces with a glaze of more than one color, these rundlets
are highly desirable and tend to be expensive. The piece
illustrated was used very little and is in mint condition, factors
that also raise the price. Look for chips or cracks; they may
decrease the value of a piece as much as 75 percent, depending
on their location and extent. Ultraviolet light often reveals hard-
to-spot repairs.

Yellowware rundlet

Description
Small, barrel-shaped keg with bunghole that has protruding stem; small air hole on one side of bunghole; 2 decorative rings incised above and below bunghole; 3 rings incised near slightly recessed top and bottom of keg. Back of rundlet slightly flattened. *Variations:* Air hole may be absent. Back sometimes rounded.

Materials and Dimensions
Yellow earthenware with clear alkaline glaze on upper part, brown Albany slip on lower sides and bottom; interior glazed with brown Albany slip. Wheel-thrown; top, bottom, and bunghole stem separately shaped and applied. Similar pieces molded. Height: 5–6″. Diameter: 4–4½″.

Locality and Period
New Jersey and Ohio. c. 1860–90.

Comment
The rise in popularity of yellowware coincided with the decline in popularity of the rundlet, and consequently few were made of yellow earthenware. Wheel-thrown examples with flattened backs like the rundlet illustrated are especially rare. Most of the yellowware rundlets available today were cast in the form of water kegs, complete with hoops and rivets.

Hints for Collectors
Do not confuse early 19th-century thrown rundlets with cast 20th-century examples. The latter were part of liqueur sets that came with 6 small, matching, barrel-shaped cups. These cast, or molded, rundlets, which are common and inexpensive, have a stemless bunghole and a second hole in the top. They are made of a dark yellow-brown clay and are decorated with vertical scratches in imitation of tree bark.

Bottles, Jugs, and Flasks

 Bottles, jugs, and flasks are among the earliest ceramics produced by American potters. They were intended to store all kinds of liquids, including water, wine, ginger beer, molasses, and whiskey.

Bottles

In the late 18th and early 19th centuries, ceramic bottles were modeled after the sack, or wine, bottles made of glass. These pieces have a squat body and a long neck, which usually terminates in a thick, shaped rim. Redware examples often have a clear lead glaze, although examples can be found glazed with black or multicolored slip. Similar bottles were made of stoneware, which, because of its strength, gradually became preferred to fragile red earthenware. After 1850, bottles tended to be tall and cylindrical, with a shoulder that angles in to a thick, doughnut-shaped rim. Known as "ginger beer bottles" because they were designed to hold ginger beer and other carbonated beverages, they were only rarely decorated and very few bear the mark of a pottery. Similar bottles that were designed to store ink may have a small pouring spout.

Jugs

Among the most beautiful examples of American pottery are the graceful, ovoid jugs made before 1800. Tall and elegant, these pieces have U- or ear-shaped handles placed high on the shoulder, and finely tooled rims. After 1800, these ovoid pieces were gradually replaced by squatter forms; after 1830, most jugs were cylindrical. Toward the end of the 19th century, the cylindrical body was topped by a ledge; above the ledge, the shoulder sloped in to a short neck. Although all of these jugs were intended primarily for storage of water or whiskey, they were also used for wine, cooking oil, vinegar, molasses, cider, milk, and even kerosene.

Jugs were made of both red earthenware and stoneware; some, mostly miniatures, were fashioned from yellow earthenware as well. Although incised and impressed decoration were occasionally employed before 1820, most pieces after that were hand-decorated with cobalt-blue slip or with spongework. Toward the end of the 19th century, inexpensive stenciled decoration was introduced; because it could be executed quickly and required little skill, it soon became popular. The stoneware jugs made around the turn of the century were usually covered with a simple coat of brown or brown and white slip. An interesting decorative variation can be seen in the work of some southern potters. Instead of relying on slip decoration, sponging, or stenciling, they applied hand-shaped facial elements to their jugs. Still being produced today, these "face jugs" are also sometimes embellished with applied snakes.

Flasks

Potters fashioned flasks out of both red earthenware and stoneware. These portable containers, which usually held whiskey or rum, are mostly flattened and ovoid, designed to fit easily into a hip pocket. Most stoneware flasks have a simple salt glaze and can store about a pint. Redware examples come in a greater variety of sizes and may have a clear, black, or multicolored glaze. Neither type was popular after about 1850.

71 Stoneware ink bottle

Description
Tall, cylindrical vessel with high shoulder and long neck. Neck
tapers slightly to ring, then flares out to rim with pinched spout.
"WM. ALLEN & CO N.Y. LEDGER INKS" impressed just above plain
base. *Variations:* Similar pieces may lack spout or may be
squatter.

Materials and Dimensions
Stoneware with white Bristol glaze; similar pieces with light
brown glaze. Molded; rim and spout hand-shaped. Height: 8–12″.
Diameter: 3–4″.

Locality and Period
Probably New York City. Similar pieces from the East and
Midwest. c. 1850–90.

Comment
Ink bottles were common during the 19th century. The example
shown is a large "master" bottle, in which ink was stored in bulk
and then transferred to smaller individual ink bottles. The
smaller ink bottles, often no more than 4″ high and without a
pouring spout, are more common than the master ink bottles.
Redware ink bottles with various glazes were also produced,
although they are rare.

Hints for Collectors
The mark on this bottle is that of the ink manufacturer that
ordered it for its product. Few ink bottles bear potters' marks,
and those that do are quite valuable. If you have an ink bottle
with a name and location on it, you may be able to determine if it
is a pottery mark by checking with the local library or historical
society of the town listed in the mark. If they can determine
when the potter or merchant was in business, you will be able to
date the bottle approximately.

Stoneware ginger beer bottles

Description
4 cylindrical bottles with high shoulder and thick, rounded rim. Plain base. Impressed (left to right): "FAIRBANKS & BEARD/ HOWARD ST.," "RUMROY & HALL," "E. HUBBARD," and "COWDEN & WILCOX." *Variations:* Impressions vary. Rim may be in form of tapered cone.

Materials and Dimensions
Stoneware; exterior with salt glaze; interior glazed with brown Albany slip. Similar pieces sometimes touched or partially covered with cobalt blue. Wheel-thrown; later examples molded. Height: 6–10″. Diameter: 2½–4½″.

Locality and Period
Right, Cowden, Wilcox & Company, Harrisburg, Pennsylvania. c. 1850–80. Other pieces from New England west to Indiana, south to Maryland. c. 1850–1900.

Comment
Heavy stoneware bottles for ginger beer, sarsaparilla, and other beverages were made by nearly every American stoneware manufacturer. The vast majority bear the mark of the company for whom they were made, rather than that of the pottery. Ginger beer bottles, sometimes simply called beer bottles, were inexpensive. In 1850 the Bennington, Vermont, stoneware pottery sold them for only $1.00 per dozen.

Hints for Collectors
Ginger beer bottles are still common and inexpensive. Collectors frequently dig them up by the dozen as they explore old dumps. The choicest examples include those with blue decoration and, particularly, those rare pieces, like the Cowden & Wilcox bottle illustrated here, that bear the mark of a pottery rather than a bottler.

Redware ginger beer bottle

Description
Tall vessel with sides that angle outward slightly to high waist.
Above waist, shoulder tapers to narrow neck with thick, shaped
rim. Plain base. "S. DUSTIN" impressed above shoulder.
Variations: May be cylindrical. Rim may be in form of tapered
cone. Neck may have ring.

Materials and Dimensions
Red earthenware with clear lead glaze. Wheel-thrown; rim
separately shaped and applied. Height: 7–10″. Diameter:
3½–4½″.

Locality and Period
New England west to Ohio, south to Virginia. c. 1840–70.

Comment
Although ginger beer bottles made of stoneware are common,
redware examples are relatively rare. Since these vessels held
carbonated beverages that had to be kept under pressure,
stoneware, which is stronger than redware, was no doubt the
preferred material. Also, these pieces were usually shipped in
large quantities and probably banged about in a wagon or ship's
hold. Redware, which is fragile, could not withstand such rough
treatment.

Hints for Collectors
Although ginger beer bottles are often marked, the names are
rarely those of a potter. Instead most bear the name of the
bottler. A ginger beer bottle made of redware is uncommon and
worth purchasing; if it should bear an identifiable potter's mark,
it would be quite valuable.

Redware flask

Description
Flattened, jarlike storage vessel with rounded shoulder and short neck with shaped rim. Below shoulder, sides taper gradually to plain base. Front and back flattened. Bottom has label printed "W. Oakley Raymond/–Collection–." *Variations:* May lack shaped rim.

Materials and Dimensions
Redware with clear lead glaze splotched with black manganese; similar pieces without manganese; base unglazed. Wheel-thrown in 2 pieces and then joined. Height: 6–8″. Width: 4–5″. Depth: 3–4″.

Locality and Period
New England south to Pennsylvania. c. 1780–1840.

Comment
Flasks like this were once popular with workers and travelers. The "refreshment" they contained might be anything from rum to brandy or even plain drinking water. By the mid-19th century they had been almost entirely replaced by cheaper and lighter glass bottles and tin hip flasks. The absence of glaze at the base of the piece indicates where the potter held the flask when he dipped it into the glaze.

Hints for Collectors
The bottom of this piece bears an old label that indicates the flask was once owned by W. Oakley Raymond, a pioneer collector of pottery. If a well-known collector or an authority on pottery has owned a piece, its value will almost always be enhanced. Never remove this kind of label. If one is loose, it may be glued, shellacked down, or covered with a small piece of transparent plastic.

Stoneware flask

Description
Flattened vessel has high shoulder and short neck. Incised line beneath crudely shaped rim. Below shoulder, sides taper gradually to small, plain, oval base. Bottom slightly recessed. *Variations:* Some flasks are squatter. Some have thick, rounded rim. Some have cobalt-blue or incised decoration or a combination of both.

Materials and Dimensions
Stoneware; exterior with salt glaze; interior glazed with ocher slip; traces of ocher slip on rim and neck. Wheel-thrown. Height: 6–9″. Width: 3½–5″. Depth: 2–3½″.

Locality and Period
New England west to Ohio, south to the Carolinas. c. 1790–1860.

Comment
Like redware flasks, those made of stoneware were designed to hold liquids, usually whiskey. They were often carried in a coat pocket; hence the flattened shape. The incised line beneath the rim was used to anchor a string or wire, which bound down the cork. The finer examples were made to order and often bore the owner's name or initials as well as other decoration; today these decorated pieces are rare and expensive.

Hints for Collectors
Undecorated stoneware flasks are easy to find, especially in rural shops throughout New York, Pennsylvania, and Connecticut. Most are reasonably priced, but even the smallest amount of blue decoration usually results in a sharp increase in price. Examples bearing the mark of a potter are extremely rare.

Stoneware bottle

Description

Tall bottle with swelling shoulder and long, narrow neck. Thick, shaped rim. Sides taper gradually from shoulder to plain base. Marked "GOODALE/&/STEDMAN/HARTFORD" on shoulder.
Variations: Most pieces unmarked. Many have shorter necks and stouter bodies.

Materials and Dimensions

Stoneware with light brown ocher glaze. Wheel-thrown. Height: 7–10″. Diameter: 4–5″.

Locality and Period

Goodale & Stedman, Hartford, Connecticut. c. 1822–25. Similar pieces from New England, New York, and the Middle Atlantic states. c. 1800–30.

Comment

Long-necked stoneware bottles closely imitated the green glass whiskey bottles of the same period, although the stoneware was much heavier and, of course, opaque. The limited number that have survived make it clear that most customers preferred glass. Examples like this one that bear the mark of a pottery are quite uncommon. Other examples were marked by Paul Cushman, who worked in Albany, New York, in the early 19th century.

Hints for Collectors

Don't confuse these rare and early long-necked bottles with the many ginger beer bottles made in the mid- and late 19th century. The latter are extremely abundant, inexpensive, and usually bear the mark of the ginger beer or sarsaparilla producer for whom they were made. An early bottle with a potter's mark will be inexpensive only if its owner doesn't know what it is.

Redware bottle

Description
Squat vessel with sides that taper from low shoulder to long neck with flaring, shaped rim. Sides taper slightly from shoulder to plain base. *Variations:* Neck may be shorter. Body may be cylindrical. Base may be chamfered.

Materials and Dimensions
Red earthenware with clear lead glaze; similar pieces with multicolored glaze. Wheel-thrown. Height: 6–8″. Diameter: 3–4″.

Locality and Period
New England west to Ohio, and south to the Carolinas. c. 1790–1840.

Comment
Redware bottles are even less common than those made of stoneware. Examples like the piece illustrated resemble the sack, or wine, bottles of the first quarter of the 19th century, while later 19th-century examples look more like stoneware ginger beer bottles. Marked examples are almost unknown, but pieces with a documented history have been traced to New Hampshire, Connecticut, and New York.

Hints for Collectors
Among the most desirable pieces of redware are those with unusual glazes. Although the bottle illustrated has a clear lead glaze, its rich hue and pebbled surface make it especially appealing. The irregularity of the surface occurred during firing, when the glaze bubbled or blistered. Since all redware bottles are scarce, even a chipped or cracked example is often worth purchasing.

Stoneware corker

Description
Squat, bulbous jar. Above shoulder body curves in to short neck defined by small ridge. Thick, shaped rim. Beneath shoulder sides taper slightly to plain base. *Variations:* Body may be more elongated.

Materials and Dimensions
Stoneware glazed with brown Albany slip. Wheel-thrown; upper neck and rim separately shaped and applied. Height: 6–9″. Diameter: 5½–7″.

Locality and Period
New Jersey west to Missouri, south to Arkansas and Texas. c. 1860–1900.

Comment
These jars were commonly referred to as corkers, since, unlike other canning jars, they could be closed with a common cork. A wire or string was tied around the cork, then under the ridge on the neck. Although price lists do not indicate what was customarily stored in corkers, it seems likely that they held soft foods such as preserves and stewed tomatoes that could easily be poured through the narrow mouth.

Hints for Collectors
Corkers are less common than preserve jars with wide mouths, but they remain inexpensive because few collectors seem interested in them. They make practical household containers and are a necessary part of any canning jar collection. Unlike most stoneware, corkers were seldom, if ever, fired with a salt glaze. Marked examples are rare and especially desirable.

Miniature stoneware jugs

Description
Small jugs with ear-shaped handles and plain bases. Sides taper slightly from high shoulder to base (left and right) or from rounded shoulder to base (center). Rim thick and shaped (left and center) or plain (right). Inscribed across front (left) "Centennial/July 4th/1876." *Variations:* Shapes differ. Inscriptions vary.

Materials and Dimensions
Stoneware glazed with brown Albany slip. Left and center: wheel-thrown. Right: modeled. Left, height: 2¾–3½"; diameter: 1¾–2¼". Center, height: 3–3½"; diameter: 2–2¾". Right, height: ¾–1"; diameter: ½–¾".

Locality and Period
New England west to Missouri, south to Kentucky. c. 1860–1910.

Comment
Most stoneware miniatures have a brown glaze. Although the origins of many have not been established, several incised jugs have been traced to Bennington, Vermont. Most of these have patriotic inscriptions relating to the Battle of Bennington or the 1876 Centennial. A group of similar jugs advertising liquor dealers and taverns comes from Lexington, Kentucky.

Hints for Collectors
Assembling a collection of brown stoneware miniatures decorated with inscriptions is a real challenge. Look for sayings such as "Little Brown Jug," "Merry Christmas, 1877," and "Columbian Exposition, 1893." Although difficult to find, these pieces are not especially expensive: the brown glaze has not been a popular one among collectors of miniatures.

Redware jug

Description
Tall vessel with high shoulder and short, narrow neck with shaped rim. Ear-shaped handle attached at rim and low on shoulder. Below shoulder sides taper to plain base. *Variations:* Earlier examples are more rounded, with narrower semicircular handles.

Materials and Dimensions
Red earthenware with black glaze. Wheel-thrown; handle separately shaped and applied. Height: 6–11″. Diameter: 5–7″.

Locality and Period
New England west to Pennsylvania. c. 1780–1870.

Comment
Jugs covered with a dull or shiny black glaze were made in many places during the 18th and 19th centuries, but they were especially common in Connecticut and Pennsylvania. They come in several sizes with the smallest and largest examples being least common. These jugs were rarely marked, and it is usually impossible to determine their exact origin.

Hints for Collectors
Like other redware pieces with a black glaze, jugs are often reasonably priced. Avoid examples with flaking glaze, since it is particularly conspicuous and unattractive on this type of pottery. Dampness and sudden temperature changes cause this kind of damage, so store your collection in a dry place with a stable temperature. If you own pieces that have flaking glaze, it is possible to disguise the damage. Cover the areas where the red earthenware is visible with black paint, then coat them with clear epoxy. This usually retards further damage.

Stoneware jugs

Description
Ovoid jugs with sides that taper sharply from broad waist to narrow neck with tall, shaped rim. Below waist sides taper to plain base. Ear-shaped handle attached near rim and on shoulder. *Variations:* Neck may have several concentric rings. Body may be squatter.

Materials and Dimensions
Stoneware glazed with tan to brown Albany slip. Wheel-thrown; handles separately shaped and applied. Height: 6–14″. Diameter: 5–9″.

Locality and Period
New England west to Indiana, south to Delaware. c. 1800–40.

Comment
Among the most beautiful pieces of American stoneware are the graceful ovoid jugs produced in quantity during the first half of the 19th century. Although most of them are not marked, it has been established that the majority were made in New York and New England. Very early pieces with brown glaze have a reddish-brown ocher finish; brown-glazed examples from the mid-19th century are rich chocolate. In about 1820 the form became shorter and blockier, and by 1850 the sides were nearly straight.

Hints for Collectors
Today most collectors prefer decorated pottery, and as a consequence, it is expensive and sometimes clearly overpriced. Appealing alternatives are these ovoid jugs, which though highly esteemed by some collectors can often be purchased at reasonable prices. Keep an eye out for marked examples, usually worth twice as much as unmarked jugs.

Redware jug

Description
Squat vessel with gently rounded shoulder and pinched neck
with shaped rim. Below waist sides taper gradually to plain base.
Ear-shaped handle with decorative central groove attached at
rim and on shoulder. Stamped on rim "A. WILCOX/W.
BLOOMFIELD." *Variations:* Shape varies from ovoid to cylindrical.
Handle may be attached in 2 places at shoulder. Rim may be
plain.

Materials and Dimensions
Red earthenware with clear lead glaze. Wheel-thrown; handle
separately shaped and applied. Height: 5–13″. Diameter: 4–10″.

Locality and Period
Alvin Wilcox, West Bloomfield, New York. c. 1840–50. Similar
pieces from New England west to Pennsylvania, south along the
mid-Atlantic coast to the Carolinas. c. 1780–1850.

Comment
The mark on this piece indicates that it was made at the shop of
Alvin Wilcox, who worked near Rochester, New York, from the
1830s to the late 1850s. Few redware pieces bear potter's marks.
Since they were customarily sold near the pottery where they
were produced, buyers usually knew who had made them.
Except for the mark, this jug is typical of those made throughout
the Northeast in the second quarter of the 19th century.

Hints for Collectors
Because of its scarcity, marked redware often commands many
times the price of similar unmarked pieces. Along with Wilcox,
John Bell of Waynesboro, Pennsylvania, Anthony W. Baecher of
Winchester, Virginia, and Solomon Bell of Strasburg, Virginia,
are among the potters who marked their redware.

Miniature redware jug

Description
Small jug with high shoulder and plain neck and rim. Beneath
shoulder sides taper gradually to shaped base. Arched handle
attached at rim and shoulder. Stenciled "SOUVENIR 1902/
CAMBRIDGE/FAIR" on lower side. Painted flowers opposite handle.
Variations: Inscriptions vary and may be incised.

Materials and Dimensions
Red earthenware, unglazed; some examples glazed. Oil-painted
flowers added at a later date. Wheel-thrown; handle separately
shaped and applied. Height: 2–4″. Diameter: 1½–2″.

Locality and Period
Probably New York. c. 1902. Similar examples from New
England west to Ohio, south to Kentucky. c. 1870–1910.

Comment
Miniature jugs were a common product of many different
potteries toward the end of the 19th century. The inscription on
the one shown here suggests that this jug was a souvenir of the
agricultural fair held in Cambridge, New York, in 1902. Many
similar commemorative inscriptions were used, almost always on
unglazed miniature jugs. Glazed redware miniature jugs, on the
other hand, were rarely inscribed; most were probably intended
as toys.

Hints for Collectors
Besides being fun to collect, souvenir miniatures are also
interesting historically because they commemorate fairs, historic
sites, or important occasions like the Philadelphia Centennial of
1876. Since they are fairly uncommon, miniature redware jugs
with inscriptions may be expensive. In shops or at shows, both
the glazed and unglazed miniatures can probably be found among
antique toys.

Miniature stoneware jug

Description
Squat vessel with high, rounded shoulder encircled by incised
line. Neck curves in then out again to form flared rim. Below
shoulder sides taper gradually to plain base. Ear-shaped handle
attached below rim and at shoulder. *Variations:* Some miniature
jugs have incised or cobalt-blue decoration. Others are
cylindrical.

Materials and Dimensions
Stoneware with salt glaze. Wheel-thrown; handle separately
shaped and applied. Height: 2–4″. Diameter: 2–3″.

Locality and Period
New England west to Ohio, south to Kentucky. c. 1850–1900.

Comment
Miniature jugs may have been used by salesmen as samples. No
doubt some were toys for children, and others were sold or given
away as souvenirs. In Kentucky these small vessels were
inscribed with the name of a local tavern and filled with whiskey
—an early form of the "sampler" we are all so familiar with
today.

Hints for Collectors
Jugs are by far the most common of pottery miniatures, and an
interesting collection can be formed with these alone. Unless
they are decorated in blue or with incised patterns they are often
surprisingly inexpensive. Marked examples are rare, although
some with the stamp of the well-known Bennington, Vermont,
stoneware pottery are known. Do not confuse these old pieces
with contemporary stoneware miniatures; although they may be
decorated with cobalt, they usually bear the mark of a 20th-
century pottery.

Stoneware jug

Description
Tall jug with rounded shoulder defined by incised lines. Short neck terminates in incised ring and shaped rim. Semicircular handle applied at neck and high on shoulder. Sides taper from waist to plain base. Impressed "BOSTON" on shoulder opposite handle. *Variations:* Similar pieces marked "BOSTON 1804."

Materials and Dimensions
Stoneware with 2-tone ocher glaze. Wheel-thrown; handle separately shaped and applied. Height: 8–12″. Diameter: 5–8″.

Locality and Period
Frederick Carpenter, Boston, Massachusetts. c. 1804–10.

Comment
Considered by many collectors the most beautifully shaped of all early American stoneware, pieces bearing the Boston mark were made at 2 Boston potteries. The first examples were produced from around 1793 to 1796 by Jonathan Fenton and Frederick Carpenter. These pieces are marked with capital letters that are all the same size. Later examples were made from around 1804 to 1810 by Carpenter at a pottery in Charlestown, the oldest section of Boston. In these early 19th-century pieces, the "B" is taller than the other letters, as in the jug illlustrated. Both types are characterized by superb form and a 2-tone tannish-brown glaze.

Hints for Collectors
If a piece of pottery is glazed with ocher rather than Albany slip, it was probably made before the 1830s, when Albany slip became widely used. Albany slip is darker and more lustrous than ocher, and quickly became the preferred interior glaze. Pieces such as this one where ocher is used as a surface glaze are uncommon.

Description
Large jug with bulging waist. Sides taper to narrow neck. Rim shaped, with double ring. Incised line high on shoulder. Lower body tapers to shaped base. Ear-shaped handle attached at shoulder and beneath rim. *Variations:* Usually lacks elaborate rim.

Materials and Dimensions
Red earthenware; exterior with lead-based yellow, brown, and green glaze; interior with clear lead glaze. Similar pieces with plain lead glaze or in combinations of green, brown, yellow, black, red, and purple. Wheel-thrown; handle separately shaped and applied. Height: 6–15″. Diameter: 4–11″.

Locality and Period
New England west to Ohio, south to Virginia. c. 1750–1850.

Comment
Jugs like the one illustrated were the most common items made by early potters. They were not easy to make, and a finely shaped example is the mark of a master. As a general rule, the earlier the jug, the more elongated the ovoid body is. By the 1830s bodies had become squatter, and after 1850 the form was seldom made.

Hints for Collectors
Two unglazed finger marks on the base of this jug indicate where the potter held the jug as he dipped it into the glaze tank. Since craftsmen tried to avoid marking wares in this manner, finger marks are relatively rare. Early jugs often had areas where the glaze has flaked away, exposing the raw red clay surface. Such unsightly areas affect value significantly. The problem can be helped a bit by covering the exposed clay with epoxy to form a clear, shiny surface.

Stoneware jug

Description
Storage vessel with sides that taper sharply from bulbous waist to narrow neck. Neck terminates in collar with plain rim. Ear-shaped handle attached just below rim and on waist. Lower body tapers sharply to plain base. Impressed below rim "N. CLARK & CO./ MOUNT MORRIS." Incised and painted representation of small steamship alongside floral decoration on upper body. *Variations:* Decoration varies. Earlier pieces more elongated.

Materials and Dimensions
Stoneware; exterior with salt glaze; interior glazed with brown Albany slip. Incised design highlighted with cobalt-blue slip; decoration on similar pieces may lack cobalt blue or, rarely, may have manganese-brown highlights. Wheel-thrown; handle separately shaped and applied. Height: 9–12″. Diameter: 8–10″.

Locality and Period
Nathan Clark & Company, Mount Morris, New York. c. 1835–46. Similar pieces from New England west to Ohio, south to Virginia. c. 1820–50.

Comment
Incised decoration appeared on American stoneware from the 18th century until the early 1840s, although a few later 19th-century examples exist. Typically, it was highlighted in blue. The squat, ovoid body shown here was common from about 1820 to 1840. Earlier shapes were more elongated, and after 1840 gradually became straight-sided.

Hints for Collectors
Stoneware pieces decorated with incised ships are rare and extremely desirable. Most of the ships are unidentifiable, but a few represent particular naval or commercial vessels, giving such pieces historical importance.

Stoneware jug

Description
Tall jug with high shoulder. Sides curve in to narrow neck with
ridge and shaped rim. Heavy handle attached at neck and high
on shoulder. Below shoulder body tapers gently to plain base
defined by incised line. On front of jug incised design of 7-petaled
flower filled with blue. *Variations:* Handle may be attached
lower on neck and may be U-shaped. Rim usually plain.

Materials and Dimensions
Stoneware; exterior with salt glaze; interior with ocher glaze.
Incised decoration filled with cobalt-blue slip; similar pieces may
be decorated with manganese-brown slip or may lack color.
Wheel-thrown; handle separately shaped and applied. Height:
9–13″. Diameter: 6–9″.

Locality and Period
Probably New York or New Jersey. c. 1790–1820. Similar pieces
from New England west to Ohio, south to the Carolinas.
c. 1790–1840.

Comment
Incised decoration on early jugs varies greatly. Some examples
have simple or elaborate floral patterns, while others depict
subjects such as fishes, birds, sailing ships, or, in rare cases,
entire scenes.

Hints for Collectors
Since incised decoration was done freehand, these pieces are
always one of a kind, and consequently command high prices.
But don't pay a lot for any old jug: Not all of the workmen who
decorated these pieces had talent. Be discriminating and get
what you pay for. Incised decoration filled with blue is more
valuable than that which lacks color; incised decoration filled with
manganese-brown slip is rarest of all.

Stoneware jug

Description
Squat, bulbous vessel with bulging waist. Shoulder defined by 2 incised lines. Short neck curves out to shaped rim. Heavy, ear-shaped handle applied at rim and shoulder. Below waist body tapers to plain base. Front slip-decorated with flower and featherlike leaves. Above flower, impressed "HULL & BACH/ BUFFALO." *Variations:* Rim may be plain.

Materials and Dimensions
Stoneware; exterior with salt glaze; interior glazed with brown Albany slip. Decoration cobalt blue; similar pieces rarely with manganese brown or combination of blue and brown. Wheel-thrown; handle separately shaped and applied. Height: 10–14″. Diameter: 9–11″.

Locality and Period
Hull & Bach Company, Buffalo, New York. c. 1835–40. Similar pieces from New England west to Indiana, south to Virginia. c. 1830–50.

Comment
Broad, squat stoneware jugs of this era provided more decorative area than earlier types. Most often, the decoration consisted of a single flower, often a tulip or poppy, which could be executed easily by an unskilled artist. After 1860, decoration became much more sophisticated.

Hints for Collectors
Underpriced and easy to find at present, these flower-decorated jugs offer the collector a chance to acquire an early 19th-century jug for a reasonable price. Pieces with birds, ships, and human figures are rarer and more expensive.

Stoneware presentation jug

Description
Squat storage vessel with high shoulder and narrow neck. Neck with heavy, shaped rim. Ear-shaped handle attached at rim and shoulder. Lightly shaped base. Impressed below rim "WM. E. WARNER/WEST TROY." Front of jug decorated with stylized floral motif above the painted initials "F.L.V." *Variations:* Shape may be more ovoid.

Materials and Dimensions
Stoneware; exterior with salt glaze; interior glazed with brown Albany slip. Cobalt-blue decoration. Wheel-thrown; handle separately shaped and applied. Height: 9–12″. Diameter: 7½–9″.

Locality and Period
William E. Warner, West Troy (Watervliet), New York. c. 1850–55. Similar examples from New England west to Ohio, south to the Carolinas. c. 1850–1900.

Comment
Decorated stoneware with initials or names on it was often specially made as a gift or presentation piece. Such initials may be found on both earlier (pre-1840) ovoid-shaped stoneware and later straight-sided pieces such as the example shown. The elaborate, calligraphic decoration seen here is characteristic of examples made near Albany in West Troy (Watervliet).

Hints for Collectors
Names or initials, like dates, enhance the value of a jug. Unfortunately, it is often impossible to determine why and for whom a piece was made. However, if one is interested, names can be researched in local business directories and census records. What you uncover may enrich the history of your piece and, consequently, its value.

91 Stoneware jug

Description
Jug with high shoulder and narrow neck with shaped rim. Ear-shaped handle attached at rim and high on shoulder. Plain base. Decorated with bird resting on stylized branch with flower and leaf. Shoulder impressed "WHITES, UTICA" beneath number " 9."
Variations: Varied floral, geometric, and figural designs.

Materials and Dimensions
Stoneware; exterior with salt glaze; interior glazed with brown Albany slip. Decoration cobalt blue; rarely manganese brown or a combination of blue and brown. Wheel-thrown; handle separately shaped and applied. Height: 10–16″. Diameter: 6–11″.

Locality and Period
White's Pottery, Utica, New York. c. 1865–77. Similar pieces from New England to Ohio, south to Virginia. c. 1845–1900.

Comment
From the late 1840s, decoration grew increasingly sophisticated and abstract, and elaborate designs became commonplace in the 1860s. Based on the Spencerian script that was then taught in many schools, the decoration was often applied by women or schoolchildren. Previously, potters had decorated their wares themselves.

Hints for Collectors
Look for pieces with a well-balanced blue design and a minimum of damage. Most stains on stoneware are under the glaze and permanent. The brown rust stain on the breast of the bird seen here cannot be removed—it won't "wash right off"—and detracts from the value of the jug.

92 Stoneware jug

Description
Squat jug with high shoulder and collarlike neck. Neck marked by deeply incised line. Heavy, ear-shaped handle attached at rim and high on shoulder. Plain base. Front decorated with simple blue leaf. Front shoulder impressed: "E. NORTON & CO/ BENNINGTON VT." *Variations:* Neck may lack collar.

Materials and Dimensions
Stoneware; exterior with salt glaze; interior glazed with brown Albany slip. Decorated with cobalt blue. Wheel-thrown; handle separately shaped and applied. Height: 9–14″. Diameter: 7–9″.

Locality and Period
Edward Norton & Company, Bennington, Vermont. c. 1883–94. Similar pieces from Maine south to Texas and Virginia. c. 1850–1910.

Comment
The simplicity of the decoration on the jug shown here is typical of such pieces from the late 19th century. The impressed mark is one of the most common of those on Bennington stoneware.

Hints for Collectors
Jugs with straight sides and simple blue designs are by far the most common type of decorated stoneware. Examples with deer, eagles, or houses are rarer and more expensive than pieces with simple blue leaves, flowers, or geometric designs. Marked stoneware, especially that of the Bennington, Vermont, stoneware factory, usually costs more. Many people associate the costly porcelain and Rockinghamware made by the United States Pottery Company in Bennington with the less expensive products from the stoneware factory there. Products from both potteries are much in demand. Even the stoneware examples with simpler decoration tend to be expensive.

Redware face jug

Description
Squat vessel with applied facial features. Sides slope out slightly
from plain base, then in sharply from high shoulder to narrow
neck with plain rim. Ear-shaped handle attached high on neck
and at shoulder. *Variations:* Body may be straight sided. Facial
features sometimes more elaborate, with applied snakes.

Materials and Dimensions
Red earthenware with brown metallic glaze. Similar pieces
stoneware with alkaline or salt glaze. Fragments of porcelain
dish for teeth. Wheel-thrown; features and handle separately
shaped and applied. Height: 6–10″. Diameter: 6–8″.

Locality and Period
Throughout the South, especially North and South Carolina and
Georgia. c. 1850–1920. Similar stoneware pieces throughout the
South. 1850–present.

Comment
Face jugs, or "grotesque" jugs as they are often called, were
produced mostly in the South, and it seems likely that black
potters made at least some of them. Most are of alkaline-glazed
stoneware. They are among the few types of American ceramics
that are anthropomorphic; the finest of them can rightly be
thought of as folk art.

Hints for Collectors
As with other pottery, signs of wear and age such as chips,
smooth bases, and a fine spidering of the glaze will indicate the
earlier pieces. Clever touches, such as the use of broken
porcelain for teeth, are especially desirable. Although the early
jugs, particularly examples in red earthenware, bring high
prices, the stoneware pieces being made today are reasonably
priced.

Stoneware molasses jug

Description
Bell-shaped vessel with high shoulder and short, narrow neck.
Neck has flaring, shaped rim, pulled to form spout. Opposite
spout, large, ear-shaped handle attached at neck and just below
shoulder. Plain base. *Variations:* Shoulder may be squared.

Materials and Dimensions
Stoneware glazed with brown Albany slip; rare examples with
salt glaze. Wheel-thrown; handle and spout separately shaped
and applied. Later examples molded. Height: 9–12″. Diameter:
7–9″.

Locality and Period
New England west to Missouri, southwest to Texas, and south to
Virginia and the Carolinas. c. 1860–1920.

Comment
Commonly called molasses jugs, vessels like the one shown here
were actually used to store a wide variety of liquids, including
whiskey, vinegar, and cooking oil. They were intended primarily
for thicker substances like molasses, which pours better from a
spout. Such jugs were not developed until the mid-19th century.
A price list issued by the Norton stoneware pottery at
Bennington, Vermont, did not list them in 1858, but the same
pottery advertised molasses jugs in 3 sizes in 1867: ½-, 1-, and
2-gallon jugs at prices ranging from $2.75 to $6.50 a dozen.

Hints for Collectors
Molasses jugs are inexpensive and readily available. Many bear
the marks of eastern or midwestern potteries, and although
these are sometimes no more costly than unmarked examples,
such pieces are more likely to appreciate in value over the years.
A real novelty to watch for is the rare salt-glazed molasses jug;
most examples have a brown glaze.

Miniature yellowware jug

Description
Cylindrical vessel with high rounded shoulder and short neck terminating in crudely formed rim. Ear-shaped handle attached at rim and just below shoulder. Plain base. *Variations:* May have flattened oval body.

Materials and Dimensions
Yellow earthenware; exterior with clear alkaline glaze; interior unglazed. Similar pieces with dark brown glaze. Molded; handle separately shaped and applied. Height: 1½–2″. Diameter: ½–¾″.

Locality and Period
Probably Bennington, Vermont. c. 1850–90. Similar pieces made in the East and Midwest. c. 1870–1900.

Comment
Records from the Bennington pottery in the second half of the 19th century refer to miniatures such as the one shown here, which were probably made in quantity. Identical pieces with a heavy brown glaze over a yellow clay body are even more common, and these were made in places as far apart as Kentucky and Ohio. No marked examples are known; indeed, it would be difficult to mark so small an item.

Hints for Collectors
Unmarked miniatures like this can be hard to identify. One approach is to study documented examples in museum collections for comparison. The Bennington Museum in Vermont, for example, has various miniatures known to have been made at the potteries there; similarities in shape and glaze are good evidence of a common source.

Stoneware jug

Description
Tall, cylindrical vessel with straight sides. Shoulder angles sharply to short neck with 2 shaped rings separated by channel. Ear-shaped handle attached at top and bottom of shoulder. Plain base. *Variations:* Neck may lack rings. Handle may be attached at neck and shoulder.

Materials and Dimensions
Stoneware; exterior glazed with white Bristol slip and brown Albany slip; interior glazed with brown Albany slip. Molded; handle separately shaped and applied. Height: 11–12″. Diameter: 6–7″.

Locality and Period
New York, New Jersey, and Ohio. c. 1880–1920. A few similar examples from Texas and the Midwest. c. 1880–1920.

Comment
Cast in molds at large potteries, these vessels were used by distillers and by manufacturers of cooking oil, vinegar, and molasses, all of whom needed large, sturdy containers for the bulk shipment of their products. Some bear stenciled merchants' marks or marks that indicate what they contained, but pottery marks are practically unknown.

Hints for Collectors
These easy-to-recognize and inexpensive jugs are ideal for the beginning stoneware collector. Most antiques dealers who specialize in stoneware regard them as too recent to bother with, so look for them in country shops and at yard sales and rural house auctions. Because they are so common, collectors can be choosy and select only examples in excellent condition.

Stoneware jug

Description
Heavy, cylindrical vessel with sides that rise to ledge. Above
ledge, shoulder curves in to neck with plain rim. Ear-shaped
handle attached just below rim and at shoulder. "ZUCKER &
STEIN,/PASSAIC, N.J." inscribed in blue on front.

Materials and Dimensions
Stoneware; exterior glazed with white Bristol slip; interior
glazed with brown Albany slip. Similar pieces have exterior
glazed with both brown and white slip; some have interior glazed
with white Bristol slip. Molded; handle separately shaped and
applied. Height: 9–12″. Diameter: 6–8″.

Locality and Period
New Jersey and Ohio. c. 1880–1920. Similar pieces occasionally
from Texas and the Midwest. c. 1880–1920.

Comment
Whiskey jugs such as this were mass produced in large factories
in the late 19th and early 20th centuries. Because they had
straight sides they were easy to pack and ship, and this no doubt
contributed to their popularity. They eventually replaced the
wheel-thrown jugs of the preceding decades.

Hints for Collectors
A rather ordinary piece like this can be surprisingly valuable. It
appeals not only to the pottery enthusiast but also to the
collector of advertising memorabilia. Keep an eye out for jugs
marked with the names of firms, especially popular names such
as Park & Tilford, Slazangers', and other well-known distilleries.
These jugs are also of interest to collectors who specialize in
whiskey bottles.

Spongeware jug

Description
Cylindrical vessel with sides topped by ledge. Above ledge, shoulder slopes in to incised line at neck with plain rim. Ear-shaped handle attached at neck and shoulder. Plain base. *Variations:* May lack ledge. Handle may be smaller and U-shaped.

Materials and Dimensions
Stoneware; exterior glazed with yellow slip decorated with green sponging; interior glazed with brown Albany slip. Molded; handle separately shaped and applied. Height: 10–12″. Diameter: 6–7″.

Locality and Period
New Jersey and Ohio. c. 1890–1920.

Comment
Except for their sponged decoration, which was a touch of luxury, these utilitarian vessels resemble other mass-produced molded jugs of the period. All were manufactured at large potteries, mostly in New Jersey and Ohio. The sponged jugs were never as common as the plain ones since they took longer to decorate. Occasionally these pieces will be stamped with the names of businesses, but most simply have spongework.

Hints for Collectors
Although jugs are perhaps less attractive than other spongeware forms, they are just as collectible, at least in part because of spongeware's current popularity. In addition, there are fewer sponge-decorated jugs than bowls, plates, and deep dishes. Relative scarcity may raise their price. Dealers unaware of their worth sometimes price these pieces just as they would plain brown-and-white jugs.

Pitchers, Teapots, Coffeepots, and Related Objects

All of these incredibly varied pieces have a pouring spout and a handle. They range from simple miniature stoneware pitchers to elaborate porcelain coffeepots; some are unadorned, while others are richly decorated with hand painting and gilding. The earliest examples are wheel-thrown; pieces produced after 1850 are usually molded.

In pitchers, the spout forms part of the rim. Wheel-thrown pitchers usually have simple spouts, shaped by hand when the clay was wet. In molded examples, the spout may be more complex, sometimes even animal-shaped. Unlike pitchers, coffeepots and teapots have a tubular spout that is usually attached toward the base of the piece. In most examples, the spout is S-shaped; in a few it is straight. Although coffeepots and teapots resemble one another, teapots are almost always shorter and squatter. Batter jugs also have tubular spouts, but unlike most coffeepots and teapots they have thick, bulbous bodies and a wire handle. Sauce boats, which usually have a small, shaped pouring spout, are low, with an oval body.

Because these pieces vary so greatly in shape, the best clues to identification and dating are clay type, method of manufacture, and decoration.

Wheel-thrown Pieces
Most of the stoneware and redware pieces featured here are wheel-thrown pitchers. A few from the 18th century have survived, but most examples available today were made after the mid-19th century. Bulbous, with a low waist, stoneware pitchers are typically large, with a simple salt glaze; most redware pieces are smaller, with a clear or polychrome glaze. Batter jugs were also made of stoneware; like the pitchers, they have a bulbous body. Among the most desirable of the stoneware pieces are those with painted or slip-trailed cobalt-blue designs and those with incised decoration. The most sought-after redware pitchers have elaborate multicolored glazes.

Molded Pieces
By the mid-19th century, molding techniques had become fairly sophisticated, facilitating mass production. Molded pitchers, teapots, and coffeepots made from about 1850 to 1900 are often adorned with floral and geometric patterns, or with animal and human forms. Yellow earthenware, ironstone, and porcelain were the materials favored by most potteries. In addition to the embossed designs that embellish many of these molded vessels, some yellowware examples have a rich tortoiseshell Rockingham glaze or a striking flint-enamel finish. Ironstone pieces are frequently decorated with inexpensive transfer printing, while porcelain objects might be hand painted and gilded.

At the same time that these elaborate pieces were being made, factories were producing simple, cylindrical pitchers as well. Typically made of yellow earthenware or ironstone, these pieces rarely had any decoration other than sponging.

Modern Examples
Among the most inexpensive pieces included in this section are those that were mass-produced in the late 19th and early 20th centuries. Although often referred to as "art pottery," most of these pitchers and coffeepots were made in large quantities by major factories rather than by hand in small studio potteries. Variously shaped, and with a variety of bright, attractive finishes, these pieces are still affordable and continue to increase in value.

99 Stoneware pitcher

Description
Tall pitcher with low waist. Sides curve in from waist to flaring rim. Front of rim pulled down and out to form spout. 2 incised lines above waist. Opposite spout, ridged, ear-shaped handle attached below rim and just above waist. Below waist sides curve sharply in to shaped base. Opposite handle double tulip design in blue. *Variations:* May be squatter.

Materials and Dimensions
Stoneware; exterior with salt glaze; interior glazed with brown Albany slip. Decorated with cobalt blue. Wheel-thrown. Height: 9–12″. Diameter: 7–9″.

Locality and Period
New England west to Ohio, south to Virginia. c. 1780–1890.

Comment
Although stoneware pitchers with salt glaze appeared in the 18th century, most examples available today date from the mid-19th century or later. Some early pitchers have incised decoration, but blue painted designs were much more common, especially after 1850. Floral motifs were the favored subject; more rare are human and animal figures and even houses. Dates and initials or names also sometimes appear, and potters' marks are fairly common, particularly on pieces dating from 1850 to 1890.

Hints for Collectors
These pitchers are popular and are getting expensive, particularly if they are marked and bear dates or names. Brown-glaze examples are more affordable. However, if you must have a blue-decorated piece, look for it in large city shops. Prices should be lower there because city dealers tend to be less interested in country pieces like these.

Redware pitcher

Description
Small pitcher with low waist. Sides slope in from waist to wide neck decorated with incised lines. Above neck, sides curve out slightly to shaped rim and short, pulled spout. Sides curve down and in to shaped base. Ear-shaped handle made of 2 intertwined pieces of clay attached just above neck and at waist. *Variations:* Handle usually plain. Rim usually plain.

Materials and Dimensions
Red earthenware with clear lead glaze; areas around base unglazed; exterior splotched with brown and green slip. Wheel-thrown; handle separately shaped and applied. Height: 4–6″. Diameter: 2¾–4½″.

Locality and Period
New England west to Ohio, south to the Carolinas. c. 1790–1840.

Comment
Small pitchers were widely produced for many years, but few have such an elaborate handle. Its form, derived from English creamware of the same period, resembles those on 18th-century mugs and teapots from the Moravian pottery at Salem, North Carolina.

Hints for Collectors
Always look closely at how a piece of pottery is constructed. Although resembling other American pitchers in shape, this piece is distinguished and made more valuable by the unusual handle and the incised decoration. Large chips in the rim like those shown here do decrease value, but small glaze chips on the body are of no consequence.

Stoneware pitcher

Description
Pear-shaped vessel with low, swelling waist. Sides curve in to shoulder marked by incised line, then out again to slightly flaring rim with long, pinched spout. Ear-shaped handle attached just below rim and at waist. Below waist sides taper to plain base. *Variations:* Shape of spout and handle may vary.

Materials and Dimensions
Stoneware with light brown glaze; areas near base unglazed; similar pieces with different glaze colors. Wheel-thrown; handle separately shaped and applied. Height: 7–10″. Diameter: 6–9″.

Locality and Period
New England west to Missouri, southwest to Texas, and throughout the South. c. 1830–1910.

Comment
Almost all 19th-century stoneware factories made pitchers in large quantities, and most, especially outside the Northeast, were glazed with brown slip. Some of these pitchers were used on the table for milk, water, or cider, while others held such things as pancake batter.

Hints for Collectors
Most stoneware pitchers are around 9″ to 10″ high. Smaller ones are hard to find and very desirable, especially those with an interesting glaze. Brown slip varies from flat and dull-looking to rich and shiny. A grouping of brown-glazed pitchers in different sizes can be quite attractive. Marked examples, although not difficult to find, are more expensive but still a valuable investment.

Redware pitcher

Description
Large, bulbous vessel with sides that taper from waist to high collar. Collar flares out to plain rim with small, pinched spout at front. Opposite, ear-shaped handle attached just below rim and at waist. Lower body tapers to slightly protruding base.
Variations: Body may have straight sides.

Materials and Dimensions
Red earthenware; exterior with mottled red, yellow, green, and brown glaze; interior with clear lead glaze. Wheel-thrown; handle separately shaped and applied. Height: 9–12″. Diameter: 7–9″.

Locality and Period
Upper New York State. Similar examples from New Hampshire to New Jersey and south to North Carolina. c. 1800–80.

Comment
Pitchers with a mottled, multicolored glaze were never common, since they called for a substantial amount of expensive glazing materials. Consequently, few potteries regularly used this type of decoration; others did so only at special request, usually limiting themselves to the less costly black glaze for red earthenware.

Hints for Collectors
Do not confuse early multiglaze pieces with the much later art pottery forms; the latter are not glazed but made from several types of colored clay mixed together. Art pottery examples, made by potteries such as Niloak, have several colors on the interior of the piece as well as the exterior.

Miniature stoneware pitcher

Description
Small pitcher with sides that taper from pronounced waist to neck with wide, flaring collar. Collar slightly pinched at front to form shallow spout. Opposite, ear-shaped handle attached at waist and collar. Below waist sides taper to plain base.
Variations: Some examples have smaller collars and deeper spouts.

Materials and Dimensions
Stoneware with light tan glaze. Wheel-thrown; handle separately shaped and applied. Height: 3–4″. Diameter: 2¾–3¼″.

Locality and Period
New England west to Ohio. c. 1820–70.

Comment
This piece is large enough to serve as an individual creamer, but it was probably intended as a toy or a miniature. Records show that these small pieces were made at the Bennington, Vermont, stoneware pottery as well as at other potteries in the East and Midwest. Although relatively few were manufactured, most have probably survived, since they were always treated as curiosities rather than as functional pieces of pottery.

Hints for Collectors
Miniatures were often made in sets, so you may eventually find a matching sugar bowl or several similar pieces. However, even pieces in matched sets will vary slightly in size and shape, in part because it is much more difficult on a wheel to shape a small piece than a large one. Look for these pitchers in collections of porcelain and ironstone miniatures, with which they are often mixed.

Stoneware pitcher

Description
Large vessel with bulbous body. Sides swell up and out to
sloping shoulder. Embossed collar with shaped rim and long
spout. Below shoulder, sides slope in to shaped base. Elongated
handle in the form of a greyhound is attached over rim and below
shoulder. Lower body covered with embossed scene of dogs
pursuing stag through woods; collar decorated with grapes and
vines. Bottom marked "J.B. CAIRE & CO./POKEEPSIE/N.Y."
Variations: Position of dog on handle varies.

Materials and Dimensions
Stoneware glazed with brown Albany slip; similar examples with
green or blue and white glaze. Molded; handle separately shaped
and applied. Height: 8–11″. Diameter: 6–8″.

Locality and Period
John B. Caire and Company, Poughkeepsie, New York. c. 1842–
52. Similar pieces from West Troy, New York; Burlington,
Vermont; and East Liverpool and Tiltonville, Ohio. c. 1840–65.

Comment
The popular hound-handled pitcher is most often found in a
Rockingham glaze; less common are stoneware examples with a
brown glaze, as shown here, or a matt green or delftlike blue-
and-white glaze. The latter 2 were produced by the Vance
Faience Pottery Company of Tiltonville, Ohio, in the 1880s.

Hints for Collectors
Always check the bottom of any stoneware pitcher for a maker's
mark; most decorative pitchers are marked there. Marked
hound-handled pitchers such as the one illustrated here are rare
and expensive.

105 White earthenware commemorative creamer

Description
Bulbous pitcher with rounded shoulder. Collar, rim, and spout in form of eagle. Ear-shaped handle in form of knotted piece of rope attached just below rim and at waist. Decorated on side with transfer-printed portrait of Admiral Dewey, on the other with representation of his flagship, *Olympia*. Marked on bottom, "COOK POTTERY CO. JULY PATENTED 1895 TRENTON, N. J." *Variations:* Decoration may commemorate other important 19th-century events and people.

Materials and Dimensions
White earthenware with clear alkaline glaze. Decorated with transfer-printed designs and hand-painted and gilded flags. Molded. Height: 4–4½". Diameter: 3½–4".

Locality and Period
Cook Pottery Company, Trenton, New Jersey. c. 1895. Similar pieces from New York, New Jersey, Ohio, and Maryland. c. 1876–1918.

Comment
The Cook Pottery Company, the manufacturer of this piece, was active in Trenton, New Jersey, from 1894 until after 1900. The creamer commemorates Admiral Dewey's victory over the Spanish fleet at the battle of Manila Bay. Other such pieces bear likenesses of presidents and scenes from other important battles.

Hints for Collectors
Commemorative pottery is popular with some collectors, yet unless a piece is associated with a popular figure such as Lincoln or Washington, prices are not particularly high. Since many people who live in rural areas have preserved these pieces over the years, country shops and auctions are especially good places to look for them.

Porcelain creamer

Description
Squat pitcher with bulbous body. Sides curve in from waist to wide neck marked by raised line. Above, collar with slightly flaring rim and short spout. Ear-shaped handle attached at neck and waist. Plain base. Body with band of blue flower forms and embossed linked circles and vertical ribbing. Collar decorated with embossed scrolls. *Variations:* Body may lack vertical ribbing.

Materials and Dimensions
Porcelain with clear alkaline glaze. Decorated with cobalt blue. Molded; handle separately shaped and applied. Height: 3½–3¾". Diameter: 3¼–3½".

Locality and Period
Attributed to the United States Pottery Company, Bennington, Vermont. c. 1850–58. Similar examples from New York and New Jersey. c. 1860–90.

Comment
Porcelain pitchers were made in large quantities, and small cream pitchers, or creamers, like the one shown here often followed the pattern of the larger pitchers. Although attributed to Bennington, this piece resembles examples made in several American and English factories. English examples, however, tend to be more delicate and skillfully made.

Hints for Collectors
Creamer collections can be interesting, and many kinds of creamers are available. Most are unmarked but their origin can occasionally be determined by comparing them with authenticated examples in museums and elsewhere.

Hand-painted porcelain pitcher

Description
Pitcher with sides that curve in sharply from shoulder to wide neck. Above, collar flares out to shaped rim and large spout. Elongated ear-shaped handle attached high on rim and low on shoulder. Shaped base. Embossed decoration above base; other embossed decoration on spout and where handle joins body. Elaborately decorated with landscape and with floral and geometric forms. Gilding on rim, handle, and sides. *Variations:* Painted decoration varies. Spout may lack embossed decoration.

Materials and Dimensions
Hand-painted porcelain with clear alkaline glaze. Gilded details. Molded; handle separately shaped and applied. Height: 9–9½″. Diameter: 7–8″.

Locality and Period
American China Manufactory, Philadelphia, Pennsylvania. c. 1826–38. Similar examples from Vermont, New Jersey, and Pennsylvania. c. 1825–50.

Comment
During the decade of its operation in Philadelphia, William Tucker's American China Manufactory was the most successful American porcelain company of the first half of the 19th century. Its products, like the piece shown here, are characterized by simple shapes and restrained decoration.

Hints for Collectors
Tucker porcelain is expensive and seldom appears on the market. Examples marked "Tucker & Hulme" or "William E. Tucker" in gold and red ink are known. Collectors should always watch for unrecognized examples. If in doubt about a piece, consult a museum curator or porcelain authority.

Ironstone presentation pitcher

Description
Large, bulbous pitcher with low waist. Sides slope in from waist to wide neck. Neck flares out to scalloped rim and spout. Large, ear-shaped handle with angled brace at bottom attached at rim and high on waist. Lower body tapers to shaped base. Gilded details and painted decoration, including inscription "Mrs. Lucy Forbes." *Variations:* Inscriptions vary.

Materials and Dimensions
Hand-painted ironstone with clear alkaline and pink glaze. Gilded details. Similar pieces with different glaze colors. Molded; handle separately shaped and applied. Height: 4¾–9¾". Diameter: 3¾–7".

Locality and Period
Attributed to the United States Pottery Company, Bennington, Vermont. c. 1850–58. Similar pieces from New York to Ohio. c. 1840–90.

Comment
Vessels like that shown here were commonly called presentation or sweetheart pitchers. Intended as gifts, they came in various sizes and bear either the name or initials of the recipient: women, hotels, even fraternal organizations. Pictorial decoration is less common.

Hints for Collectors
American presentation pitchers are rarely marked. Examples from the United States Pottery Company at Bennington can be recognized by the curling brace or bridge at the foot of the handle. Similar pieces, also attributed to Bennington, have a large floral medallion at the base of the handle.

Porcelain presentation pitcher

Description
Squat vessel with sides that curve in from low waist to wide
neck. Plain rim and flaring spout. Ear-shaped handle in
embossed branch form attached at top of rim and at neck. Below
waist, sides taper to shaped base. Embossed motifs embellished
with gilding. Painted shield with "To The Assembly" written in
gold leaf. "Presented by the M&M Union" and "Of the State of
New York" on sides. *Variations:* Decoration varies greatly.

Materials and Dimensions
Hand-painted porcelain with clear alkaline glaze. Decorated with
gilding. Molded; handle separately shaped and applied. Height:
12–13″. Diameter: 9–9½″.

Locality and Period
Attributed to Charles Cartlidge & Company, Greenpoint, New
York. c. 1844–56. Similar examples from New York, Vermont,
and New Jersey. c. 1850–70.

Comment
The Cartlidge firm, which made soft paste porcelain until about
1850 and hard paste after about 1856, did not mark its wares,
making them hard to identify. Most pieces attributed to
Cartlidge have documented histories.

Hints for Collectors
Because presentation pitchers were popular after around 1860,
enough examples remain to provide an interesting collection.
Business directories and census records may reveal information
about an inscription, enhancing a piece's value.

Rockingham pitchers

Description
Massive pitchers with low, heavy waists marked by incised lines.
Above waist, sides curve inward and then out again to form
scrolled rim with scooplike spout. Opposite spout, elongated
handle in form of dog peering over rim of pitcher. Handle
attached at rim and lower body. Bulbous base. Embossed scene
of deer and rabbit with floral border on each side of pitcher.
Variations: Many variations in hound-shaped handle and
embossed decoration.

Materials and Dimensions
Yellow earthenware with Rockingham glaze. Molded; handle
separately shaped and applied. Height: 6–10″. Diameter: 5–7″.

Locality and Period
New England west to Ohio, south to Maryland. c. 1850–1900.

Comment
The so-called hound-handled Rockingham pitchers were made in
many different cities, including Bennington, Vermont;
Poughkeepsie, New York; and East Liverpool and Tiltonville,
Ohio. The embossed decoration on the sides ranges from the
rather bucolic scene on the examples illustrated to a scene of
hounds hunting down a deer, found on Bennington pieces and
some from Ohio. The form of these pieces is English in origin.

Hints for Collectors
Although many mistakenly believe all hound-handled pitchers
are from the pottery at Bennington, no marked Bennington
pieces have been found. Bennington examples have been
identified by pottery records and by history of ownership.
Marked pieces from both Ohio and New York are known, as well
as examples from a pottery in Burlington, Vermont.

Rockingham creamer

Description
Small pitcher with low waist from which sides curve in to wide neck. Neck flares out to scalloped rim and short spout. Below waist, sides taper sharply to shaped base. Ear-shaped handle attached high on rim and at waist. Sides decorated with embossed tulips and leaves; embossed wreath under spout. *Variations:* May be shorter and wider. Decoration varies.

Materials and Dimensions
Yellow earthenware with Rockingham glaze. Molded; handle separately shaped and applied. Height: 4–5″. Diameter: 3½–4″.

Locality and Period
Vermont west to Ohio, south to Maryland. c. 1830–90.

Comment
Rockingham creamers similar to that shown here were offered by various midwestern potteries during the 1860s and 1870s for as little as $2.00 per dozen. True Rockingham has a mottled tortoiseshell surface, as on this piece, formed by spattered glaze. Some later 19th-century examples were dipped to produce an overall dull brown glaze, a faster, cheaper method that gave a less attractive result.

Hints for Collectors
Small creamers are common but rarely marked. Look for examples with a minimum of damage or wear and a good glaze. The dull brown examples are less valuable today than pieces with a true Rockingham glaze. A collection of creamers in different sizes but with identical decoration can be both interesting and valuable.

Rockingham pitcher

Description
Bulbous pitcher with low, swelling waist. Above waist, sides
curve in to wide neck. Neck swells to scalloped rim with large,
shaped spout. Below waist, sides curve in to shaped base. Ear-
shaped handle in form of curving branch attached at top of rim
and at waist. Upper body embossed with grapes and vines in
vertical panels; lower body embossed with acanthus leaves.
Variations: Embossing varies greatly, may include human and
animal figures, geometric and floral devices.

Materials and Dimensions
Yellow earthenware with Rockingham glaze. Molded; handle
separately shaped and applied. Height: 7–11″. Diameter: 6–7½″.

Locality and Period
Attributed to the United States Pottery Company, Bennington,
Vermont. c. 1852–58. Similar forms from New England west to
Ohio, south to Maryland. c. 1840–90.

Comment
Bulbous Rockingham-glazed pitchers with varied embossed
decoration were made at many potteries. Floral patterns are
most common, but geometric forms also appear. Some examples
are decorated with arches and columns, motifs derived from the
Victorian Gothic Revival style.

Hints for Collectors
The rare "paneled grapevine" pattern, seen on the pitcher
illustrated, is associated with the Bennington pottery; it makes
this example much more valuable than most floral-decorated
pitchers. A collector familiar with floral patterns can spot the
better values.

Stoneware pitcher

Description
Simple, octagonal pitcher with sides that slope in from very low waist to wide neck. Sides slope out from neck to shaped rim and spout. Below waist, sides angle in sharply to octagonal, shaped base. Elongated, ear-shaped handle in form of vine attached at rim and waist. Embossed floral design on sides. *Variations:* Embossed decoration differs. Handle may be plain rather than vinelike.

Materials and Dimensions
Stoneware glazed with brown Albany slip. Molded; handle separately shaped and then applied. Height: 9–11″. Diameter: 7–9″.

Locality and Period
Western New York, probably Syracuse. c. 1850–60. Similar pieces from Maine to Ohio and south to Maryland. c. 1830–80.

Comment
Before 1900 cast stoneware pitchers were not common; technical problems and the cost of molds limited production to a few large companies. There are marked examples from potteries in Poughkeepsie and Geddes (Syracuse), New York; Portland, Maine; Burlington, Vermont; and Baltimore, Maryland.

Hints for Collectors
Any cast stoneware pitcher made prior to 1900 is a rarity, but a marked one is a real find. To avoid marring the surface, potters almost always placed their mark on the bottom of such pitchers. A few examples are marked under the handle.

Porcelain pitchers

Description
Tall pitchers with sides that curve in from very low waist to wide
neck, then gradually out to flaring, shaped rim and spout. Below
waist, sides curve in to shaped base. Elongated handles
embossed with leaf forms and attached high on rim and low on
body. Surface embossed with human figures and palm trees and
other vegetation against stippled background. Bottom of pitcher
at left marked "T.J. & J. MAYER" enclosed in a ribbon. Bottom of
pitcher at right marked "U.S.P." enclosed in ribbon. *Variations:*
Embossed decoration differs widely.

Materials and Dimensions
Porcelain covered with blue slip and clear alkaline glaze. Molded;
handle separately shaped and applied. Height: 9–11½".
Diameter: 5–6".

Locality and Period
Left: Thomas, John, and Joseph Mayer, Hanley, England.
c. 1840–60. Right: United States Pottery Company, Bennington,
Vermont. c. 1852–58.

Comment
With decoration based on a popular, 19th-century moralistic tale,
these pitchers were widely made in England and America.
English examples are distinguished by sharper, more detailed
embossing and 2 dots of blue glaze among the leaves at the tip of
the spout, where Bennington pieces are solid white.

Hints for Collectors
Marks on such pitchers require close inspection. American
potteries often imitated English marks to attract buyers who
preferred English porcelain. For example, the marks on the
pieces illustrated are superficially similar.

Porcelain pitcher

Description
Large pitcher with sides that taper gradually from base to shaped rim with heavy spout. Slightly protruding base. Large, ear-shaped handle with knoblike projections attached to top of rim and lower body. Surface covered with embossed tulips and sunflower plants; embossed palm trees below spout. Bottom marked "U.S.P." enclosed in ribbon. *Variations:* Grotesque mask or scalloped band may appear below spout.

Materials and Dimensions
Porcelain with clear alkaline glaze. Molded; handle separately shaped and applied. Height: 7½–8¾". Diameter: 5–5½".

Locality and Period
United States Pottery Company, Bennington, Vermont. c. 1852–58. Similar pieces made in Massachusetts, New York, and in Portugal. c. 1860–90.

Comment
Although this piece is identified by the mark on its bottom, almost identical pieces were made from about 1873 to 1883 by the New England Pottery Company of East Boston, Massachusetts. Later, a Portuguese firm made similar pieces. Both imitators used colored glazes, which were never put on Bennington pitchers.

Hints for Collectors
The similarity between this expensive piece of Bennington porcelain and later reproductions should stand as a warning to collectors: Always check marks. Compare size, design, and material with those of identified examples. If possible, get a written statement of authenticity.

Description
Tall vessel with sides that slope out gradually to form curving rim with large, pulled spout. Shaped base. Elongated, ear-shaped handle with shaped base attached just below rim and on lower body. Sides decorated with pairs of vertical lines and with embossed flowers, leaves, and stems. Impressed on bottom "Weller Pottery/since 1872."

Materials and Dimensions
White earthenware with pale green glaze; embossed design decorated with white, yellow, brown, and dark green slip. Molded; handle separately shaped and applied. Height: 11–13″. Diameter: 4½–6″.

Locality and Period
Weller Pottery, Zanesville, Ohio. c. 1930–40.

Comment
Art pottery sets often included a pitcher and several matching tumblers or goblets. Weller produced many lines that are very similar to those of other potteries.

Hints for Collectors
Water pitchers are distinguished from other types of pitchers by their elongated form. Some have a shaped spout that prevents ice from falling into a glass as it is filled. Although intact sets consisting of a pitcher and matching tumblers are uncommon, it is not too difficult to assemble a set by buying a marked pitcher and then finding tumblers that match both its pattern and glaze colors. These pieces were usually produced in quantity, so they should be easy to find in secondhand stores and at rummage sales.

Description
Left: Vessel in form of human figure with feet and legs and one hand tucked inside coat, sitting on oval base with embossed decoration. Hat-shaped rim with spout. Handle with embossed floral decoration attached at back of hat and midway down figure's back. Marked on base "Reproduction Bennington Museum." Right: Vessel in form of bust of figure with one hand tucked into coat. Hat-shaped rim with pouring spout. Handle with embossed floral decoration attached at base of hat and high on figure's shoulder. Plain base. Embossed medallion on hat. *Variations:* Figures vary in placement of hands, facial features, and shape and placement of handle.

Materials and Dimensions
Yellow earthenware with Rockingham glaze. Molded; handle separately shaped and applied. Height: 5¾–7″. Diameter: 4–5½″.

Locality and Period
Left: Bennington, Vermont. c. 1970–80. Right: Attributed to United States Pottery Company, Bennington, Vermont. c. 1849–58. Similar examples from England and New Jersey. c. 1840–90.

Comment
The toby pitcher, a traditional English form, was also popular in America—the Bennington pottery alone produced 5 types. Since few pieces are marked, it is usually difficult to determine where a particular item was made.

Hints for Collectors
Nineteenth-century toby pitchers have been widely reproduced. The example shown on the left is clearly marked as a reproduction, but not all are so explicit. The collector should become familiar with identified examples and look for the usual signs of age.

Yellowware figural pitcher

Description
Squat vessel in the form of President Herbert Hoover. Plain rim and small spout. Arms extend at an angle with hands gripping arms of chair. Shoes protrude below hands, forming base. Bracket-shaped handle attached to back of head and back of chair at shoulder level. Facsimile Hoover signature on base.
Variations: Many different political and theatrical figures are depicted.

Materials and Dimensions
Yellow earthenware with clear alkaline glaze; signature in black slip. Molded. Height: 5½–6½″. Diameter: 4½–5½″.

Locality and Period
Syracuse China Company, Syracuse, New York. c. 1928–32. Similar pieces from New Jersey west to Ohio. c. 1925–40.

Comment
The manufacturer of the pitcher illustrated has been a ceramics producer since the late 19th century, specializing in ironstone china and fine porcelain. This figural piece follows the tradition of many such political subjects in pottery and glass made in America during the past 150 years.

Hints for Collectors
Don't avoid pottery and porcelain because it was made only 50 years ago. Political figures like this that combine topical interest and the potter's skill are bound to increase in value. They interest both collectors of political memorabilia and ceramics enthusiasts, and were usually made in a limited quantity. Today demand exceeds the number of examples available.

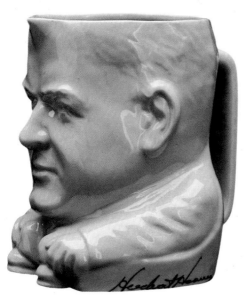

Stoneware sewer-tile pitchers

Description
Left: Pitcher with sides tapering slightly to plain rim. Spout
adorned with classical mask. Shaped base. Twig-shaped handle
attached at lower edge of rim and lower body. Incised lines on
body imitate bark with applied knoblike disks. Right: Pitcher
with sides that taper slightly to plain rim. Spout with applied
frog. Plain base. Ear-shaped handle attached below rim and
midpoint on body. Incised lines on body with applied
representations of wreath, man with pipe, and knoblike disks.
Variations: Applied decoration always varies.

Materials and Dimensions
Stoneware with dark brown glaze. Wheel-thrown; handles
separately shaped and applied; decorative details cast in molds
and applied. Height: 6–9″. Diameter: 4½–5½″.

Locality and Period
New York, Pennsylvania, and Ohio. c. 1880–1915.

Comment
What is called sewer-tile or sewer-pipe pottery represents the
last labors of the traditional potter. By the 1880s many of the
older kilns were closed, and the potters who had worked in them
got jobs producing drainage and sewer tile. In their spare time
they made complex, one-of-a-kind pieces like the examples shown
here, which were made from the same clay as the tiles and were
probably intended as presents.

Hints for Collectors
Until recently sewer tile pottery did not interest most collectors,
but it is beginning to find buyers. Look for it in the 3 states
where most examples were made.

Art pottery pitcher

Description
Tall vessel with sides that curve in from shoulder marked by an impressed line. Plain rim and small spout. Long, ear-shaped handle attached at shoulder and low on body. Below, sides slope in sharply to rimmed base. Embossed decoration: floral motif on shoulder and lower body; kingfisher with trees and grass on side panels; cattails on front and back.

Materials and Dimensions
White earthenware with dark blue glaze. Molded; handle separately shaped and applied. Height: 7½–9″. Diameter: 5½–6½″.

Locality and Period
Weller Pottery, Zanesville, Ohio. c. 1925–40. Similar examples from Ohio and New Jersey. c. 1920–50.

Comment
This piece is an example of the Weller Zona Kingfisher pattern. Jars, bowls, and basket forms were also made in this line. Unlike much art pottery, these pieces were durable, practical, and intended for household use. The glaze on the pitcher illustrated here was applied thinly in places to allow the white body to show through, creating contrasting highlights.

Hints for Collectors
This glazing technique makes some collectors think the glaze is wearing off and that the piece is defective. Where the glaze has worn off, the body will have a rough surface. If the glaze is intact, both light and dark areas will feel equally smooth.

121 Ironstone pitcher

Description
Tall, cylindrical pitcher that tapers slightly from base. Rim has 2
raised bands and terminates in short spout. Ear-shaped handle
decorated with embossed knob at top and bottom and incised
vertical line. Raised band above projecting base. Bottom bears
transfer print "MELLOR & CO." beneath representation of lion,
shield, crown, and unicorn. *Variations:* May have bulbous body
swelling toward base. Embossed floral decoration.

Materials and Dimensions
Ironstone with clear alkaline glaze. Molded. Handle separately
cast and applied. Height: 4–7″. Diameter: 3–5″.

Locality and Period
Cook Pottery Company, Trenton, New Jersey. c. 1894–1910.
Similar examples from large potteries in the East and Midwest,
particularly New Jersey and Ohio. c. 1880–1910.

Comment
This pitcher bears one of the marks of the Cook Pottery
Company, a firm in Trenton, New Jersey, that made ironstone
from 1894 until the early 1900s. The "MELLOR & CO." mark was
adopted so that their wares would not be confused with those
produced by Cook & Hancock, another Trenton pottery. The
form is typical of mold-cast pitchers made at many factories in
the East and Midwest. Identical pieces were sometimes
produced in several shops, since potters often owned their own
molds and took them with them when they moved.

Hints for Collectors
Collectors are just beginning to become aware of American
ironstone, which is less abundant than ironstone made in
England. In both countries the larger pieces were most often
marked, especially pitchers, large serving bowls, and platters.

Spongeware pitchers

Description
Vessels with sides that taper slightly to plain rim (left), collarlike
rim (center), or scalloped rim (right). Spout short and pulled (left
and center) or scrolled (right). Base plain (left), slightly shaped
(center), or rimmed (right). Handle elongated and ear-shaped
(left and right) or rectangular (center); attached below rim and
midway down body. Left pitcher has embossed floral decoration.
Variations: Many other shapes and handle types.

Materials and Dimensions
Stoneware with cream glaze; similar pieces ironstone or
stoneware with colored glaze. Decorated with spongework in
various combinations of green, gray, and brown; also found in
blue and white. Molded; handles separately shaped and applied.
Height: 6–11″. Diameter: 4½–6″.

Locality and Period
New York to Ohio; primarily New Jersey and Ohio.
c. 1890–1925.

Comment
The 3 pieces shown here give some idea of the variety found in
spongeware pitchers. They were made in large quantities at the
turn of the century. Only a few appear to have been marked, and
any specific attribution is difficult.

Hints for Collectors
Popular blue-and-white spongeware pitchers are usually more
expensive than those in other colors. Acquiring pitchers with
different shapes in the same color combination can be an
interesting approach to collecting. Note the crack on the rim of
the center pitcher; this kind of damage can lessen the value of a
piece by as much as 75 percent.

Spongeware creamer

Description
Small cream pitcher with sides that taper from bottom to shaped rim. Short, pulled spout. Opposite spout, ear-shaped handle attached just below rim and at midpoint on body. Plain base. *Variations:* Many have squat, bulbous bodies. Some have embossed decoration.

Materials and Dimensions
Ironstone with cream glaze; some examples stoneware. Decorated with spongework in green and tan. Molded; handle separately shaped and applied. Height: 2½–4″. Diameter: 2–3″.

Locality and Period
New Jersey and Ohio. c. 1890–1930.

Comment
Small spongeware creamers, or cream pitchers, are relatively uncommon; certainly they are seen far less often than large pitchers. Many of the surviving examples appear to have been made to match covered sugar bowls. Their form and spongework decoration often parallel that of the larger cider or milk pitchers produced at the same time. Creamers, however, are less likely to be embossed, since the smaller surface area is difficult to decorate. In contrast, many of the larger pitchers were decorated with embossing.

Hints for Collectors
Spongeware creamers are popular and expensive, not only because they are scarce, but also because many people collect cream pitchers. Others like to collect pitchers in different sizes that have the same shape and decoration. Don't confuse creamers with the much smaller miniature pitchers. The latter are only 1″ to 2″ tall and do not have room to hold enough cream for even a single cup of coffee.

Yellowware pitcher

Description
Small pitcher with sides that taper slightly from base to rim.
Shaped rim pulled forward at front creating short spout. Slightly
recessed base. Ear-shaped handle attached below rim and above
base. *Variations:* Some pitchers have bulbous bodies.

Materials and Dimensions
Yellow earthenware with clear alkaline glaze. Wheel-thrown;
handle separately shaped and applied. Similar pieces usually
molded. Height: 5–8″. Diameter: 4–6″.

Locality and Period
Massachusetts west to Ohio, south to Maryland. c. 1860–1920.

Comment
This pitcher was thrown on a wheel rather than cast in a mold,
which was the traditional method for producing yellowware
pottery. Its basic shape imitates that of white earthenware and
ironstone pitchers, a common characteristic of yellowware
pieces. Although few examples of yellowware were marked,
factory catalogues indicate that most were produced in New
Jersey, Ohio, and Maryland.

Hints for Collectors
To determine whether a piece of yellowware is cast rather than
wheel-thrown, examine the outside for thin vertical lines, which
usually run down the front near the spout or down the back near
the handle. These are seam lines created by a mold. If you can
feel rough concentric horizontal ridges inside the piece, it was
wheel-thrown. Such ridges are made by the potter's hands as the
piece turns on a wheel.

Modern pitcher

Description
Large vessel with sides that curve out from base to high
shoulder and rolled rim. Short, narrow spout. Square handle
with incised markings attached just below shoulder and low on
body. Plain base. Marked "FRANKOMA" on bottom. *Variations*
Shape and decoration vary.

Materials and Dimensions
Red earthenware with opaque green and brown glaze. Molded.
Height: 7½–9″. Diameter: 6½–7½″.

Locality and Period
Frankoma Pottery, Sapulpa, Oklahoma. c. 1950–60. Similar
examples from New Jersey and Ohio. c. 1930–60.

Comment
The rolled rim seen here is often called an ice lip. It was designed
for lemonade, ice-tea, and water pitchers to prevent large chunks
of ice from falling into the glass being filled. Ice lips were used on
silver-plated pitchers in the late 19th century, but it was not
until well after 1900 that they appeared on pottery examples.
The simple lines of the piece illustrated recollect the Art Deco
style popular in the 1930s.

Hints for Collectors
Many enthusiasts collect Frankoma and other ceramics made
from around 1930 to 1960. Pieces made by Frankoma are
inexpensive and abundant. They are a good choice for an
adventurous collector more concerned with developing his own
taste than with the prestige of collecting expensive modern
pottery.

Stoneware pitcher

Description
Barrel-shaped pitcher with sides tapering from waist to rim and base. Wide, slightly raised decorative bands above and below waist and at plain rim and shaped base. Small, pinched spout opposite ear-shaped handle; handle attached below rim and above base. Entire piece covered with incised lines simulating tree bark. *Variations:* Sides may be straight. Embossed decoration may include flowers or animals.

Materials and Dimensions
Stoneware with green glaze; similar examples with blue, brown, red, yellow, or tan glaze, or various combinations. Molded; spout and handle separately shaped and applied. Height: 8–10″. Diameter: 6–7″.

Locality and Period
New York, New Jersey, and Ohio. c. 1900–20.

Comment
Molded stoneware was made in large quantities from the turn of the century to the 1930s, primarily in large, mechanized factories located in New Jersey and Ohio. In the pitcher illustrated, the traditional barrel shape is combined with a popular late 19th-century decorative motif, the simulated bark surface. Other pitchers were decorated with scenes of the outdoors, people, animals, houses, or floral motifs.

Hints for Collectors
Early 20th-century mold-cast stoneware is beginning to attract notice; it is a good time to start collecting it. Prices remain reasonable, especially for pieces in glazes other than blue. Look for pieces with interesting form and decoration and try to acquire several examples in the same pattern but in different sizes or glaze colors.

Redware creamer

Description
Small vessel with low waist. Above waist sides slope in gradually to narrow, slightly raised band at neck. Flaring rim with shallow, pulled spout. Rim has interior ridge. Ear-shaped handle attached at rim and waist. Below waist sides taper sharply to shaped base. *Variations:* Shape and rim vary considerably. May have matching lid.

Materials and Dimensions
Red earthenware with cream and brown glaze. Wheel-thrown; handle separately shaped and applied. Height: 3–4". Diameter: 3½–5".

Locality and Period
New England west to Missouri, south to the Carolinas. c. 1790–1880.

Comment
Redware creamers are distinguished from other pitchers by their small size and relatively squat form. The shape of the rim on this pitcher suggests that it may once have had a lid that fit within its curled edges. Although creamers don't appear on early price lists and inventories, references to "little pitchers" probably include such pieces.

Hints for Collectors
Like other small, fragile redware items, these creamers are rare today, though they were produced in large quantities. Such pieces will be expensive, especially if they are in good condition. Although there is a small chip on the rim of the piece illustrated, it would still be an important acquisition.

Yellowware pipkin

Description
Bulbous vessel with sides that curve in from high, rounded
shoulder to wide neck. Slightly flared collar with plain rim and
pinched spout. Hollow, tubular handle with slightly flared end.
Plain base. Lid (not illustrated) flat, with knoblike handle.
Variations: Slight variations in shape. May lack spout.

Materials and Dimensions
Yellow earthenware with clear alkaline glaze. Wheel-thrown;
handle separately shaped and applied. Height: 5–7″. Diameter:
4–6″.

Locality and Period
New England to Pennsylvania. c. 1850–90.

Comment
A pipkin is a baking vessel with a large, round handle that is
usually hollow, opening into the interior, allowing steam to
escape. The pipkin was used primarily for baking beans.
Yellowware and Rockingham pipkins were made at the United
States Pottery Company in Bennington, Vermont, in the 1850s
and 1860s; as late as 1890, stoneware examples were being made
at the Brown pottery in Huntington, New York.

Hints for Collectors
Pipkins are seldom seen in pottery collections because of their
rarity, and collectors should be on the lookout for them.
Although many pipkins were made, they were short-lived
because their hollow handles were easily broken. Examples have
been found bearing the impressed "1849" stamp of the United
States Pottery Company at Bennington, Vermont; no other
marks on pipkins are known.

Stoneware batter jug

Description
Squat vessel with low waist. From waist, sides slope gently in to
shaped rim. At each side, triangular ear present, pierced to hold
wire bail handle with wooden grip. At front, short, thick spout
set at an angle. Below waist body tapers sharply to plain base.
At rear just above base, U-shaped handle present. *Variations:*
Some pieces may lack rear handle. Most have tin covers for top
and spout. Some may be straight sided and less bulbous.

Materials and Dimensions
Stoneware glazed with brown Albany slip; earlier examples with
salt glaze. Wheel-thrown; spout, handle, and ears separately
shaped and applied. Height: 8–10″. Diameter: 6–7″.

Locality and Period
New England west to Missouri and into Texas. c. 1860–1910.

Comment
Batter jugs were traditionally kept on kitchen stoves with a little
batter left in them in order to form yeast for the next day's
baking. The handle at the rear facilitated lifting and pouring
from the heavy jug.

Hints for Collectors
Although the jug shown here lacks the tin covers for its top and
spout, this is not a serious loss. Some batter jugs did not have
them, and if covers are missing, replacements are often easily
found. If, however, the wire bail handle is missing, this is a
serious defect and will lower the value of the piece considerably.
A replacement handle, shaped from wire and a drilled wooden
dowel, makes an incomplete jug both more functional and
salable.

Stoneware batter jug

Description
Squat vessel with sides that taper from low waist to ringed neck.
Tin cover with wire bail handle fits over collar. At each side of
neck, applied ear holds wire bail carrying handle with wooden
grip. At front, tubular spout with plain rim and tin cap. Painted
bird below spout. Below waist sides taper gradually to plain
base. Semicircular handle at rear above base. *Variations:* May
lack rear handle. May be undecorated.

Materials and Dimensions
Stoneware; exterior with salt glaze; interior glazed with brown
Albany slip. Front decorated with cobalt blue. Wheel-thrown;
spout, handles, and ears separately shaped and applied. Height:
8–11″. Diameter: 7–8″.

Locality and Period
New England west to Ohio, south to Maryland. c. 1840–80.

Comment
The batter jug is an early stoneware form—an 18th-century
example from New York City's Crolius pottery is still in
existence. However, few examples dating prior to 1830 are now
found. Many salt-glazed stoneware batter jugs bear the mark of
a potter, usually one from New York or Pennsylvania, and some
of them, like this example, are decorated.

Hints for Collectors
Although brown-glazed stoneware batter jugs are common, salt-
glazed examples are harder to come by, and a piece with blue slip
decoration like the one shown here is a real find. These jugs can
still be used for their original function, but they also make
interesting containers for flowers or can serve as pitchers.

Modern carafe

Description
Bulbous water vessel with high waist, from which sides slope in to shoulder marked by slight ridge. Above, long, narrow neck with flaring rim and pulled spout. Below waist, sides taper to slightly shaped base. Hook-shaped wooden handle attached at neck by metal band. Marked on bottom "BAUER/LOS ANGELES." Matching lid slightly dome-shaped with acorn-shaped handle.

Materials and Dimensions
White earthenware with opaque orange glaze; similar pieces with green or blue glaze. Molded. Height: 9–9½″. Diameter: 7–7½″.

Locality and Period
J. A. Bauer & Company, Los Angeles, California. c. 1930–40. Similar examples from New Jersey and Ohio. c. 1925–50.

Comment
The pottery that made this piece was established in the early 20th century and became a large concern with 4 active kilns and complete lines of stoneware, redware, and white earthenware. Sleek, modern pieces like the pitcher illustrated were usually made of white earthenware.

Hints for Collectors
Decorative California pottery is not as common as that from other states such as Ohio and New Jersey, and little is found in the East and Midwest. One of its unusual and interesting characteristics is the occasional combination of wood, metal, or other materials with the ceramic body. The novelty of such pieces may someday make them more valuable but today they are often overlooked by collectors and reasonably priced.

Description
Tall vessel with sides that taper slightly from low waist to plain rim and triangular spout. Below rim, several concentric decorative bands. Below waist sides taper more sharply to flaring base decorated with several concentric bands. Ear-shaped handle with incised lines attached just below rim and at waist. Matching dome-shaped lid with tufted knoblike handle and concentric band decoration.

Materials and Dimensions
White earthenware with opaque turquoise glaze; similar examples with red, yellow, blue, light and dark green, white, ivory, chartreuse, and gray. Molded; handle separately shaped and applied. Height: 8–8½″. Diameter: 4½–4¾″.

Locality and Period
Homer Laughlin Company, Newell, West Virginia. 1936–69.

Comment
The example illustrated is the most common kind of coffeepot in the Fiesta line. An after-dinner coffeepot, called the "A.D. coffeepot" in Homer Laughlin's catalogues, had a similarly shaped body, but in place of the ear-shaped handle, it had a sticklike handle set at a slight angle on the side rather than at the back of the pot.

Hints for Collectors
Produced in all Fiesta colors, the coffeepot is a popular and increasingly valuable item, especially in red and blue. Pots in pastel shades like gray, ivory, and light green are beginning to attract collector attention and are a good alternative to the more expensive pieces in red and blue.

Art pottery teapot

Description
Teapot with high, rounded shoulder. Short neck with plain rim.
Tubular spout protrudes at an angle from shoulder. Below waist,
sides slope out to plain base. Elongated, ring-shaped handle
attached at neck and shoulder. Matching lid with simple, acorn-
shaped handle.

Materials and Dimensions
White earthenware with green glaze; areas of base unglazed.
Molded; handle and spout separately shaped and applied. Height:
5½–6½". Diameter: 4–4½".

Locality and Period
Clifton Art Pottery, Clifton, New Jersey. c. 1905–08. Similar
examples from the Denver China and Pottery Company, Denver,
Colorado. c. 1900–05.

Comment
The glaze on this piece is known as crystal patina, and was
created to resemble the patina of old bronze. It was developed by
the pottery pioneer and innovator William Long and first used at
his Denver pottery. Clifton pieces are often impressed "CLIFTON
POTTERY COMPANY," sometimes with a date.

Hints for Collectors
While much art pottery was marked, this piece was not.
Unmarked pieces can be identified by comparison with similar,
marked Clifton pieces. Although made in fairly small quantities
and not particularly common today, Clifton art pottery can often
be purchased reasonably.

Art pottery coffeepot

Description
Covered vessel with sides that slope out slightly to shaped rim
and swell slightly above shaped base. Tubelike spout protrudes
at angle from upper body. Elongated, ear-shaped handle
attached at rim and base. Decorated with incised geometric
forms. Matching lid with central knoblike handle and gilding.
Variations: Bodies are sometimes bulbous. Spouts and handles
differ greatly.

Materials and Dimensions
White earthenware; exterior with yellow glaze; interior with
clear alkaline glaze. Gilded decoration. Molded; handle and spout
separately shaped and applied. Height: 6–7″. Diameter: 4½–5½″.

Locality and Period
Attributed to the Clifton Art Pottery, Clifton, New Jersey.
c. 1905–08.

Comment
Very few art potteries produced coffeepots and it was not until
the 1920s and 1930s that large factories began producing
utilitarian examples in a streamlined modern form. Although
produced by a company that specialized in art pottery, the gilded
edges on the coffeepot illustrated align it with traditional
tableware.

Hints for Collectors
Loss of a matching lid can substantially reduce the value of a
piece of modern pottery. Consequently, collectors and dealers
are always trying to match separated pots and lids. When
buying, always check carefully to see that the lid matches the pot
in clay type, style, and color, and that it fits correctly.

Porcelain coffeepot

Description
Octagonal vessel with sides that taper to neck. Shaped, gilded band below neck. Shaped, flaring rim. Elongated spout attached on lower body. Shaped base. Ear-shaped handle with branchlike knobs attached at gilded band and spout level. Matching dome-shaped lid with stylized finial. Gilded details. *Variations:* Gilding varies or may be absent.

Materials and Dimensions
Porcelain with clear alkaline glaze. Gilded decoration. Molded; handle and spout separately shaped and applied. Height: 8¾–9½″. Diameter: 6¼–7″.

Locality and Period
Attributed to the United States Pottery Company, Bennington, Vermont. c. 1850–58. Similar pieces from New York west to Ohio, south to Maryland. c. 1850–1900.

Comment
This coffeepot belongs to a set of matching tableware. Sets of dinnerware were made by many American firms, particularly large factories located, for example, in Brooklyn, New York; Liverpool, Ohio; and Trenton, New Jersey. Without a pottery mark or specific history it is usually not possible to determine the origin of such pieces. The coffeepot illustrated is attributed to the Bennington pottery based on its style and known history.

Hints for Collectors
Because it can seldom be attributed, unmarked American porcelain often sells for less than marked European examples. A careful collector can assemble a matching set of plates, serving dishes, and other tableware for a surprisingly small amount of money.

Flint-enamel coffeepot

Description

Octagonal vessel with low waist. Sides curve in to neck marked by 3 shaped ridges. Shaped, flaring rim. Wide spout attached at waist. Lower body tapers to plinthlike, octagonal base. Branch-shaped handle attached just below neck and at waist. Impressed on bottom "Lyman Fenton & Co./Fentons/ENAMEL/PATENTED/ 1849/BENNINGTON, Vt." Matching lid with fluted, acornlike finial. *Variations:* Lid may be dome-shaped.

Materials and Dimensions

Yellow earthenware with clear alkaline glaze; exterior sprinkled with brown manganese oxide, green copper oxide, and cobalt-blue oxide. Molded; spout and handle separately shaped and applied. Height: 11–13″. Diameter: 5¼–6″.

Locality and Period

United States Pottery Company, Bennington, Vermont. c. 1849–58. Similar examples from New Jersey and Ohio. c. 1850–70.

Comment

Often bearing the "1849" Bennington mark, these spectacular coffeepots were made exclusively at the United States Pottery Company. Similarly shaped coffeepots with the Rockingham glaze were made at New Jersey and Ohio factories.

Hints for Collectors

A tea- or coffeepot lid usually has 1 or 2 protuberances that match notches along the rim of the pot to hold it in place. If these do not match, it is likely that the lid was not made for the piece. On the other hand, slight differences in glaze color should not be used as a determining criterion in matching pieces, as these often varied slightly after firing.

Flint-enamel teapot

Description
Gourd-shaped vessel with low, bulbous waist. Shoulder marked by shaped double ring. Wide neck decorated with embossed acanthus leaves. Shaped rim slightly scalloped. Long, curved spout with ribbed surface attached at waist. Below waist, sides curve in to shaped base. Ear-shaped handle with branchlike knobs attached at rim, shoulder, and waist. Lower body decorated with embossed rib pattern. Matching lid with flat, rounded handle. *Variations:* May have floral embossing. Shape of handle varies.

Materials and Dimensions
Yellow earthenware with clear alkaline glaze; exterior sprinkled with brown manganese oxide and touches of green copper oxide. Molded; handle and spout separately shaped and applied. Height: 6½–8½″. Diameter: 6–7″.

Locality and Period
Attributed to the United States Pottery Company, Bennington, Vermont. c. 1849–58.

Comment
The flint-enamel process was patented in 1849 by Christopher Webber Fenton of Lyman, Fenton & Co., which in that year became the United States Pottery Company. Pots with this decoration appear to have been made exclusively at Bennington.

Hints for Collectors
It is often difficult to distinguish flint enamel from Rockingham glaze, since manganese oxide, used for both, produces a similar mottled brown finish. When the other coloring agents used in flint enamel are lightly applied, as in the teapot illustrated, the colors they leave are barely noticeable.

Rockingham teapot

Description
10-sided vessel with sides tapering gradually from bottom to high, rounded shoulder. Above shoulder, collar with plain rim. Sides curve in to recessed base. Large spout with scroll at tip and foliate decoration at base attached low on body. Ear-shaped handle attached at shoulder and above base. Embossed scene with woman and jug at open well on both sides. Matching dome-shaped lid with acornlike handle. *Variations:* Shapes vary greatly. Some pieces marked "Rebecca At The Well" on lower body. Form of woman varies and may appear on only 1 side.

Materials and Dimensions
Yellow earthenware with Rockingham glaze. Molded; handle and spout separately cast and applied. Height: 8–10″. Diameter: 6–7″.

Locality and Period
New York west to Ohio, south to Maryland. c. 1860–1900.

Comment
Many different sorts of Rockingham teapots were made during the 19th century, but the most common was the type illustrated. Mistakenly believed by some to have been produced at the Bennington, Vermont, pottery, where they were never made, these teapots were turned out by many large potteries. The earliest known examples, made c. 1860, are from the Edwin Bennett's pottery of Baltimore.

Hints for Collectors
Avoid buying Rebecca teapots without matching lids; if a lid is missing, it is very unlikely that you will find a correct replacement. So many different versions were manufactured that few lids will fit more than a single model. Pots with a darker brown glaze, like the one illustrated, are less desirable than those with a mottled yellow-brown, or tortoiseshell, glaze.

Yellowware coffeepot

Description
Ornate coffeepot with low waist. Above waist sides curve in to neck marked by scalloping and indented line. Collar with shaped rim. Below waist sides curve in to shaped, stepped base. Spout in form of goose's neck and head attached at waist. Elaborate ear-shaped handle attached below neck and at waist; embossed with form of man whose head forms finial. Embossed floral motifs on body. Marked on bottom "D. & J. HENDERSON/JERSEY/CITY." Matching dome-shaped lid with acorn-shaped handle. *Variations:* May have straight sides. Decoration varies.

Materials and Dimensions
Yellow earthenware with clear alkaline glaze. Molded. Height: 11–12″. Diameter: 7–8″.

Locality and Period
Jersey City Pottery Company, Jersey City, New Jersey. c. 1829–33. Similar pieces from New Jersey and Ohio. c. 1840–70.

Comment
The Henderson firm was one of the first American makers of yellowware and Rockingham. Its products were based on European models familiar to the English potters employed by the firm. Henderson's products were far more elaborate than most American coffeepots made later in the 19th century.

Hints for Collectors
The Henderson mark is rare, and coffeepots made by the firm are rarer still. Pieces similar to the one pictured here were made in England, and it is easy to confuse them with Henderson products. Always check the bottom for the Henderson mark. In such rare American-marked pieces, damage such as a cracked lid or reglued spout would be acceptable.

Redware teapot

Description
Vessel with low waist marked by embossed line. Above waist,
sides slope in to wide neck decorated by embossed floral motifs.
Rim slightly rolled. Fluted lower body curves in to shaped base.
Slightly curved spout attached below waist. Elaborate ear-
shaped handle attached at rim and just below waist. Matching
dome-shaped lid, with floral embossing and acorn-shaped handle,
rests on ridge within rim. *Variations:* Some have simple round
shape. Some lack embossed decoration.

Materials and Dimensions
Red earthenware with shiny black glaze; base unglazed. Molded;
spout and handle separately shaped and applied. Height: 6–7″.
Diameter: 3½–4½″.

Locality and Period
John Mann, Rahway, New Jersey. c. 1830–50. Similar examples
from New England south to North Carolina. c. 1780–1870.

Comment
Black-glazed teapots were made in substantial numbers during
the 18th and 19th centuries, although few examples with marks
or reliable histories have survived. These black-glazed teapots
are mentioned in a 1789 North Carolina pottery inventory, and
they were made in both Troy, New York, and Whately,
Massachusetts, in the 1820s. The only known marked examples
are stamped "John Mann/Rahway N.J." on the bottom.

Hints for Collectors
In England, teapots like this one were common; they were based
on models made of silver, and usually had a black glaze, although
some lustreware examples exist as well. Unless it is marked or
has a documented history of American manufacture, a teapot
with this shape and decoration should be regarded as English.

Harlequin sauceboat

Description
Low, elongated vessel with sides that angle outward to rim. Rim slopes inward and has deep, pulled spout. Slightly flaring, rimmed base. Triangular handle attached at rim and lower body. Embossed rings encircle upper body.

Materials and Dimensions
White earthenware with opaque orange glaze. Similar examples in all Harlequin colors except ivory. Molded. Length: 6¾–7½". Width: 3½–3¾". Height: 3–3½".

Locality and Period
Homer Laughlin Company, Newell, West Virginia. c. 1938–64.

Comment
Harlequin was introduced by Homer Laughlin as a less expensive version of its popular Fiesta line; like Fiesta, its design is in the Art Deco style. However, as a rule Harlequin pieces are more elongated and more sharply angled. The Fiesta sauceboat, for example, has a bulbous body.

Hints for Collectors
Some confuse Harlequin with Fiestaware. It is not, however, difficult to tell them apart. Original Harlequin is never marked, while Fiesta often is. The set of decorative rings or bands on Harlequin pieces are placed a distance below the rim of the piece, while those on Fiesta run up to the rim. Also, Harlequin plates and other flat pieces lack the center decoration of several concentric circles found on Fiesta examples. In the 1970s, Homer Laughlin reissued its Harlequin line for the F. W. Woolworth Company to celebrate Woolworth's 100th anniversary. Although for the most part these new pieces are identical to the original line, the dinner plates bear the company name and the date of production.

Modern gravy boat

Description
Low, oval serving vessel with attached, saucerlike dish. Sides of
bowl slope out to wide mouth with shaped rim. At each end of
rim, downcurving spout. Shaped base. Attached dish has
irregular, oval rim and collar with embossed curvilinear
decoration. Dish has shaped base. Bottom marked "Lu-Ray
Pastels/U.S.A." *Variations:* Similar gravy boats may be round.
Some have separate saucers.

Materials and Dimensions
White earthenware with pale yellow glaze; similar pieces with
other pastel glazes. Molded in 2 pieces and joined before firing.
Length: 6¾–7″. Width: 5–5½″. Height: 3–3½″.

Locality and Period
The Midwest. c. 1950–60.

Comment
Gravy boats with attached saucers are common 20th-century
forms, although a few 19th-century pieces were made in this
manner. Unlike handled sauceboats, which have spouts for
pouring, the spouts of this piece serve as resting places for
spoons, an unusual feature among American pottery.

Hints for Collectors
Recent 20th-century ceramics are beginning to appear in
antiques shops and at shows, but the best places to look for them
are junk shops, secondhand stores, and yard or house sales. One
should still be able to pay very little for such collectibles. Since
they are so common, select only those examples that are in
excellent condition, without chips, cracks, or cracked glaze.

Transfer-decorated ironstone gravy boat

Description
Boat-shaped vessel with body elongated on one side to form a
deep spout. Opposite, ear-shaped handle attached to shaped rim.
Flaring base with deeply recessed bottom. Blue transfer-printed
Masonic symbol on each side. Base marked "STERLING VITRIFIED
CHINA EAST LIVERPOOL OHIO" in a banner-shaped area.
Variations: Body may be rounder or lower. Many examples are
decorated with floral or geometric motifs.

Materials and Dimensions
Transfer-decorated ironstone with clear alkaline glaze. Molded.
Length: 7–10″. Width: 2½–3½″. Height: 3–5″.

Locality and Period
Sterling Pottery Company, East Liverpool, Ohio. c. 1900–20.
Similar examples from New York west to Ohio, south to
Maryland. c. 1870–1940.

Comment
American-made gravy, or sauce, boats appeared soon after the
Civil War. At that time, local earthenware manufacturers began
to compete with their English and continental rivals, whose
exports had long stifled the American market. It was not,
however, until late in the century that such specialized pieces
were common. They are, of course, still made.

Hints for Collectors
The most interesting thing about this piece is the transfer-
printed Masonic symbol of rule and calipers that appears on each
side. This indicates that the piece was probably made especially
for use in the dining hall of a Masonic lodge. Since some
collectors specialize in wares related to fraternal orders, pieces
like the one shown here are usually more in demand than plain
examples.

Modern creamer

Description
Asymmetrical vessel with sides that taper slightly from waist to slightly incurving rim set on diagonal. Elongated spout at front. Lower body curves in to narrow, shaped base. Elaborate, ear-shaped handle with S-shaped base attached just below rim and on lower body. Marked on bottom "HULL, U.S.A."

Materials and Dimensions
White earthenware with mottled pink glaze; handle with darker metallic pink glaze. Molded; handle separately shaped and applied. Length: 4–6″. Width: 3–4″. Height: 3–5″.

Locality and Period
A. E. Hull Pottery Company, Crooksville, Ohio. c. 1917–52.

Comment
At one point the Hull pottery manufactured 3 million pieces a year. Most examples are in a more modern, pared-down style than this piece, which reflects a blend of modern Bauhaus design and traditional 18th-century elements. Creamers, or cream pitchers, were also produced by many art potteries, and marked examples have been found from Roseville, Weller, Van Briggle, and other well-known factories.

Hints for Collectors
A grouping of modern creamers would form an interesting collection; creamers in general have always appealed to collectors. Hull creamers have not yet attracted the attention given to examples from better-known potteries and are, consequently, quite inexpensive. Look for matching sugar bowls and for the matching trays, teapots, and coffeepots that were sometimes produced. A complete set will be worth more.

Cups, Mugs, Tumblers, and Goblets

Most ceramic drinking vessels were modeled on fashionable silver forms. However, the clay versions were usually much more simplified than those made of silver or other metals.

Porringers

Among the first to become common in America was the porringer, a cuplike container used for both beverages and soft foods like gruel. Although silver porringers had 1 or 2 wide, flat handles, which were attached horizontally, this fragile grip was impractical for earthenware vessels. Instead, potters attached U-shaped or ear-shaped handles similar to those used later on cups. Made of red earthenware, porringers were usually covered with a clear lead glaze.

Cups

The first cups used in this country had no handles. They were intended to hold tea, which was then poured in small amounts into a deep saucer. The cup was placed on a glass plate while the tea drinkers slowly sipped the hot beverage from the saucer. This custom was never accepted by the upper classes, and by the mid-19th century, cups were almost always made with handles. Produced by large factories, such cups, with matched saucers, were usually part of a full line of matching dinnerware. Among the earliest American examples are those made of white earthenware and ironstone, which were often painted by hand or decorated with transfer printing. Finer pieces from New York, New Jersey, and Ohio factories were made of porcelain or brightly colored majolica. These pieces were often quite ornate, with embossed organic or sculptural designs. During the 20th century, simple and inexpensive mass-produced cups and saucers became increasingly common.

Mugs

Mugs are heavy, cylindrical vessels with a large handle that is easy to grasp. Widely used in taverns, hotels, and other public places as well as in homes, the earliest mugs were made of red earthenware; thrown on a wheel, these were often glazed with dark green or black slip. Since redware is fragile, stoneware rapidly became the preferred clay for these utilitarian pieces. Many of these durable stoneware mugs were decorated with cobalt-blue slip.

Mugs were cast in molds as well as wheel-thrown. Today many are available in yellow earthenware, often with a Rockingham glaze, and in ironstone and porcelain. Although most of these pieces are in the traditional shape, there exist interesting variations, such as shaving mugs and soda-fountain mugs. Some of the most desirable mugs are those produced around the turn of the century by art potteries. These decorative pieces are often embellished with underglaze painting and embossed designs.

Beakers, Tumblers, and Goblets

In addition to cups and mugs, a few beakers and tumblers are included in this section. Never as popular as glass examples, these ceramic pieces are usually similar in shape to contemporary examples in glass.

Like beakers and tumblers, ceramic goblets are uncommon. Used to hold wine or water, these pieces have a cuplike section that rests on a tall, thin stem mounted on a broad foot. Some were cast in molds by major mid-19th century factories; other one-of-a-kind examples were handmade by potters working in sewer-tile factories at the turn of the century. Because the tall stem was fragile, very few goblets have survived.

145 Porcelain beaker

Description
Drinking vessel with fluted sides sloping out to plain rim decorated with gilded bands over row of gilded dots. Scalloped base. Upper body hand-painted with swag and rosebud decoration. *Variations:* Shape and decoration vary greatly.

Materials and Dimensions
Hand-painted porcelain with clear alkaline glaze. Gilding. Molded. Height: 3–4″. Diameter: 2¾–3″.

Locality and Period
Lenox, Inc., Trenton, New Jersey. c. 1920. Similar pieces from New York, New Jersey, and Ohio. c. 1870–1930.

Comment
Established in 1889 as the Ceramic Art Company, the Lenox company became one of the major producers of fine American porcelain during the first half of the 20th century. Lenox specialized in traditional forms with decoration derived from fine European porcelain. Beakers of porcelain are relatively uncommon; they were usually made of glass. Porcelain examples usually came in sets of 8 to 12 matching pieces.

Hints for Collectors
Most pieces of Lenox china can be identified by the firm mark, which is usually stamped on the bottom. It consists of a wreath enclosing the initials "L" or "LC" over the word "LENOX." Because American porcelain was always expensive and made in a relatively limited quantity, it is worth collecting today, even those pieces that are only a few decades old.

Fiesta tumbler

Description
Drinking vessel with sides sloping out to plain rim. Upper body decorated with embossed rings that are widest near rim. Plain base. Bottom marked "Fiesta/HLC USA."

Materials and Dimensions
White earthenware with opaque yellow glaze. Similar pieces glazed in green, red, blue, ivory, or turquoise. Molded. Height: 4½–4¾". Diameter: 3⅜–3½".

Locality and Period
Homer Laughlin Company, Newell, West Virginia. c. 1936–46.

Comment
This type of tumbler was produced for only 10 years, perhaps because ceramic tumblers were never as popular as those made of glass. Fiesta tumblers are often associated with a wheel-shaped "disk" pitcher; in fact, the pitcher did not appear until 1939 and was made until 1973, long after the tumblers had stopped being produced.

Hints for Collectors
The 10-ounce tumblers were made in all the original Fiesta colors, and only the turquoise examples are scarce today. There is little danger of confusing them with Harlequin tumblers, also made by Homer Laughlin. Unlike Fiesta pieces, which angle out slightly near the rim and have a continuous series of rings on the upper body, Harlequin examples have straight, tapering sides and a wide, undecorated band between the rim and ring decoration. All tumblers may have chipped or rough areas near the rim; since these pieces are fairly abundant, only buy examples that are in good condition.

Spongeware soda fountain mug

Description
Tall drinking vessel with sides that slope out to plain rim.
Embossed rings below rim and above slightly flaring base.
Elongated, bracket-shaped handle attached just below rim and
above base. *Variations:* Body may be cylindrical. Handle may be
shorter.

Materials and Dimensions
White earthenware with clear alkaline glaze; exterior with blue
and brownish-pink sponging. Similar pieces have sponging in
other colors. Molded; handle separately shaped and applied.
Height: 5½–7″. Diameter: 3½–4″.

Locality and Period
New Jersey west to Ohio, south to Maryland. c. 1890–1930.

Comment
Large mugs like this were used at soda fountains and in homes
for ice cream sodas and sundaes. Their size and shape
distinguishes them from coffee mugs, which are usually smaller.
Since they were heavy when full, the large handle was designed
to provide a firm grip. These mugs were not marked and
apparently never made in large quantities.

Hints for Collectors
Since most spongeware was made within the past century, age is
rarely a factor in establishing its worth. Instead, color, condition,
and rarity determine value. The mug pictured here is a highly
desirable piece because soda fountain mugs are rare. In addition,
this mug is in excellent condition and has unusual 2-color
spongework.

Art pottery mug

Description
Tall drinking vessel with sides sloping in to plain rim from 2 ridges near slightly flaring, shaped base. Semicircular handle attached below rim and slightly below center. Upper body decorated with glaze-painted cherries and leaves.

Materials and Dimensions
Hand-painted white earthenware with rich brown glaze. Molded; handle separately shaped and applied. Height: 6½–7″. Diameter: 4½–5″.

Locality and Period
Weller Pottery, Zanesville, Ohio. c. 1893–1918.

Comment
The Weller Pottery company was established by Samuel A. Weller in 1873 and began producing art pottery in 1893. The mug illustrated is in one of the most popular Weller styles, Louwelsa, which is characterized by an underglazing of fruit, flowers, Indian portraits, and other subjects combined with a rich brown glaze. The glazing technique was developed by William Long at his own Lonhuda Pottery in Steubenville, Ohio; the subjects depicted and the glazing methods mimicked those used on the more expensive art pottery produced by Rookwood. Weller worked briefly with Long perfecting the glazing technique, then used it to turn out inexpensive versions of the high-quality Rookwood ware.

Hints for Collectors
Along with the dozens of individual decorator's marks, the Weller company also used about a dozen impressed factory marks and several ink marks. Most marked pieces from the pre-1930 period bring good prices, especially Louwelsa examples.

Stoneware commemorative mug

Description
Cylindrical mug with plain rim and simple, shaped base that
extends slightly beyond body of mug. Front of mug has complex
machine-impressed design and inscription, including phrase
"SYRACUSE. GUT HEIL. N.Y. 1896." Decorative bands above and
below inscription. Ear-shaped handle has hole at top for pin to
secure pewter cover. Base of handle with mark "C.N.Y. POTTERY
UTICA N.Y." Impressed design, bands, and handle decorated with
blue. *Variations:* Similar mugs commemorate meetings of other
organizations. Some are barrel-shaped. Decoration varies.

Materials and Dimensions
Stoneware with salt glaze. Decorated with cobalt blue. Molded.
Height: 4–6″. Diameter: 3–4″.

Locality and Period
Central New York Pottery, Utica, New York. 1896. Similar
examples from New York and New Jersey. c. 1880–1910.

Comment
This complex molded and machine-impressed small stein reflects
the application of sophisticated techniques that became common
toward the end of the 19th century. Pieces such as the one shown
here were made in large quantities to the order of various
fraternal and benevolent societies. Since the molding and
decoration were done by machine, all pieces were more or less
identical.

Hints for Collectors
This stoneware mug has many of the characteristics that
collectors look for. It is dated, it has the mark of an identifiable
pottery, and it is elaborately decorated. Since it was made for
the annual meeting of the Turners, a German-American athletic
organization, it would also appeal to collectors of fraternal items.

Stoneware mug

Description
Barrel-shaped drinking vessel with plain rim and base. Incised bands, filled with blue, below and above base. Ear-shaped handle attached just below rim and above base. *Variations:* Some mugs are cylindrical. Some are undecorated. Early examples may have more elaborate incised decoration.

Materials and Dimensions
Stoneware; exterior with salt glaze; interior glazed with brown Albany slip. Decorated with cobalt blue. Wheel-thrown; handle separately shaped and applied. Height: 4–6″. Diameter: 3–4″.

Locality and Period
New England west to Ohio, south to Virginia. c. 1790–1860.

Comment
Hand-thrown stoneware mugs were once used in almost all American taverns and public houses, at least in part because they were far sturdier than blown-glass or porcelain vessels. Some examples bear men's names, and it seems likely that these were made especially for patrons of a hotel or tavern. After 1850, light and sturdy pressed-glass beer mugs became available, which eventually drove stoneware mugs from the market.

Hints for Collectors
American stoneware mugs may be confused with English and German examples, which were imported into this country in the 18th and early 19th centuries. American mugs are roughhewn and sturdy and rarely bear the mark of a potter. Imported English and German beer mugs have thinner sides, are more skillfully shaped, may have the maker's mark, and almost always have a stamped capacity mark (in liters) under the handle or on the base.

Redware mug

Description
Delicate, cylindrical drinking vessel with plain rim. Ear-shaped handle attached below rim and on lower body. Plain base. *Variations:* Body may be bulbous rather than straight-sided. Base may be slightly shaped.

Materials and Dimensions
Red earthenware with opaque dark green glaze; base unglazed. Similar pieces with clear lead glaze or mottled red-and-black glaze. Wheel-thrown; handle separately shaped and applied. Height: 5–8″. Diameter: 3½–4½″.

Locality and Period
New England west to Ohio, south to the Carolinas. c. 1750–1870.

Comment
Redware mugs were once quite common. A pottery inventory from 1786 lists them in 3 sizes; the largest, with a quart capacity, cost 6 pence, and the 2 smaller sizes sold for 3½ and 4½ pence. In the 1820s the potter John Corliss of Woolrich, Maine, sold redware mugs for 10 cents. Most of these vessels held either a pint or a quart.

Hints for Collectors
Once very common, redware mugs are now rare and are frequently found damaged or repaired. Check for handles that have been glued on or replaced and for repairs around the rim. Pieces with an unusual glaze, like the dark green shown here, are particularly desirable even if they show minor damage. Green and other colored glazes are uncommon because the glazing materials were quite costly.

Redware mug

Description
Cylindrical drinking vessel with plain rim. Thin, ear-shaped
handle attached just below rim and below center. Shaped base.
Variations: Body may be bulbous. Base may be plain or more
heavily shaped. May have incised or coggled decoration.

Materials and Dimensions
Red earthenware with manganese-black glaze. Wheel-thrown;
handle separately shaped and applied. Height: 4–6″. Diameter:
3½–4″.

Locality and Period
New England west to Ohio, south to Virginia. c. 1780–1870.

Comment
Black-glazed redware mugs were made primarily for taverns and
public houses. Since they are fragile and were probably used
almost every day, only a relatively small number survive. The
capacity of many of these mugs suggests that beer was often
served by the pint.

Hints for Collectors
Early redware mugs are becoming increasingly more expensive.
Check the handles carefully before you buy; a mug with a
reglued or replaced handle is worth only a fraction of what you
would pay for an undamaged example. Rim chips, which are
common, are less of a problem if not unsightly. Since mugs were
hardly ever marked, an example with a potter's mark would be a
real prize. Pieces with incised or coggled decoration are also in
great demand, as are miniature redware mugs, which
occasionally appear on the market.

153 Porcelain presentation mug

Description
Cylindrical drinking vessel. 12-sided upper portion with shaped rim that is gilded and outlined in blue. Below, embossed decoration of spear-shaped leaves tipped with gilding. Ear-shaped handle with scroll at top is outlined in blue and attached just below rim and low on body. Shaped base outlined in gilding and blue. Inscribed on front "Mrs. B. Golden." *Variations:* Shape of handle varies. Decoration and embossing vary greatly.

Materials and Dimensions
Porcelain with clear alkaline glaze; similar pieces ironstone. Cobalt-blue and gilded decoration. Molded; handle separately shaped and applied. Height: 3½–4½″. Diameter: 3–4″.

Locality and Period
Vermont west to Ohio, south to Maryland. c. 1850–1900.

Comment
The inscription on the front of the mug shown here indicates that it was probably made as a gift or presentation piece. Many potteries produced plain mugs, called blanks, that could be decorated to order as presentatin pieces. Since these pieces were made in both Europe and the United States, it is difficult to tell where an example was produced if it is not marked.

Hints for Collectors
Presentation mugs are uncommon. When possible, learning something about the person whose name appears on a presentation mug makes it easier to date the piece and determine where it was made.

Ironstone mug

Description
Drinking vessel with sides that slope out from middle to rolled rim and shaped base. Elaborate ear-shaped handle, scrolled at top and bottom and attached below rim and above base. *Variations:* Handles often less ornate. Body may be cylindrical. Base may be plain.

Materials and Dimensions
Ironstone with clear alkaline glaze. Molded; handle separately shaped and applied. Height: 3½–4½″. Diameter: 3½–4½″.

Locality and Period
New York west to Illinois, south to Maryland. c. 1860–1920.

Comment
Like much American ironstone, the mug shown here is unmarked. In contrast, after 1891 British manufacturers were required to mark similar pieces they exported to America. Because many consumers favored this imported ironstone, the Americans who did mark their wares often chose trademarks that resembled those used by their English competitors.

Hints for Collectors
There are many different types of ironstone mugs, and they can often be purchased quite reasonably. Especially interesting are those decorated with names of people or places, and those that bear dates. Particularly desirable and often quite expensive are mugs that bear inscriptions relating to occupations; these were made for doctors, lawyers, and other professionals. Avoid discolored examples, as stains can seldom be removed. Do not confuse these mugs with shaving mugs, which always have a shallow ledge over one side of the mouth.

155 Yellowware mug

Description
Cylindrical mug with slightly flaring, rolled rim. Embossed ring slightly above flaring base. Ear-shaped handle attached just below rim and at embossed ring. Decorative band of black slip around body flanked above and below by 3 thinner, matching white bands. *Variations:* Decorative banding may vary.

Materials and Dimensions
Yellow earthenware with clear alkaline glaze; decorated with white and black slip. Molded; handle separately cast and applied. Height: 2½–3½". Diameter: 3–4".

Locality and Period
Vermont west to Ohio, south to Maryland. c. 1880–1910.

Comment
Yellowware mugs, more common than their Rockingham counterparts, were made in large factories throughout the United States, but they were also imported in substantial quantities from English potteries. Since these pieces are rarely marked, it is extremely difficult to distinguish American- from English-made pieces. Both are enthusiastically collected in the United States. As a general rule, English examples have thinner walls and more elaborate decoration.

Hints for Collectors
Mugs, especially smaller ones, are popular and expensive collectibles. Look for pieces with attractive banding, such as the example illustrated. Avoid chipped or cracked mugs, as these have little resale value. Several mugs with the same decoration but in different sizes will be worth more together than a set of similar mugs with different colored banding. Most desirable is a set of mugs that are the same size with identical decoration.

Rockingham mug

Description
Drinking vessel with sides that slope out gradually from middle to plain rim and elaborately shaped base. Ear-shaped handle attached just below rim and slightly above base. *Variations:* Base may be plain.

Materials and Dimensions
Yellow earthenware with Rockingham glaze. Molded; handle separately shaped and applied. Height: 3–5″. Diameter: 3–4″.

Locality and Period
Vermont west to Ohio, south to Maryland. c. 1870–1900.

Comment
Many of the larger American potteries made mugs with a Rockingham glaze during the second half of the 19th century. Most mugs were relatively small and intended for coffee or tea rather than beer. The 1896 price list of one New York pottery indicates that they were available in ½-, ¾-, and 1-pint sizes, at a price of from 65 to 85 cents per dozen. It is usually impossible to tell where these mugs were made, because they were rarely marked and potters often carried molds with them from one pottery to another.

Hints for Collectors
Because Rockingham mugs are so popular with collectors, they now bring substantial prices, especially those rare examples that are marked. Look for pieces like the mug illustrated with interesting glaze patterns. However, if a handle has been replaced or repaired, the value of a piece can be substantially diminished.

157 Spongeware mug

Description
Small drinking vessel with sides curving out gradually from center to slightly flaring rim with traces of gilding and slightly flaring base. Elongated, ear-shaped handle attached just below rim and slightly above base. *Variations:* May have straight sides. Handle may be gilded.

Materials and Dimensions
Ironstone with yellow glaze. Decorated with green spongework and gilding. Similar pieces with clear glaze decorated with blue or brown spongework. Molded; handle separately shaped and applied. Height: 4–5″. Diameter: 3–4″.

Locality and Period
New Jersey and Ohio. c. 1890–1920.

Comment
Although plain white ironstone mugs are relatively common, those decorated with sponging are not. Like most American spongeware, this mug is unmarked. The gilding often seen on the rims of these mugs is a typical turn-of-the-century touch often found on spongeware; in many cases, as the example shown, the gilding has worn off. Although regilding is possible, most collectors prefer to let the wear show.

Hints for Collectors
Keep an eye out for spongeware mugs that bear stenciled advertisements, including slogans and store names. They were apparently given away by grocers and other merchants. Because these mugs appeal to collectors of advertising items as well as to pottery enthusiasts, they bring a premium.

Redware porringer

Description
Cuplike vessel with squat body. Sides curve inward from waist, then flare out to plain rim. Below, sides curve in sharply to shaped base. U-shaped handle attached below rim and at waist. *Variations:* Earlier examples lower and wider. Handle may be ear-shaped.

Materials and Dimensions
Red earthenware with clear lead glaze. Exterior decorated with spongework in yellow, green, and black. Wheel-thrown; handle separately shaped and applied. Height: 2–3″. Diameter: 3–4½″.

Locality and Period
New England west to Ohio, south to North Carolina. c. 1750–1850.

Comment
The porringer often looks like an oversized modern drinking cup, but it is an ancient vessel used to hold food that was eaten with a spoon, such as soup, stew, or porridge. Large and small porringers are mentioned in a 1786 inventory of Massachusetts potters' wares. The 1789 list from the Moravian pottery at Wachovia, North Carolina, includes porringers made in 3 sizes that sold for 5, 6, and 8 cents. By the mid-19th century they had been replaced by bowls and teacups.

Hints for Collectors
Porringers in good condition are hard to come by. Like mugs, their handles should always be checked for repair or replacement, which can substantially lessen their value. Most examples found have a multicolored or black glaze; multicolored porringers are by far the more popular and expensive.

Redware porringer

Description
Small cuplike vessel with sides that slope in above waist, then out to plain rim. Heavy, ear-shaped handle attached at rim and very low on waist. Shaped base. *Variations:* Handle usually smaller.

Materials and Dimensions
Red earthenware with clear lead glaze; base unglazed. Wheel-thrown; handle separately shaped and applied. Height: 2½–3″. Diameter: 2¾–3¼″.

Locality and Period
New England west to Illinois, south to the Carolinas. c. 1780–1860.

Comment
Simple redware porringers such as this were once found in every home. They are mentioned in contemporary records and appear in paintings of the period. They did not come with matching saucers. Since porringers were never marked, it is seldom possible to identify their makers. The great majority, however, were produced in the northeastern states before 1840.

Hints for Collectors
The tiny chips on the rim of this porringer are typical of the type of damage common on early cups. The deeper and more noticeable the chips, the more the piece is devalued. Since this kind of damage has often been skillfully repaired, it may be necessary to use ultraviolet light to detect it. The potter who made this porringer gripped the base as he dipped the piece into the glaze; the value of the piece is not diminished, however, because the base is unglazed.

Art pottery cup

Description
Small drinking vessel with sides curving out from plain base to
plain rim. Sides decorated with impressed, vertical lines. Thick,
ear-shaped handle attached just below rim and above base.
Incised on bottom "AA./Col. Spgs." *Variations:* Shape varies.
Handle usually thinner.

Materials and Dimensions
White earthenware with blue-green glaze streaked with white.
Molded; handle separately shaped and applied. Height: 1¾–2".
Diameter: 3¼–3¾".

Locality and Period
Van Briggle Pottery, Colorado Springs, Colorado. c. 1920–30.

Comment
The "AA." cypher incised on the cup shown here stands for
Artus and Anne Van Briggle, who established the Van Briggle
Pottery in 1901. Since the Van Briggles were among the first to
employ molds extensively in the making of art pottery, their
original products continued to be made even after the designer,
Artus, died in 1904. In later years, the designs became more
simplified and the colors less unusual. These late pieces are not
as valuable as those produced before 1910.

Hints for Collectors
The quality and condition of a glaze are always important in
evaluating art pottery. The rich matt glazes found on many Van
Briggle pieces have certainly contributed to their popularity.
Since flaking or chipped glaze substantially reduces value,
damaged surfaces are sometimes treated with paints or epoxies.
Ultraviolet light is helpful in spotting these repairs.

Transfer-decorated ironstone cup

Description
Drinking vessel with gently rounded sides rising to plain rim.
Ear-shaped handle attached just below rim and toward plain
base. Upper section with blue decoration in Oriental manner of
trees, houses, pagodas, and flying birds. Handle decorated with
blue fish-scale pattern. *Variations:* Decoration varies. Cup may
be taller. Handle may be longer.

Materials and Dimensions
Transfer-decorated ironstone with clear alkaline glaze. Similar
pieces decorated in red and green. Height: 2½–3″. Diameter:
3¾–4″.

Locality and Period
New Jersey west to Ohio, south to Maryland. c. 1900–30.

Comment
White pottery and porcelain with blue decoration like this
originated in China in the 18th century. Often referred to as
"willowware," these pieces depicted scenes with people, villages,
mountains, and trees. The type became popular in both the East
and West, yet it was not until the mid-19th century that
American manufacturers began to produce it in quantity, usually
decorating just part of a piece rather than covering it with an
overall design as was the custom on Chinese examples and those
produced in 19th-century England.

Hints for Collectors
Although Chinese and Japanese blue-and-white willowware has
long been popular with collectors, pieces produced in America
have been largely ignored. Many bear the marks of large, turn-
of-the-century potteries in New Jersey, Pennsylvania, and Ohio.
These pieces are abundant and inexpensive, so it is easy to
acquire a complete set of matching tableware.

Modern cup and saucer

Description
Matching cup and saucer. Sides of cup curve out to plain rim.
Ear-shaped handle attached below rim and below midpoint.
Shaped base. Saucer shallow, with widely flaring sides and plain
rim; rimmed base. Cup and saucer impressed on bottom "Lu-Ray
Pastels/USA."

Materials and Dimensions
White earthenware with opaque pink glaze. Molded; handle
separately shaped and applied. Cup height: 2¼–2½"; diameter:
3½–3¾". Saucer height: ¾–1"; diameter: 5½–6".

Locality and Period
The Midwest. c. 1950–60.

Comment
During the 1950s, manufacturers produced lines of pastel ceramic
tableware, which soon inspired similar pieces in plastic. Made in
pale blues, grays, pinks, yellows, and greens, Luray ceramics
have only recently begun to attract the attention of collectors.
Relatively common today, these pieces are bound to become
harder to find with time.

Hints for Collectors
Now is the time to collect Luray ceramics and similar pieces
made after World War II. They are abundant and inexpensive,
so be sure to choose examples that are in excellent condition.
Whether you do so piecemeal or all at once, try to acquire a
complete set. Items such as covered serving dishes are usually
the most difficult to find, since lids often break or are misplaced.
Look for these pieces in secondhand shops and at house sales;
they should be easy to find.

Description
Matching cup and saucer with embossed fruit and leaf
decoration. Sides of cup curve slightly out to plain rim. Ear-
shaped handle with branchlike embossing attached just below
rim and above rimmed base. Saucer flares out from rimmed base
to plain rim. *Variations:* Similar pieces may be embossed with
seaweed, fishes, crabs, and other wildlife.

Materials and Dimensions
Coarse white earthenware with thick, polychrome glaze. Molded;
handle separately shaped and applied. Cup height: 2½–2¾";
diameter: 3–3¼". Saucer height: ¾–1"; diameter: 5¾–6¼".

Locality and Period
Griffen, Smith & Hill, Phoenixville, Pennsylvania. c. 1880–93.
Similar pieces from New Hampshire, New York, New Jersey,
Maryland, and Ohio. c. 1870–1900.

Comment
Majolica, a brightly colored, coarse-bodied ware, was popular
during the last quarter of the 19th century. Examples made by
Griffen, Smith & Hill usually bear an impression on the bottom,
either "ETRUSCAN MAJOLICA" in a circle surrounding the
intertwined initials "G.S.H." or simply "ETRUSCAN" or "ETRUSCAN
MAJOLICA." Typical majolica forms included leaf-shaped relish
dishes, ice-cream platters shaped like straw hats and festooned
with ribbons, and cabbage-shaped teapots.

Hints for Collectors
Much more majolica was produced in England than America. To
find American examples, look for marks of firms such as
Morrison & Carr of New York City and Baltimore's Chesapeake
Pottery. Since majolica is fragile, chips, cracks, and worn glaze
are common.

Fiesta demitasse cup and saucer

Description
Matching cup and saucer. Cup has sides curving gently out to
plain rim. Sticklike handle attached just below midpoint. Slightly
flaring, rimmed base. Saucer has wide, slightly flaring border
decorated with concentric rings; small rimmed base.

Materials and Dimensions
White earthenware with opaque, dark blue glaze. Found in all
Fiesta colors except for medium green. Molded; handle
separately shaped and applied. Cup height: 2¼–2½″; diameter:
3½–3¾″. Saucer height: ¾–1″; diameter: 5¾–6″.

Locality and Period
Homer Laughlin Company, Newell, West Virginia. c. 1936–51.

Comment
Demitasse sets consisting of cups, saucers, and coffeepots were
among the earliest pieces in the Fiesta line. Production of the
demitasse coffeepots, which were only made in green, blue,
yellow, red, white, and turquoise, was discontinued in 1943. Like
the cup illustrated, the pot had a stick handle, which was more
difficult to grip than the ear-shaped handle found on standard
coffeepots, and this may have contributed to its limited
popularity.

Hints for Collectors
Probably the 2 most popular Fiesta glazes are deep blue and
brilliant orange-red, and pieces in these colors usually command
more than similar examples in other colors. Pieces in red can be
especially difficult to find. One of the principal components of the
red glaze was depleted uranium oxide; in 1943, the Federal
government took over control of the substance, and Homer
Laughlin withdrew the glaze from production. Only in 1959 was
its manufacture resumed.

Porcelain cup and saucer

Description
Elaborate, matching cup and saucer. Cup has slightly flaring rim.
Handle in form of modeled figure of Liberty attached just below
rim and at base. Shaped base has footlike projections. Saucer has
wide rim that angles down and outward. Shaped base also with
footlike projections. Exterior of cup and saucer with embossed,
painted, and gilded floral, figural, and geometric decoration,
including figure of Justice. *Variations:* Most cups do not have
figural handles.

Materials and Dimensions
Hand-painted porcelain with clear alkaline glaze. Gilded. Molded;
handle separately shaped and applied. Cup height: 3¾–4";
diameter: 3½–3¾". Saucer height: 1¼–1½"; diameter: 6¾–7".

Locality and Period
Union Porcelain Works, Greenpoint, New York. c. 1876–77.
Similar pieces from New York, New Jersey, Ohio, and
Maryland. c. 1876–80.

Comment
In honor of America's Centennial celebration in 1876, some of the
major American porcelain manufacturers produced pieces with
patriotic or commemorative themes. The Union Porcelain Works
was one of the most notable of these firms. It employed the
sculptor, Karl Müller, creator of this piece, to design a number of
items that incorporated historical figures, such as Washington,
and patriotic scenes, such as the Boston Tea Party.

Hints for Collectors
Although many of the pieces made to commemorate the
Centennial were one of a kind or produced in limited numbers,
this cup and saucer set was made in some quantity and collectors
still occasionally encounter it. However, it is expensive.

Art pottery compote

Description
Large, goblet-shaped compote with thick stem in form of tree trunk and circular foot. Bowl decorated with embossed leaves and branches and supported by 4 branch-shaped brackets that rise from stem. Shaped rim. *Variations:* Decoration is usually less naturalistic.

Materials and Dimensions
White earthenware with a matt green glaze. Molded. Height: 9–10″. Diameter: 6–7″.

Locality and Period
New Jersey and Ohio. c. 1910–20.

Comment
Compotes and centerpieces were popular art pottery forms and were manufactured by such well-known firms as the Weller and Roseville potteries. Relatively few of them were made in the Art Nouveau style seen here. In America most pieces in that style were produced between 1910 and 1920, a decade after it was popular in Europe, where it originated. The goblet shape seen here is unusual, since most compotes were bowl-like in shape, designed to hold fruit.

Hints for Collectors
After several decades of neglect, Art Nouveau began to become popular with collectors in the late 1950s and it is still escalating in popularity today. Ceramics in this style are usually still reasonably priced and offer a real opportunity for the collector. Unmarked pieces usually cost much less than marked examples and can be bargains. The appealing shape and glaze seen here make this example a particularly good investment.

Rockingham goblet

Description
Drinking vessel with tubular stem and flaring foot. Cup with plain rim. Foot hollow. Incised line between cup and stem and between stem and foot. *Variations:* Some goblets are lower and squatter. Some have ear-shaped handle.

Materials and Dimensions
Yellow earthenware with Rockingham glaze. Molded. Height: 4–6″. Diameter: 3–4″.

Locality and Period
Attributed to the United States Pottery Company, Bennington, Vermont. c. 1848–58. Similar pieces from New Jersey, Maryland, and Ohio. c. 1840–65.

Comment
Although several major Rockingham manufacturers produced goblets, few have survived, probably because the hollow foot was fragile and could break easily. They were seldom marked by their makers. These goblets come in a variety of sizes and shapes, and a group of them form an interesting and attractive collection. The goblet seen here is attributed to the United States Pottery Company in Bennington on the basis of illustrations in the pottery's catalogues.

Hints for Collectors
Rockingham goblets are popular today and bring good prices on the market. Since they are easily broken, be sure to check condition before you buy. Broken fragments have sometimes been reattached with glue, and chipped rims may show signs of repair with epoxy.

Stoneware sewer-tile goblet

Description
Drinking vessel with hexagonal foot and stem. Sides of stem
curve out to chamfered bottom of goblet. Plain rim. Sides of cup
embossed with vertical, leaflike pattern alternating with Gothic
arches filled with squares and X shapes. 3 horizontal bands of
squares and X shapes around cup bottom.

Materials and Dimensions
Stoneware with brown glaze. Molded. Height: 5–7″. Diameter:
3½–4″.

Locality and Period
New York, Pennsylvania, and Ohio. c. 1880–1915.

Comment
Potters working in the sewer-pipe and sewer-tile factories made
ceramic objects in their spare time as a sideline or for their own
use or to be given as gifts. This piece was modeled after the
pressed-glass goblets and spoon holders produced by many
American glass factories during the Victorian era. It was
probably too heavy to be used as a drinking vessel; it may have
been employed as a vase. Since sewer-tile objects were not
production pieces, their construction was a matter of whimsy. It
is often difficult to determine what they were used for.

Hints for Collectors
Like much pottery of the early 19th century, sewer-tile pieces
were one-of-a-kind objects and were often signed by their
makers. Always check the bottom for names and dates. Even if
unsigned, they are unique examples of the potter's art and
should be collected. A group of these goblets would be a valuable
addition to a pottery collection.

Plates, Platters, and Serving Dishes

Most ceramic plates are circular, usually between 7″ and 15″ in diameter, with low sides. Those that have taller sides were intended for baking, although they probably doubled from time to time as all-purpose dishes. Platters are generally larger, sometimes as much as 2′ in length, and are usually oblong, oval, or rectangular. The earliest pottery plates and platters were either drape-molded or wheel-thrown; by the middle of the 19th century almost all were cast in molds.

Redware Plates and Platters

In the 18th century, plates and platters were typically made of red earthenware. Produced in quantity, most of these pieces were richly decorated. Throughout much of the Northeast, potters trailed colored slip across the clear-glazed red surface, forming abstract designs or names, dates, and sayings. In Pennsylvania, potters also used sgraffito decoration. In this technique, the body was first coated with opaque slip; the decorator then cut or scraped through the slip to expose the red clay body. Both slip and sgraffito decoration were employed until almost the middle of the 19th century.

Ironstone and White and Yellow Earthenware Plates

With the introduction of sophisticated molding techniques in the mid-19th century, redware plates generally fell out of favor, although they were produced in rural areas as late as the 1880s. Yellow and white earthenware soon became the preferred clays for tableware. Yellowware examples were either covered with a clear glaze or with the popular Rockingham finish. Manufactured in both England and America, ironstone and white earthenware plates often had a simple clear glaze; however, many examples, especially those made of earthenware, were decorated with sponging, transfer printing, or hand painting. Ironstone examples were often embellished with embossed floral or geometric motifs. Plates with sponging and the rarer spattered decoration were apparently preferred in rural areas. Hand-painted pieces became less common toward the end of the 19th century, when the inexpensive transfer-printing technique became popular.

Serving Dishes

In the late 19th century, it was common for factories to produce lines of matching tableware that might include plates in several sizes, as well as cups, saucers, soup bowls, serving dishes, platters, and miscellaneous pieces like bone dishes, which were designed to hold bones and other remains of elaborate dinners. Each place setting might contain as many as 8 pieces. Some of these tableware sets were expensive, made of porcelain, and elaborately decorated by hand; others, of ironstone, were simple and sturdy, made for use in hotels and homes. By the early 20th century, many large companies were producing inexpensive tableware meant for everyday use. With their simple lines and bright glazes, some of these pieces are eagerly collected today in spite of the fact that they hardly qualify as antiques.

Miscellaneous Dishes

In addition to plates and platters, this section includes miscellaneous serving pieces ranging from fanciful oyster plates to elegant bonbon dishes. The most elaborate of these pieces are made of fine porcelain cast in unusual shapes and then painted and gilded by hand.

Redware pie plate

Description
Circular baking dish with low sides that curve slightly to coggled rim. Plain base. Interior inscribed in yellow with name "Wildey." *Variations:* Rim may be plain. Base may be slightly shaped.

Materials and Dimensions
Red earthenware; exterior unglazed; interior with clear lead glaze. Inscription in yellow slip; similar pieces occasionally with white, green, or black inscription. Drape-molded; similar pieces sometimes wheel-thrown. Diameter: 7–15″.

Locality and Period
Philadelphia. c. 1830–40. Similar pieces from Connecticut, New York, New Jersey, and Pennsylvania. c. 1800–70.

Comment
Pie plates and larger circular serving dishes, sometimes called chargers, were made in large quantities in Connecticut and Pennsylvania. Some were inscribed with such phrases as "Mince Pie" and "Clams and Oysters," suggesting their function. Others bore inscriptions that were probably intended as a joke, such as "Cheap Dish" and "Cheap Money," or those that advertised a pottery. Finally, those inscribed with names or initials were most likely intended as gifts. The Wildey family, whose name appears on this dish, was prominent in politics in Philadelphia.

Hints for Collectors
More common than inscribed platters, slip-decorated name pie plates are becoming expensive. Choice examples are those with green or black slip decoration, and those inscribed with uncommon phrases, like "Pony Up the Cash," or place names. Like inscribed platters, many of these plates have been reproduced.

Redware pie plate

Description
Circular baking dish with low, curving sides and coggled rim.
Plain base. Inscribed on interior in green and yellow, "Why Will
You Die." *Variations:* Rim may be plain. Base may be slightly
shaped.

Materials and Dimensions
Red earthenware; exterior unglazed; interior with clear lead
glaze. Inscription in yellow and green slip; similar pieces
decorated with white, black, or a combination of white and black.
Drape-molded; similar pieces sometimes wheel-thrown.
Diameter: 7–15".

Locality and Period
Possibly John B. Gregory, Clinton, New York. c. 1808–31.
Similar pieces from Connecticut, New York, New Jersey, and
Pennsylvania. c. 1800–70.

Comment
Pie plates decorated with complete phrases are much rarer than
those with a name or 1 or 2 words; examples slip-painted in more
than 1 color are rarer yet. Inscriptions like the one seen here and
others such as "Cheap as Dirt" probably had a special
significance for the potter that is lost to us. Particularly
interesting are miniature examples.

Hints for Collectors
Slip-decorated redware pie plates were very rarely, if ever,
impressed with a pottery mark, although a few examples were
decorated in slip with names associated with someone who owned
or worked for a pottery. An example with a pottery mark would
be a find of major importance. Chips on the rims of these plates
have often been repaired. Use ultraviolet light to check for
clever restorations.

Redware pie plate

Description
Circular baking dish with sides curving slightly outward to plain
rim. Plain base. Multicolored curvilinear decoration on interior.
Variations: Rim may be coggled or notched. Base may be
slightly shaped.

Materials and Dimensions
Red earthenware; exterior unglazed; interior with clear lead
glaze. Decorated with white, black, and green slip; similar pieces
usually decorated with single color. Drape-molded; similar pieces
occasionally wheel-thrown. Diameter: 7–15″.

Locality and Period
New England. c. 1820–40. Similar pieces from Pennsylvania
south to the Carolinas. c. 1770–1880.

Comment
Slip decoration on pie plates may vary from a few simple lines in
yellow or white to a rather complex pattern of several colors, as
seen here. Some of the plates with the most complex and
exuberant decoration come from Pennsylvania.

Hints for Collectors
Slip-decorated pie plates were made in large quantities and
remain fairly common. However, they were put to hard use. The
combination of heat from the oven and contact with knives and
other utensils when the pie was cut and served has often worn
away much of the original slip. Unless the decoration is quite
unusual, such wear devalues a piece. Although somewhat worn,
the decoration on the plate seen here has a handsome, strong
design, and the plate would still be a good investment.

Redware sgraffito plate

Description
Circular plate with sides that curve gently outward to coggled rim. Plain base. Interior decorated with incised and painted design of 2 birds perched on leaves of large potted plant. *Variations:* Rim may be plain.

Materials and Dimensions
Red earthenware glazed with cream slip. Incised decoration with touches of green slip. Drape-molded; similar pieces wheel-thrown. Diameter: 11–13″.

Locality and Period
Pennsylvania. c. 1800–30. Similar pieces from New Jersey, Pennsylvania, and North Carolina. c. 1770–1850.

Comment
Used primarily in Pennsylvania, sgraffito decoration involved covering the body of a piece of pottery with an opaque slip, which was usually white. Then the potter cut or scraped through the slip to the red clay beneath, producing a contrasting color scheme. As here, other colors, especially green and black, were often painted on the surface. Plates with sgraffito decoration are most common, but other objects such as jars and bowls were also decorated.

Hints for Collectors
Authentic sgraffito pottery is rare, highly prized, and expensive. Watch out for reproductions: First made during the 1920s and 1930s, some are still being made today. They can be recognized by the lack of surface crazing and wear that is found on antique pottery. Some reproductions will be distinguished by a mark, but if in doubt, get a letter of authenticity from the dealer.

173 Redware deep dish

Description
Large cooking or serving dish with sides that curve up and out to wide, flaring rim. Plain base. Interior covered with floral and abstract slip decoration. *Variations:* Rim may be plain, not flaring. Decoration varies.

Materials and Dimensions
Red earthenware with dark brown glaze. Decorated with yellow and black slip. Drape-molded. Diameter: 12–14″.

Locality and Period
Salem, North Carolina. c. 1800–40. Similar pieces from North Carolina and Pennsylvania. c. 1770–1860.

Comment
Plates with elaborate slip decoration were made in large numbers by the Moravian potters of North Carolina. Today, based on differences in shape, they are called pans, deep dishes, or plates. The Moravians referred to them all as dishes; after 1821, examples such as the one seen here were referred to as flowered dishes. Moravian slip-decorated ware is similar to that produced in Pennsylvania by other Germanic settlers, but it is distinguished by its more abstract design and a general lack of the pictorial elements that were favored by Pennsylvania potters.

Hints for Collectors
Moravian pottery is in great demand and brings high prices, but it is rarely marked. Pieces should be identified by comparison with known examples in public collections and in the standard reference books listed in the bibliography. Don't buy a reputed Moravian piece without a guarantee of authenticity. Some minor damage is acceptable with such rare pieces.

Rockingham pie plate

Description
Circular baking dish with sides that angle out to plain rim. Plain
base. *Variations:* Some examples have rolled rims. Others have
small footlike knobs on bottom.

Materials and Dimensions
Yellow earthenware with Rockingham glaze. Similar pieces with
clear alkaline glaze. Molded; earlier examples drape-molded.
Diameter: 7–10″.

Locality and Period
Vermont west to Ohio, south to Maryland. c. 1845–1900.

Comment
Rockingham pie plates were made in many different potteries,
particularly in Vermont, New York, New Jersey, Ohio, and
Maryland. Examples made at the various potteries are quite
similar, and it is practically impossible to identify the maker
without a mark or reliable history of origin. Factory prices for
pie plates were based on size. For example, 7″ plates retailed at
one pottery for 75 cents per dozen, while 10″ examples brought
$1.05 per dozen.

Hints for Collectors
Rockingham pie plates are popular with collectors, and some
dealers maintain they all come from the famous Bennington,
Vermont, pottery. Most, in fact, do not. Unless a piece has a
Bennington mark (usually with the date "1849"), don't pay the
premium that is charged for Bennington pieces. Avoid pieces
that have cracks, chips about the rim, or areas where the glaze
has worn off. These defects are common in utilitarian pieces such
as pie plates, and do reduce their worth.

175 Yellowware pie plate

Description
Circular baking dish with low sides that angle out to plain rim. Plain base. *Variations:* Some plates are deeper. Sides may be set at different angles.

Materials and Dimensions
Yellow earthenware with clear alkaline glaze. Drape-molded; earlier pieces wheel-thrown. Diameter: 8–12″.

Locality and Period
Massachusetts west to Ohio, south to Maryland. c. 1860–1900.

Comment
Many yellowware baking dishes were made during the second half of the 19th century, since it was customary, particularly among farm families, to serve pie two or even three times a day. While early 19th-century yellowware plates were thrown on a wheel, later examples were shaped over a wooden form, trimmed, and then fired. Such pie plates replaced the redware ones that had been popular prior to 1850. Although both stoneware and ironstone examples are occasionally found, neither medium was ever used extensively for this form. Rockingham pie plates, however, are common.

Hints for Collectors
Yellowware pie plates come in several sizes, are easy to find, and are relatively inexpensive. A fine crazing, or spidering, on the surface is common in older examples and is no detriment. On the other hand, plates with cracks should be avoided. Look for unusually small or large examples and for the very few that bear the mark of a pottery; the latter were usually made in Ohio or New Jersey. Some use these plates for baking, but only do so with caution. They can easily break—especially if they are cracked—when they are exposed to high temperatures.

Ironstone pie plate

Description
Circular plate with low sides that angle out from plain base to plain rim. Impressed on bottom "WARRENTED/COPY RGT./COOK & HANCOCK." *Variations:* Sides may rise at a sharper angle.

Materials and Dimensions
Ironstone with clear alkaline glaze. Molded. Diameter: 8–11″.

Locality and Period
Crescent Pottery Company, Trenton, New Jersey. c. 1881–1902. Similar wares from New York west to Ohio, south to Maryland. c. 1860–1920.

Comment
The bottom of the piece shown is impressed with a mark used by the Crescent Pottery Company. Founded in Trenton, New Jersey, in 1881 by Charles H. Cook and W. S. Hancock, the pottery produced yellowware and earthenware as well as ironstone china, and was active until the early 1900s. This mark is one of the more common of several different impressions the company used.

Hints for Collectors
Ironstone pie plates were never as popular as yellowware examples, and they are not often seen today. However, the relative lack of interest has kept prices low, and an ironstone pie plate is usually quite affordable. It is possible to assemble a nest of 3 or 4 ironstone pie plates in different sizes. It would be a real achievement if all bore the same mark of an American pottery; American factories tended to mark only the more important pieces, such as coffeepots, tureens, and serving bowls.

Spatterware plate

Description
Large, circular plate with sides that slope out to wide, flaring rim. Interior decorated in spatter with 2 bands surrounding circle, creating a bull's-eye effect. Rimmed base. *Variations:* Center of plate may have transfer-printed or hand-painted motif such as a rose or peafowl.

Materials and Dimensions
White earthenware with clear alkaline glaze; interior spattered with blue slip; similar examples with red, green, or black slip. Exterior may be similarly spattered or, as here, undecorated. Molded; similar pieces sometimes drape-molded. Diameter: 9–11″.

Locality and Period
Probably England. c. 1840–80.

Comment
Although spatterware resembles spongeware, the 2 types differ. Spatter decoration is more concise and is usually applied in a more distinctive pattern. Large open areas, which are seen around and between sponged motifs, are generally lacking in spatterware. Although the name "spatterware" refers to the belief that color was applied by spattering with a brush, it may have been applied with a sponge, or even with stencils or by transfer-printing. Whatever the actual method, the term is an accepted one for pieces like the example illustrated.

Hints for Collectors
Being both older and less common than spongeware, spatterware is usually more valuable. Collectors visiting England should look for examples in the shops and flea markets there. American-made spatterware is extremely rare, but can be seen in a few museum collections.

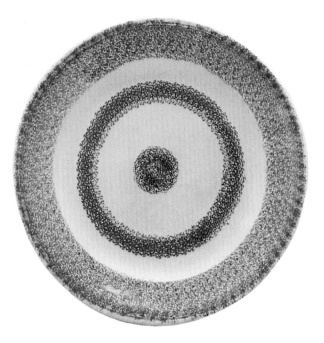

Spongeware plate

Description
Circular plate with sides that curve out to slightly flared rim. Rimmed base. *Variations:* Base may lack rim. Angle of sides varies.

Materials and Dimensions
Ironstone with clear alkaline glaze; exterior undecorated; interior covered with heavily mottled blue sponging. Molded; some examples drape-molded. Diameter: 9–10½".

Locality and Period
England; also New Jersey and Ohio. c. 1860–90.

Comment
Plates were among the earliest pieces with sponged decoration, and apparently they were not made for as many years as other forms, such as bowls and pitchers. Most are unmarked, but a few bear the impressions of English potteries such as Edge, Malkin & Company, and the Middleport Potteries of Burslem. The rare American marks are those of Ohio or New Jersey companies.

Hints for Collectors
A marked spongeware plate is a welcome and unusual find, and even the mark of an English pottery does not lessen the value of the piece in the American market. Since both English and American plates of this sort were used in the States, both are considered equally desirable by collectors. The most sought-after examples have strong, well-defined decoration. Avoid plates with chipped edges or long scratches caused by knives and forks, and be especially wary of pieces with conspicuous cracks. They may break on the slightest impact.

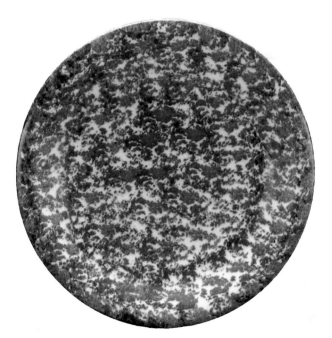

179 **Ironstone plate**

Description
Circular plate with wide border and shaped rim. Rimmed base below 2 incised concentric lines. Bottom slightly recessed. Marked "1862 GREENWOOD CHINA/TRENTON N.J./1876 REG US PAT OFF." *Variations:* Some plates have transfer decoration. Most are unmarked.

Materials and Dimensions
Ironstone with clear alkaline glaze. Molded. Diameter: 5–10".

Locality and Period
New Jersey. 1876. Similar examples throughout the East and Midwest. c. 1860–1920.

Comment
Ironstone plates are tough, durable, and inexpensive. At the turn of the century they were used not only in homes but also in restaurants, where they were so common that they were often referred to as hotel china. Although English ironstone is almost always marked, many American pieces are not. The great majority, however, were made in large factories in major ceramics centers, such as Trenton, New Jersey, and Liverpool, Ohio.

Hints for Collectors
Look for pieces with unusual marks. This plate is desirable because its mark not only contains the date the pottery was founded, 1862, but also the year in which the piece was produced, 1876, the nation's Centennial. Some collectors are willing to pay more for pieces produced in that year. A set of 2 to 4 matching pieces of ironstone is always more valuable than the same number of unmatched pieces.

Porcelain commemorative plate

Description
Circular plate with wide border and plain rim. Rimmed base. Decorated with painted bands and garlands surrounding polychrome painting of the Dorflinger glass factory and home at White Mills, Wayne County, Pennsylvania. *Variations:* May picture individuals, scenes, or historic events.

Materials and Dimensions
Hand-painted porcelain with clear alkaline glaze. Molded. Diameter: 9¼–9½".

Locality and Period
New Jersey, Pennsylvania, and Ohio. c. 1870–75. Similar pieces from New York west to Ohio, south to Maryland. c. 1865–1900.

Comment
During the second half of the 19th century merchants and captains of industry commissioned paintings of such things as their homes, factories, and ships. Most of these works were simply hung in the home, but some served as illustrations for local business directories or advertisements. Adapting such a painting to decorate a commemorative plate was an even more unusual format. The plate shown here features a factory, an ornate Victorian home, and the countryside along the old Delaware and Hudson Canal.

Hints for Collectors
Since ceramics are rarely decorated with industrial scenes, this plate is a valuable example. Do not confuse these 19th-century pieces with 20th-century souvenir plates. The latter are often decorated with picturesque sites such as Niagara Falls or landmarks such as the White House and always have the mark of a 20th-century American or European pottery on the bottom. In addition, they are seldom painted by hand.

Description
Circular plate with border and scalloped rim. Beaded base.
Central design of transfer-printed sailing ship with date "FEBY
25th 1902." Ship flanked at left and right by American eagle with
shield and imperial German eagle. Border with embossed floral
design and printing "SOUVENIR/LAUNCHING OF SCHOONER YACHT
METEOR BUILT FOR H.I.M./THE EMPEROR OF GERMANY/TOWNSEND-
DOWNEY Ship Building Co/NEW YORK U.S.A." Impressed on back
"O.P.W." *Variations:* Decoration varies.

Materials and Dimensions
White earthenware with clear alkaline glaze. Decorated with
transfer designs in green. Molded. Diameter: 9–10″.

Locality and Period
Onondaga Pottery Company, Syracuse, New York. c. 1875–1900.
Similar pieces from New York, New Jersey, and Ohio. c. 1870–
1940.

Comment
Commemorative plates have been popular in America since the
last quarter of the 19th century. Most were produced in limited
numbers by large potteries with facilities for transfer printing
and decoration. The decoration on this plate commemorates the
building of a yacht for a German emperor by an American firm.

Hints for Collectors
While plates commemorating major historical events such as the
1876 Centennial and the Columbian Exposition of 1893 are
relatively easy to find, those relating to less significant
occurrences are rare. Look for late 19th-century American
commemorative plates in shops specializing in Danish Christmas
plates and souvenir pottery; they are often sold together. Almost
all American examples are marked.

Transfer-decorated white earthenware plate

Description
Shallow plate with border and scalloped rim. Rimmed base. Decorated with blue transfer printing: border with alternating panels of floral and pictorial decoration; interior edged with swag-and-tassel motif enclosing landscape with ruins, urns, gondola, plants, and trees. Ink-stamped on bottom "American Pottery Manufacturing Co./Canova/Jersey City" in an oval ribbon with words encircling urn. *Variations:* Rim may be plain.

Materials and Dimensions
White earthenware with clear alkaline glaze. Decorated with transfer designs in blue. Molded. Diameter: 9–9½".

Locality and Period
American Pottery Manufacturing Company, Jersey City, New Jersey. c. 1840–42.

Comment
The American Pottery Manufacturing Company was the first firm to introduce the English technique of transfer decoration into this country. Plates such as this are the American version of English blue Staffordshire, and were produced to compete with the imported ware. But early domestic pieces, while of high quality, were more expensive than the English imports, and production was soon discontinued. It did not resume in volume until after the Civil War.

Hints for Collectors
Early 19th-century American transfer-decorated white earthenware is rare and quite valuable; however, it is easily mistaken for English products. The Canova pattern seen here, for example, was adapted from a very similar design made by the John Ridgway firm of Hanley, England. Always check the bottoms of such plates for makers' marks.

183 Hand-painted white earthenware plate

Description
Octagonal dinner plate with border and plain rim. Plain base.
Shallow interior decorated with 2 multicolored sprays of flowers.
Bottom stamped in ink, "HC/HOMER LAUGHLIN/MADE IN U.S.A."
Variations: May be undecorated or transfer decorated.

Materials and Dimensions
Hand-painted white earthenware with clear alkaline glaze.
Molded. Diameter: 8½–9½".

Locality and Period
Homer Laughlin Company, Newell, West Virginia. c. 1910–30.
Similar pieces from New York west to Ohio, south to Maryland.
c. 1870–1950.

Comment
Although most plates and saucers are circular, square and
octagonal examples exist as well. The English made octagonal
ones in the 18th century, as did the Chinese for export. In the
19th century, potters in Pennsylvania produced some in red
earthenware. The plate illustrated was manufactured by Homer
Laughlin, a major American producer of white earthenware. The
decoration was done freehand, which was more time consuming
and expensive than stencil decoration or transfer printing.

Hints for Collectors
Hand-decorated white earthenware was produced in some
quantity from 1880 to around 1930, and it is still possible to
assemble a dinner service consisting of a number of pieces in the
same pattern. Currently inexpensive, this ware is just beginning
to attract collectors' attention. Look for it not only in antiques
shops but also in secondhand stores and at garage and yard sales.

84 Transfer-decorated porcelain saucer

Description
Shallow saucer with sides that slope up and out from rimmed base to plain rim. Interior decorated with floral sprays, gilded band, and floral band with birds. Bottom marked "L" in wreath, with "LENOX/MADE IN U.S.A." below. *Variations:* Decoration varies or is absent.

Materials and Dimensions
Transfer-decorated porcelain with clear alkaline glaze. Gilding. Molded. Diameter: 5¼–5¾″.

Locality and Period
Lenox Inc., Trenton, New Jersey. c. 1910–30. Similar pieces from New York west to Ohio, south to Maryland. c. 1900–30.

Comment
This transfer-decorated dish has an Oriental flavor, popular in this country at the turn of the century. By 1900 few firms could afford to maintain a staff of painters to hand-decorate their wares, and instead employed the transfer method, which had been discovered in the mid-18th century. Such items were designed for the middle-income market, but the finest, most expensive porcelain continued to be hand-painted.

Hints for Collectors
Cups and saucers often become separated, but the collector should acquire single pieces with the hope of finding a match. Avoid pieces that are in any way damaged or repaired or that show wear to the decoration. These have practically no value, and early 20th-century porcelain is abundant, allowing the collector to be selective.

Fiesta plates

Description
Circular plates with slightly raised, shaped rim. Series of
concentric circles just inside rim and at center of each plate.
Slightly raised, rimmed base. Bottom impressed "Fiesta/HLC
USA."

Materials and Dimensions
White earthenware with opaque glaze; examples here red, gray,
ivory, yellow, and light green. Similar examples in all standard
Fiesta colors. Molded. Diameters (large to small): chop plate, 12–
12½"; dinner plate, 10–10¼"; luncheon plates, 9–9¼"; bread and
butter plate, 7–7¼".

Locality and Period
Homer Laughlin Company, Newell, West Virginia. c. 1936–69.

Comment
There are several types of Fiesta plates, including a large 15"
chop plate that was discontinued in 1959, and a 6" dessert plate.
All types are relatively common, except for the largest chop
plate and the 10" dinner plate. Dark colors, with the exception of
red and blue, are more common than the pastels that first
appeared in the 1950s.

Hints for Collectors
Fiesta plates are practical and plentiful enough for one to be
selective. Choose only examples in good, undamaged condition
and, preferably, those bearing one of the several Fiesta marks on
the bottom. Marked examples will, of course, be of greater
value. If you want inexpensive examples, choose those in the
pastel shades; although they are not as plentiful as the darker
colors, they are not particularly popular. Red and blue pieces are
more expensive, but will probably continue to increase in value.

Fiesta compartment plates

Description
Circular plates with wide, slightly angled borders, decorated
with series of concentric rings. Interior of plate divided into 3
areas by 2 raised ridges forming a T shape. Rimmed base.
Bottom impressed "Fiesta/HLC USA."

Materials and Dimensions
White earthenware with opaque glaze; examples here blue,
green, yellow; similar pieces in all standard Fiesta colors.
Molded. Diameter: 10½–11⅝".

Locality and Period
Homer Laughlin Company, Newell, West Virginia. c. 1936–59.

Comment
Designed for more efficient serving, compartmentalized plates
were among the first items to be manufactured in the Fiesta line,
and appeared in catalogues until the late 1950s. Although they
were used in homes, restaurants, and institutions, they were
never as popular as traditional Fiesta plates and are harder to
find today.

Hints for Collectors
It is especially difficult to find chartreuse compartment plates;
their rarity makes them more expensive than those with other
glazes. No turquoise examples are known. Yet while color is a
factor in determining the value of Fiesta pieces, object type and
even size can be important. For example, although catalogues
listed compartment plates in 2 sizes, with diameters of both 10½"
and 11⅝", the latter is practically unknown. It is a good idea to
carry a tape measure, especially when odd sizes are known to
exist.

Fiesta tray

Description
Tiered serving piece consisting of 2 plates of different sizes
mounted one above the other on a metal shaft with circular finial.
Each plate has series of concentric bands below slightly raised
rim. Concentric circles at center of each plate. Rimmed base.
Both plates with bottom impressed "Fiesta/HLC USA."
Variations: May consist of 3 plates arranged in same manner.
Connecting rod may be baluster-shaped brass.

Materials and Dimensions
White earthenware with opaque yellow and light blue glaze;
similar pieces in various combinations of yellow, light blue, light
green, turquoise, rose-pink, and gray. Molded. Plate diameters:
8½–13". Height of assembled tray: 9–15".

Locality and Period
Homer Laughlin Company, Newell, West Virginia. c. 1939–43.

Comment
These trays, which cost only 98 cents, were made as promotional
items to encourage sales during the Second World War. The
plates were produced by the Homer Laughlin Company and the
trays assembled at metal factories. The lighter Fiesta colors,
such as those seen here, were popular during this period; they
are currently the focus of renewed collector interest.

Hints for Collectors
One can often find the separate parts that make up these trays,
such as a group of plates with drilled center holes but no metal
shaft or finial. It is worth accumulating such parts until a
complete unit can be assembled, as these trays are not
particularly common.

Yellowware baking dish

Description
Rectangular serving or baking vessel with straight sides angling slightly outward to plain rim. Plain base. *Variations:* Some examples may be more oblong in shape.

Materials and Dimensions
Yellow earthenware with clear alkaline glaze. Molded; similar pieces drape-molded. Length: 9–12″. Width: 7–9″. Height: 2–3″.

Locality and Period
New York west to Ohio, south to Maryland. c. 1860–1900.

Comment
Rectangular dishes are relatively uncommon in yellowware. The piece shown here could have been used either for serving or for baking in a coal- or wood-burning oven. Because of its large size, it seems likely that this dish was designed for baking. Also, most yellowware serving forms were derived from comparable shapes in ironstone, and no examples of American ironstone serving dishes in this shape exist. These pieces were apparently never marked, so it is almost impossible to determine where a particular example was produced.

Hints for Collectors
It is often difficult to determine how a bowl or dish was used, but one may find a clue by checking the bottom of the piece. If the bottom shows darkened or burnt areas, the piece was probably used for baking. On the other hand, a bowl with many fine lines on the bottom of the interior may have been used for serving food. The scratches or lines would be caused by the constant contact with a serving spoon.

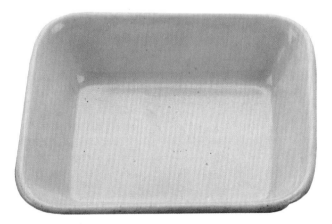

Redware platter

Description
Rectangular serving dish with sides that slope out to coggled rim. Plain base. Interior inscribed in yellow with "Emma," enclosed by decorative lines. *Variations:* Shape may be more oblong. Rim sometimes plain.

Materials and Dimensions
Red earthenware; exterior unglazed; interior with clear lead glaze. Decorated with yellow slip; similar pieces with white or green decoration. Drape-molded. Length: 10–18″. Width: 7–11″.

Locality and Period
Connecticut; Long Island, New York; New Jersey; and Pennsylvania. c. 1800–60.

Comment
Platters like the one pictured here were probably made to order as gifts for friends or loved ones. Similar platters decorated with abstract curvilinear designs were for the most part production pieces. Inscriptions found on these platters include names like "Finetta Wheeler," "Lafayette," and "Susan," and memorable slogans like "Good Enough for Rich Folks."

Hints for Collectors
Name platters and the more common slip-decorated name pie plates are extremely popular with collectors today and bring very high prices. Many are chipped or cracked, particularly around the rim. But if the damage does not affect the design, a platter is still probably worth buying. Be wary of recent reproductions, which will have shiny surfaces and bottoms that are light and clean rather than darkened from use in the oven.

Redware platter

Description
Oblong dish with sides that slope out to coggled rim. Plain base. Painted yellow linear decoration with leaflike forms on interior. *Variations:* Shape may be rectangular. Rim may be plain. Sometimes decorated with inscriptions; rarely with pictorial scenes.

Materials and Dimensions
Red earthenware; exterior unglazed; interior with clear lead glaze. Decorated with yellow slip; similar pieces with white, green, or black decoration; rare pieces decorated with a combination of 2 or 3 colors. Drape-molded. Length: 12–22″. Width: 8–12″.

Locality and Period
Connecticut; Long Island, New York; New Jersey; and Pennsylvania. c. 1800–60.

Comment
These platters were decorated with a slip cup, a hollow receptacle with 2 to 4 tubes protruding from its base. Slip in the cup could be released by moving one's fingers, which were held over the tube spouts. Various curvilinear patterns were created as the potter moved his hand over a surface. The example shown illustrates a particularly skilled use of the slip cup.

Hints for Collectors
These platters should not be confused with 2 other types of platters sometimes seen. English combware has a redware body decorated with long parallel lines of white slip resembling marks made by the teeth of a comb. Canadian redware has a deep red clay body and a plain, undecorated white interior.

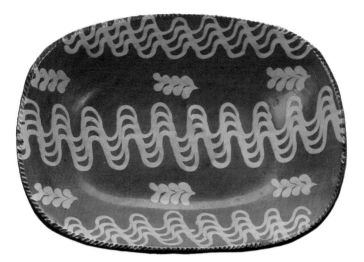

Ironstone platter

Description
Oval serving dish with border and shaped rim. On border, raised and recessed walls create panels of varying widths. Plain base. *Variations:* Decoration varies or is absent. Interior may have transfer decoration.

Materials and Dimensions
Ironstone with clear alkaline glaze. Molded. Length: 10½–14″. Width: 7½–9″.

Locality and Period
Massachusetts west to Ohio, south to Maryland. c. 1860–1920.

Comment
Like most American ironstone, this platter is unmarked, but it probably came from Ohio or New Jersey. Large quantities of ironstone were produced in these areas in the late 19th and early 20th centuries. Durable and generally resistant to acids and staining, ironstone was popular in the home as well as restaurants and public institutions. It was commonly referred to as hotel china.

Hints for Collectors
Ironstone may show discoloration, particularly about the base and rim; check to see if this is surface dirt that can be scrubbed off. The stains may result from oils and other materials that have entered the clay through cracks in the glaze. They can sometimes be removed by soaking the piece in ammonia, but often they are permanent. Avoid stained, cracked, or chipped examples; ironstone is plentiful, allowing the collector to be selective.

Transfer-decorated white earthenware bone dish

Description
Shallow oval dish with sides that curve up and out to plain rim. Interior with embossed cartouchelike devices at 4 points just below rim, and 4 blue abstract designs at ends and midpoints. Plain base. Bottom stamped "E.E.P. CO./MADE IN OHIO/CHINA" in green ink and "T.C. RAINE CO., INC./NEW YORK/CITY" in gilt. *Variations:* May be undecorated.

Materials and Dimensions
Transfer-decorated white earthenware with clear alkaline glaze. Molded. Length: 7–8″. Width: 5½–6″.

Locality and Period
East End Pottery, East Liverpool, Ohio. c. 1880–1900. Similar pieces from New York west to Ohio, south to Maryland. c. 1870–1920.

Comment
In the late 19th century, shallow oval dishes were commonly placed alongside dinner plates in order to accommodate the bones and other remains of an elaborate Victorian meal. A bone dish was often included as part of the standard place setting, which might consist of as many as 8 or 9 pieces.

Hints for Collectors
Note that this piece has 2 marks on the bottom: that of the maker, East End Pottery, and that of the New York City department store that sold the pattern. This practice was common in the late 19th and early 20th centuries, when large department stores and shops specializing in china might order thousands of place settings and direct that their names appear on the tableware.

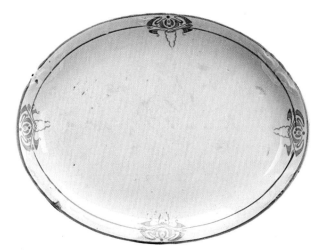

193 Porcelain oyster plate

Description
Shallow dish in form of clamshell. Sides slope up and out to shaped rim. Plain base. Interior embossed in forms of and painted with oysters, mussels, a lobster claw, various seashells, seaweed, and floral motifs. *Variations:* Decoration varies or is absent.

Materials and Dimensions
Hand-painted porcelain with clear alkaline glaze. Gilded details. Molded. Length: 8–9″. Width: 6½–7″.

Locality and Period
Union Porcelain Works, Greenpoint, New York. c. 1880–90. Similar pieces from New York, New Jersey, and Ohio. c. 1870–1910.

Comment
Oyster plates were, of course, intended for the serving of shellfish, which would fit neatly into their depressions, along with hot sauce and other condiments. Oysters were popular in this country as early as the 17th century. Reports from the 18th century describe oysters from New York Bay that were as large as a man's hand. The Union Porcelain Works, which produced this plate, was one of the major American porcelain manufacturers of the late 19th century.

Hints for Collectors
Union Porcelain Works china was often marked, usually with some variation of the logo "U.P.W./UNION/PORCELAIN/WORKS/N.Y." The output of the firm was large, and it is still possible to find marked examples. The factory also produced ironstone pieces, which bear similar marks.

Rockingham relish dish

Description
Shallow serving vessel with low sides that curve out to ridged and scalloped rim. Rimmed base. Interior embossed with small acanthus leaf and flowers at one end from which wavelike ridges radiate outward in leaf form.

Materials and Dimensions
Yellow earthenware with Rockingham glaze. Molded. Length: 9¾–10″. Width: 5½–5¾″.

Locality and Period
Attributed to the United States Pottery Company, Bennington, Vermont. c. 1849–58.

Comment
Leaf-shaped relish dishes are quite common in white earthenware, and a substantial number were made in England. However, the form is not a common one for Rockinghamware. An 1852 price list from the Bennington pottery lists these relish, or pickle, dishes at $1.75 per dozen, but few have survived. Most likely they were not popular, and only a small number were produced.

Hints for Collectors
Don't confuse these Rockingham relish dishes with similar forms made during the past 10 years. These later pieces are similar in shape and purpose but are made of white earthenware, have thicker walls, and are covered with a dark brown glaze. English and continental porcelain examples of leaf-shaped dishes can be readily distinguished by their translucent white body and polychrome glaze.

Belleek bonbon dish

Description
Shallow serving dish in form of seashell. Thin sides taper out
from shaped base to scalloped rim. *Variations:* May be
decorated, usually with embossed floral motifs.

Materials and Dimensions
Belleek porcelain with clear alkaline glaze; similar pieces
sometimes hand-painted with blue or other colors. Molded.
Diameter: 4¾–5″.

Locality and Period
Knowles, Taylor & Knowles, East Liverpool, Ohio. c. 1888–89.
Similar pieces from New Jersey and West Virginia. c. 1882–
1905.

Comment
Belleek is a type of porcelain developed in Ireland and
characterized by extremely thin walls and a shiny, off-white
body. Ott & Brewer of Trenton, New Jersey, first produced it in
America in 1882. In 1887, Knowles, Taylor & Knowles, an
important midwestern china manufacturer, hired an Irishman,
Joshua Poole, to develop and adapt Belleek for them. They had
been producing it for only a year when a fire destroyed their
factory. They subsequently began manufacturing a similar type
of porcelain, Lotus Ware, which had thicker walls than true
Belleek and was fired at a lower temperature. A similar product
made by the Wheeling Pottery Company in West Virginia was
called Cameo Ware.

Hints for Collectors
Collectors should watch for pieces with the Knowles mark: a
circle bearing a crown with the words "LOTUS WARE" printed
around the circumference. Since American Belleek can be
confused with Irish examples, marks should always be inspected.

Porcelain sweetmeat dish

Description
2-tiered serving dish. Lower unit has 3 shell-shaped dishes with ribbed interiors and scalloped rims. Dishes rest on short, tapered legs and are joined to central column decorated with applied shell motifs. Mounted on top of column, circular bowl with scalloped rim and ribbed exterior. Interiors of all vessels painted with blue floral motifs. *Variations:* Decoration varies.

Materials and Dimensions
Hand-painted porcelain with clear alkaline glaze. Molded, then joined by hand. Height: 5–5½″. Diameter: 7–8″.

Locality and Period
Attributed to Bonnin & Morris, Philadelphia. c. 1770–72.

Comment
This piece is attributed to the first moderately successful American porcelain factory, that of Gousse Bonnin and George Morris, which was established around 1770 at Southwark, an area of Philadelphia. Unfortunately, the factory failed after only a few years. Pieces that have been attributed to it include examples marked with an incised "P." Bonnin & Morris porcelain resembles comparable examples made in England during the same period. The English examples are lighter and more delicate.

Hints for Collectors
Never discount the possibility that rare and valuable pieces will show up in unexpected places. In 1981, a sweetmeat dish similar to the one seen here and also probably made by Bonnin & Morris was found at a Long Island, New York, yard sale. Purchased for just a few dollars, it was later sold at auction for $60,000.

Bowls and Related Objects

Made in numerous sizes and shapes, and in virtually every type of native clay, these pieces range from simple redware soup bowls to elaborate hand-painted porcelain examples. The earliest bowls were probably drape-molded, but very few of these have survived. Pieces made before 1850 of red earthenware and stoneware were usually wheel-thrown; later examples in ironstone, white and yellow earthenware, and porcelain were generally cast in molds.

Mixing Bowls
Mixing bowls are probably the most familiar kind. Made from about 1850 well into the 20th century, most were of yellow earthenware decorated with bands of white or brown slip; a few redware mixing bowls with similar decoration exist. These bowls are relatively low and broad, often with a wide-rimmed base; they may have a thick, rolled rim or a collar. Most came in stacking sets with pieces from 4½″ to 13″ in diameter. In addition to the typical banded decoration, some yellowware examples have a Rockingham glaze or sponged or embossed decoration. Stoneware mixing bowls are usually heavier and squatter than their yellowware counterparts; most have a collar.

Baking Dishes
Similar to mixing bowls, baking dishes were simply called "bakers" in 19th-century price lists. They generally have straight rather than curved sides; many have a tall collar, and in some a wire bail handle is attached to the collar. Matching, dome-shaped lids that usually have a central, knoblike handle often came with baking dishes. The decoration on these pieces resembles that on mixing bowls. Other bowl-shaped pieces include deep dishes, which were used for cooking, especially for baking pies. They have low sides that angle out to either a plain rim or a thick collar. Made of white, yellow, or red earthenware as well as ironstone and stoneware, most of these pieces are plain.

Serving Bowls
Before the middle of the 19th century, cooking bowls were probably used for table service as well. By about 1850, however, specialized pieces became available for serving vegetables and other side dishes. Many of these serving bowls were modeled on English ironstone examples and frequently came as part of a set of matching dinnerware. Most serving bowls are oval or round and have low, sloping sides. Made of all the standard clays, some are plain, while others are decorated with transfer printing, gilding, or embossed designs.

Soup and Salad Bowls
In the late 18th and early 19th centuries, potters throughout the country produced small redware bowls. Most had a clear glaze, although some were decorated with splotches of manganese black. Records indicate that these wheel-thrown bowls were once produced in quantity, yet today they are rare, no doubt because redware is so fragile. After 1860, small bowls for individual helpings of salad or soup were often part of a matching dinnerware set. The finest of these pieces are elaborately hand-painted porcelain.

Miscellaneous Bowls
Miscellaneous bowls are also featured in this section. They range from batter bowls, which resemble mixing bowls but have a large pouring spout, to milk pans, into which milk was poured to separate the cream.

Ironstone vegetable bowl

Description
Shallow, oval vessel with sides that rise at angle to shaped rim. Plain base. On bottom, impressed in oval "GLASGOW CHINA/ VITRIFIED/TRENTON, N.J." *Variations:* May have transfer decoration or embossed decoration. Base may be plain.

Materials and Dimensions
Ironstone with clear alkaline glaze. Molded. Length: 5½–6½". Width: 4–4¼". Height: 1¼–1½".

Locality and Period
Glasgow Pottery, Trenton, New Jersey. c. 1882–84. Similar pieces from New York west to Ohio, south to Maryland. c. 1870– 1910.

Comment
At the turn of the century, small bowls like this were commonly used to serve individual portions of vegetables and other side dishes. They were made by both British and American manufacturers. Although British ironstone was nearly always marked, American manufacturers frequently left their pieces unmarked in the hope that they would be mistaken for the more popular British ware. Other American manufacturers used marks designed to be confused with those of English potteries.

Hints for Collectors
Although British and American ironstone is almost identical, American collectors tend to prefer the imported pottery. Consequently a variety of interesting American pieces are available at quite reasonable prices. Look for hard-to-find forms such as sugar bowls, covered tureens, and coffeepots.

Modern serving bowl

Description
Large oval serving vessel with heavy, flaring rim that has handlelike protrusion at each end. Protrusions decorated with embossed floral garland. Plain base. Bottom stamped with ink "Lu-Ray Pastels/U.S.A." *Variations:* May lack embossed decoration. Rim may be plain rather than flaring, without handlelike extensions.

Materials and Dimensions
White earthenware with pale blue glaze; similar pieces with other pastel glazes. Molded. Length: 10–10½". Width: 7¼–7¾". Height: 2–2½".

Locality and Period
The Midwest. c. 1950–60.

Comment
Almost all table services include serving bowls and platters in various sizes. The example shown here has an appealing combination of a pastel glaze, popular in the mid-20th century, and a more traditional form than that of most modern ceramics. Its shape and embossed decoration are quite Victorian in feeling.

Hints for Collectors
Many 20th-century manufacturers published descriptive catalogues that are invaluable to the collector who wishes to assemble a complete set of matching tableware. Even a costly catalogue will usually be well worth purchasing. Specialized book stores carry these catalogues as well as price lists, and antiques dealers can often help you find these shops.

Description
Shallow, oval serving bowl with scalloped, gilded rim. Interior of rim embossed with simple, triangular motifs. Plain base. Stamped on bottom "K.T.&K./S--V/CHINA." *Variations:* Rim may be plain. Some bowls have undecorated rim, others have hand-painted or transfer-printed motifs on rim.

Materials and Dimensions
Ironstone with clear alkaline glaze. Gilded details. Molded. Length: 7–9″. Width: 6–7″. Height: 1¾–2½″.

Locality and Period
Knowles, Taylor & Knowles, East Liverpool, Ohio. c. 1872–90. Similar examples from New Jersey and New York west to Ohio and south to Maryland. c. 1870–1920.

Comment
Knowles, Taylor & Knowles was one of the largest producers of American ironstone during the late 19th and early 20th centuries. The firm produced dozens of patterns and used many different marks, one of which appears on the piece illustrated.

Hints for Collectors
The gilding about the rim of this serving bowl is worn, a common problem with often-used pieces that still have their original gilding. Although regilding is possible, such restored pieces are generally worth less than unrestored originals. Pieces made by Knowles, Taylor & Knowles and other major manufacturers are relatively easy to find and inexpensive, so buy pieces that have the gilding intact. With persistence a collector can assemble complete table settings.

Hand-painted porcelain salad bowl

Description
Deep, circular serving dish with plain, slightly flaring rim.
Interior of rim decorated with repeating floral pattern and 3
larger floral motifs set in ovals. Large cabbage painted on base of
interior. Narrow, rimmed base. Bottom transfer printed "U.P.W."
above eagle's head clutching letter "S." *Variations:* Decoration
varies.

Materials and Dimensions
Hand-painted porcelain with clear alkaline glaze. Molded.
Height: 3½–4″. Diameter: 9½–10½″.

Locality and Period
Union Porcelain Works, Greenpoint, New York. c. 1880–85.
Similar pieces from New York west to Ohio and south to
Maryland. c. 1870–1940.

Comment
The bowl illustrated was made by a company well known for its
hand-decorated wares. The firm continued to make them even
when many manufacturers had turned to transfer printing to cut
costs. Choosing the relatively mundane cabbage for decoration is
unusual, perhaps inspired by the same motive that led majolica
makers to cast their wares in the form of vegetables.

Hints for Collectors
Since American porcelain often resembles porcelain made in
Europe, the 2 types are often mixed together at shows and in
shops. Check any piece bearing a mark that looks vaguely
English. In an attempt to have their products mistaken for the
more fashionable imported wares, many American
manufacturers designed marks based on British examples.

Ironstone soup bowl

Description
Shallow, circular bowl with central depression and wide, flaring rim. Plain base. On bottom, impressed "GREENWOOD CHINA/ TRENTON, N.J." *Variations:* May be slightly deeper.

Materials and Dimensions
Ironstone with clear alkaline glaze. Molded. Height: 1½–2″. Diameter: 7–10″.

Locality and Period
Greenwood Pottery Company, Trenton, New Jersey. c. 1886–1910. Similar pieces from New York west to Ohio and south to Maryland. c. 1860–1920.

Comment
The Greenwood Pottery Company was established by Stephens, Tams & Co. in 1861 and was in operation until after 1900. It was one of the major producers of household wares and, like many other companies, made porcelain as well as ironstone. Since soup bowls like the one illustrated were made in large numbers by many companies, unless they are marked it is usually impossible to determine where they were made. There are many similar English ironstone bowls, but these usually bear recognizable English marks.

Hints for Collectors
Pottery companies often changed their marks over the years. If you know when a particular mark was in use, you can tell approximately when a piece with that mark was made. For example, Greenwood Pottery first used the mark "GREENWOOD CHINA" in 1886; the bowl illustrated was obviously made in 1886 or after that year.

Fiesta deep plate and cream soup cup

Description
Deep plate has wide, flaring rim. Rim and center decorated with concentric rings. Narrow, rimmed base. Cream soup cup has plain rim and 2 flat, U-shaped handles that are ridged near ends. Narrow, rimmed base decorated with concentric rings.

Materials and Dimensions
White earthenware with opaque green glaze. Made in all Fiesta colors. Molded; handles separately shaped and applied. Deep plate diameter: 8–8¼". Cream soup cup height: 2¼–2½"; diameter: 4¾–5¼".

Locality and Period
Homer Laughlin Company, Newell, West Virginia. Deep plate c. 1936–69. Cream soup cup c. 1936–59.

Comment
Deep plates and cream soup cups were both used as soup bowls, although the deep plate could easily double as a salad or dessert bowl. They were made in all the standard Fiesta colors, originally red, ivory, dark blue, light green, yellow, and turquoise. Rose, gray, chartreuse, dark green, and medium green were added later as the line became more popular.

Hints for Collectors
Fiesta deep plates and cream soup cups are easy to find, so buy only those in good condition. Check the fragile handles and base of the soup cup. Cups glazed with medium green are rare, since that color was introduced in 1954, the year the cups were discontinued. Despite their rarity, medium green examples usually cost less than those with the extremely popular dark blue and deep red glazes.

Harlequin oval baking dish

Description
Oval vessel with sides that angle up and out to plain rim. 2 triangular handles with shaped bases set horizontally beneath rim. Just above handles, concentric rings encircle body. Rimmed base. Matching stepped lid (not illustrated) decorated with concentric circles and with a central, upright, triangular handle.

Materials and Dimensions
White earthenware with opaque yellow glaze. Similar pieces in all Harlequin colors. Molded. Height: 3–3¼″. Diameter: 8½–9″.

Locality and Period
Homer Laughlin Company, Newell, West Virginia. c. 1938–64.

Comment
Harlequin pottery was Laughlin's inexpensive alternative to its Fiesta line. Thinner-bodied and more fragile than Fiestaware, it sold for 20 to 30 percent less and was marketed by the F. W. Woolworth Co. stores. The piece illustrated is one of the 2 baking dishes produced in this line. Light-bodied earthenware like this was not especially popular for baking.

Hints for Collectors
Oval baking dishes are among the most attractive of Harlequin pieces and not easy to find. Search for them at house and yard sales, church bazaars, even in secondhand stores. Placing ads in rural and small-town newspapers may produce results. Although these baking dishes are less common than other Harlequin pieces, they remain reasonably priced. Especially desirable are examples that have their matching lids.

Yellowware batter bowl

Description
Large bowl that curves gradually from base to thick, shaped rim with large spout. Broad, rimmed base. Slightly recessed bottom. Heavily embossed floral decoration. *Variations:* May be embossed with geometric panels or may lack embossing.

Materials and Dimensions
Yellow earthenware with clear alkaline glaze. Similar pieces stoneware with salt glaze. Molded. Height: 4–6″. Diameter: 9–12″.

Locality and Period
New York west to Ohio, south to Maryland. c. 1870–1910.

Comment
Bowls without spouts are often found with embossed patterns identical to those on spouted examples. The embossed surface decoration was produced by pouring liquid clay into a mold, the interior of which had been carved in an elaborate floral or geometric pattern. Embossing is relatively uncommon in yellowware; even less common are marked bowls with such decoration.

Hints for Collectors
Batter bowls were produced in 3 to 4 different sizes, making it possible to assemble a small nest of matching pieces. Examples with embossed panels are especially appealing. These pieces are not particularly popular with collectors, perhaps because they come only in solid colors. Nevertheless, they can be attractive and inexpensive additions to any collection.

Ironstone compote

Description
Bowl-like compote with sides that rise at slight angle to rolled rim. Pedestal-like base has flaring foot. Slightly recessed bottom marked "STONE CHINA COXON & CO." *Variations:* Sides may be lower and more flared. Most pieces unmarked.

Materials and Dimensions
Ironstone with clear alkaline glaze. Molded. Height: 5–7″. Diameter: 8–11″.

Locality and Period
Coxon and Company, Trenton, New Jersey. c. 1863–84. Similar pieces from New York, New Jersey, Maryland, and Ohio. c. 1860–1900.

Comment
The Coxon firm, founded in 1863, was a major producer of various types of ironstone, including transfer-decorated pieces. Most of the ware consisted of the usual table pieces such as plates, bowls, and platters, and compotes were made only in limited numbers. Compotes were decorative pieces, meant to be filled with fruit and placed in the center of a table or on a sideboard. Most compotes were not marked, so one with a manufacturer's name is a valuable find.

Hints for Collectors
This piece is heavily crazed, that is, covered with minute lines or "spidering" caused by the separation of the glaze as it ages. Although some collectors find crazing attractive, and potters have occasionally induced it as a decorative device, most collectors avoid pottery with this kind of damage, which usually reduces the value of a piece.

Redware pot

Description
Squat, round vessel with thick sides that taper slightly to thick, rolled rim. Below, sides curve in to plain base. Impressed on side "A. WILCOX/G. HULBERT/WEST BLOOMFIELD." *Variations:* Rim may be plain rather than rolled.

Materials and Dimensions
Red earthenware; exterior unglazed; interior with clear lead glaze. Wheel-thrown. Height: 5–7″. Diameter: 8–10″.

Locality and Period
Alvin Wilcox, West Bloomfield, New York. c. 1855–62. Similar pieces from New England west to Ohio, south to the Carolinas. c. 1790–1890.

Comment
Pots such as this one were made by many different shops and may have been used as baking dishes or mixing bowls. The thick, rolled rim seen here makes it likely that these pots were also used for food storage; a paper or cloth cover could be anchored beneath the rim.

Hints for Collectors
Never dismiss a piece just because it looks ordinary—always check for distinguishing marks. Hard to see but present on the piece shown is the stamp of an extremely rare upper New York State pottery, active from about 1855 to 1862. The presence of this pottery stamp increases the value of an otherwise plain piece considerably. Since some companies marked their wares with very light impressions that may have worn down with wear, it is sometimes helpful to examine pieces with a magnifying glass.

Stoneware batter bowl

Description
Large bowl with gently sloping sides and thick, shaped rim
drawn out slightly at front to form shallow spout. 2 lug handles
with tapering ends attached on sides. Plain base. Number "4"
impressed on front beneath spout. *Variations:* May be plainer.
May lack spout. May lack handles.

Materials and Dimensions
Stoneware glazed with brown Albany slip; rare examples salt
glazed. Wheel-thrown; handles separately shaped and applied.
Height: 5–7″. Diameter: 8–10″.

Locality and Period
New England west to Ohio and south to Virginia. c. 1850–90.

Comment
Most batter bowls glazed with salt or brown Albany slip were
made by eastern and midwestern potteries, but very few bear
makers' marks. These pieces are not common. The number "4"
impressed on this piece may represent an actual capacity, as it
often did in the West, or an arbitrary size designation, as it
occasionally did in the East.

Hints for Collectors
Uneven heat during firing caused the attractive variation in glaze
color on the piece shown. Higher temperature yielded the lighter
shade. These subtle gradations are often extremely attractive,
yet many collectors do not recognize or appreciate them, and
consequently pieces with this kind of irregularity can often be
purchased quite reasonably.

Art pottery bowl

Description
Circular vessel with sloping sides and lightly shaped rim. Plain base. Bottom impressed "FULPER." *Variations:* Art pottery bowls vary in shape and surface decoration.

Materials and Dimensions
Stoneware with pink glaze covered with thick, dark blue glaze. Wheel-thrown. Height: 7–9″. Diameter: 4–5″.

Locality and Period
Fulper Pottery Company, Flemington, New Jersey. c. 1910–29.

Comment
Originally established as a commercial tile and stoneware pottery factory in 1805, the Fulper company began to make a line of art pottery known as Vasekraft in 1910. The firm produced vases, lamps, bowls, and even cigarette boxes in a variety of matt and high-gloss glazes and a number of forms. Some forms were simple, but more often they were exaggerated versions of classical Greek or Roman styles. The company's numerous marks were impressed or stamped in ink or printed on paper labels, which were then applied. In 1916, in its February issue, *The American Magazine of Art* referred to Fulper products as "clay wrought into odd—sometimes too odd—forms."

Hints for Collectors
In the 1970s Fulper rose in popularity. Today the ware is in less demand, and prices have declined. On the other hand, high quality pieces made by Rookwood, Ohr, and Weller have continued to increase in value. Well-made wares by these recognized firms are usually a sounder investment than products that have suddenly become fashionable to collect.

Yellowware bowls

Description
Circular bowls with sloping sides and thick, shaped rim. Rimmed base. Trademark "PACIFIC" stamped in ink on bottom.

Materials and Dimensions
Yellow earthenware with reddish-brown, yellow, green, and black glazes. Molded. Height: 4–6″. Diameter: 7–10″.

Locality and Period
Pacific Clay Manufacturing Company, Riverside, California. c. 1890–1910.

Comment
The pottery that produced these bowls was founded at Elsinore, California, in 1884. The factory was later moved to south Riverside, where it remained in operation until well into this century. The multiglaze finish is different from anything on other American yellowware. Another major California manufacturer, J. A. Bauer & Company of Los Angeles, also produced marked yellowware in the early 20th century. Its pieces were quite similar to those produced in the East and Midwest.

Hints for Collectors
The worn and cracked glaze in the bottom of the bowl at the right is caused by age and use. This kind of wear helps reveal a vessel's age but does not significantly devalue a piece. While fairly common on the West Coast, California yellowware is not often seen in other areas and may not be recognized when it appears. It usually costs much less in the East and Midwest. Look for the "PACIFIC" trademark and the distinctive multicolored glaze.

Spongeware serving bowl

Description
Large, circular bowl with flat, slightly flaring rim. Lower body has slight ridge near plain base. *Variations:* May have fluted sides.

Materials and Dimensions
White earthenware; exterior sponged with tan and green slip over cream-colored slip and with tan band around rim; interior with cream-colored glaze. Height: 5–6″. Diameter: 10–11″.

Locality and Period
New Jersey, Ohio, and Maryland. c. 1890–1930.

Comment
Most spongeware serving bowls are circular, although there are occasional examples that are oval or rectangular. Forms closely resemble those of contemporary ironstone. Some bear the marks of Ohio and New Jersey potteries, but marked examples are uncommon. The combination of cream interior and sponged exterior on the bowl illustrated is somewhat unusual; spongeware bowls were usually sponged inside and outside.

Hints for Collectors
Bowls, mugs, platters, sugar bowls, creamers, pitchers, and even piggy banks are available with tan-and-green spongework on a cream-colored ground, making it a good choice for those who wish to assemble complete sets. And since most collectors prefer blue-and-white spongeware, pieces decorated with tan and green are relatively inexpensive. In addition, they are usually fairly easy to find.

Redware mixing bowl

Description
Round, thin-walled bowl with sides that curve gently up and out to rolled rim. Incised line encircles body at shoulder. Lower body curves in and then out slightly to shaped base. *Variations:* Sides may be lower, may flare more. Base may be plain.

Materials and Dimensions
Red earthenware with mottled green glaze. Wheel-thrown. Height: 4–6″. Diameter: 7–9″.

Locality and Period
New England west to Missouri and throughout the Southeast. c. 1780–1850. Examples with clear lead glaze from Utah. c. 1870–80.

Comment
Throughout the 18th century, redware bowls were in great demand, but they were replaced in the mid-19th century by factory-made white earthenware and yellowware bowls. William Jackson, a potter in the Lynn, Massachusetts, area, advertised pint and quart bowls in 1814, while other potters referred to "large and small" bowls. These vessels sold for just a few pennies each. Marked examples are rare, although there are a few pieces bearing the impressed mark of Samuel Bell & Sons, active in Strasburg, Virginia, in the late 19th century.

Hints for Collectors
Although once abundant, redware bowls in good condition are now real finds. Many are decorated with slip, which may cover the entire surface, making it hard to tell at first if a piece is redware. Since bottoms were rarely glazed, the red clay will usually be visible there. On the bowl illustrated, the green glaze mottled in firing, producing an unusual finish that resembles sponged decoration.

Rockingham mixing bowl

Description
Circular vessel with sides that curve up and out to heavy shaped rim. Lower body curves in to rimmed base. Embossed band in beaded pattern encircles body below rim and above base; sides decorated with overall pattern of embossed arcs. *Variations:* Embossed patterns may differ or be absent.

Materials and Dimensions
Yellow earthenware with Rockingham glaze. Molded. Height: 3–6″. Diameter: 4–12″.

Locality and Period
New England west to Ohio, south to Maryland. c. 1840–1910.

Comment
Rockingham mixing or kitchen bowls could serve a variety of purposes and were made by many different eastern and midwestern potteries. In the late 1890s one New York State factory offered them in 10 nesting sizes ranging from ¾-pint to 3-gallon capacity. Prices per dozen wholesale ranged from 50 cents to $4.50. While a few of these bowls bear the impressed mark of Ohio potteries or the famous United States Pottery Company at Bennington, Vermont, the great majority are unmarked and their origins cannot be traced.

Hints for Collectors
The ever popular Rockingham mixing bowls have many different embossed surface patterns, so it is possible to gather a nested set in any one of several designs. When buying make sure that the embossed pattern on the piece you are choosing exactly matches that of your group. Many seemingly identical bowls vary in such ways as the shape of the rim, placement of the decoration, or type of base.

Spongeware serving bowl

Description
Tall, circular bowl with shaped, collarlike rim and rimmed base. Bottom of interior stenciled "RASMUSSEN GROCERY/GOOD THINGS TO EAT/ RAVENNA, NEB." *Variations:* May be shorter and wider.

Materials and Dimensions
Stoneware with white glaze. Exterior decorated with reddish-brown and blue spongework. Molded. Height: 6–8″. Diameter: 3½–5″.

Locality and Period
New Jersey, Ohio, and California. c. 1890–1930.

Comment
Tall bowls like this would have been impractical for mixing and catalogues indicate they were designed primarily as serving pieces. The majority were made in large potteries in New Jersey and Ohio. Around 1900, the Elsinore Pottery Company in Elsinore, California, was producing spongeware bowls remarkably like this one. The same form was made in several glaze combinations and with a plain white glaze.

Hints for Collectors
Messages like that from the Nebraska grocer at the bottom of this bowl are uncommon and therefore enhance the value of a piece. It is unlikely that such bowls were retailed; they were probably given away as advertisements. Some may have held products such as butter and cheese, since similar containers were used for that purpose. They were covered with waxed cardboard or paper. Combinations of colors like the reddish-brown, white, and blue of this piece make for prize spongeware.

Spongeware mixing bowl

Description
Circular container with sides that slope gently from rolled rim to rimmed base. Recessed bottom. *Variations:* Some pieces lack recessed bottom or rolled rim.

Materials and Dimensions
Stoneware with white alkaline glaze; exterior decorated with blue sponging. Similar pieces ironstone. Color combinations vary. Molded. Height: 2–6″. Diameter: 4–12″.

Locality and Period
The Midwest, chiefly Ohio; also England. c. 1900–35.

Comment
A large quantity of spongeware was produced in the early 20th century in both the United States and England, but few such pieces were marked, and it is virtually impossible to ascertain their origin. Unlike yellowware mixing bowls, spongeware examples do not appear to have been made in nesting sets, although several sizes can be found in any given color combination. Other common spongeware forms include pitchers and spittoons.

Hints for Collectors
Collectors find it difficult to distinguish between unmarked American and English examples, but American spongeware is generally more valuable. Although the many differences in glaze combinations (some pieces have 4 colors) are appealing, most collectors favor sponged blue on white. Consequently, pieces with this decoration are at a premium, while other colors can often be picked up at bargain prices. Green and yellow or brown and yellow examples are often quite reasonably priced. Pieces having 3 or more colors (such as red, brown, and green) will almost always be more expensive.

Stoneware serving bowl

Description
Circular bowl with heavy, shaped rim. Lower body slopes in sharply to rimmed base. Exterior has floral transfer decoration between 2 thin bands of blue. *Variations:* Decoration varies or may be absent.

Materials and Dimensions
Stoneware with white Bristol glaze. Decorated with cobalt blue. Molded. Height: 6–8″. Diameter: 3½–4½″.

Locality and Period
New York to Ohio. c. 1890–1930.

Comment
The decoration on this serving bowl resembles that found on other stoneware kitchenware, such as rolling pins, spice jars, salt and pepper shakers, and other bowls. Matching sets of kitchen utensils were very popular around the turn of the century and continue to be so today. The simple form of the bowl illustrated and its inexpensive transfer decoration indicate that it was probably mass produced.

Hints for Collectors
Although these Bristol-glazed bowls are not too popular, the combination of blue and white is in demand in every collecting field. If, as seems likely, such bowls begin to get the attention they deserve, a collector who has stocked up on them will be ahead of the game. Since the bowls were made in several sizes, stackable matching sets can be assembled. A matching set is always more valuable than a group of dissimilar pieces.

Yellowware bowl

Description
Circular mixing bowl with thick, shaped rim. Lower body curves sharply in to heavy, shaped base. Decorated with wide white band, thinner blue band, and sponged seaweed decoration. *Variations:* Base may be plain.

Materials and Dimensions
Yellow earthenware with clear alkaline glaze. Decorated with white Bristol slip and cobalt blue. Similar pieces decorated with white and green. Molded; earlier examples wheel-thrown. Height: 5–7″. Diameter: 6–10″.

Locality and Period
New Jersey, Ohio, and Maryland. c. 1870–1910.

Comment
Sponged seaweed decoration on American yellowware bowls is similar to the delicate tracery on English mochaware, but American examples are cruder; designs are often blurred. Such bowls are seldom, if ever, marked.

Hints for Collectors
Seaweed-decorated yellowware is in great demand among collectors, especially the rare covered crocks. Damage, like the long hairline crack on the piece shown, may reduce the value by as much as 50 percent. Because of their popularity, even damaged pieces are worth purchasing if they are reasonably priced. These bowls are found in several sizes and with either blue or green decoration, so it is possible to form a nest of 3 or 4 matching pieces.

Description
Circular bowls with rolled rim and sides that slope in to rimmed base. Decorated with 3 concentric white bands. *Variations:* Placement and thickness of white bands vary. Rim may be thicker or more collarlike. Base may be plain.

Materials and Dimensions
Yellow earthenware with clear alkaline glaze; decorated with white slip. Molded; earliest examples wheel-thrown. Height: 3½–7″. Diameter: 4½–13″.

Locality and Period
New England west to Ohio, south to Maryland. c. 1840–1940.

Comment
Although yellowware mixing bowls come in various sizes and with several kinds of decoration, bowls like the ones illustrated with 3 narrow white bands are the most common and most popular. The Syracuse Stoneware Company in Syracuse, New York, advertised these bowls in 1896. They came in 10 sizes from ½ pint to 3 gallons and sold at prices ranging from 40 cents to $3.00 per dozen. Bowls decorated with 2 wide white bands are also common, as are those with a single white band between 2 brown bands. All types continued to be made into the 1930s.

Advertisements in women's magazines such as *Ladies' Home Journal* frequently picture a smiling housewife using the bowls to prepare cakes and other baked goods. During the 1930s similar bowls appeared in pastel shades, but these are of little interest to collectors at present. Except for a few pieces impressed "U.S.A." on the bottom, yellowware bowls are seldom marked, and it is usually impossible to determine the maker of an individual piece.

Hints for Collectors
Bowls like those shown here are relatively easy to find. Keep an eye out for examples over 10″ in diameter. Although manufacturers advertised them, they are extremely hard to find today. Don't be concerned if the placement and width of the white bands vary from bowl to bowl. Since they were made in many different potteries, it is almost impossible to find a nest with decoration that matches perfectly. These bowls are fairly plentiful, so don't buy examples that are cracked or have chipped glaze.

Redware mixing bowls

Description
Circular vessels with thick, shaped, collarlike rim. Lower body curves in sharply to rimmed base. Larger bowl has "WELLER" impressed on base. Decorated with white bands. *Variations:* May be undecorated. Height of rimmed base varies. Size and number of white bands varies.

Materials and Dimensions
Red earthenware with clear alkaline glaze; decorated with white slip. Molded. Height: 2½–7″. Diameter: 5–13″.

Locality and Period
Left: Weller Pottery, Zanesville, Ohio. Right: Probably Ohio. c. 1890–1930.

Comment
The Weller Pottery, which produced the bowl on the left, was established in 1872 at Fultonham, Ohio. In 1888 it moved to nearby Putnam, which is today Zanesville, where it remained active until 1948, becoming well known for its art pottery. Around the turn of the century many bowls were cast in the shapes seen here, but few were made of redware, which was relatively fragile.

Hints for Collectors
Since redware breaks easily, bowls in good condition are fairly hard to find. Undamaged examples—especially those bearing the mark of the Weller Pottery—should be reserved for display. Unmarked pieces with minor damage can be used for everyday service. Although they are likely to break with constant use, they are common and can be replaced without much difficulty.

Stoneware mixing bowls

Description
Squat, heavy, circular vessels with thick collar and plain rim.
Lower body tapers sharply to rimmed base. *Variations:* Sides
may be fluted. Collar may be thinner.

Materials and Dimensions
Stoneware with brown Albany glaze; rim and narrow band under
collar unglazed. Identical pieces with white Bristol glaze.
Molded. Height: 3–5″. Diameter: 7–11″.

Locality and Period
New York to Ohio. c. 1900–40.

Comment
Heavy stoneware mixing bowls like those illustrated were also
used as baking dishes. Stoneware was well suited for both
purposes since it was sturdy and could withstand high
temperatures. Its weight, however, was a disadvantage; once it
was filled, a bowl might weigh several pounds. The bowls came
in several nesting sizes. The Syracuse Stoneware Company of
Syracuse, New York, listed 5 sizes in its 1899 price list. They
ranged from ¼ to 1½ gallons at prices from 42 cents to $1.26 per
dozen wholesale. They were referred to as round-bottom pans,
and their glaze was described as Rockingham, although it
technically is not.

Hints for Collectors
Still largely neglected by collectors, these brown-glazed bowls
are both readily obtainable and inexpensive. Some have "U.S.A."
impressed on the bottom, and most have various numbers
impressed or incised there as well. These numbers refer to the
molds in which the pieces were cast and neither help to identify
examples nor enhance their value.

Yellowware mixing bowl

Description
Heavy vessel with sides that angle outward to heavy collar.
Broad base. 3 cobalt-blue bands encircle collar; 3 slightly
narrower bands on lower body. Body also decorated with rows of
embossed motifs. *Variations:* Embossed design may vary or may
be absent. Banding may differ or be absent.

Materials and Dimensions
Yellow earthenware with clear alkaline glaze. Bands of cobalt-
blue slip. Molded. Height: 3–6″. Diameter: 4–10″.

Locality and Period
Throughout the Northeast and Midwest, particularly New
Jersey and Ohio. c. 1880–1930.

Comment
Molded yellowware mixing bowls with embossed surface
decoration and banding, usually in cobalt-blue slip, were
produced by many potteries from the turn of the century well
into the 1900s. Like the earlier, hand-thrown bowls of the same
material, they can be found in nesting sets of graduated sizes.
However, most molded sets consist of 4 or 5 bowls, rather than
the 7 to 10 typical of thrown sets. Molded bowls usually have
some sort of floral or geometric design embossed on the surface.

Hints for Collectors
Embossed yellowware mixing bowls are inexpensive, and most
sizes are rather easy to find. A complete set, or nest, is
especially desirable. Be sure to seek out the smallest bowl made
for a set; it may be no more than 3″ tall. Since these diminutive
pieces are fairly scarce, even an example with a chip or small
crack is worth buying.

Spongeware covered bowl

Description
Circular vessel with matching lid. Sides of bowl rise at slight angle to thick collar with plain rim. Lower body curves in sharply to plain base. Exterior decorated with blue spongework. Dome-shaped lid rises gradually to flattened, mushroom-shaped handle. Blue band and spongework on lid. *Variations:* Sides may be fluted or have other embossed decoration.

Materials and Dimensions
Stoneware with white glaze; rim and area under collar unglazed. Exterior and lid decorated with cobalt blue. Similar examples with white glaze only. Molded. Height: 8–9″. Diameter: 10–12″.

Locality and Period
New Jersey and Ohio. c. 1890–1930.

Comment
Contemporary advertisements indicate that covered bowls like this were used primarily for baking. They could be used as serving dishes as well, especially for foods that were taken directly from the stove to the table. They were made in several Ohio potteries and came not only with spongework, but also with a plain white glaze.

Hints for Collectors
These bowls were often stacked rim to rim in the kiln, and consequently the rim and the bottom were not glazed. If the parts that touched had been glazed, the glaze would have "glued" the pieces together. Even though they were originally meant to be used in ovens, these pieces are now likely to break if exposed to high temperatures, especially if they are already cracked.

Spongeware baking dish

Description
Heavy, circular baking dish with fluted sides angling outward to high collar. Iron-wire bail handle with turned wooden grip set into 2 holes, one at each side of rim. Lower body tapers to rimmed base. Exterior decorated with sponging; single band of sponging encircles interior below rim. *Variations:* May have matching, dome-shaped lid with circular knob. Sides may be plain rather than fluted.

Materials and Dimensions
Stoneware; heavy ironstone more common. Decorated with blue sponging; other examples with green or brown sponging. Molded. Height: 6–7″. Diameter: 11–12″.

Locality and Period
The East and Midwest, particularly New Jersey and Ohio. c. 1880–1930.

Comment
Heavy spongeware pots for baking or stewing were made in substantial numbers at the turn of the century. Most had matching pottery lids, although glass lids were also occasionally used. Such vessels are generally unmarked, although a few bear the impressed names of midwestern potteries.

Hints for Collectors
After these pieces have lost their handles, they can usually be bought at a substantial discount; since it is not difficult to have a replacement handle made, these discounted dishes are well worth buying. Lids, too, can usually be found; collectors often purchase them and then search for dishes that match. It's a good idea to note down the dimensions of lids or baking dishes you need and to carry a measuring tape to size prospective purchases.

Stoneware baking dish

Description
Deep, circular baking dish with thick collar. 2 semicircular
projections on collar hold heavy, semicircular wire handle. Below
collar, sides curve gently to rounded base. Bottom has 8 knobs
protruding ⅛" from surface; "STAR FIRE CLAY ACID PROOF"
embossed on bottom. *Variations:* Some examples lack bottom
knobs or have 6 or 7 knobs. May have matching lid.

Materials and Dimensions
Stoneware with clear alkaline glaze; some examples with salt
glaze or brown Albany slip. Molded. Height: 4–6". Diameter:
8–12".

Locality and Period
The East and Midwest. c. 1910–50.

Comment
These baking dishes were made by various large potteries,
primarily in New Jersey and Ohio, and many pieces are marked.
Intended for use in the oven, casseroles were designed to
withstand high temperatures and are extremely durable. Some
were made with lids; even if the lid is missing, these can be
distinguished by a shallow ridge just inside the rim where the lid
rested.

Hints for Collectors
These pieces represent a type of factory-made stoneware that
has been largely ignored by collectors; consequently it is both
inexpensive and plentiful. Look for examples with complete
handles, matching lids, and potters' marks. These pieces are
common enough for the collector to be selective.

Stoneware deep dish

Description
Heavy circular vessel with sides rising at angle to heavy collar.
Plain base. *Variations:* Collar may be thinner. Bottom may be
slightly recessed.

Materials and Dimensions
Stoneware; exterior with salt glaze; interior glazed with brown
Albany slip. Molded; earlier examples wheel-thrown. Height:
3–5″. Diameter: 9–12″.

Locality and Period
New York west to Indiana, south to Arkansas. c. 1870–1910.

Comment
Like their counterparts in yellowware and white earthenware,
stoneware deep dishes were used for baking. Although much
stronger than the other clays, stoneware is also much heavier,
and consequently only a limited number of deep dishes in this
material were made. Molded examples like the one shown here
were produced by machine at large factories, primarily in New
Jersey and Ohio. They are seldom marked, and it is usually
impossible to determine their exact place of origin.

Hints for Collectors
You can often distinguish wheel-thrown stoneware pieces from
those that are molded by running your fingers along the inside of
the vessel. If you feel ridges on the inside of the wall, the piece
has been wheel-thrown—the ridges were left by the potter's
fingers as he shaped the piece. In most cases wheel-thrown
pottery is more desirable than that which is molded, as hand-
formed objects have always had greater appeal to the collector.
Not only do they have the personal and sometimes primitive
touch of the potter, but they are also usually older than their
molded counterparts.

Yellowware covered bowl

Description
Low, rounded sugar or serving bowl with thick collar. Below collar, sides slope inward to recessed base. Matching lid is sunken around buttonlike knob. Bowl and lid decorated with thin bands of light brown separated by thicker white band.

Materials and Dimensions
Yellow earthenware with clear alkaline glaze. Decorated with light brown and white slip. Molded. Height: 3½"–4½". Diameter: 6–7".

Locality and Period
New Jersey west to Ohio, south to Maryland. c. 1870–1920.

Comment
Although it is large enough to function as a serving piece, this covered bowl bears the same decoration as some small pitchers, or creamers, and may have been intended as a sugar bowl. Brown and white bands may decorate yellowware pitchers, mugs, and small covered crocks, but they are most often seen on bowls.

Hints for Collectors
Yellowware enthusiasts often collect pieces that are similarly decorated, and those with brown and white bands are one of the most popular types. Pieces with 3 thin white bands or 2 thick white bands are also available, but usually only in a limited number of forms. Bowls are, of course, easy to find, but covered pieces are more difficult. If you find either a lid or a bottom, you should eventually be able to purchase the missing part. It's a good idea to carry a tape measure with you to size potential matches.

Stoneware mixing bowl

Description
Circular bowl with straight sides and flaring rim. Base of rim encircled by ridge. Plain base. "L. Jenison" painted in blue across exterior. *Variations:* Some examples have curving sides or sides set at more of an angle.

Materials and Dimensions
Stoneware; exterior with salt glaze; interior glazed with brown Albany slip. Decorated with cobalt blue. Similar pieces without decoration. Wheel-thrown. Height: 5–6″. Diameter: 10–12″.

Locality and Period
New England to Ohio, south to Virginia. c. 1840–80.

Comment
Salt-glazed stoneware mixing bowls were not made by many potteries, and today they are uncommon. Although early pottery price lists rarely mention them, the 1875 list of the A.J. & J.L. Russell kiln of West Troy (Watervliet), New York, has them in ½- and 1-gallon sizes at 40 and 50 cents. Most examples are neither decorated nor marked. The name on the piece illustrated is that of the owner, not the potter, and indicates that the bowl was specially made, probably as a gift.

Hints for Collectors
Don't confuse this type of mixing bowl with a cake pot. The sides of a cake pot do not flare out at the rim. Although these bowls are unusual, they don't interest most collectors, and consequently are reasonably priced. The name on the bowl illustrated makes it an unusual and valuable example; additional cobalt-blue decoration would increase its value further.

Description
Low, circular vessel with slightly concave sides and shaped rim.
2 semicircular handles attached about midway down sides.
Shaped base. Floral decoration encircles body. Matching lid (not
illustrated) flat, with button-shaped handle. *Variations:* May be
undecorated. Sides often straight, not concave. May have brown-
and-white lid. Base may be plain or chamfered.

Materials and Dimensions
Stoneware; exterior with salt glaze; interior glazed with brown
Albany slip. Decorated with cobalt blue; similar examples with
white glaze. Wheel-thrown; handles separately shaped and
applied. Height: 4–6". Diameter: 7–10".

Locality and Period
New England west to Ohio, south to Virginia. c. 1850–1900.

Comment
Used for the storage of cakes and other perishable foods, cake
pots were always sold with a matching lid. Although they
strongly resemble larger crocks such as butter pots, cake pots
are always squatter. In 1875 the West Troy (Watervliet), New
York, pottery offered them in 1- to 5-gallon sizes, retailing for 50
cents to $1.50. Because they were so low, few have elaborate
decoration. Typically they are embellished with floral sprays or
leaflike decoration, although some have bands of cobalt blue.

Hints for Collectors
Very few cake pots still have their matching lids. Those that do
are valuable, especially if they have blue decoration. Most of the
marked examples found today were made in Pennsylvania.

Spongeware covered serving dish

Description
Oval container with matching lid. Dish has slightly sloping sides
and flaring rim. Interior of mouth has small ridge. Plain base.
Dome-shaped lid has oval handle. *Variations:* May have
embossed decoration. May have gilding around rim and on
handle.

Materials and Dimensions
Heavy white earthenware with yellow glaze; similar pieces in
stoneware. Decorated with green spongework; similar pieces
with blue or brown spongework. Molded. Length: 9–11″. Width:
7–8″. Height: 3–4″.

Locality and Period
New Jersey or Ohio. c. 1880–1920.

Comment
Covered dishes of this sort were primarily used for serving foods
and sometimes for baking. The type illustrated was part of a set
that included a butter dish, sugar bowl, creamer, and other
related items. Like much spongeware, this piece loosely
resembles the porcelain and plain white earthenware dishes
popular around the turn of the century.

Hints for Collectors
Serving dishes decorated with spongework lack the sturdy
country feel of similarly decorated mixing and baking bowls, and
consequently are not particularly popular with collectors. This is
especially true of pieces that are gilded or that don't have the
favored blue-and-white combination. Such dishes often go for
bargain prices.

Spatterware deep dish

Description
Circular dish with tall sides angling out to plain rim. Plain base.
Decorated on exterior and interior with band of circular motifs.
Larger band of similar motifs encircles bottom of interior.
Variations: Circular motifs not always present.

Materials and Dimensions
White earthenware; exterior spattered with blue glaze; interior
spattered with blue and tan glaze. May also be spattered in red,
green, black, or combinations; usually found in only 2 colors.
Molded. Height: 2–3″. Diameter: 8–10″.

Locality and Period
Probably England. c. 1840–70.

Comment
While pieces of spatterware bearing English pottery marks are
fairly common, few marked American examples have come to
light—the type may seldom have been made in this country.
Nevertheless, it was imported in large quantities during the mid-
19th century, and today is widely collected here. Plates and
platters are the most common forms, but other types such as
serving dishes, cups and saucers, and even coffeepots are found.

Hints for Collectors
Spatterware is often difficult to distinguish from common
spongeware, to which it is closely related. Spatterware tends to
have a more distinct pattern, while sponging creates a more
smudged effect in a design. The more elaborate the design, the
more desirable a piece of spatterware is. The presence of 2-tone
spattering makes this a particularly choice example.

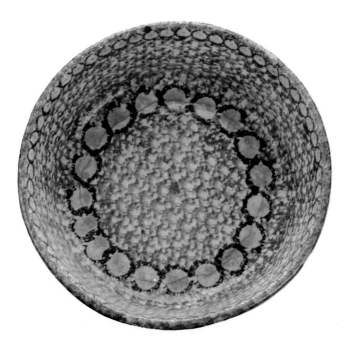

Redware deep dish

Description
Heavy dish with sides that slope slightly out to rolled rim.
Encircled by an incised line just above plain base. *Variations:*
Sides may be straight rather than slightly sloping. Most
examples lack incised line.

Materials and Dimensions
Red earthenware with clear lead glaze. Decorated with splashes
of black manganese. Similar pieces with clear lead glaze on
interior and unglazed exterior. Wheel-thrown. Height: 4–5″.
Diameter: 8–11″.

Locality and Period
New England west to Pennsylvania, south to the Carolinas.
c. 1750–1880.

Comment
Deep dishes like this were often used to make pudding. The
account book of John Parker, a Charlestown, Massachusetts,
potter, indicates that he made "pudn pans" as early as 1753. In
1864, the A. E. Smith pottery of Norwalk, Connecticut,
produced them in 4 sizes. Prices ranged from 90 cents to $2.00
per dozen, depending on size. The mottled decoration of the piece
illustrated is characteristic of Norwalk and other western
Connecticut potteries.

Hints for Collectors
Although not a particularly interesting form to look at, the deep
dish, or pudding pan, is important for its long history. They have
been used for cooking since the 18th century, and appear in early
illustrations of American home life. Multiglazed examples like
this one are less common and especially desirable. Like most
redware, such pieces were seldom marked.

Redware milk pan

Description
Large, bowl-like vessel with sloping sides and heavy, rolled rim. Rim and upper body marked by several incised lines. Lower body tapers to plain base. Impressed on bottom "HOW & CO." *Variations:* Sides may be lower and may angle more sharply. Base may be chamfered. Examples from the South may have small lug handles.

Materials and Dimensions
Red earthenware; exterior unglazed; interior with clear lead glaze. Similar pieces may have clear lead glaze on exterior; rarely, interior decorated with trailing lines in white slip. Wheel-thrown. Height: 3–5″. Diameter: 11–15″.

Locality and Period
Probably New York. c. 1830–40. Similar pieces from Maine west to Missouri, south to the Carolinas. c. 1790–1870.

Comment
Milk pans were made in large quantities throughout much of the United States. Milk was placed in them so that the cream could separate and rise. As early as 1789 the pottery at a Moravian settlement in Wachovia, North Carolina, carried in its inventory milk pans in 6 sizes priced from 4 pence to a shilling. The majority of these pieces were plain and unadorned.

Hints for Collectors
Like many early pans, this one no doubt served several purposes. The flaking on its interior was probably caused by a spoon or chopper, indicating that it was used both as a milk pan and as a mixing and chopping bowl. The mark on the bottom is probably that of an unidentified pottery; if the location of the pottery and the period it was in operation could be determined, the value of the piece would increase substantially.

Ironstone deep dish

Description
Circular baking or serving dish with sides that angle out to plain rim. Plain base. Bottom slightly recessed. *Variations:* Angle of sides may vary.

Materials and Dimensions
Ironstone with clear alkaline glaze. Molded. Height: 2–4″. Diameter: 6–12″.

Locality and Period
New York west to Ohio, south to Maryland. c. 1870–1920.

Comment
Deep dishes made of ironstone and white earthenware were manufactured by large potteries in several areas of the East and Midwest. Most were produced in New Jersey and Ohio. Unlike their yellowware cousins, they were often marked with the name of the pottery at which they were produced. Most examples are around 9″ to 10″ in diameter. They were used both for baking and as mixing bowls, and although in a pinch they might have been used for serving food, contemporary records make it clear that they were not intended for that purpose.

Hints for Collectors
Like yellowware deep dishes, ironstone examples can be collected in different sizes to complete a matching stack. Avoid pieces that have brown or yellow stains beneath the glaze. Occasionally these stains can be removed if the dishes are soaked in bleach or ammonia, but this is not always effective; consequently, discolored ironstone is a bad investment.

Yellowware deep dish

Description
Circular dish with sides sloping gently to plain rim. Plain base.
Bottom slightly recessed. *Variations:* May have 3 knoblike
projections on bottom.

Materials and Dimensions
Yellow earthenware with clear alkaline glaze; rare pieces with
white glaze on interior. Molded; some early examples wheel-
thrown. Height: 2–4″. Diameter: 6–12″.

Locality and Period
New England west to Indiana, south to Maryland. c. 1870–1920.

Comment
Period advertisements indicate that yellowware deep dishes
were often referred to as nappies. In the late 19th century these
dishes were sold wholesale at 80 cents to $3.00 per dozen, and
most companies sold 7 sizes. Similarly shaped deep dishes have a
Rockingham glaze. Examples with white glaze on the interior
may be Canadian, since such pieces were also produced there.
Unlike yellowware bowls, these deep dishes were never
decorated with bands of slip.

Hints for Collectors
Next to mixing bowls, deep dishes are the most plentiful and
popular of yellowware forms. Like bowls, they come in a range of
sizes, so matching pieces can be stacked in a nest. A complete set
of matching dishes is always more valuable than the same
number of unmatched pieces. The hardest to find are the largest
and the smallest dishes in the set, but even these are relatively
common. Don't buy chipped or cracked examples.

Yellowware serving bowl

Description
Heavy, oval serving dish with sloping sides and flaring, shaped rim. Plain base. *Variations:* Sides may be gently rounded. Rim may be plain.

Materials and Dimensions
Yellow earthenware with clear alkaline glaze. Molded. Length: 8–10″. Width: 6–8″. Height: 2–3″.

Locality and Period
Massachusetts west to Ohio, south to Maryland. c. 1870–1900.

Comment
Simple yellowware serving bowls were patterned on the more popular examples in white earthenware and ironstone. The bowl illustrated is almost identical to ironstone examples made in both this country and England. It is, indeed, possible that the yellowware pieces were shaped in molds intended for white earthenware and ironstone. Very similar Rockingham serving pieces were also made, although these are far less common than those made from white earthenware and ironstone. A few yellowware pieces bear the mark of an Ohio pottery.

Hints for Collectors
Marked yellowware is uncommon and valuable, so always check the base for the mark of a potter. In most cases, marks were impressed with a stamp while the clay was still soft. In some cases, however, the mark was transfer-printed. Since transfer-printed marks have often worn away in part, they can be especially difficult to trace.

35 Decorated white earthenware serving dish

Description
Shallow, oval vessel with sloping sides and flaring, shaped rim. Plain base. Interior and exterior transfer-decorated; exterior with band of brown florets, interior with similar band along inner rim above a band of blue flowers alternating with brown leaves. Bottom has transfer-printed mark "Mayer Pottery/Beaver Falls, Pa." *Variations:* Some dishes are wider. Some have higher sides. Decoration varies greatly.

Materials and Dimensions
White earthenware with clear alkaline glaze. Cut-sponge decoration with brown, blue, and yellow slip. Molded. Length: 8–11″. Width: 6–8″. Height: 2–3½″.

Locality and Period
Mayer Pottery, Beaver Falls, Pennsylvania. c. 1880–1900. Similar pieces made from Massachusetts west to Ohio, south to Maryland. c. 1870–1920.

Comment
Oval serving dishes in white earthenware and ironstone were popular in both the United States and England. Most were undecorated or had simple floral decoration, usually in green or blue. The type of blue and brown work on the dish shown here is often termed "cut-sponge" decoration. It is believed that small pieces of sponge were cut into various patterns, dipped in glaze, and then applied to the unfired surface.

Hints for Collectors
With its unusual decoration and potter's mark, this serving dish is an especially desirable piece of American white earthenware. Pieces like this are bound to increase in value as more collectors become interested in the ironstone and white earthenware made in America.

Rockingham baking dish

Description
Shallow, oval bowl with gently curving sides and flaring, rolled rim. Plain base. *Variations:* Some dishes are wider. Some have slightly recessed bottom. Sides may have embossed decoration.

Materials and Dimensions
Yellow earthenware with Rockingham glaze. Molded; earlier examples wheel-thrown. Length: 8–11″. Width: 7–9″. Height: 2–3″.

Locality and Period
New England west to Ohio, south to Maryland. c. 1845–1900.

Comment
Pieces similar to the dish shown here were described as oval bakers in the 1852 price list of the United States Pottery Company at Bennington, Vermont. They came in 6 sizes and ranged in price from $2.25 to $4.00 per dozen. Although listed as bakers, period illustrations indicate that they could double as serving pieces, and today that is how they are often used by Rockingham collectors.

Hints for Collectors
Look for marked examples of these bowls, which are worth 3 to 4 times as much as those that are unmarked. Some bear the "1849" mark of the United States Pottery Company. Others have the marks of potteries in East Liverpool, Ohio, and Baltimore. On these Rockingham pieces, the thick glaze often filled the impressed marks, making them very difficult to see. Since these pieces varied little from pottery to pottery, it is practically impossible to determine where a piece was produced if it lacks a mark.

Redware soup bowl

Description
Shallow, circular vessel with sloping sides and slightly shaped rim. Plain base. *Variations:* Some have higher sides. Some are octagonal.

Materials and Dimensions
Red earthenware with clear lead glaze. Decorated with splotches of manganese black. Wheel-thrown; octagonal bowls drape-molded. Height: 2–4″. Diameter: 6–8″.

Locality and Period
New England west to Utah and throughout much of the South. c. 1750–1880.

Comment
So few small redware bowls have survived that it is difficult to realize their importance to frontier families. Unable to buy European porcelain or sometimes even tin plates, they depended on locally produced redware. A letter written in 1814 by the potter Norman Judd of Rome, New York, describes how he worked from dawn until late at night to meet the demand for his pottery, noting that "ware here is ready cash. . . . I have just done turning bowls . . . have burned 8 kilns since the 5th of last May." As late as the 1870s, isolated Mormon settlements in Utah were dependent on red earthenware for their bowls.

Hints for Collectors
Because they are small, these rare and expensive redware eating bowls may occasionally be overlooked by dealers and collectors. Look for them at rural house sales and local auctions, and don't hesitate to buy a chipped or cracked example if the price is right. They are fragile, so few have survived without some minor damage.

Kitchenware

Many of the familiar kitchen items that are now made of glass, metal, wood, and plastic were once manufactured from clay. Featured here are such diverse ceramic objects as baking molds, rolling pins, funnels, and egg cups.

Among the most familiar baking molds are the large, doughnut-shaped examples with a fluted interior. Because of their resemblance to a turban, these pieces are called "Turk's cap molds." The earliest examples, of red earthenware, often have a mottled black glaze; many later yellowware pieces have a Rockingham finish. Smaller oval, oblong, and circular molds with plain or fluted sides may have an embossed design on the interior, usually a sheaf of wheat or an ear of corn. These little molds were used to bake sponge cakes and corn bread, and are most often made of yellow earthenware.

Like molds, small custard cups were produced throughout much of the 19th century, usually in yellow earthenware with a clear glaze, a Rockingham finish, or decorated with spongework; less common are examples in white earthenware and stoneware. Almost all are circular, with slightly flaring sides; rare pieces bear embossed decoration.

Popular around the turn of the century, ceramic rolling pins in yellow earthenware and stoneware were ideally suited to rolling pastry. After being exposed to cold, they remained cool much longer than wooden ones, so dough was less likely to stick to them. The most attractive ceramic rolling pins are often part of a matching set of kitchen implements and are decorated with transfer printing.

Less common ceramic kitchen objects include funnels, meat tenderizers, and colanders. Such pieces are rare today, no doubt because they were subjected to heavy use. Red earthenware and stoneware funnels date from the early part of the 19th century; stoneware meat tenderizers from the middle of the 19th century; and yellow earthenware colanders, from around the turn of the century.

Among the miscellaneous objects included in this section are soap dishes, egg cups, salt and pepper shakers, and spice jars. Most of these pieces are readily available today, with a wide variety of decoration, and they are among the least expensive of ceramic collectibles.

Yellowware colanders

Description
At left, large bowl with thick collar and plain rim. 2 holes in side; groups of 7 holes about base and in bottom. Rimmed base. Decorated with thin white bands between thicker blue bands. At right, low bowl with thick, rolled rim. 2 holes in side; evenly spaced holes in lower half of body and in bottom. Plain base. *Variations:* Spacing of holes differs. Shape of rim and base varies.

Materials and Dimensions
Yellow earthenware with clear alkaline glaze. Bowl at left decorated with blue and white slip; color combinations vary. Molded; pieces similar to bowl at right sometimes wheel-thrown; holes hand-punched. Left, height: 5–6″; diameter: 11–13″. Right, height: 3–4″; diameter: 9–11″.

Locality and Period
New Jersey, Ohio, and Maryland. c. 1880–1920.

Comment
Most yellowware colanders were fashioned by punching holes in standard mixing bowls before they were fired. Colanders with straight, slanting sides like the one on the left are less common than those with gently rounded sides. None of these pieces bear the mark of a pottery.

Hints for Collectors
Because of their extreme scarcity, such colanders are choice collectibles, and most dealers charge accordingly. Look for them in yard and house sales and at country auctions. Even chipped or cracked examples are worth purchasing.

Yellowware mold

Description
Deep, oval cake mold with sides slanting in from plain rim to plain base. Base of interior has embossed design of ear of corn. Bottom slightly recessed. *Variations:* Base of interior may be plain or may be embossed with sheaf-of-wheat or other design.

Materials and Dimensions
Yellow earthenware with clear alkaline glaze. Molded. Height: 4–5″. Length: 5–7″. Width: 4–4½″.

Locality and Period
Massachusetts to Ohio and Maryland. c. 1880–1930.

Comment
When corn bread or sponge cakes were baked in molds like this, the embossed design was impressed on top of the loaf. Most yellowware molds are the size and shape of the example illustrated. Variations in the embossed design indicate that the molds were made by many different potteries, yet practically no known examples have potters' marks.

Hints for Collectors
On many yellowware molds the glaze has begun to flake, especially on the interior. Since examples in good condition are plentiful and inexpensive, don't buy molds with this kind of damage. If you already own a piece with flaking glaze, you can disguise the damage partially by covering affected areas with clear epoxy. The epoxy creates a clear, glazelike surface and seals the damaged areas, preventing further flaking. If a piece has been treated with epoxy, it should not be washed or exposed to heat. Repaired pieces are, of course, worth less.

Yellowware mold

Description
Circular mold with central, hollow, cone-shaped projection. Sides rise gently to plain, flattened rim. Interior has 15 fluted channels that become increasingly smaller toward bottom, then join central projection in a counterclockwise direction. Exterior mirrors the interior fluting. Plain base. *Variations:* May lack fluting. Fluting may not extend up central projection. May have rimmed base.

Materials and Dimensions
Yellow earthenware with clear alkaline glaze. Molded. Height: 3–4″. Diameter: 8–10″.

Locality and Period
New York west to Ohio, south to Maryland. c. 1860–1900.

Comment
Because of their turban shape, these pieces are popularly called Turk's cap molds. Used to make cakes, they were manufactured for many years in Europe and England before they were introduced into America. Still popular today, most modern examples are of aluminum.

Hints for Collectors
European redware and stoneware Turk's cap molds exported to America can be confused with examples made in this country. However, plain yellowware molds like the one illustrated were made only in the United States. Because they were never marked, it is usually impossible to pinpoint the manufacturer. Since these molds vary both in size and in internal design, it is possible to assemble an interesting group of related pieces.

Redware molds

Description
Circular molds with central, hollow, cone-shaped projection. At left, interior with 18 fluted channels spiraling in a clockwise direction to plain flattened rim. Plain base. At right, 12 fluted channels curve out to plain, flattened rim. Plain base.
Variations: Number of channels may vary. Central projection may be plain, not fluted.

Materials and Dimensions
Red earthenware; mold at left with clear lead glaze touched with manganese-black sponging; mold at right with variegated mustard-colored, lead-based glaze. Wheel-thrown; later examples molded. Left, height: 3–4″; diameter: 8–9″. Right, height: 3½–4½″; diameter: 8–10″.

Locality and Period
New England west to Ohio, south to Virginia. c. 1800–60.

Comment
Yellowware and Rockingham Turk's cap molds gradually replaced those made of redware in the second half of the 19th century. In mid-century, all three types were being produced. Most small manufacturers made redware molds on a potter's wheel; larger firms such as Mauldine Perine & Company of Baltimore had begun casting them in plaster molds by 1850.

Hints for Collectors
Redware molds of this sort are attractive, common, and relatively inexpensive. Consequently, they are favorites among redware collectors. European imports are generally similar but have thicker walls and are made of darker clay.

Rockingham mold

Description
Circular, bowl-shaped vessel with slightly rolled rim. Interior with 15 fluted channels and short, hollow, central projection. Plain base. *Variations:* Central projection may be higher and may not be hollow. Number of fluted channels and their pattern varies.

Materials and Dimensions
Yellow earthenware with Rockingham glaze. Molded. Height: 3–4". Diameter: 6–9".

Locality and Period
Attributed to the United States Pottery Company, Bennington, Vermont. c. 1848–58. Similar pieces from New England to Ohio, south to Maryland. c. 1845–85.

Comment
Often referred to as Turk's cap molds from the fancied resemblance between their fluting and a turban, these cake molds are found in redware and plain yellowware, and less commonly with a Rockingham glaze. Because they were made in many different potteries and almost never marked, it is practically impossible to determine where or when a particular example was produced.

Hints for Collectors
A group of molds makes an interesting collection. Many prefer to display them at an angle, so that their fluting can be seen. They can, of course, be used in baking, but high temperatures may cause them to crack or lose their glaze. Most molds like the example illustrated were not marked, but an attribution may be possible by comparison with identified pieces.

Yellowware mold

Description
Very small, circular, bowl-shaped mold with thick, slightly rolled rim. Short, plain base and recessed bottom. Interior with 10 deep, fluted channels that alternate with shallow channels and extend almost to the bottom. Bottom of interior stepped, with ear-of-corn pattern impressed in center. *Variations:* Mold may have plain interior or have different design on bottom.

Materials and Dimensions
Yellow earthenware with clear alkaline glaze. Molded. Height: 3½–4½". Diameter: 2–2½".

Locality and Period
New Jersey west to Ohio. c. 1880–1920.

Comment
These molds are small enough to be thought of as miniatures, but they were probably molds for individual cakes and corn muffins. Since they are about the size of a custard cup they may also have been used as forms for individual custards. They are less common than the larger oval and octagonal molds.

Hints for Collectors
Yellowware molds usually come in 3 basic forms: round, oval, and octagonal. Their interiors vary from plain to elaborate, with corn, sheaf-of-wheat, and leaf patterns most common. These are often combined with geometric designs. Pieces with complex interiors are the most desirable. Figural designs on the interior bottom are very rare, but molds with impressed cows and eagles are known. A group of molds in different shapes with similar interior designs can form an interesting collection.

Miniature stoneware mold

Description
Small, rectangular mold with rounded corners. Body slopes in toward base and then swells out to shaped, oval base. Troughlike interior has 5 ridges that create fluted effect. *Variations:* Some examples lack interior fluting. Number of flutes varies. Base may be rectangular.

Materials and Dimensions
Stoneware with light tan glaze. Modeled. Length: 3–3½". Width: 2–2½". Height: 1¾–2".

Locality and Period
Northeastern United States, particularly New York and New Jersey. c. 1830–60.

Comment
Miniature stoneware molds are uncommon. Although an example like the one shown here may be a true miniature, it could also be used as a mold for a very small cake or cookie. Authorities usually regard them as miniatures or perhaps children's toys rather than as practical kitchen accessories. The shiny tan glaze seen here was often used in the mid-19th century on larger pieces of stoneware, particularly crocks and jugs. These little molds are not mentioned in pottery price lists and were probably made in small quantities.

Hints for Collectors
While miniature jugs and crocks are fairly common, other miniature forms are relatively rare. Consequently, a piece like that shown here would be a choice find. Like most miniatures, this mold does not bear a potter's mark, probably because the wood or metal stamps used to mark larger pots were much too big for the smaller pieces.

Description
At left, oval dish with embossed decoration below rolled rim. Interior slopes inward, terminating in a flat platform with 16 small holes surrounding larger central hole. Rimmed base. At right, roughly oblong dish with shaped body and thick, shaped rim. Platformlike interior with 12 small drainage holes. Shaped base. *Variations:* May be square or round. Number of drainage holes varies.

Materials and Dimensions
Yellow earthenware with Rockingham glaze. Similar pieces white earthenware with clear alkaline glaze. Molded. Left, length: 5–6″; width: 3–4″; height: 2–3″. Right, length: 4–5″; width: 3–4″; height: 1½–2″.

Locality and Period
New England west to Ohio, south to Maryland. c. 1850–1900.

Comment
Referred to in price lists as soap drainers, these inexpensive household items were made in many different eastern and midwestern potteries and were apparently never marked. In 1896 the Syracuse Stoneware Company of Syracuse, New York, sold them for $1.25 per dozen.

Hints for Collectors
Many collectors use these Rockingham soap dishes for their original function; others prefer to display a varied group. Certain forms, although unmarked, are attributed to the United States Pottery Company in Bennington, Vermont. These can be identified by reference to books on that kiln. They will generally bring higher prices than similar pieces from other potteries.

Yellowware custard cups

Description
At left, small vessel with slightly shaped rim and plain base. Decorated with 3 blue bands. At right, bowl-shaped vessel with shaped rim and rimmed base. *Variations:* Shapes vary. Some examples are cone-shaped. Rim and base may be plain. Number of bands varies.

Materials and Dimensions
Yellow earthenware with clear alkaline glaze; interior of cup at right glazed with white Bristol slip. Cup at left decorated with cobalt blue; similar pieces decorated with white and brown slip. Molded. Height: 1¾–3″. Diameter: 3–4″.

Locality and Period
New England west to Ohio, south to Maryland. c. 1870–1930.

Comment
Many manufacturers produced these small yellowware custard cups, and, although they are almost never marked, certain forms are associated with specific potteries. For instance, cone-shaped cups were produced at the United States Pottery Company in Bennington, Vermont. Plain examples with a clear glaze are less common than those decorated with bands. Cone-shaped custard cups are rarest of all.

Hints for Collectors
Because of the variety of shapes, custard cups form interesting collections. Cone-shaped examples are particularly desirable and hard to find. Some collectors use these cups for their original purpose; others prefer to display them or use them as vases. If you choose to use them as vases, be sure to protect the glaze with a waterproof lining.

Spongeware custard cups

Description
Circular cups with thick, shaped rim and plain base. Central cup has fluted body. *Variations:* Shape varies. Rim may be plain. Base may be rimmed. Bottom may be marked "USA" and may have mold number and letter.

Materials and Dimensions
Yellow earthenware with clear alkaline glaze. Left cup with brown spongework; central cup with green and brown spongework; right cup with green spongework. Similar pieces white earthenware with blue spongework. Molded. Height: 2–3″. Diameter: 3–4″.

Locality and Period
New Jersey and Ohio. c. 1890–1940.

Comment
Custard cups are among the most common forms decorated with spongework. Most examples have brown sponging like the cup on the left, but there are various other combinations as well. The impression "USA" often appears on the bottom, indicating that they were made in America. This mark appears after 1891, the year a tariff act was passed requiring imported goods to be marked with their country of origin. American manufacturers often followed suit to promote American-made goods.

Hints for Collectors
Although custard cups are alike in shape, their varying decoration can add interest to a group. Look for pieces in different color combinations, or with embossing or fluting. The impressed numbers and letters on the bottom of these cups designate the molds in which they were formed. They differ considerably, making it apparent that the cups were produced at a large number of potteries.

Redware apple butter pots

Description
Vessels with sides that curve gently out to incised ring slightly below thick, rolled rim. Plain base. *Variations:* May have straighter sides. Base may be chamfered.

Materials and Dimensions
Red earthenware; pot on left with clear lead glaze; pot on right with unglazed exterior, clear lead glaze on interior. Rare examples with multicolored glaze. Similar pieces stoneware. Wheel-thrown. Height: 6–7″. Diameter: 5–5½″.

Locality and Period
New Jersey to Pennsylvania, south to Virginia. c. 1790–1890.

Comment
These small pots held apple butter, a sweet favored by German settlers, particularly in Pennsylvania. A piece of cloth or waxed paper covered the mouth, protecting the apple butter. The covering was anchored by a string that fit under the heavy rim. Some potters, such as the Bell family of Strasburg, Virginia, and Waynesboro, Pennsylvania, made examples with multicolored glazes, usually in cream, brown, and green, but most were glazed only on the interior. Rare examples bear the marks of potteries in Pennsylvania and New Jersey.

Hints for Collectors
Except for the multiglazed and marked examples, apple butter pots are common and inexpensive. Attractive forms in good condition make fine containers for cut or dried flowers. If you use one as a vase, be sure that it has a waterproof liner to protect the glaze.

Yellowware custard cup

Description

Octagonal custard cup tapering slightly from top to bottom. Slightly raised band around rim of cup. Each side with embossed triangular decoration enclosing treelike motif. Rimmed base. Bottom slightly recessed. *Variations:* Some custard cups are round. Some are decorated with raised floral patterns. Most have a plain base.

Materials and Dimensions

Yellow earthenware with clear alkaline glaze. Molded. Height: 2½–3″. Diameter: 3–3½″.

Locality and Period

New York and New Jersey west to Ohio, south to Maryland. c. 1880–1920.

Comment

While mold-cast custard cups are common, this octagonal form is not. Although the geometric pattern refects the Gothic Revival style of the 19th century, it was rarely used in yellowware. The design of this piece also indicates the presence of far more sophisticated molding machinery than was required to make the usual yellowware bowl, and suggests that the cup was produced at a large factory, probably in Ohio.

Hints for Collectors

The octagonal form of this cup makes it uncommon and therefore desirable. At antiques shops and markets, search for unusual pieces, which are sometimes mixed in among the stacks of ordinary examples. They are worth buying even if they have small cracks or chips; however, damaged pieces should cost less than those in good condition.

Fiesta egg cup

Description
Cuplike vessel with plain rim and sides that curve in to flaring base. Beneath rim and on base embossed bands present. Bottom recessed and embossed "Fiesta/HLC/USA."

Materials and Dimensions
White earthenware with opaque ivory-white glaze; also available in other Fiesta colors. Molded. Height: 3–3¼". Diameter: 3¼–3½".

Locality and Period
Homer Laughlin Company, Newell, West Virginia. c. 1936–58.

Comment
Egg cups, among the first items in the Fiesta line, remained in production for over 20 years. They were bigger than traditional egg cups and large enough for poached eggs and even bits of toast. Despite the recessed bottom, nearly all of these egg cups bear one of the Fiesta marks.

Hints for Collectors
Even though they were made for many years, Fiesta egg cups are relatively scarce. Examples in yellow and turquoise are more common than those in cobalt blue, rose, and dark green. In the early 1940s the Hankscraft Company produced a line of egg cups that they promoted as "Genuine Fiesta." They are easy to distinguish from true Fiesta pieces because they have a white-glazed interior. Individual egg cups in Homer Laughlin's Harlequin line had a tall, footed stem. The Harlequin line also had a double egg cup. Shaped somewhat like an hourglass, one end was large enough to accommodate 2 eggs, while the other end held just 1 egg.

White earthenware egg cup

Description
Small egg cup with thick, rolled rim. Wide, flaring base. Deeply recessed bottom. *Variations:* May have transfer decoration. May have plain rim. Base may be shorter and may flare less widely.

Materials and Dimensions
White earthenware with clear alkaline glaze. Molded. Height: 3–4″. Diameter: 2–3″.

Locality and Period
New England west to Ohio, south to Maryland. c. 1870–1930. Similar pieces from Europe. c. 1850–1930.

Comment
Egg cups are seldom used today, but they were popular from the turn of the century to as late as the 1950s. They were rarely marked, and it is difficult to distinguish American examples from those made in England and elsewhere in Europe. Further, since the basic form changed little over the years, a late 19th-century cup looks much like one made in the 1920s. These cups were also made in glass and metal.

Hints for Collectors
Like other pieces made of white earthenware, egg cups often have fine lines or cracks in the glaze caused by aging. Although some find this spidering attractive, it's best to avoid such pieces. Dirt and oil can penetrate the cracks, causing discoloration that is difficult to remove. Cracked egg cups should never be used for their original purpose. Some collectors use them as match or toothpick holders. Others seek out examples with varying shapes and interesting decoration for display.

Harlequin salt and pepper shakers

Description
Tall, cone-shaped vessels with slightly raised central section at top. Several small, round holes in center of top. Several embossed bands present below top. Flaring base. Bottom deeply recessed. Large, central hole in bottom accommodates cork.

Materials and Dimensions
White earthenware with opaque blue glaze; similar pieces in all standard Harlequin colors. Molded. Height: 2¾–3¼″. Diameter: 1¾–2″.

Locality and Period
Homer Laughlin Company, Newell, West Virginia. c. 1938–64.

Comment
These cone-shaped, thin-bodied pieces are typical of the best in the Harlequin line. Like all other Harlequin pieces, they were sold exclusively at F. W. Woolworth Co. stores, where they were carried until the late 1950s. Inexpensive, yet brightly colored and with an attractive, streamlined design, the Harlequin line was an extremely popular alternative to high-priced dinnerware.

Hints for Collectors
Although no longer as inexpensive as they once were, Harlequin pieces are still affordable and easy to find. Favorites with collectors who admire the Art Deco style, Harlequin ceramics are usually more readily available than pieces in Homer Laughlin's popular Fiesta line. Watch for the rarer colors like pastel shades and deep blue. Homer Laughlin's Fiesta line also had salt and pepper shakers. Available in all Fiesta glazes, they are round with a flaring, circular base and have 7 small holes in the top. Imitation Fiesta shakers have the holes in the side.

Transfer-decorated stoneware spice jar

Description
Small, covered container with matching lid. Plain rim. Lower
body curves inward and has embossed, swirling flutes. Rimmed
base. Interior of mouth has small ledge to support matching lid.
Lid rises in 3 levels to a buttonlike knob. Decorated with
transfer-printed bands of blue, floral devices, and the word
"PEPPER." *Variations:* May lack embossing. Decoration varies.

Materials and Dimensions
Stoneware with white glaze. Decorated with cobalt blue. Height:
3–4". Diameter: 2–3".

Locality and Period
New Jersey and Ohio. c. 1900–40.

Comment
Like mixing bowls, rolling pins, and other kitchenware, these
spice jars were mass produced in the first half of the 20th
century. Usually they were part of a complete canister set that
included containers for items like salt, sugar, and flour. Transfer
printing permitted much quicker and cheaper decoration than
had previously been possible for stoneware factories.

Hints for Collectors
Although English and continental factories produced containers
much like this one, pottery catalogues indicate that they were
also made in Ohio and New Jersey. The many pottery catalogues
and price lists circulated during the first half of the 20th century
often reveal where pieces were manufactured, so always
purchase these lists when they are available. Look for them in
stores that specialize in used books and magazines.

Stoneware rolling pin

Description
Cylindrical body with floral decoration. Each end recessed
slightly to round, centered hole. Turned wooden handle baluster-
shaped with ball-like ends; handle fits through holes in body.
Variations: Decoration may vary or be absent.

Materials and Dimensions
Stoneware glazed with white slip. Decorated with blue transfer-
printed floral devices; similar pieces undecorated. Molded.
Length: 13–15″. Diameter: 2¾–3¼″.

Locality and Period
New Jersey and Ohio. c. 1890–1930.

Comment
Ceramic rolling pins were preferred by many to wooden ones
because they are smoother than wood and easier to work with.
Since ceramic pins have a cooler surface than wood, dough is less
likely to stick to them, especially if they are refrigerated before
use. Earlier 19th-century examples were made in yellowware but
were relatively fragile; stoneware pins were found to be more
durable although heavier. The decorative pattern shown here
also appears on other kitchen utensils such as covered spice jars
and custard cups.

Hints for Collectors
White-glazed stoneware utensils like the rolling pin shown here
are readily available, inexpensive, and worth collecting, even
though of relatively recent vintage. Moreover, many pieces are
in good enough shape to be used as well as admired. A small
group of various utensils with similar decoration would be an
attractive addition to any collection.

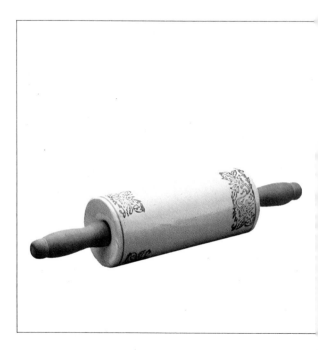

Yellowware rolling pin

Description
Cylindrical body. Each end slightly concave with central hole.
Hand-carved wooden rod that fits through holes has knoblike
ends and thicker center section. *Variations:* Carving of handles
varies.

Materials and Dimensions
Yellow earthenware with clear alkaline glaze. Molded. Length:
7–9″. Diameter: 3–3½″.

Locality and Period
New Jersey to Ohio. c. 1870–1910.

Comment
Yellowware rolling pins, especially those from the late 19th
century, are not common. Through hard use over the years,
many were broken or damaged. Chipping and flaking of the glaze
is especially common.

Hints for Collectors
Yellowware rolling pins, although uncommon and usually
expensive, are desirable additions to any collection. Look for
them in antiques shops specializing in kitchenware. Rolling pins
that have lost their handles sometimes pass unrecognized
through shops and shows. The handles were designed in 2 pieces
and intended to be screwed together inside the rolling pin; once
separated it was difficult to find a replacement. However, rolling
pins are well worth purchasing even if they have lost their
handles, for new handles can be made easily. Many of these
utilitarian pieces show chips or glaze damage. Affected areas can
be filled with plastic wood, then stained yellow. A coat of clear
epoxy will seal the restoration. This kind of repair is primarily
cosmetic; a restored rolling pin is still worth substantially less
than one in good condition.

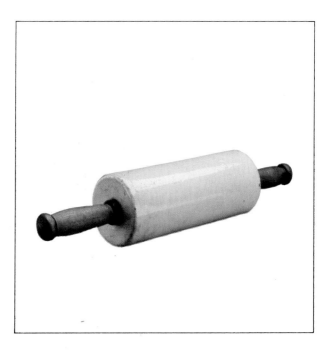

Description
Cone-shaped funnel with heavy, tubular handle and heavy, rolled rim. Funnel tapers from rim to narrow spout. Funnel encircled by 2 incised lines. Handle with knoblike end attached to body between rim and incised lines. *Variations:* Funnel may angle out near spout. Handle is often shorter and lighter.

Materials and Dimensions
Red earthenware with clear lead glaze. Decorated with sponged orangish-brown slip. Wheel-thrown; handle separately shaped and applied. Length: 6–10″. Diameter: 4–6″.

Locality and Period
Bucks County, Pennsylvania. c. 1840–50. Similar pieces from New England to Ohio, south to the Carolinas. c. 1800–50.

Comment
Funnels were subject to hard use; most people preferred metal ones, but when they were not available, they made do with ceramic funnels. They were probably never made in quantity, and because they do not appear on surviving pottery price lists, they were no doubt made to order. Marked examples are exceedingly rare.

Hints for Collectors
Redware funnels appear so seldom on the market that both collectors and dealers may fail to recognize their rarity and worth. As with other uncommon forms, cracks and chips that would disqualify an ordinary piece are perfectly acceptable, but substantial damage does justify a reduction in price. Frequently, the handles on these pieces have broken off and then been reglued or even replaced.

Description

Cylindrical object with body deeply incised horizontally and vertically, forming small oblongs; each oblong section embossed in a raised X shape. Top slightly rounded, with central hole; interior of hole threaded. Long, baluster-turned wooden handle has threaded end that screws into end of ceramic body. Flattened bottom impressed "PAT'D DEC 25, 1877." *Variations:* May be rectangular with incurving sides. Handle hole may run completely through body.

Materials and Dimensions

Stoneware with salt glaze. Molded, then hand-finished. Height: 8–10″. Diameter: 3–4″.

Locality and Period

Probably Ohio. c. 1877. Similar examples from New York to Ohio. c. 1865–85.

Comment

Heavy and as hard as steel, although without steel's tensile strength, stoneware at first seems a natural material for the heavy work of pounding tough meat. However, stoneware tends to chip when it strikes another object. Few such pieces were made, probably because they were never very popular, and they are scarce today.

Hints for Collectors

Like funnels, these tenderizers are often overlooked because the form is so obscure. They are valuable, especially when marked or dated. The mark on this piece is extremely unusual; very few bear a manufacturer's name. Since the handle can be replaced easily, never hesitate to buy a tenderizer that is missing that part.

Redware churn

Description
Tall churn with sides gradually sloping in to flaring rim. 2 embossed bands on sides. 2 heavy lug handles attached slightly below rim. Heavy, shaped base. Mouth has narrow interior ledge to support matching lid. Separate lid has flat rim and tall, central section with curving sides and central hole for dasher.
Variations: May be cylindrical. Cover may lack tall, central section.

Materials and Dimensions
Red earthenware with black glaze. Wheel-thrown; handles separately shaped and applied; cover separately shaped. Height: 12–16″. Diameter: 6–9″.

Locality and Period
New England west to Ohio, south to the Carolinas. c. 1780–1850.

Comment
Redware churns were listed on the price lists of some potteries, but always as items that could be made on special request. Typically they sold for 3 to 6 cents per gallon. Since churns had to withstand constant battering by the wooden dasher, and since redware is fragile, few redware churns lasted very long, which may explain why they were never standard production items. By 1850, stoneware and tin churns were readily available, and redware examples were less often made.

Hints for Collectors
A redware churn is a real find. Almost certainly the rim will be chipped, and the interior will have chips, gouges, and glaze loss caused by the dasher. Nevertheless, these pieces are sufficiently uncommon to justify overlooking the damage.

Description

Large, 2-piece water cooler with matching lid. Tall, upper section rests on small base. Upper section embossed with paneled and acanthus-leaf decoration and with a double ring. Above ring, flaring rim. 2 leaf-shaped handles attached just below double ring. Lower body slopes in to double ring. Round hole with short stem accommodates pewter spigot. Separate base has shaped top and flaring footlike bottom and is embossed with acanthus-leaf decoration. Matching lid stepped, with flat, button-shaped handle. *Variations:* Embossed decoration differs and may be less elaborate.

Materials and Dimensions

Yellow earthenware with Rockingham glaze. Molded. Height: 16–19″. Diameter: 11½–14″.

Locality and Period

Attributed to the United States Pottery Company, Bennington, Vermont. c. 1848–58. Similar pieces from New York to Ohio. c. 1850–80.

Comment

Rockingham-glazed water coolers were never common, though they appear to have been produced at several potteries. Their large size and relatively complex construction made them expensive.

Hints for Collectors

The individual parts that make up these coolers occasionally turn up. Learn to know what the base looks like, since without the upper section it can be difficult to recognize. Although the extensive repairs noticeable on this piece diminish its beauty, it is still worth owning because of its rarity.

Pitchers and Washbowls, Chamber Pots, Spittoons, and Related Objects

In the days before indoor plumbing, every home probably had several pitcher-and-washbowl sets and chamber pots. These practical necessities were no doubt among the first ceramic forms made in America. The pitcher and washbowl were displayed on top of a commode or washstand that usually had a cupboard in its base to conceal the chamber pot. Spittoons were used in homes and public places throughout most of the 18th and 19th centuries. Made in great quantities, these pieces were also a necessity in an age when tobacco chewing was common.

Most pitcher-and-bowl sets produced before 1850 were hand-thrown and made of red earthenware. Some were decorated with colored slip, but most were covered with a clear lead glaze. After 1850 they were usually cast in molds and made of white or yellow earthenware or ironstone; a substantial number of these sets were imported from England. Because they were kept on display, many were embellished with decoration; the most desirable sets are those decorated with spongework or with a Rockingham glaze. A few miniature pitcher-and-bowl sets were also made; these rare pieces are in great demand today.

Early chamber pots were made of clear-glazed red earthenware or salt-glazed stoneware and usually not decorated. Potters may have fashioned them by simply attaching a handle to a wheel-thrown bowl. Throughout the 19th century, however, chamber pots became increasingly ornate even though they were probably concealed in cupboards or under the bed. Made of yellow earthenware or ironstone and cast in molds, a number were produced as part of a matching set of toilet items that included a pitcher and washbowl. These chamber pots frequently had attractive glazes or bore sponged or transfer-printed decoration.

Although ceramic spittoons were made throughout most of the 18th and 19th centuries, many of the examples available today date from after 1850. The earliest examples were made of red earthenware in various shapes; later ones were produced in yellow and white earthenware and stoneware. Those made for such public spaces as clubs and restaurants might be as large as a foot in diameter and were usually made of sturdy stoneware, while the smaller pieces preferred for home use were sometimes made of decorated porcelain. Some of the most attractive spittoons have lavish embossed decoration and a Rockingham finish.

Other specialized personal items, including bedpans, a footbath, and a foot warmer, are also featured in this section.

Scroddledware pitcher and bowl

Description

Matching pitcher and bowl set. 12-sided pitcher with faceted sides embossed in diamond pattern. Sides taper from low, bulbous waist to neck defined by shaped ring. Above ring sides curve out to shaped rim and spout. Ear-shaped, branch-form handle attached at rim and midbody. Lower body curves in to shaped base. Circular bowl has flaring, 12-sided rim and tall rimmed base. *Variations:* Body may be squat. Small beads may surround diamond facets. Sides may not be faceted.

Materials and Dimensions

Brown and white earthenware with clear alkaline glaze. Molded; handle separately shaped and applied. Pitcher height: 8¾–10½"; diameter: 6–7". Bowl height: 4¼–4¾"; diameter: 12–13".

Locality and Period

United States Pottery Company, Bennington, Vermont. c. 1853–58.

Comment

Scroddledware is made of 2 or more clays that fire to different colors, typically pink, white, gray, and shades of brown. The clays are mixed together before they are placed in the mold. Apparently scroddledware was made only at Bennington, although the well-known 20th-century Niloak pottery was made by a similar process.

Hints for Collectors

Scroddledware and marbledware are sometimes confused. Marbledware has multicolored glazes on the outside, but the interior is usually 1 solid color. Clay striations pass completely through a piece of scroddledware and are visible on the interior. Marked scroddledware is expensive, but unmarked examples are sometimes overlooked and reasonably priced.

Spongeware pitcher and bowl

Description
Bulbous pitcher with matching bowl. Sides of pitcher taper sharply from low waist, then swell out to flaring rim with large spout. Large, ear-shaped handle attached opposite spout at rim and just above waist. Below waist, sides taper sharply to plain base. Sides of bowl slope out to rolled rim. Bowl has rimmed base. Bowl and pitcher decorated with blue bands and spongework. *Variations:* Pitcher may be narrower, with gently curving sides.

Materials and Dimensions
Stoneware glazed with white slip. Decorated with cobalt blue; similar pieces sponged and decorated in other colors. Molded; earlier examples wheel-thrown; handle separately shaped and applied. Pitcher height: 11–13″; diameter: 7–8″. Bowl height: 4–6″: diameter: 13–15″.

Locality and Period
New Jersey west to Ohio. c. 1870–1910.

Comment
Pitcher and bowl sets made of white earthenware are quite common, but fewer were made of stoneware. Examples with sponging are relatively rare, especially those as well-decorated as the set illustrated.

Hints for Collectors
Pitcher and bowl sets are among the most desirable pieces decorated with blue spongework, and consequently they command high prices. Avoid buying a "married" set, one in which undamaged pieces have been substituted for broken ones even though they don't quite match. The proportions of the pitcher should be harmonious with those of the bowl, and the sponging and banding should match exactly.

Miniature Rockingham pitcher and bowl

Description
Tiny pitcher with matching bowl. Sides of pitcher curve in from waist, then flare out to shaped rim and spout. High, ear-shaped handle attached at rim and just below waist. Lower body tapers to shaped base. Sides of bowl slope out to plain rim. Lower body slopes in sharply to rimmed base.

Materials and Dimensions
Yellow earthenware with Rockingham glaze. Molded; handle separately shaped and applied. Pitcher height: 1⅝–1¾"; diameter: 2¾–3". Bowl height: 1⅝–1¾"; diameter: 3¾–4".

Locality and Period
Vermont west to Ohio, south to Maryland. c. 1850–90.

Comment
Miniatures made of yellow earthenware with a Rockingham glaze are much less common than those made of stoneware or redware. Since they are far too small to mark, most miniatures are anonymous and can only be identified if their history is known or through contemporary references such as price lists. These pieces were usually intended as gifts, especially at Christmas, and were never produced in quantity.

Hints for Collectors
Miniatures are in great demand and often cost more than their full-size counterparts. Although a matching set like the one illustrated is much more valuable than the pitcher or bowl alone, either would be worth buying separately because these pieces are so rare. These objects are sometimes confused with doll house furnishings, so look for them in stores that specialize in dolls and doll houses.

Redware pitcher and bowl

Description
Large, circular bowl with matching pitcher. Pitcher curves in from low waist to shoulder marked by incised line. Wide neck with collar and plain rim with pulled spout. Ear-shaped handle attached at rim and waist. Lower body tapers to plain base. Sides of bowl slope out to flaring, overhanging rim. Lower body curves in to broad base. Decorated with brown splotches.
Variations: Handle attachment and spout vary.

Materials and Dimensions
Red earthenware with yellow glaze; rim of bowl unglazed. Decorated with brown manganese. Wheel-thrown; handle separately shaped and applied. Pitcher height: 10–13"; diameter: 7–8½". Bowl height: 3½–4½"; diameter: 14–15".

Locality and Period
Attributed to Virginia. c. 1860–80. Similar sets from Pennsylvania to North Carolina. c. 1850–90.

Comment
During the Victorian era almost every bedroom contained a large pitcher-and-washbowl set, many of them made in England of ironstone. American-made examples in the same medium were available by the mid-19th century. However, in certain isolated areas, primarily the South, sets were made of richly glazed, native redware. A few such pieces, notably those from the Strasburg, Virginia, area, bear potters' marks, but most are unidentified.

Hints for Collectors
These sets were made in several sizes with the same kind of decoration. Consequently, sets have been mixed up over the years. In buying a set, be sure that the color and decoration match and that the proportions are harmonious.

Flint-enamel chamber pot

Description
Squat, octagonal vessel. Sides slope in from low waist to neck defined by heavy ring and to flaring, octagonal rim. Ear-shaped handle in form of bent branch attached below rim and above waist. Lower body curves in sharply to plinthlike, octagonal base. Matching, dome-shaped, octagonal lid has acorn-shaped handle.

Materials and Dimensions
Yellow earthenware with clear alkaline glaze sprinkled with brown manganese, green copper, and blue cobalt metallic oxides. Molded; handle separately shaped and applied. Height: 7–9″. Diameter: 10–11″.

Locality and Period
United States Pottery Company, Bennington, Vermont. c. 1849–58.

Comment
Chamber pots with a Rockingham glaze were made at potteries from New England west to Ohio and south to Maryland. Those with a flint-enamel finish were produced only at the United States Pottery Company; they often bear the firm's "1849" mark. The decoration used on this piece is called the scalloped rib pattern; it appears on other toilet articles, such as pitcher and bowl sets, soap dishes, and toilet boxes.

Hints for Collectors
Pieces with the flint-enamel finish are uncommon and expensive. Because chamber pots are unpopular with collectors, they are usually the least expensive of flint-enamel objects, especially if they are missing their lids. Collectors often use them as planters.

Yellowware chamber pot

Description
Large, cup-shaped vessel with gently rounded sides and
flattened, flaring rim. Ear-shaped handle attached just below rim
and at waist. Rimmed base. Decorated with 3 white bands
enclosed by 2 slightly wider brown ones. *Variations:* May be
lower and wider. May be undecorated or decorated with single
wide white band or with 2 white bands.

Materials and Dimensions
Yellow earthenware with clear alkaline glaze. Decorated with
brown and white slip. Molded; handle separately shaped and
applied. Height: 4–6″. Diameter: 7–10″.

Locality and Period
Probably western New York. c. 1890–1900. Similar pieces from
New York west to Ohio, south to Maryland. c. 1860–1910.

Comment
Chamber pots almost identical to this one in style and decoration
were sold by the Syracuse Stoneware Company of Syracuse,
New York, in 1896. They came in 4 sizes, with diameters ranging
from 7″ to 10″, and cost $1.75 to $4.25 per dozen. Although these
pieces were almost always concealed, the decorative banding on
them sometimes matches that found on bowls, crocks, and other
kitchenware.

Hints for Collectors
Chamber pots made of yellowware and decorated with banding
tend to be somewhat more popular than other types of chamber
pots, perhaps because of their decoration. A collection of diverse
pieces with similar banding would be incomplete without a
chamber pot. Matching lids for the "chambers" were available,
but they are rare today, possibly because they were sold
separately for half the price of the pot.

Stoneware chamber pot

Description
Squat, cup-shaped vessel with incised line at shoulder and flaring, flattened rim. Plain base. U-shaped handle attached at rim and waist. *Variations:* May have rimmed base.

Materials and Dimensions
Stoneware; exterior with salt glaze; interior glazed with brown Albany slip. Wheel-thrown; handle separately shaped and applied. Height: 5–6″. Diameter: 7–8″.

Locality and Period
New England west to Texas, south to Virginia. c. 1850–1900.

Comment
Usually referred to on price lists as "chambers," these items were also made of white earthenware, and of yellow earthenware, occasionally with a Rockingham or flint-enamel finish. In 1845, the stoneware pottery in Bennington, Vermont, sold them in two sizes for $1.00 and $2.00 per dozen. Examples with anything but the simplest decoration are practically unknown; most stoneware chamber pots have a plain salt glaze. It seems likely that potters simply attached handles to the standard bowls they produced to make the type of chamber illustrated here.

Hints for Collectors
Stoneware chamber pots have limited appeal and are inexpensive, although not especially common. Those made before 1850 usually have thick, heavy walls. Thinner and simpler examples like the one illustrated date from the second half of the 19th century. Look for the rare chambers that have the mark of a pottery, usually one located in New York or Pennsylvania.

Stoneware spittoon

Description
Massive, circular vessel with flattened rim and shaped base.
Interior slopes in to round hole in center. Round discharge hole
in upper side. Blue band below rim, 2 more above base.
"STAMFORD, N.Y." painted in decorative script around body.
Variations: Spittoons are usually smaller. Placement of
discharge hole varies.

Materials and Dimensions
Stoneware; exterior with salt glaze; interior glazed with light
brown Albany slip. Decorated with cobalt blue. Wheel-thrown.
Height: 4–7″. Diameter: 8–12″.

Locality and Period
Probably New York State. c. 1840–70. Similar pieces from New
England to Ohio, south to Virginia. c. 1830–80.

Comment
Like the piece shown, which was once used in a Stamford, New
York, hotel, these large stoneware cuspidors were kept in the
lounges and barrooms of hotels and in restaurants. They were
seldom intended for use in private homes, where smaller models,
often made of porcelain, were preferred.

Hints for Collectors
Although spittoons are not especially popular with collectors, an
example like this one is appealing because of its decoration.
Pieces that bear the name of a town or city are especially popular
with collectors from that region. They usually command
substantially higher prices in the area where they were made or
used than elsewhere.

Redware spittoon

Description
Spool-shaped vessel with sides that flare slightly outward to form
flaring rim and base. Top recessed, sloping down from edges to
center hole. Just below rim, discharge hole at one side.
Variations: Sides may be straight. Discharge hole may be in a
different location.

Materials and Dimensions
Red earthenware glazed with yellow and light brown slip.
Wheel-thrown. Height: 4–5″. Diameter: 7–9″.

Locality and Period
New England west to Pennsylvania. c. 1790–1850.

Comment
Most redware spittoons have a black or brown finish, but a few
multiglazed examples can be found. These come primarily from
New England and western New York and date from the first half
of the 19th century. Some marked pieces are known, particularly
those from the Morganville, New York, pottery, but spittoons
were seldom considered important enough to merit a maker's
mark.

Hints for Collectors
Spittoons, or cuspidors, are seldom of much interest to
collectors. However, a redware example with a variegated glaze
has importance and value because of its rarity, and the addition
of a maker's mark could elevate its price substantially. Never
dismiss a piece with an unusual glaze just because it is an
unappealing form; less popular types are often better buys.

Yellowware spittoon

Description
Octagonal cuspidor with curving sides, squared rim, and
plinthlike base. Interior slopes downward in 8 wedge-shaped
sections to circular hole at center. Triangular drainage hole at
one corner. Bottom slightly recessed. *Variations:* May be
circular.

Materials and Dimensions
Yellow earthenware with clear alkaline glaze; scattered spots of
dark brown glaze, probably due to kiln accident. Molded. Height:
3–4″. Diameter: 7–8″.

Locality and Period
Massachusetts west to Ohio, south to Maryland. c. 1850–90.

Comment
It is difficult for us today to comprehend the number of spittoons
used in the 19th century. But back then, when nearly every man
chewed tobacco, there were hotel lounges that had as many as 40
of these pieces. Apparently plain yellowware spittoons, or
cuspidors, were never common since few have survived. Most
examples found are made of stoneware or have a Rockingham
glaze.

Hints for Collectors
Since Victorian-era pieces like chamber pots, foot warmers, and
spittoons hold almost no interest for most collectors, they are
usually inexpensive. An attractive geometric form such as the
one illustrated would be a nice addition to any yellowware
collection. The scattered brown spots in the glaze, probably
caused by an accident in the kiln, are an interesting feature;
details like this appeal to some collectors.

Description
Squat, circular spittoon with bulbous body. Embossed decoration around upper edge consists of 12 seashells linked by rope. Interior has shaped raylike pattern and slopes down to hole in center. Oval or triangular drainage hole at midpoint on side. Plain base. *Variations:* Some examples lack rope between shells. Overall decoration may vary.

Materials and Dimensions
Yellow earthenware with Rockingham glaze. Molded. Height: 3½–4″. Diameter: 9–10″.

Locality and Period
Vermont west to Ohio, south to Maryland. c. 1850–70.

Comment
Known among collectors as "shell cuspidors," pieces like the one illustrated are among the most attractive of all spittoons. Many were made by the United States Pottery Company in Bennington, Vermont, from 1850 to 1858, and often bear the factory's "1849" mark. The United States Pottery Company was formed that year, and "1849" continued to be used as one of the pottery's marks. Similar spittoons were also made in Ohio and at the Bennett pottery in Baltimore.

Hints for Collectors
Despite the popularity of ware with a Rockingham glaze, spittoons in this material have not attracted collectors' attention any more than those made of stoneware or redware. Spittoons are thus some of the best buys of all Rockingham pottery. A Bennington Rockingham spittoon with the "1849" mark may be half the price of any other pottery form with the same impression.

Miniature redware spittoon

Description
Small, circular spittoon with high waist, sharply flaring collar, and plain rim. Lower body squat. Bottom slightly recessed.
Variations: May be gilded, or decorated with gilding and paint.

Materials and Dimensions
Red earthenware. Unglazed. Wheel-thrown. Height: 2–3″. Diameter: 3–3½″.

Locality and Period
New England to Pennsylvania. c. 1870–1910.

Comment
In the late 19th century, hand-thrown pottery gradually declined in popularity, replaced by wares made of glass, tin, or machine-cast ceramic. Many potteries turned to the manufacture of small novelty items to meet this challenge. Miniature spittoons, jugs, and banks were sold in the forerunners of the modern five-and-dime store, and at county fairs as conversation pieces or mantel ornaments. Novelty miniatures were also sold or given away as souvenirs of historic sites or at the annual conventions of fraternal organizations; these commemorative pieces are sometimes dated or bear inscriptions. Since spittoons were so abundant around the turn of the century, it is not surprising that they were popular miniatures, particularly for men's organizations.

Hints for Collectors
Except for glazed examples, which are very uncommon, miniature redware spittoons are inexpensive and relatively easy to find, especially in Maine and Massachusetts, where they may have been produced. The most interesting examples have original gilding and painted decoration.

Spongeware spittoon

Description
Squat, circular spittoon with high waist. Above waist, sides slope in sharply, then out sharply to wide, flaring collar with plain rim. Below waist, sides curve in gently to shaped base. Bottom slightly recessed. Decorated with wide, pale blue band at waist and with thinner bands at neck and below waist. Collar and lower body covered with random sponged designs. *Variations:* Collar may be narrower, less flaring. Base may be plain. Number of bands varies.

Materials and Dimensions
Stoneware with clear alkaline glaze; similar pieces white earthenware with white glaze. Decorated with cobalt blue. Height: 5–6″. Diameter: 7–8″.

Locality and Period
New Jersey west to Ohio. c. 1870–1910.

Comment
Many spittoons have sponged decoration, most often blue sponging on a white ground. Combinations such as green and white or brown and white were less frequently employed. It is likely that the heavy, durable clay body made stoneware particularly suitable for spittoons; the combination of blue and white has always been a favorite with potters.

Hints for Collectors
Almost the only spittoons that are popular are those that have decorative spongework. The best examples have strong, vibrant sponging. Collectors often use them as flowerpots or as vases for cut flowers. A waterproof liner should always be inserted, however, since soil and water can easily damage the glaze. Never drill a drainage hole in the bottom of the spittoon. This kind of alteration substantially reduces value.

Redware spittoon

Description
Circular spittoon with high waist. Above waist, flaring collar.
Below, sides curve out to plain rim. Crudely trimmed, bell-
shaped base. *Variations:* May have taller base. Collar may flare
less widely.

Materials and Dimensions
Red earthenware with shiny black glaze. Molded; earlier
examples sometimes wheel-thrown. Height: 4–5″. Diameter:
6–7″.

Locality and Period
New England to New York. c. 1870–1900.

Comment
These rather crude spittoons were manufactured at many
different eastern potteries during the second half of the 19th
century. Most were molded. According to the price lists of
several New England potteries, they were the most inexpensive
type and often sold for less than half the price of contemporary
Rockingham pieces. No marked examples have been found, and
it is almost impossible to determine where any one piece was
made.

Hints for Collectors
These common and inexpensive spittoons are of little interest to
most collectors, not only because of their original purpose but
also because of their simple shape and lack of decoration.
Accordingly, like bean pots and apple butter pots, they represent
good pieces for the beginning collector or for the collector with a
limited budget. Because they are plentiful, one need not settle
for a cracked or chipped piece.

Flint-enamel footbath

Description
Oblong, tublike vessel. Sides faceted, with 14 vertical panels. Sides curve in from waist to flaring, shaped rim. Below waist, body slopes in to shaped base. 2 bracket-shaped handles curving out from body attached just above waist.

Materials and Dimensions
Yellow earthenware with clear alkaline glaze sprinkled with variously colored metallic oxides. Molded; handles separately shaped and applied. Length: 16–20″. Width: 12–14″. Height: 7–9″.

Locality and Period
United States Pottery Company, Bennington, Vermont. c. 1849–58.

Comment
In America footbaths apparently were made only at the United States Pottery Company and only with a flint-enamel finish. The firm's 1852 price list shows 2 sizes, selling for $24.00 and $26.00 a dozen. Their design, the scalloped rib pattern, is seen in other Bennington wares, such as pitchers and bowls and chamber pots.

Hints for Collectors
Since footbaths are relatively uncommon, they may pass unrecognized by dealers and collectors, who sometimes confuse them with jardinieres or planters. If you are uncertain about the original function of a piece, compare it with the pictures in one of the books on Bennington pottery. A footbath like the one illustrated would be worth more if it was part of a set bearing the same scalloped rib pattern.

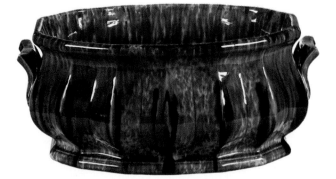

Rockingham foot warmer

Description
Large, hollow, shovel-shaped vessel with 2 foot-size recesses.
Recesses separated by ridge. Short neck has circular spout with
plain rim. Rear curved. *Variations:* Usually barrel-shaped with
flattened rear.

Materials and Dimensions
Yellow earthenware with Rockingham glaze. Molded; spout
separately shaped and applied. Length: 9½–11″. Width: 8–9″.
Depth: 6–7″.

Locality and Period
Ohio. c. 1850–65. Similar pieces from New England south to
Maryland. c. 1845–65.

Comment
In many parts of the country in the mid-19th century, homes
relied on small stoves or fireplaces for heat, making specialized
devices such as foot warmers an important convenience. A foot
warmer was filled with hot water or sand and then used either in
the home or in wagons and carriages. The spout was sealed with
a cork or corn cob, or even with a piece of whittled wood.

Hints for Collectors
Most people don't know what these odd-looking pieces are. They
are not common; barrel-shaped foot warmers are encountered
more frequently. Despite their relative scarcity, they are in
limited demand and may often be purchased quite reasonably.
Most examples are marked on the bottom. Although the example
illustrated is not marked, the history of its ownership strongly
suggests that it was made in Ohio.

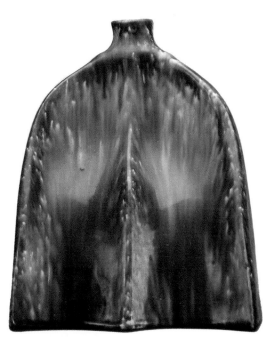

Rockingham bedpan

Description
Large receptacle with sloping, oval body. At one end, curved
tubular spout with shaped rim. Circular opening, opposite spout,
below which body terminates in blunt, rectangular foot.
Variations: May be squatter. Spout may be shorter. May have
ring at base of spout.

Materials and Dimensions
Yellow earthenware; exterior with sponged Rockingham glaze;
interior with clear alkaline glaze. Molded; spout separately
shaped and applied. Length: 14–16″. Width: 10–12″. Depth: 5–6″.

Locality and Period
New England west to Ohio, south to Maryland. c. 1845–1900.

Comment
Rockingham bedpans were being made as early as 1849 by the
United States Pottery Company in Bennington, Vermont, and
some bear the "1849" mark of that firm. In 1896 the Syracuse,
New York, stoneware company sold them at $9.00 per dozen, a
dollar more than was charged for the same dozen in yellowware
without the Rockingham glaze. They were made in quantity for
hospital and home use.

Hints for Collectors
Bedpans are now often used as planters by collectors. Despite
such ingenuity such pieces are considered unattractive and are
not popular. Good examples may be purchased at reasonable
prices. Of marked Rockinghamware, bedpans and spittoons are
the least costly. A marked example can be helpful in studying the
glazes and clay types used by a pottery.

Yellowware bedpan

Description
Large receptacle with sloping, oval body. At one end, curved
tubular spout with shaped rim curves up from body. Large, oval
opening above blunt, rectangular foot. *Variations:* May have
large ring around base of spout. May be larger. Spout may be
longer.

Materials and Dimensions
Yellow earthenware with clear alkaline glaze. Molded; spout
separately shaped and applied; early examples hand-shaped.
Length: 17–19″. Width: 10–12″. Depth: 4–6″.

Locality and Period
New England west to Ohio, south to Maryland. c. 1860–1910.

Comment
Although redware bedpans appear in price lists dating from as
early as the 1820s, few of these pieces remain. Most were made
of yellow earthenware, apparently in large quantities. Some have
a Rockingham glaze, while still others were made of white
earthenware. By 1900, most were made of enameled tin or glass.
Ceramic bedpans were fairly expensive, both because of the
quantity of clay used and because they were difficult to
manufacture. They were cast in 2 separate molds and then joined
together. Rarely marked by potteries, it is seldom possible to
determine where they were manufactured.

Hints for Collectors
Surprisingly common, such pieces are understandably of little
interest to most collectors and are consequently quite
inexpensive. Yet every comprehensive yellowware collection
should include one.

Miscellaneous Objects

Not only did American potteries produce countless types of jars, jugs, crocks, and tableware, they also manufactured numerous miscellaneous objects that range from trinket boxes to doorknobs. Some of the widely diverse pieces included here, such as pipes, are plentiful and inexpensive, while others, such as a Rockingham desk set, are rare and costly.

Ceramic desk accessories were produced by many companies during the 19th century. Ink was customarily stored in a large master bottle with a pouring spout, which was usually made of stoneware. Ink was then poured into small individual ink bottles or inkwells. The inkwells have a large central hole for ink storage and several smaller holes in which to place quill pens. To blot the ink after writing, it was a common practice to sprinkle fine white sand on the page. The ceramic vessels that held the sand were called sanders; rare today, they date mostly from before 1850. By then they had been replaced by tin and wooden sanders, which were easier to fill. Ink bottles, inkwells, and sanders are usually simple and undecorated, yet some potteries also produced elaborate desk accessories. In the desk set featured here, inkwell and sander are nested in one piece that also provides storage space for sealing wax and other writing necessities. This rare desk set typifies the specialized, multipurpose objects that became common in the second half of the 19th century.

Both simple and fancy banks were produced throughout the 19th century. Despite the fact that most had to be broken to retrieve the savings they contained, many have survived, indicating how common they once must have been. The simplest, made of stoneware or redware, are inexpensive today, while those made of porcelain or decorated with spongework cost substantially more.

Other common 19th-century ceramic objects are tiles. By the end of the century, many companies specialized in their manufacture, while others made them in limited quantities. Some examples are plain and functional with simple glazes, while others have elaborate molded and glazed decoration. Among the most interesting pieces are large panels consisting of numerous tiles that together form a picture or abstract design. Also in demand are tiles that commemorate historical events or figures and those that bear the mark of a pottery.

This section also features inexpensive doorknobs and ashtrays as well as elegant porcelain trinket boxes. Together these pieces are representative of the vast range of ceramic products manufactured by American companies in the past two centuries.

Art pottery tile

Description
Large, rectangular tile with embossed scene of forest and 2 crows. Word "ROOKWOOD" above crow at base. Decorator's initials "ST" at lower left. *Variations:* Other Rookwood tiles with crow motif have single bird against undefined background above word "ROOKWOOD."

Materials and Dimensions
Coarse white earthenware hand-decorated with polychrome glaze; back unglazed. Molded. Height: 14½–15″. Width: 7–8″.

Locality and Period
Rookwood Pottery, Cincinnati, Ohio. c. 1903–13.

Comment
In 1880 Maria Longworth Nichols founded Rookwood, one of the earliest and most famous American art potteries. She took the firm's name and logo from the crows, or rooks, that filled the woods near her father's country home. From 1902 until 1930 Rookwood produced mantel, fireplace, and wall tiles. Among the best known are the tiles made in 1903 for the walls of the New York City subway system. Unlike most art pottery tiles, some that Rookwood produced were as tall as 18″.

Hints for Collectors
Most of the decorators at Rookwood marked the pieces they painted. The initials on the tile illustrated are those of Sallie Toohey, a decorator at Rookwood from 1887 to 1931. Although the mark of a well-known decorator enhances the value of a piece, age, scarcity, condition, and artistic merit are also important in arriving at a price.

Art pottery tile

Description
Thick, square tile with representation of a ship with 3 sails blowing in wind and long pennant flying from central mast. Sea has undulating, white-capped waves.

Materials and Dimensions
Coarse white earthenware hand-decorated with polychrome matt glaze; back unglazed. Molded. Height: 6–6¼".

Locality and Period
Grueby Faience and Tile Company, Boston. c. 1900–10. Similar pieces from New England to the Midwest. c. 1895–1940.

Comment
An important early American art pottery, the Grueby Faience and Tile Company was established in 1897 by William H. Grueby. Previously, Grueby had worked for the Low Art Tile Works of Chelsea, Massachusetts, and tiles remained among the most important of his firm's products. Grueby tiles and other wares are characterized by simple, flowing forms and rich matt glazes, which are typically dark blue and earth colors.

Hints for Collectors
Grueby tiles bring good prices. Many have impressed marks, usually either "GRUEBY" in a rectangle or "GRUEBY TILE BOSTON" in a circle. Since the rich, thick glaze and the somewhat abstract floral or figural decoration are so characteristic, unmarked pieces can often be identified by comparing them with identified examples. Look for these tiles in the Boston area, where many are still in homes.

Description
Square tile with overall embossed design of flowers and leaves.
Raised mark "A.E.T. Co." on back.

Materials and Dimensions
White earthenware with mustard-colored glaze; back unglazed.
Molded. Height: 5–7″.

Locality and Period
American Encaustic Tiling Company, Zanesville, Ohio. c. 1881–
1935. Similar pieces from New York west to Ohio. c. 1880–1940.

Comment
For many years the American Encaustic Tiling Company was
one of the largest producers of American art tiles; by the time it
closed in 1935, it had manufactured thousands of them. Some of
its tiles were unglazed, others glazed in a solid color, and still
others decorated with complex designs inspired by subjects as
diverse as ancient legends and modern American industry. Most
of the tiles were marked with one of several variations of the
company's initials.

Hints for Collectors
In addition to its decorative tiles, the American Encaustic Tiling
Company also produced souvenir and commemorative tiles
bearing the likenesses of such figures as Admiral George Dewey,
William Jennings Bryan, and President William McKinley. Other
potteries manufactured similar pieces. These commemorative
tiles were made in limited editions for short periods of time and
consequently are both harder to find and more valuable than
most tiles. Further, tiles featuring well-known figures appeal not
only to pottery collectors but also to those who specialize in
miscellaneous commemorative objects.

Art pottery tile

Description
Square tile with overall embossed design of an animal, probably a rabbit, set against a leafy background. Back impressed "MORAVIAN."

Materials and Dimensions
Red earthenware with cream and green glaze; back unglazed. Molded. Height: 4–6″.

Locality and Period
Moravian Pottery and Tile Works, Doylestown, Pennsylvania. c. 1910–25. Similar pieces from New York and New Jersey west to Ohio. c. 1900–40.

Comment
In the early 1900s Henry Chapman Mercer established the Moravian Pottery and Tile Works. He took the firm name from the Moravian decorative motifs he used on some of the early wares. In addition, the pottery used medieval, Indian, English, and European designs to adorn fireplace, floor, and wall tiles. It also produced large decorative panels comprising many individual tiles that together created a picture. Early tiles were made of red earthenware; later tiles had a white earthenware body.

Hints for Collectors
Since most tiles have floral or geometric designs, pictorial examples like the one illustrated here are especially desirable. Even more valuable are the large decorative panels, most of which were installed around fireplaces or on walls. Many of these panels were destroyed when the buildings in which they were placed were torn down. The "MORAVIAN" mark on the back of these tiles is sometimes accompanied by Mercer's initials, "HCM."

Rockingham desk set

Description
Tower-shaped desk set consisting of 4 stacking units. Large
bottom unit has central inkwell and small hole for quill pen in
each corner. Smaller unit above has square hole for sealing wax
or stamps. Third unit, a sander, has drilled holes. Top (not
illustrated) is hollow and steeple-shaped. All units have corner
posts and are shaped at top and base; middle units have attached
finials; bottom unit has short, stumplike legs.

Materials and Dimensions
Yellow earthenware with Rockingham glaze. Molded. Height:
12–13″. Width: 5½–5¾″.

Locality and Period
Attributed to the United States Pottery Company, Bennington,
Vermont. c. 1854–55.

Comment
Since only a very few such pieces are known, this desk set was
probably made to order rather than as a standard production
item. Small inkstands were also sometimes made to order, as
were such things as water coolers and miniatures. Because of
their fragile nature, most of these desk sets are damaged in some
way; the finials, for example, are usually broken or chipped.

Hints for Collectors
Although sets like this seldom appear on the market, it is
important to be familiar with them, especially since they consist
of several sections. Occasionally one or more of the units become
available. Since very few of these sets were made, even isolated
units are worth buying.

Rockingham and flint-enamel book flasks

Description
Whiskey flasks shaped like books. Top inset slightly and has circular spout with rolled rim. Rim has circle of raised dots around base. Spine of larger flask impressed "DEPARTED SPIRITS"; spine of smaller flask impressed "HERMIT'S COMPANION." Bottom of small flask impressed "Lyman Fenton & Co./Fentons/ENAMEL/ PATENTED/1849/BENNINGTON, Vt." *Variations:* Inscriptions vary.

Materials and Dimensions
Yellow earthenware; larger flask with Rockingham glaze; smaller flask with clear alkaline glaze sprinkled with metallic oxides. Molded; spout separately shaped and applied. Height: 6–8″. Width: 3¾–5¾″. Depth: 2–3″.

Locality and Period
United States Pottery Company, Bennington, Vermont. c. 1849–58. Similar pieces from Ohio and from England. c. 1840–70.

Comment
Intended for the storage of whiskey, book flasks often had humorous titles, such as those seen here. Others that were popular include "Bennington Ladies," "Suffering and Death," and "Life of Kossuth." Although the larger of the flasks illustrated does not have a pottery mark, it can be attributed to the United States Pottery Company because of its similarity to marked Bennington examples. These flasks were produced in the pint and 2-quart sizes illustrated and in a 4-quart size.

Hints for Collectors
Book flasks made at Bennington always have a circle of beaded dots about the spout. These dots distinguish Bennington pieces from those made elsewhere in the United States or in England. And, of course, any flask with a title like "Bennington Ladies" may safely be attributed to that pottery.

Description

Doughnut-shaped vessel decorated with notch carving. Body square in cross section. Short, square neck with chamfered edges rises to plain rim. Short, rectangular legs set at angle to body. *Variations:* Most ring flasks are round in cross section. Most lack legs.

Materials and Dimensions

Red earthenware with clear lead glaze; similar pieces stoneware with salt glaze. Wheel-thrown; neck and legs separately shaped and applied. Diameter: 4–8″. Depth: 1–2″.

Locality and Period

New England west to Pennsylvania, south to the Carolinas. c. 1790–1840.

Comment

Ring flasks do not appear in the price lists of early potteries and were apparently never common. They held water or spirits and could be taken to the field or the workshop like a canteen. Because they were circular they could be carried over an arm or looped over the pommel of a saddle. In the South, stoneware ring flasks were made for use on saddles even at the end of the 19th century. After 1850 redware examples were no longer produced, perhaps because they were too fragile to be practical.

Hints for Collectors

Redware ring flasks are coveted by collectors, and examples in good condition often bring substantial prices. Yet because of their rarity, they may be passed over by those unfamiliar with the form. Learn to spot unusual pieces; you may be able to purchase one for much less than its market value.

Stoneware ink bottles

Description
Small, cylindrical bottles with slightly angled shoulder and short neck with rolled rim. Plain base. *Variations:* Some examples lack rolled rim.

Materials and Dimensions
Stoneware with light brown glaze; similar pieces with tan or salt glaze. Molded; early examples wheel-thrown. Height: 3–6″. Diameter: 2–3″.

Locality and Period
New England west to Ohio, south to Maryland. c. 1830–80. Similar pieces from England. c. 1830–80.

Comment
These small, individual ink bottles were designed to be inkwells as well as storage bottles. Intended to be used until the ink was gone and then thrown away, they sold for a few cents a dozen and were made in large quantities. Larger ink bottles with spouts, called master inks, stored ink until it was poured into inkwells. Both types of bottles were made at most eastern and midwestern potteries. Since they were nearly always unmarked, it is extremely difficult to determine their origin.

Hints for Collectors
Although American and English ink bottles are quite similar, the latter can sometimes be distinguished by a potter's mark, often that of the pottery in Lambeth, which reads "LAMBETH POTTERY" impressed in an oval. Ink bottles are small and attractive and popular among collectors, at least in part because they are so practical and inexpensive. They make excellent containers for herbs and spices.

Spongeware bank

Description

Small, jug-shaped bank with short neck and plain rim. U-shaped projection on each side of shoulder; wire bail handle with wooden grip passes through projections. Vertical slot on shoulder. Plain base. Decorated with 2 thin, blue bands and spongework.

Materials and Dimensions

Stoneware with white Bristol glaze; similar pieces ironstone. Decorated with cobalt blue. Molded. Height: 3¾–4¼". Diameter: 2½–3".

Locality and Period

New Jersey west to Ohio, south to Maryland. c. 1880–1920.

Comment

Jug-shaped banks decorated with spongework are uncommon and may have been made only to order. They are never marked and could have been made at any of the numerous potteries that produced spongeware. The wire and wood handle seen here helps to date this bank, since similar handles were used on many housewares such as pails and kettles around the turn of the century.

Hints for Collectors

Blue and white spongeware is in great demand, and a rare form like the bank illustrated may bring a surprisingly high price, even with minor cracks in the glaze caused by age. Many pieces that originally came with wire bail handles have lost them over the years. Since it is easy and inexpensive to manufacture a reasonable facsimile, pieces without their handles are still desirable.

Porcelain bank

Description
Large bank with bulbous center and tall, shaped finial. Finial has
ring-shaped projections separated by reel-shaped depressions
and acorn-shaped tip. Horizontal slot near top of shoulder.
Lower body curves in to thin ring, then out to flaring base with 4
holes. Body decorated with applied face. Bottom incised
"Benjamin Colvell/Bennington, Vt."

Materials and Dimensions
Porcelain with clear alkaline glaze. Wheel-thrown; finial lathe-
turned; applied decoration molded. Height: 7–7½". Diameter:
4½–5".

Locality and Period
Attributed to the United States Pottery Company, Bennington,
Vermont. c. 1849–58.

Comment
Porcelain banks were made to order, probably as gifts for
children. They are rare, since porcelain was too expensive to be
used for something a child might break open to retrieve a few
pennies. Banks were often incised with the name of the owner,
usually on the bottom. Since no potter by the name of Benjamin
Colvell is known to have worked at Bennington, the name on the
example illustrated is probably that of the child for whom this
bank was made.

Hints for Collectors
This piece would be a choice addition to any bank collection, not
only because porcelain banks are rare, but also because the
Bennington inscription ensures that it was made in America.
Without the inscription, it might easily be taken for a European
piece because of the applied decoration and elaborate finial.

Description
Rounded bank with buttonlike finial and 2 incised lines encircling shoulder. Long, horizontal slot cut in body just below finial. Below waist, body curves in to stumplike base. *Variations:* Banks may be jug- or log-cabin-shaped. May be decorated.

Materials and Dimensions
Stoneware; exterior with light brown glaze; similar pieces with salt glaze and sometimes with cobalt-blue decoration. Wheel-thrown. Height: 3–4″. Diameter: 3–3½″.

Locality and Period
New England west to Ohio, south to Virginia. c. 1820–70.

Comment
Many banks must have been made in the 19th century. To retrieve the large copper pennies that were usually stored in these banks, they had to be broken, yet a large number survive today. Stoneware banks were less varied than their redware counterparts, and most seen today are round or jug-shaped. The few examples that bear children's names were probably made to order or as gifts for members of the potter's family.

Hints for Collectors
Banks are easy to store and display, and make an interesting collection. Since most stoneware examples have a brown glaze, look for those with a salt glaze. Variations in size and shape are also desirable, particularly such unusual forms as log cabins with removable roofs. These, however, are generally expensive. Dealers who specialize in miniatures, novelties, and toys often carry banks. They may also be found in collections of larger stoneware.

Redware bank

Description
Small, thin vessel with gently sloping sides and simple peaked finial. Shoulder, defined by coggled line, has vertical slot. Lower body tapers to chamfered base. *Variations:* May be squatter or jug-shaped. May be painted or dated, or inscribed with names or initials.

Materials and Dimensions
Red earthenware; unglazed. Wheel-thrown. Height: 3–4″. Diameter: 2½–3½″.

Locality and Period
New England west to Missouri, south to Virginia. c. 1800–1900.

Comment
Simple penny banks such as the one seen here were made by many potteries, either to order or at special times of the year, like Christmas, when they were in demand. In its 1837 price list, the firm of Clark and Fox in Athens, New York, referred to them as "money jugs," while other shops called them "banks" or "safes." They seldom sold for more than a few pennies each, and were meant to be broken to remove the savings they held. That so many have survived indicates the large numbers that must have been produced.

Hints for Collectors
These plain banks are among the least costly of all redware. Although they are not true miniatures, they fit well in a collection of redware miniatures. Look for interesting examples. Some owners added gilded or painted decoration, and some banks were inscribed and dated.

Rockingham doorknobs

Description
At left, 8-sided doorknob with rounded sides and flat top. Short, columnar shaft and flaring base separated by molded rings. Hole for iron shaft in base; smaller hole for screw in side. At right, circular, mushroom-shaped doorknob with rounded top. Flat back with hole for iron shaft. *Variations:* Columnar shaft may be shorter.

Materials and Dimensions
Yellow earthenware with Rockingham glaze; similar pieces with solid brown glaze. Molded. Left, height: 1¾–2¼″; diameter: 2¼–2¾″. Right, height: 1–1½″; diameter: 2¼–2¾″.

Locality and Period
Massachusetts west to Ohio, south to Maryland. c. 1845–1900.

Comment
Doorknobs with a Rockingham glaze were produced at many potteries and for a long period of time. Since they were never marked, it is often impossible to determine where they were made. Like modern doorknobs, they came in sets of 2, which were connected by an iron shaft and held in place by screws. Examples with columnar shafts are less common than the mushroom-shaped ones.

Hints for Collectors
Doorknobs are by far the least expensive of all Rockingham-glazed objects and can often be picked up at junk shops or even found on doors in old houses. Anyone restoring a Victorian house would find these knobs a handsome, authentic addition to its interior.

Stoneware sander

Description
Small sander with flaring, cup-shaped top. Top, with plain rim and 15 small holes at center, rests on hollow pedestal with swelling waist. Above waist, body tapers to thick neck. Below waist, body tapers, then slopes out to shaped base. *Variations:* May be plainer and shaped like an hourglass. Number of holes varies.

Materials and Dimensions
Stoneware glazed with light brown Albany slip; similar pieces with salt glaze and decorated with cobalt-blue slip. Wheel-thrown. Height: 3–4″. Diameter: 2½–3½″.

Locality and Period
New England south to Pennsylvania and the Carolinas. c. 1790–1840.

Comment
These vessels held fine white sand, which was sprinkled over a page to blot the ink left by a quill pen. Examples excavated at the Moravian settlement in Bethabara, North Carolina, are believed to date from the 18th century. After 1850 tin and wood sanders replaced those made of stoneware, perhaps because stoneware sanders were so difficult to fill: The sand had to be poured through the little holes in the cuplike section.

Hints for Collectors
Sanders are hard to come by today, and even examples with minor damage like the chipped rim seen here are worth purchasing. Since most were made in New England and Pennsylvania, look for them there. Advertising in local newspapers is often a good way to search for unusual pieces. Since even pottery collectors may be unfamiliar with sanders such as this one, be sure to describe what you are looking for.

Description
Small, circular inkwell with straight sides and plain rim. Central hole surrounded by 3 smaller holes. Interior well cone-shaped. *Variations:* Number of small holes varies. May be decorated.

Materials and Dimensions
Red earthenware with green, orange, and brown glaze; clear lead glaze more common. Wheel-thrown; top separately shaped and applied; holes made with stylus or dowel. Some later examples molded. Height: 1½–2″. Diameter: 2½–3½″.

Locality and Period
New England south to the Carolinas, west to Ohio. c. 1790–1870.

Comment
Redware inkwells, not as common as similar pieces in stoneware, seldom appear in potters' inventories or price lists, and were probably made only to special order. Ink was poured into the well through the large center hole, and one or more quill pens were stored in the surrounding smaller holes, which were not filled with ink.

Hints for Collectors
Pottery marks on these wells are almost unknown. However, since they were usually made to order, redware inkwells may be decorated, or incised with names or dates. Consequently, they are very desirable pieces. Many are chipped around the rim, but because of their bulky construction they are seldom seriously damaged. If they are shallow, rim chips will not greatly diminish the value of these inkwells.

Stoneware inkwell

Description
Circular container with straight sides and large hole in center of top. On each side of central hole, a small hole. Incised circle on top. Interior of well cone-shaped. *Variations:* Some inkwells are decorated with other incised designs or names; some are highlighted with cobalt blue. Top may have 2–3 incised concentric circles. Number of small holes varies.

Materials and Dimensions
Stoneware with salt glaze; similar examples with brown glaze. Wheel-thrown. Height: 1–2″. Diameter: 2–4″.

Locality and Period
New England west to Ohio, south to the Carolinas. c. 1770–1860.

Comment
The typical pottery inkwell had a large center hole into which ink was poured. Quill pens were stored in the small holes around it. Larger, rectangular pieces, termed inkstands, might contain 2 inkwells and a pen rest. These are now quite rare. By the mid-19th century, inkwells and inkstands of stoneware and redware were almost completely replaced by less expensive glass, tin, and porcelain ones.

Hints for Collectors
Inkwells are interesting small collectibles. Plain examples, like the one illustrated, are quite reasonable, but pieces with incised or blue decoration bring high prices. Occasionally one will see European, usually German, stoneware inkwells. Even if not marked they can be distinguished by their more ornate form and more extensive use of blue decoration.

Porcelain trinket boxes

Description
Small containers with matching lids. Containers have slightly curving sides and shaped rim and base. Sides embossed with roses. Lids decorated with embossed flowers and leaves; lid at left also embellished with applied bunch of grapes and leaves. *Variations:* Embossed decoration varies.

Materials and Dimensions
Left, porcelain partially glazed with blue slip. Right, parian porcelain. Molded; grapes and leaves separately shaped and applied. Length: 5–5½". Width: 2¾–3". Height: 2¼–2¾".

Locality and Period
Attributed to the United States Pottery Company, Bennington, Vermont. c. 1850–58. Similar pieces from New York, New Jersey, and Ohio, and from England. c. 1850–90.

Comment
Trinket boxes were common 19th-century boudoir and bathroom accessories and were made in large quantities both here and abroad. It was customary to make a number of boxes using the same mold, then to decorate them in various ways. Here, for example, the basic shape of the boxes is identical, but one has been decorated with blue and white, and has been further embellished with the applied grapes and leaves.

Hints for Collectors
Since neither American nor European examples were marked, it is difficult to determine where trinket boxes were made. The boxes shown here are attributed to the United States Pottery Company because their basic pattern is among those made by the firm. Of the 130 basic patterns that have been traced to the United States Pottery Company, almost all were varied by the addition of color and applied decoration.

Flint-enamel toilet box

Description
Oblong box with matching lid, both decorated with alternating thick and thin embossed vertical ribs. Flaring rim. Sides of box curve in to central depression. Shaped base. Interior divided into 3 sections by 2 low, scalloped dividers. Lid curves up to flat top with ringlike handle. *Variations:* May lack ribs. May have octagonal handle.

Materials and Dimensions
Yellow earthenware with clear alkaline glaze sprinkled with manganese-brown and copper-green metallic oxides; similar pieces with Rockingham glaze. Molded. Length: 7½–8½". Width: 2¾–3¼". Height: 3–3½".

Locality and Period
Attributed to the United States Pottery Company, Bennington, Vermont. c. 1849–58. Similar pieces from Vermont west to Ohio, south to Maryland. c. 1845–75.

Comment
These boxes held various toilet articles and were placed on the dresser or washstand. Similar ironstone and porcelain boxes are known; these and flint-enamel examples often came with matching pieces, including additional storage boxes and powder boxes. Some sets included "hair receivers," boxes that stored hair that fell out during brushing. When enough had accumulated, it was fashioned into hair pieces or jewelry.

Hints for Collectors
Although toilet boxes resemble covered butter dishes, they can easily be distinguished by their interior dividers. Before you purchase any covered piece, make sure that the lid matches the body in glaze and surface decoration.

Art pottery ashtray

Description
Low ashtray has wide, shaped rim with groove at each corner. Lower body curves in to plain base. Bottom impressed "Van Briggle/Colo. Sp'gs."

Materials and Dimensions
White earthenware with blue matt glaze. Molded. Length: 6½–7″. Width: 3¾–4¼″. Height: 1–1¼″.

Locality and Period
Van Briggle Pottery, Colorado Springs, Colorado. c. 1920–60.

Comment
Ashtrays became common after World War I, when cigarette smoking became popular. Among the most interesting are those produced by well-known companies like Van Briggle. Founded in 1901, the Van Briggle Pottery is still in business today, although it has changed management several times. Most of its wares are vaguely Art Nouveau in style and have distinctive matt finishes. The glaze on the ashtray illustrated is characteristic of those used by the Van Briggle Company. It is called Turquoise Ming.

Hints for Collectors
Van Briggle pottery is among the most popular of all American art pottery. Most pieces are relatively easy to obtain because they were mass produced in molds. Early pieces with glazes that were used for only a short time, such as a mustard-colored glaze, or those with the "AA" mark, are the most valuable. Dated examples are worth more than undated pieces, especially those that were made before 1910.

Stoneware pipes

Description
Stoneware pipe heads, each with cylindrical, reeded body rising
to shaped ring beneath plain rim. Curved foot terminates in
short hexagonal stem with swelled end. Circular hole in end for
pipe reed. *Variations:* Pipe heads are made in many different
forms, including human and animal heads.

Materials and Dimensions
Stoneware; at left with salt glaze; at right with brown glaze.
Molded. Height: 1½–1¾″. Diameter of bowl: 1–1¼″.

Locality and Period
New England west to Missouri and throughout the South.
c. 1800–80.

Comment
Pipe heads like these were made in vast quantities during most
of the 19th century, a time when nearly all men smoked pipes.
Molds for such pieces were small and so were carried easily by
potters throughout most of the eastern United States.
Differences in glazes and stoneware clay composition led to a
wide variety of colors. Shapes ranged from simple, geometric
forms, like those shown here, to realistic human or animal heads.
Many pipe heads have been excavated at the sites of potteries
and 19th-century settlements.

Hints for Collectors
Pipe collectors are an active and growing group. Simple pipes are
still inexpensive and relatively common, but as interest in all
pipes increases, these too are bound to rise in price. Since the
variety of stoneware pipe heads is almost endless, a large and
varied collection can easily be amassed.

Flowerpots, Vases, and Candleholders

Most of the objects in this section are decorative, and designed to hold flowers and plants. Candleholders, both plain and elaborate, and sometimes combined with vases, are also included here.

Flowerpots

Cone-shaped flowerpots, made of red earthenware and stoneware, were a common product of many potteries after 1850; they were made in New England and throughout much of the South and Midwest. Many redware examples were unglazed, resembling the flowerpots produced today, but examples with a clear lead-glazed exterior are also plentiful. Stoneware flowerpots, on the other hand, were often decorated with cobalt-blue or brown slip. Both came with and without attached saucers.

Vases

Vases dating from the first half of the 19th century were typically red or yellow earthenware with a rich glaze. Their shapes frequently resembled contemporary glass forms, and like drinking goblets, they often had a stem and foot. Simple redware vases and more elaborate wall pockets for plants or cut flowers were produced in Pennsylvania and Virginia during the second half of the 19th century. Most such pieces were painted with slip, and some had more elaborate, applied decoration.

Vases came in a variety of shapes and styles, including exotically decorated Victorian examples and massive porcelain commemorative pieces produced from 1860 to 1890. These vases were usually one of a kind and are rare today. More common are the small, parian porcelain figural vases made in both America and Europe; so similar are American and European examples that it is often impossible to distinguish them.

By far the most numerous vases available to collectors are those made by art potteries in the late 19th and early 20th centuries. Their popularity reflected the rise of a well-to-do middle class who had grown accustomed to having cut flowers adorn their homes. Some examples, in the Art Nouveau style, are naturalistic, while others, in the Art Deco mode, are streamlined and modern. Rounded, bowl-like vases were also produced. Decoration ranged from hand painting and polychrome glazes to embossed and incised surfaces. Clays included stoneware, white and red earthenware, and porcelain.

Planters and Jardinieres

Art pottery planters and jardinieres, a related form, first appeared in the late 19th century. Often oblong or rectangular, they are generally larger than contemporary vases. Commonly made of red or white earthenware, they might have heavily embossed or polychrome-glazed surfaces.

Candlesticks

The earliest American candlesticks are extremely rare today; made of red earthenware, they were purely utilitarian. By 1850 candles had become less a necessity than a decorative accessory, often placed on a table or sideboard. Rockingham candlesticks, based on contemporary silver forms, were made at mid-century; in the late 19th and early 20th centuries, many decorative candleholders were produced by various art potteries. Forms varied greatly, ranging from a pair of simple matching candlesticks to pieces that combined a bud or flower vase with attached candleholders. Such pieces provided an attractive centerpiece, and remain popular today. Although examples by individual makers are rare, many of these art pottery forms were made in quantity, and can easily be found.

Art pottery vase

Description
Urn-shaped vase with high shoulder from which sides curve in to wide neck, then out to rolled, collarlike rim. Lower body tapers gradually to plain base. *Variations:* Shape varies.

Materials and Dimensions
Several types of earthenware clay mixed together, most often blue, brown, pink, cream, and green; exterior unglazed; interior with clear alkaline glaze. Wheel-thrown. Height: 4–9″. Diameter: 2½–5″.

Locality and Period
Niloak Pottery, Benton, Arkansas. c. 1909–42. Similar pieces from Gay Head Pottery, Martha's Vineyard, Massachusetts. c. 1879–80.

Comment
Niloak pottery is unlike most art pottery because it retained the natural colors of the baked clay rather than utilizing colored glazes. Clays of different hues were mixed together and then turned so that they formed a spiral design. The surface was left unglazed and sanded to a satiny finish. Both the urn shape of this vase and the marbleized effect of the clays are reminiscent of ancient pottery.

Hints for Collectors
Niloak is often impressed "NILOAK" or has a paper label reading "NILOAK POTTERY." However, unmarked examples can be recognized readily by the streaks of colored clay in their bodies. The only similar art pottery was made at the Gay Head Pottery on Martha's Vineyard; it is much rarer but easy to identify. Sun baked rather than fired, it is completely unglazed. Niloak is relatively common, still inexpensive, and popular with collectors.

Art pottery vase

Description
Massive vase with sides curving out to shoulder embossed with folded, leaflike forms. Deeply indented neck and bulbous rim. Lower body swells slightly above plain base. 7 long, handlelike strips of clay stretch down sides, attached at rim and above base. Bottom impressed with stylized lotus flower circled by "GRUEBY. POTTERY. BOSTON. U.S.A." *Variations:* Grueby vases may have only 5 clay strips on sides.

Materials and Dimensions
White earthenware with green matt glaze; similar examples with yellow, brown, gray, blue, or purple glaze. Wheel-thrown; strips of clay separately shaped and applied. Height: 10½–11″. Diameter: 8–9″.

Locality and Period
Grueby Pottery, Boston. c. 1900–10. Similar examples from New York west to Ohio. c. 1890–1930.

Comment
Grueby was one of the first American art potteries to popularize matt glazes rather than the somewhat gaudy, shiny glazes popular at the turn of the century. The duller glazes were combined with lush, naturalistic Art Nouveau shapes and hand-formed details to produce extremely sophisticated ware.

Hints for Collectors
Marked examples of Grueby art pottery are expensive and in great demand. Take care, however, not to pay high prices for similar-looking, unmarked examples. From 1905 to about 1920, many potteries copied the Grueby style and its glazes, often producing inferior, mass-produced pieces. Most authentic Grueby art pottery is clearly impressed on the bottom with one of the firm's several marks.

300 Art pottery vase

Description
Squat, ovoid vase with high shoulder that curves abruptly to plain rim. Below shoulder, sides taper to recessed base. Surface covered with incised, painted moose skulls arranged in a band encircling body.

Materials and Dimensions
Porcelain with polychrome glaze. Wheel-thrown. Height: 11¾–12″. Diameter: 9½–10″.

Locality and Period
Adelaide Alsop Robineau, Syracuse, New York. c. 1905–10.

Comment
One of the most important American art potters, Robineau is best known for her unusual decorating techniques, which involved the carving and cutting away of dry but unfired porcelain bodies to create monumental, sculptural pieces. Her most famous work is the so-called scarab vase, housed in the Everson Museum in Syracuse, New York, which reputedly took her 1,000 hours to carve. Never a success commercially, Robineau was primarily a teacher and innovator whose ideas influenced a generation of potters.

Hints for Collectors
Although any identified piece by Adelaide Alsop Robineau would be worth a great deal of money, most art pottery made by studio potters rather than larger commercial firms attracts little collector attention. This is primarily because studio potters produced a small quantity of one-of-a-kind pieces. Be wary of investing heavily in such pieces unless they are the work of important artists like Robineau. Because there are so few, there may not be enough records of auction and dealer sales to substantiate your high price later on should you decide to resell.

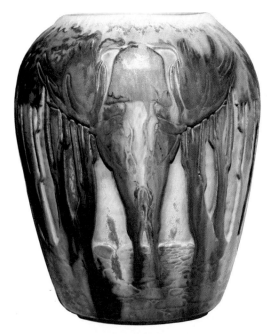

Art pottery vase

Description
Tall vase with sides that curve gracefully out to high shoulder, then in to narrow collar and plain rim. Plain base. Bottom marked with an "N" within a "C." Decorated with incised and painted landscape of tall cypress trees against a lighter background. *Variations:* Shape varies, including more squat and Oriental forms. Decoration varies and may include other forms, such as oaks, magnolias, and water lilies.

Materials and Dimensions
White earthenware with blue-green glaze over yellow glaze. Wheel-thrown. Height: 10–11″. Diameter: 4–5″.

Locality and Period
Newcomb College Pottery, New Orleans. c. 1905–10. Similar pieces from New York west to Ohio. c. 1900–15.

Comment
One of the most successful and most unusual of American art potteries, Newcomb was founded in 1895 as part of Sophie Newcomb College, now a branch of Tulane University. Pieces, some made by other potters, were decorated by the students, who received 50 percent of the profits. Most pre-1920 examples, like the vase illustrated, have a blue-green glaze and are in an Art Nouveau style. Decoration features flowers and trees found in the vicinity of the school.

Hints for Collectors
Newcomb College pottery is eagerly sought by collectors, not only for its beauty but also because prior to 1920 all pieces were one of a kind. Almost all were marked with the initials of the school as well as with impressions indicating such things as clay and glaze type and the production code number.

Art pottery vase

Description
Vase with sides that slope out to high shoulder and in to wide neck with plain rim. Plain base. Entire body, including bottom, covered with decorative pattern of stylized leaves. *Variations:* Decoration varies, including portraits of Indians and other pictorial designs.

Materials and Dimensions
Hand-painted white earthenware; exterior with iridescent polychrome glaze; interior with rich pink glaze. Wheel-thrown. Height: 8¼–8¾″. Diameter: 4¼–4¾″.

Locality and Period
Rookwood Pottery, Cincinnati, Ohio. c. 1925–26. Similar pieces from Massachusetts west to Ohio. c. 1920–30.

Comment
This piece bears the name in Japanese script of Kataro Shirayamadani, a Japanese artist who worked at Rookwood from 1887 to 1915 and again from 1925 to 1948. Shirayamadani introduced Oriental decoration and Japanese motifs to Rookwood during the firm's most vital period. Americans were very interested in Oriental styles at this time, and Shirayamadani's work was well received.

Hints for Collectors
The mark or signature of a well-known decorator on a piece of art pottery will greatly enhance its value. Even a damaged example bearing the mark of a renowned decorator will bring more than an unsigned piece in mint condition. Collectors should familiarize themselves with the marks of important decorators; most of these marks will be found on the bottom of a piece.

Art pottery vase

Description
Elongated vessel with sides that slope slightly in to curving shoulder and narrow neck with slightly flaring rim. Lower body tapers gradually to plain base. Surface decorated with hand-painted design of fish and seaweed. *Variations:* Bodies are usually more rounded, less elongated.

Materials and Dimensions
Hand-painted white earthenware with polychrome glaze. Wheel-thrown. Height: 14–15″. Diameter: 2¾–3¼″.

Locality and Period
Rookwood Pottery, Cincinnati, Ohio. c. 1893. Similar pieces from the East and Midwest. c. 1890–1910.

Comment
The elongated shape and the decoration of the vase illustrated indicate the tremendous influence Japanese design had on American art. It was transmitted through Oriental prints and bronzes, as well as ceramics. The Rookwood firm employed Japanese potters and decorators to promote and teach their native decorative styles. The fish seen here are carp, which are native to the Orient.

Hints for Collectors
Rookwood decorators often signed or initialed their work, and a piece with this mark is usually worth much more than a comparable one with the pottery mark only. Watch out for Rookwood reproductions made during the 1960s. They carry dates in the 1880s and 1890s and sometimes have forged decorators' signatures. If in doubt consult an expert.

Art pottery vase

Description
Vase with sides that slope out to slightly squared shoulder with flattened top. Collarlike neck and plain rim. Lower body tapers to plain base. Covered with painted design of fish, other sea creatures, and underwater vegetation, all encircled with heavily painted net. *Variations:* Shoulder may be gently rounded. Decoration varies.

Materials and Dimensions
White earthenware with clear alkaline glaze. Polychrome enamel-painted decoration. Wheel-thrown. Height: 28–31″. Diameter: 17–19″.

Locality and Period
Rookwood Pottery, Cincinnati, Ohio. c. 1880–84. Similar pieces from Massachusetts west to Ohio. c. 1890–1900.

Comment
This unusual piece bears the initials of Maria Longworth Nichols (1849–1932), founder of the Rookwood Pottery and active as a decorator there from about 1880 to 1890. This piece is known as the "Aladdin vase," probably because of its shape and fanciful imagery; other works by the artist have similar titles. Although Nichols designed and decorated the vase, it was thrown by a professional potter, a common practice, especially with large pieces, which are more difficult to produce.

Hints for Collectors
Early Rookwood pottery is rare and expensive, notably examples decorated by Maria Longworth Nichols. Generally, pre-1900 art pottery is scarce and desirable. Look for it in the areas surrounding art potteries, since many examples were bought or given away locally. Advertising in local papers is a good way to ferret out such treasures.

Belleek porcelain vase

Description
Ovoid vase with sides that rise gently to pronounced shoulder and then angle sharply to long, wide neck with plain rim. Plain base. At each side, a winglike decorative screen handle with elaborate, floral-form, pierced decoration extending from rim to shoulder. Body decorated with painted Oriental motifs, including flying crane, leaves, and flowers. *Variations:* Shape and decoration vary greatly.

Materials and Dimensions
Belleek porcelain; exterior with peach glaze; interior with clear alkaline glaze. Elaborately glaze-painted and gilded. Molded; screens hand-shaped, pierced, and applied. Height: 10–11″. Diameter: 4¼–4½″.

Locality and Period
Ott & Brewer, Trenton, New Jersey. c. 1883–92. Similar pieces from New York, New Jersey, West Virginia, and Ohio. c. 1885–1910.

Comment
The Oriental motifs on this piece reflect the great impact of Japanese design and decoration on Americans. While much of what was created was only a superficial parody of the Oriental models, the new designs had an important effect on American pottery making.

Hints for Collectors
Although Ott & Brewer produced Belleek in quantity, it is very popular with collectors and hard to find today. Look for it in the shops of small towns in Pennsylvania and New Jersey, especially in the vicinity of Trenton. Always examine these elaborate pieces carefully for repairs.

Porcelain commemorative vase

Description
Urn-shaped vessel with low waist girdled by embossed band.
Sides angle out to rounded shoulder and heavy neck marked by
thick, gilded band. Neck flares in and out to shaped rim; gilded
ring below rim. Elaborate decoration includes embossed animal
heads, a profile bust of Washington in relief, and historical scenes
in relief. Elaborately shaped and decorated base.

Materials and Dimensions
Porcelain with gilding and underglaze painting. Bust, animal
heads, and historical scenes in parian porcelain. Molded;
decorative elements separately shaped and applied. Height:
16–24″. Diameter: 8–12″.

Locality and Period
Union Porcelain Works, Greenpoint, New York, 1876. Similar
pieces from New Jersey and Ohio. c. 1875–77.

Comment
The Centennial of 1876 led to the creation of many
commemorative pieces, but few as complex as this. Designed by
the sculptor Karl Müller and made by the Union Porcelain Works
in Greenpoint, New York, the vase carries such scenes as the
Boston Tea Party and workers building the Brooklyn Bridge.
This piece was displayed at the Centennial exhibition in
Philadelphia.

Hints for Collectors
Pieces like this are one-of-a-kind objects. This particular vase
was made solely to exhibit the skills of a pottery and was not
intended for sale. Most such pieces are in museums. They are
important as examples of technical and artistic ability of 19th-
century American porcelain manufacturers.

Stoneware vase

Description
Tall, heavy vase with straight sides above low waist. Wide neck marked by embossed line. Flaring, scalloped rim with square-shaped pierced decoration. Below waist, sides taper to plain base. Body covered with applied and painted twining roses. *Variations:* Body may be cylindrical.

Materials and Dimensions
Stoneware; exterior unglazed; interior glazed with brown Albany slip. Decoration painted with oils. Wheel-thrown; rim hand-shaped; applied decoration similarly shaped. Height: 12–20″. Diameter: 6–10″.

Locality and Period
New England west to Indiana, south to Maryland. c. 1870–1910.

Comment
The same inspiration that led to the establishment of sophisticated art potteries in the late 19th century also led to the establishment of china painting clubs, where groups of women would assemble to paint pictures and floral designs on undecorated pottery. This practice arose out of the Arts and Crafts Movement, which was influential around the turn of the century. These plain pieces, known as "blanks" before their embellishment, were produced by most American potteries. Listed in special catalogues in the 1890s, they were issued in dozens of different sizes and shapes.

Hints for Collectors
Hand-decorated stoneware pottery can be recognized easily: The unpainted areas of the exterior are unglazed, as it was harder to paint a glazed surface; and the decoration is painted in oils, not glazed and fired. Because there is little collector interest, prices are currently low.

Parian porcelain vase

Description
Vase with sides that taper gradually from low waist to wide neck and flaring, slightly scalloped rim. Shaped base. At each side, applied ring and cluster of leaves and berries simulating a handle. On front and back, an embossed eagle with spread wings on a pedestal surrounded by floral motifs. *Variations:* Eagle may be replaced by portrait busts, additional floral motifs, or grape clusters.

Materials and Dimensions
Parian porcelain; exterior unglazed; interior with clear alkaline glaze. Similiar pieces rarely with polychrome glaze on exterior. Molded; rings, leaves, and berries separately shaped and applied. Height: 5–8″. Diameter: 3–4″.

Locality and Period
Attributed to the United States Pottery Company, Bennington, Vermont. c. 1850–58. Similar pieces from New York, New Jersey, and Ohio. c. 1850–80.

Comment
Like much American parian, this piece is unmarked. However, based on style and history it is attributed to the Bennington pottery. The prominent eagle decoration is characteristic of American decorative arts of the mid-19th century. The vessel's shape, on the other hand, is derived from European prototypes.

Hints for Collectors
The presence of an eagle, although a good indicator of American origin, does not always guarantee that a piece was made in the United States. European ceramics were also decorated with the motif. The eagle was prominently featured on Napoleonic furnishings, and a double-headed eagle was the symbol of the Austro-Hungarian Empire.

Porcelain vase

Description
Small vase in the form of a woman's right hand gripping flowerlike vase. Scalloped rim and flaring, ribbed base. Decoration includes embossed ring on little finger, bracelet of small beads encircling wrist; vase decorated with embossed and painted spray of flowers. *Variations:* Vases may be in form of left hand. Shape of vase, position of hand, and form of base varies.

Materials and Dimensions
Hand-painted porcelain; interior with clear alkaline glaze. Similar pieces usually parian porcelain. Molded. Height: 6–7″. Diameter: 2½–3″.

Locality and Period
Vermont, New York, New Jersey, and Ohio, and from English potteries. c. 1850–90.

Comment
Vases like the example illustrated were a popular Victorian novelty and were produced in quantity both in America and Europe. Since few were marked, it is seldom possible to learn the source of most pieces. In general, most American examples were in unglazed parian; European examples were usually more elaborately decorated.

Hints for Collectors
As with all unmarked ceramics, these vases should not be attributed to a given pottery without substantial history or a strong resemblance to identified pieces. Hand vases often have damage, especially around the scalloped rim and at the fingertips, and should be examined carefully before they are purchased.

Art pottery wall pocket

Description
Elongated receptacle for plants or flowers with body that slopes
out to uneven, flaring rim from knobby, rounded base. Surface
rough and embossed with vine, leaf, and berry forms; back
flattened and undecorated. Hole in back for hanging. *Variations:*
Shapes vary considerably. Most are more colorfully glazed.

Materials and Dimensions
Yellow earthenware; interior with matt green glaze; exterior
with touches of green glaze. Molded. Height: 7–9″. Width: 3½–
4½″. Depth: 2–2½″.

Locality and Period
Peters and Reed Pottery, South Zanesville, Ohio. c. 1901–20.

Comment
Peters and Reed was best known for its matt glaze pieces. One
type, called Moss Aztec, combined a red earthenware body with
a green glaze. Their pieces were often organic in shape and
embossed with flowers, vines, leaves, and trees, reflecting their
use as hanging flowerpots and vases.

Hints for Collectors
Peters and Reed wares, although seldom marked, can be
identified by the characteristic red or yellow clay body touched
with green. When the firm changed hands in 1920 it was renamed
the Zane Pottery Company; examples marked "ZANEWARE" are
often almost identical to the earlier pieces. Both types, with their
matt surfaces and organic forms, are very different from most
art pottery of the period.

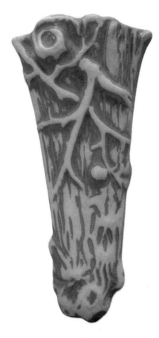

Redware wall holder

Description
Cornucopia-shaped wall pocket with bulbous upper body and long tail terminating in blunt end. Scalloped rim. Decorated with applied motifs including a bird and a stem with leaves and flowers. Impressed "BAECHER/WINCHESTER" on side. *Variations:* Shape sometimes that of deep basket, often with one side flattened, with handle.

Materials and Dimensions
Red earthenware with brown, yellow, and green glaze. Wheel-thrown; decorative motifs separately shaped and applied. Height: 6–7″. Width: 4–5″. Depth: 3–3½″.

Locality and Period
Anthony W. Baecher, Winchester, Virginia. c. 1868–89. Similar pieces from Virginia and Pennsylvania. c. 1840–90.

Comment
Some of the most appealing glazed redware comes from the Shenandoah Valley of Virginia. Besides those made by Baecher, wall pockets were made by Jacob Eberly and Solomon Bell, both of Strasburg, during the last 2 decades of the 19th century.

Hints for Collectors
The applied bird on the example illustrated originally held a worm in its beak, but most of the worm and part of the bird's beak have broken off. This damage, though significant, would not justify turning down such a rare and desirable piece. Damage must always be balanced against other factors such as scarcity, beauty, and historic importance in a decision to buy a piece. All 3 of the potteries mentioned produced both marked and unmarked wares; learning the basic forms will help you identify unmarked examples.

Redware vase

Description
Footed vessel with bulging waist marked by slightly scalloped upper edge. Above, sides angle out to neck marked by shaped band with sharply flaring rim. Below waist, thick stem mounted on heavy, shaped foot. *Variations:* Stem often much shorter and foot plainer.

Materials and Dimensions
Red earthenware with mottled green and brown glaze. Base, bulging waist, and upper portions separately wheel-thrown and joined. Height: 4–7″. Diameter: 3–5″.

Locality and Period
Pennsylvania, Virginia, and North Carolina. c. 1850–1900.

Comment
Forms such as the example illustrated are rare, and some experts believe they were designed as drinking tumblers. They do somewhat resemble the heavy, lidded, German goblets called pokals, but the flaring rim would make drinking difficult. This form is smaller than but similar to Victorian footed vases and flowerpots that were often reproduced in a slightly altered form by Pennsylvania and Virginia potters.

Hints for Collectors
Every serious collector should be familiar with rare as well as common ceramic forms. Many would not recognize a piece like this as American and might consequently pass up a great find. The glaze, however, is distinctly American; most European examples would be much more complex in coloring. This piece has been damaged and restored, something that might deter a buyer unaware of its value. The desire to buy only mint-condition pieces must sometimes be tempered by the knowledge that certain forms will not pass one's way again.

Rockingham vase or spoon holder

Description
Tall, octagonal, footed piece with fluted sides that curve out to scalloped rim. Lower body tapers to shaped ring marking waist. Below, stem flares out to octagonal, shaped foot. *Variations:* Stem may be shorter.

Materials and Dimensions
Yellow earthenware with Rockingham glaze. Upper body and hollow foot molded in 2 sections and joined at shaped ring. Height: 8½–10". Diameter: 5–6".

Locality and Period
United States Pottery Company, Bennington, Vermont. c. 1849–58.

Comment
Vases or spoon holders like this closely resemble in shape those made of pressed Sandwich glass in America during the mid-19th century; they may well have been patterned after them. Although rarely marked, these Rockingham pieces are generally attributed to Bennington. The same shape is more common with a flint-enamel finish, but there are examples in both scroddledware and ironstone.

Hints for Collectors
These pieces are among the most popular of all Bennington Rockingham and bring substantial prices when they come on the market. They are often called tulip vases, but are similar in form to spoon and celery holders. Portions of the scalloped rim may have broken off and been reglued or even completely replaced. A piece with a damaged rim may be worth 40 to 60 percent less than a vase that is intact.

314 Redware vase

Description
Vase with sides that angle out from waist to plain rim and heavy shaped base. Several incised lines encircle body. Decorated with simple, slip-trailed designs and initials "S.B." Side impressed "SOLOMON BELL/STRASBURG." *Variations:* Form may be bulbous. May be decorated with applied motifs.

Materials and Dimensions
Red earthenware with clear lead glaze; exterior decorated with yellow, brown, and green glaze. Wheel-thrown. Height: 7–10″. Diameter: 3–4″.

Locality and Period
Solomon Bell, Strasburg, Virginia. c. 1840–50. Similar pieces from Virginia and Pennsylvania. c. 1840–1900.

Comment
Although the shape of this vase is unusual, its glaze and decoration are clearly part of the American redware tradition. Solomon Bell, a master potter and member of the family of potters who were active in Maryland, Virginia, and Pennsylvania, worked at Strasburg from 1837 until his death in 1882. Since the simple vase illustrated could have been turned quickly on the wheel, large numbers were probably made. Unfortunately many have been lost, partly because of long exposure to moisture, which damages redware.

Hints for Collectors
Marked Bell pottery is eagerly sought. Look closely for marks stamped in various places on a piece—the sides, handles, and base. Heavy glaze sometimes makes it difficult to see the impression.

Redware flowerpot

Description
Cone-shaped container with sides that curve out from shaped
base to 2 thick, shaped rings below heavy, shaped rim.
Variations: Usually plainer, without shaped decoration. May
have permanently attached saucer.

Materials and Dimensions
Red earthenware with clear lead glaze; exterior splotched with
manganese black. Similar examples with various glaze colors or
unglazed. Wheel-thrown; very late examples molded. Height:
5–9″. Diameter: 5–8″.

Locality and Period
New England west to Missouri, south to the Carolinas. c. 1840–
1900.

Comment
Flowerpots, made by nearly every redware pottery, became the
sole product of many small shops as the industry waned after the
1850s. Most, as now, were unglazed, but some were glazed and
decorated. Among the best known are the spectacular green and
yellow pieces from Virginia, and the red and black pots made in
both Connecticut and Pennsylvania, like the example illustrated.
Few bear a pottery mark.

Hints for Collectors
Decorated redware flowerpots are more valuable than most other
kinds, but pieces in mint condition are rare. Chipping is common,
and so is glaze flaking from water leakage through the clay.
Examine the glaze closely; flaking areas that have been repaired
or disguised with epoxy or shellac sometimes appear yellowish.

Stoneware flowerpot

Description
Pot with attached saucer. Sides flare out to shaped rim from plain base. Saucer attached to base has plain rim and base. Drainhole in bottom. Floral decoration covers most of surface. *Variations:* Some pieces lack decoration. Some have separate saucer.

Materials and Dimensions
Stoneware hand-painted with manganese-brown glaze; similar examples decorated with brown Albany slip. Wheel-thrown; saucer separately shaped and attached. Height: 8–12″. Diameter: 7–10″.

Locality and Period
Vermont and western Pennsylvania. c. 1860–1900.

Comment
Decorated stoneware flowerpots like this may have come from either the Bennington, Vermont, stoneware works, which used this style of decoration, or western Pennsylvania, where such brown-decorated wares were made. The body of these pieces is unglazed, an unusual feature, probably intended to make the pots more absorbent. Most stoneware flowerpots are at least glazed on the exterior.

Hints for Collectors
Stoneware flowerpots were rarely decorated. In price lists where they were illustrated, they would often be the only undecorated pieces shown. A dealer unaware of this may sell a decorated pot for the generally low price most undecorated examples bring. With luck, the collector may find a real bargain.

Description
1-piece flowerpot with saucer. Sides angle out to heavy, shaped rim from plain base. Attached saucer with plain rim and plain base. Drainhole in bottom. *Variations:* Some pieces may have sides with embossed floral decoration or with geometric decoration.

Materials and Dimensions
Stoneware; exterior glazed with brown Albany slip; interior unglazed. Molded; pot and saucer sometimes separately molded and then joined. Height: 4–8″. Diameter: 6–10″.

Locality and Period
New England west to Missouri, southwest to Texas, and throughout many areas of the South. c. 1860–1930.

Comment
Nearly every pottery in the second half of the 19th century made stoneware flowerpots; brown-glazed examples were the most common. Most were made with attached saucers; for those that came without attached saucers, matching ones were always available. Surprisingly, many of these pieces were marked; potteries from Maine to Texas are known to have produced them.

Hints for Collectors
Few pieces of antique pottery are as practical as flowerpots. They are generally of higher quality than today's products and they are fairly plentiful. Marked examples are common enough to permit forming a small collection representing various stoneware potteries.

Description

Tall pot with attached saucer. Sides angle out to shaped, scalloped rim from plain base. Pairs of incised lines encircle body. Attached saucer with scalloped rim and shaped base. Drainhole in lower side of pot. *Variations:* Rim often not scalloped. May lack attached saucer.

Materials and Dimensions

Red earthenware; exterior with clear lead glaze; interior unglazed. Sponge-decorated with manganese brown. Pot and saucer wheel-thrown, then joined; scalloping hand-shaped. Height: 5–6″. Diameter: 5–6″.

Locality and Period

New England west to Ohio, south to the Carolinas. c. 1810–90.

Comment

Redware flowerpots with attached saucers were difficult and time-consuming to make and less common than plain pots. An 1821 price list from the Moravian pottery at Salem, North Carolina, offered pots for a shilling each and matching "flower dishes"—separate saucers—for 8 or 10 pence each. Marked redware flowerpots are rare, although there are pieces from such potters as Anthony Baecher of Virginia and the members of the Bell family who worked in Pennsylvania.

Hints for Collectors

Most redware flowerpots were glazed only on the outside, if at all, and water from the soil penetrated the clay through the interior, often causing the glaze to peel off. Always use an inner liner with these pots. Handworked details, like the scalloped rim on the example illustrated, add to the value of a piece.

Modern vase

Description
Bowl-like vessel with pronounced waist. Above, sides slope in
sharply to wide neck with collar. At each side of rim, 4-sided
handle forming semicircle extends down and attaches to base.
Below waist, sides curve gently in to rimmed base. Impressed on
bottom "COORS/COLORADO/POTTERY." *Variations:* Shape varies
greatly.

Materials and Dimensions
White earthenware; exterior with pinkish-tan glaze; interior with
aquamarine glaze. Similar pieces with other pastel glazes.
Molded. Height: 7–8″. Diameter: 8–9″.

Locality and Period
Coors Pottery Company, Golden, Colorado. c. 1920–40.

Comment
A modernistic, geometric form like that shown here differs from
art pottery, which was usually made in traditional or naturalistic
shapes drawn from the Art Nouveau style of the turn of the
century. Both the shape and the colors of this vase relate it to
the Art Deco style of the 1920s and 1930s. Not much is known
about the maker of this piece.

Hints for Collectors
Handles like those on the vase illustrated are easily damaged,
and they should always be closely inspected for repairs or
restoration. Damage will decrease value from 25 to 75 percent,
depending upon its extent and type. As a rule, don't buy
damaged pieces unless the example you are considering is a rare
form.

Art pottery vase

Description
Bulbous vase with narrow waist and long, wide, collarlike neck.
Neck decorated with 2 perforations extending from front to back.
Plain rim. Neck and lower body joined by curving, perforated
brackets. Swelling lower body curves in to plain base.
Variations: Art pottery vases come in many different shapes and
with many types of decoration.

Materials and Dimensions
White earthenware with matt green glaze. Molded. Height: 6–8".
Diameter: 5–6".

Locality and Period
Attributed to the J. B. Owens Pottery Company, Zanesville,
Ohio. c. 1907–09. Similar examples from New Jersey, Ohio, and
Colorado. c. 1905–30.

Comment
Owens was producing art pottery at Zanesville, Ohio, as early as
1896. The vase shown here is in Owens's Aqua Verdi line, which
was introduced in 1907. The form, based on early Chinese
bronzes, reflects the Oriental influence prevalent then. The glaze
resembles both the patina of aged bronze and the famous Chinese
celadon ceramic glaze.

Hints for Collectors
Most art pottery was made after 1910; earlier pieces, especially
those made before 1900, are somewhat more valuable. Although
unusual forms like that shown are not now widely sought, such
pieces will probably increase in value as interest in art pottery
grows.

Art pottery hanging flower basket

Description
Circular plant holder with sides rising in a gentle curve to
pronounced shoulder. Above, sides slope sharply in to plain rim.
3 equidistant holes drilled below rim. At each side, triangular
handle attached just below rim and at shoulder. Lower body
slopes in to rounded base. Surface has embossed texture with
flowers and branches. *Variations:* Most hanging planters lack
handles. Body may be ball-shaped.

Materials and Dimensions
White earthenware with matt green glaze. Decorated with pink,
white, yellow, and dark green glaze. Molded; handles separately
shaped and applied. Height: 5–7″. Diameter: 7–8″.

Locality and Period
Ohio and throughout the Midwest. c. 1920–50.

Comment
Hanging flower or plant baskets were made by many potteries,
including Roseville, Weller, and other large midwestern firms.
Most were intended for plants, although they could also be used
for cut flowers. Florists and variety stores sold them. The
retailer usually supplied brass or iron chains for hanging the
baskets.

Hints for Collectors
Unmarked art pottery can often be identified by reference to one
of the many catalogues produced by large potteries from 1900 to
1950. These catalogues show up at flea markets or old
bookstores, and some have been reproduced. Buy them
whenever they are available; they are invaluable for research.

Art pottery centerpiece

Description
Oblong display piece with low sides that angle out to irregular, flaring rim with 2 pierced keyhole-shaped decorations in each long side. At each end, ear-shaped handle with shaped decoration attached below rim and just above base. Lower body slopes in to low, rimmed base. Sides embossed with leaves and flowers. Embossed on bottom "Roseville, U.S.A." *Variations:* Centerpieces have a variety of shapes.

Materials and Dimensions
White earthenware with light blue matt glaze, touched in places with white; embossed decoration with green, pink, and white glaze. Molded. Length: 15–17″. Width: 8–9″. Height: 5–6″.

Locality and Period
Roseville Pottery, Zanesville, Ohio. c. 1939–53.

Comment
One of the larger producers of art pottery, Roseville was founded in 1885 but did not begin making artware until 1900. Later products, such as the centerpiece illustrated, are considered more commercial versions of their earlier art pottery; many collectors find them amusing.

Hints for Collectors
Because it manufactured a vast number of pieces in many different patterns, Roseville is a great favorite with collectors. For years Roseville produced wares that resemble those produced by Weller. Fortunately, almost all but the earliest Roseville is clearly marked, with different marks used for limited periods. For example, the mark on the piece shown was used from 1939 to 1953. Roseville marks are documented in reference books on the ware, and these are good sources for dating a piece.

Modern jardiniere

Description
Rectangular planter with plain rim and sides that taper to
scalloped base with short feet. Body covered with embossed
decoration. Overlapping, leaflike motifs extend down sides from
rim, and horizontal tiers of wavelike motifs rise from base.
Bottom marked "hull/U.S.A." *Variations:* Shape may be oval or
round. Decoration varies greatly.

Materials and Dimensions
White earthenware with dark green glaze on lower body and
light green glaze near rim and on interior. Molded. Length:
9–12″. Width: 5–6″. Height: 4–5″.

Locality and Period
A. E. Hull Pottery Company, Crooksville, Ohio. c. 1952–55.

Comment
Jardinieres, or planters, have long been a staple item at many of
the more commercial potteries. Firms like Hull sold a large
percentage of their output to florists and department stores. The
piece illustrated here can be given an approximate date because
the word "hull" is marked in small letters, a variation not
adopted by the firm until 1952. The leaflike motifs and decoration
on the body are reminiscent of the Art Deco style.

Hints for Collectors
Some might call this piece art pottery because of its form and
decoration. Nevertheless, it is a production piece made in large
quantities primarily by machine. The earlier wares that are
commonly referred to as art pottery, such as those made by
George Ohr, were shaped and decorated by hand. As a general
rule, collectors prefer older, handcrafted art pottery, and prices
reflect this.

Art pottery planter

Description
Plant holder or vase in form of large seashell, with sides that
curve up to irregular, partly flaring, scalloped rim. Smooth,
bulbous lower body tapers to narrow, oval base. Decoration of
concentric bands at one end. Bottom incised with Van Briggle
double "A" mark and "Van Briggle/Col. Sprgs." *Variations:*
Shell shape varies.

Materials and Dimensions
White earthenware with light blue matt glaze. Molded. Length:
8–16″. Width: 3½–8″. Height: 4–9″.

Locality and Period
Van Briggle Pottery, Colorado Springs, Colorado. c. 1930–45.
Similar pieces from New Jersey and Ohio. c. 1920–50.

Comment
Shell-shaped planters first became popular around 1900, when
the Art Nouveau style was beginning to make an impact in
America. The style drew on naturalistic forms. Unlike most
other Art Nouveau motifs, however, the shell form persisted
until well into this century. The Van Briggle catalogue of 1945
pictured the planter shown here, noting that "because of its
popularity we make this shell in three sizes." These were 8-, 12-,
and 16-inch lengths, which sold respectively for $4.30, $7.95, and
$13.75. The light blue color is Turquoise Ming, one of the most
popular Van Briggle colors.

Hints for Collectors
A scalloped edge or rim can easily be chipped. These chips,
especially if they are of some age, may be difficult to see, and
collectors should always closely examine a prospective purchase.
Depending on the extent of damage and the rarity of the piece,
chipped edges can reduce value anywhere from 20 to 75 percent.

Art pottery flower bowl

Description
Bowl with sides that flare out to wide rim. Narrow, cylindrical base terminates in 4 shaped bracket feet. Removable interior flower frog in 3-lobed leaf shape with 4 drilled holes in bulbous base for stems. Stamped in ink on bottom "FULPER"; letters arranged vertically. *Variations:* Designs vary. Some bowls have attached flower holders.

Materials and Dimensions
Yellow earthenware with mottled, pale green matt glaze; rim and underside of bracket feet unglazed. Flower frog lightly glazed in same shade. Molded. Bowl height: 3–4″; diameter: 7–8″. Flower frog height: 2–2½″; diameter; 2–2½″.

Locality and Period
Fulper Pottery Company, Flemington, New Jersey. c. 1910–25. Similar pieces from Ohio and New Jersey. c. 1900–40.

Comment
Shallow bowls like the example shown here were referred to as "flower bowls" in catalogues. During the 1920s, Fulper catalogues offered them for $3.00 to $6.00 and flower frogs for 50 cents apiece. The bowls were designed to hold short-stemmed flowers, such as water lilies, which were secured to the flower frog by their stems and allowed to float naturally in a few inches of water. Such arrangements were common table decorations during the first 4 decades of this century.

Hints for Collectors
Flower bowls and the removable frogs should match in glaze and color, but there is no such thing as a true matching set. Frogs were sold separately, and purchasers might choose from any one of several styles for a particular bowl. Although frogs were too small to carry a Fulper mark, they are valuable today.

Art Deco bowl

Description
Ball-shaped vessel with rounded sides that curve in to shaped
rim and rimmed base. Body decorated with incised, stylized
leaves and flowers against background incised to imitate bark.
Bottom impressed "WELLER." *Variations:* Shape and decoration
vary greatly.

Materials and Dimensions
White earthenware with pale blue matt glaze; highlights in
darker blue. Molded. Height: 4–5″. Diameter: 5–5½″.

Locality and Period
Weller Pottery, Zanesville, Ohio. c. 1920–25. Similar pieces from
Ohio and New Jersey. c. 1910–40.

Comment
Many bowls like the one illustrated were fragile and were
intended more for decoration than practical use. They might
serve as mantel or table ornaments or hold flowers. This bowl is
in the Paragon line, a design introduced by the Weller firm
around 1920. The shape and stylized relief decoration are typical
of the early Art Deco period and bear a striking resemblance to
certain art glass being produced at the same time in both
Germany and France.

Hints for Collectors
Weller is popular with collectors and often brings high prices,
but be wary of unmarked pieces that are attributed to the firm.
During its long period in business Weller produced dozens of
different lines, many of which closely resemble wares produced
by competitors. Don't pay a Weller price for a piece unless you
are certain it is from that pottery.

Art pottery bowl

Description
Small vessel with protruding waist marked by shaped line.
Above, body slopes in to wide, collarlike neck with plain rim.
Lower body curves in to shaped base. Impressed on bottom "G. E.
OHR/Biloxi, Miss." *Variations:* Shapes vary.

Materials and Dimensions
Red earthenware; exterior with clear alkaline glaze; interior with
black glaze. Decorated with black. Wheel-thrown. Height: 3–4".
Diameter: 4–5".

Locality and Period
George Ohr, Biloxi, Mississippi. c. 1883–1906.

Comment
George Ohr was one of America's most individualistic art
potters. His work is characterized by a remarkably sophisticated
technique, including extremely thin walls, complex shapes, and
bizarre and whimsical forms. Figural pieces often appeared in
such unlikely shapes as potatoes, a donkey's head, and hats.
Known as "the mad potter of Biloxi," Ohr did his best to live up
to his reputation, but he was also one of the finest clay craftsmen
of his generation.

Hints for Collectors
Ohr is a good example of a forgotten art potter whose work is
now in great demand and brings high prices. Virtually ignored
since he quit throwing pottery to become a car salesman more
than 60 years ago, Ohr became a minor sensation when several
thousand of his pieces came on the market in 1972.

Art pottery vase and candleholders

Description
Round bowl with sides that curve slightly in from waist to plain
rim. Bowl rests on shaped, rectangular base. At each end,
cylindrical candleholder with sides that slope out to wide, shaped
rim. Embossed leaf design joins candleholders and bowl; leaf-
encrusted base. Sides of bowl embossed with leaf and floral
decoration. *Variations:* Decoration may be less ornate.

Materials and Dimensions
White earthenware with green, pinkish-brown, and yellow matt
glaze. Molded. Length: 10–11″. Width: 5–6″. Height: 4½–5″.

Locality and Period
Attributed to the Roseville Pottery, Zanesville, Ohio.
c. 1937–50. Similar pieces from New Jersey and other Ohio
potteries. c. 1930–50.

Comment
The combination of a flower bowl with a set of candlesticks was a
20th-century innovation and one much favored by the
midwestern art potteries. Such pieces were often used as
centerpieces or mantel decorations. Although unmarked, this
piece is in the Thornapple pattern, introduced by Roseville in
1937.

Hints for Collectors
Large firms like Roseville and Weller made pottery in dozens of
different lines, and collectors should familiarize themselves with
these in order to recognize unmarked examples. Surviving
company and agents' catalogues are especially helpful in
establishing where a piece was made.

Art pottery double bud vase

Description
Binocular-shaped flower holder. 2 hexagonal bud vases with sides that taper to flaring rim from plinthlike base. 2 horizontal square bars join vases on either side of disklike medallion with embossed decoration and 2 square vertical bars at center. *Variations:* Other such vases may be curvilinear with floral decoration.

Materials and Dimensions
White earthenware; exterior with brown glaze; interior with orange glaze. Molded. Length: 7–8″. Width: 1¾–2½″. Height: 5–6″.

Locality and Period
Attributed to the Roseville Pottery, Zanesville, Ohio. c. 1924–28. Similar pieces from New Jersey and other Ohio potteries. c. 1910–40.

Comment
Known as gate, or binocular, bud vases, these receptacles were used as centerpieces or in pairs on the dining-room table. The example illustrated is in the Rosecraft Hexagon line, produced by Roseville during the 1920s. The shape is related to the Arts and Crafts style, and the brown glaze resembles oak, the wood used most often for Mission and other Arts and Crafts furniture. This vase is much more experimental than most Roseville pieces of the same period.

Hints for Collectors
Since so much later art pottery was mass-produced, it is possible to collect a variety of objects in the same line or style. Such a collection is interesting, but may take time to assemble once you have determined the pieces that the line originally included. In most cases a complete line will be worth more than a set of similar pieces from different lines.

Rockingham candlesticks

Description
Tall, cylindrical candleholders with sides that taper slightly from low waist, marked by bulbous ring, to shoulder. Shoulder with 2 shaped ridges, upper one sloping and slightly flared. Wide, shaped rim. Flaring, trumpet-shaped foot. *Variations:* Sides may be more curved. Shaped decoration varies.

Materials and Dimensions
Yellow earthenware with Rockingham glaze. Molded. Height: 7–10″. Diameter: 4–5″.

Locality and Period
Vermont west to Ohio, south to Baltimore. c. 1840–80.

Comment
Rockingham candleholders were made in several different potteries and appear not to have been marked, probably because their surface area was too small for stamping. They came in various sizes and styles. The United States Pottery Company at Bennington, Vermont, made these candlesticks in 3 sizes, which sold for $2.75, $3.50, and $4.50 per dozen. Like many ceramic candlesticks, these are modeled on examples in silver or brass.

Hints for Collectors
Single candlesticks are relatively easy to come by, but it is often difficult to find a matched pair. If you have a single stick and are looking for a match, carry the dimensions of your piece or even a color photograph with you so that you can compare it with potential purchases. Always examine the rim and foot of candlesticks closely; these areas are most often chipped or cracked.

Art pottery lamp base

Description
Cylindrical shaft in tree form that rises to shelflike shoulder covered with leaves and supported by curving branches. Above, short collar to support light bulb. Lower body swells to shaped, circular foot resembling tree roots on pedestal form. Surface rough and vertically incised to represent tree trunk. Drilled hole in base for electric cord. *Variations:* Most art pottery lamp bases are less naturalistic in form.

Materials and Dimensions
White earthenware with tan-green glaze and pink highlights. Molded. Height: 11–13″. Diameter: 5–6″.

Locality and Period
Attributed to the Weller Pottery, Zanesville, Ohio. c. 1928–30.

Comment
The Weller Pottery produced wares in hundreds of different lines. The piece shown here was part of their Woodcraft line. Although much later than its European prototype, this lamp base is clearly in the Art Nouveau tradition, popular at the turn of the century.

Hints for Collectors
Always check the neck and base to make certain that a piece was originally a lamp base and not a vase that was later converted. The neck should clearly be fitted for a lamp socket, and the base should have a drilled hole for the electric cord. In most cases a converted vase will have less value because of its alterations. Early art pottery lamp bases, generally dating before 1910, are rare, especially those that were designed to be used with kerosene.

Art pottery candlesticks

Description
Pair of candleholders with bodies that taper to narrow neck and collar with plain rim. Wide, flaring, circular foot. Bodies spiral from collar to base. Bottom impressed "BYBEE." *Variations:* Shapes vary greatly.

Materials and Dimensions
Stoneware with rich celadon-green glaze. Wheel-thrown. Height: 5–9″. Diameter: 3–4″.

Locality and Period
Bybee Pottery, Madison County, Kentucky. c. 1935–40. Similar pieces from the Carolinas and other Kentucky potteries. c. 1930–50.

Comment
The Bybee company had operated for years as a simple stoneware pottery, using local clays to produce ordinary crocks and jugs. During the 1930s the firm introduced new shapes and glazes as traditional country potters began to experiment with more sophisticated forms. Most potteries with a similar history have been located in the South; they include the Jugtown Pottery and the Pisgah Forest Pottery, both in North Carolina.

Hints for Collectors
Falling midway between traditional and art pottery, the small craft potteries of the South offer the collector an interesting field for exploration. Most of their products are stamped on the bottom with the name of the manufacturer. The variety of wares is surprisingly wide, from traditional art pottery forms like vases to complete table settings. Most are still modestly priced, especially outside the South.

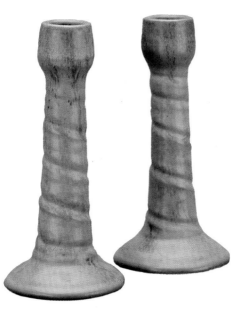

Art pottery vase

Description

Tall, cylindrical vase with low, bulbous waist. Body sweeps up and in to long, tubelike neck with plain rim. Lower body swells from waist in to plain base. Incised on bottom "MUNCIE."
Variations: Rim or base may be shaped. Lower body may be more bulbous.

Materials and Dimensions

White earthenware with matt pink glaze; thick celadon-green glaze dripped on upper body; rim and base unglazed. Similar pieces with solid green, pink, and gray glaze. Wheel-thrown. Height: 8–12″. Diameter: 4–5½″.

Locality and Period

Muncie Clay Products Company, Muncie, Indiana. c. 1922–39.

Comment

The Muncie firm produced an art pottery line that consisted primarily of vases and planters. Most of these pieces are slim, with either shiny or matt glazes. Oriental in feeling, these were sold mainly in department stores and florists' shops.

Hints for Collectors

Muncie is one of a large number of interesting art potteries that have generally been ignored by collectors. At a time when fine examples by Rookwood, Grueby, and other esteemed art potteries are selling at high prices, it is a good idea to examine quality pieces from smaller and lesser known companies. In many cases these rival those of the major firms, and they can be obtained at a fraction of the latter's cost.

Figurines

Shaped like birds, fishes, animals, and even humans, ceramic figurines have been popular in America since the 18th century. Besides being decorative, some of these pieces are quite practical.

Functional Figurines

Among the most common kinds of figurines are those meant to hold liquids. Small drinking flasks in the shape of fishes or birds date from the early 1800s and are typically made of brightly glazed red earthenware. Larger pieces, made of yellow earthenware with a Rockingham glaze and called "toby bottles," are shaped like a cloaked man with a hat. Common from the mid-19th century, they were modeled after the humorous "coachmen" bottles popular in England earlier in the century. English models also provided the inspiration for the cow-shaped yellowware and Rockingham creamers that were produced in the 1850s. Animal forms remained popular well into the 20th century as companies created colorfully glazed teapots in the form of roosters and other animals.

Bookends, inkwells, banks, and toys are among the other functional pieces included here. Some, such as doorstops and paperweights, were displayed as well as put to use. Many paperweights are shaped like eagles, lions, or other animals, usually with the figure resting on a heavy base. These objects were made of such diverse materials as glazed earthenware and porcelain. Similar to paperweights in that they are often placed on a heavy base, bookends first appeared in quantity in the middle of the 19th century. Most are flat on one side to support a row of books, and many are shaped like animals, including dogs and elephants.

Decorative Figurines

Among the earliest known decorative figures are those shaped like animals. Dating from the first half of the 19th century and made of clear-glazed red earthenware either molded or shaped by hand, these small pieces were produced in Pennsylvania, Virginia, and the Carolinas. In great demand today, the best of them are regarded as folk art. By the middle of the 19th century, Rockingham or brown-glazed stoneware animals, notably spaniels and lions, became popular table centerpieces.

At the same time, a number of major potteries began to produce small porcelain figures that were inspired by English Staffordshire examples. Subjects for these human figures were frequently chosen from classical to contemporary folk tales and literature. Other factories produced cruder versions of these pieces in Rockingham or brown-glazed stoneware. Toward the end of the 19th century, several eastern and midwestern potteries produced porcelain busts and figurines. Probably intended to resemble marble sculpture, many were designed by artists who assisted as the pieces were cast in molds. Designed as memorials or as conversation pieces, they adorned the parlors of well-to-do Victorian homes.

Modern Examples

Modern figural pieces include such inexpensive art pottery products as perfume lamps and cookie jars that were mass-produced in the early 20th century and often fashioned after popular cartoon and storybook characters. In the past 3 decades elegant porcelain birds and other animals have become popular. Complete with an appropriate setting, these figurines are still being made today.

White earthenware paperweight

Description
Paperweight in form of crouching eagle with outspread wings; head turned to right so beak touches right wing. American shield on breast. Rocklike formation at eagle's feet. Shaped, rectangular base. *Variations:* Rarely decorated with gilding.

Materials and Dimensions
Ironstone with clear alkaline glaze. Molded. Height: 2¾–3". Length: 3¾–4". Width: 2¾–3".

Locality and Period
Attributed to the United States Pottery Company, Bennington, Vermont. c. 1850–58. Similar pieces from New York west to Ohio, south to Maryland. c. 1850–80.

Comment
Figural paperweights were made with a variety of glazes by many potteries. Because few were marked, it is hard to identify the manufacturer of a particular piece. Since the paperweight illustrated here closely resembles others known to have been made at the United States Pottery Company, it has been attributed to that company. Paperweights with the eagle motif were made in other materials, such as cast iron, pot metal, pressed glass, and even pressed paper. They were also made by English potteries for sale in America.

Hints for Collectors
Collecting pottery shaped like eagles or decorated with them can be interesting; the collector can choose from a wide range of objects. Be sure, though, to examine these small and often fragile pieces carefully for chips and reglued fragments. These may not always be evident to the naked eye, but an ultraviolet light will usually reveal repairs and restorations.

Modern bank

Description
Bank in form of American eagle with outspread wings; head
turned to right. Eagle sits squarely on rectangular platform with
shaped edges and recessed top. Slot for coins in eagle's back.
Hole in bottom covered with removable tin and cork. Front panel
decorated with 3 embossed stars. Embossed on back "EMIGRANT
INDUSTRIAL SAVINGS BANK."

Materials and Dimensions
White earthenware with yellow, white, and brown glaze.
Molded. Height: 7–8″. Length: 6–7″. Width: 3–3½″.

Locality and Period
McCoy Pottery Company, Roseville, Ohio. c. 1950–60.

Comment
Modern ceramic banks are not common, but a few were made
from 1930 to 1960, usually in the shape of animals, airplanes, or
globes. The piece illustrated was made as a premium to be given
away to depositors by New York City's Emigrant Savings Bank.
Although most such products were unmarked, many were
manufactured by potteries like McCoy, which mass-produced
similar pieces for other banks.

Hints for Collectors
Pottery made to order as premiums or souvenirs, or in
commemoration of a special event, such as the Columbian
Exposition of 1893 or the 1941 New York World's Fair, is always
worth collecting. It was generally made in a limited quantity
over a short period of time and is consequently somewhat scarce.
Even contemporary pieces, such as the bank illustrated, will
usually appreciate in value, often in a relatively short time.

Redware whistle

Description
Toy whistle in shape of game bird with neck erect and head turned slightly to side. Incised lines on back and tail simulate feathers; incised eyes and mouth and applied topknot. Horizontal slit near end of tail and hole in tip of tail leading to hollow interior. Oval base with curved sides decorated with linked-chain motif. *Variations:* May be shaped like other birds, dogs, cats, and humans.

Materials and Dimensions
Red earthenware with light brown glaze; clear lead glaze more common. Modeled; base and topknot separately shaped and applied. Height: 3–4″. Length: 3½–4½″. Width: 2–3″.

Locality and Period
Pennsylvania. c. 1840–60. Similar pieces from New Jersey west to Ohio, south to North Carolina. c. 1820–70.

Comment
Although redware toys were made in some quantity, few have survived. Records indicate that as early as the 17th century a New York City potter, Dirck Claesen, was producing them. By the early 1800s, Pennsylvania potters were manufacturing such redware pieces as marbles, tops, whistles, and small flutes. A few pottery whistles were glazed in several colors, but most had a simple lead glaze.

Hints for Collectors
Early 19th-century redware whistles in good condition bring extremely high prices. But do not confuse them with redware whistles currently made in Mexico. These are made of pale pink clay and are usually unglazed. Instead, they are fired at low heat and then painted; their bright colors lack the wear of the Pennsylvania examples.

Art pottery teapot

Description
Teapot in form of crowing rooster with head upturned and open mouth creating spout. Body embossed with featherlike decoration. Slablike tail with scalloped edge placed perpendicular to body. Oval handle attached high on tail and at base. Scalloped base. Matching dome-shaped lid with curlicue-shaped handle fits in center of back. Perforated tea strainer in interior wall. *Variations:* May be in other animal forms.

Materials and Dimensions
White earthenware with yellow glaze. Molded in 3 pieces and then joined; cover separately molded. Height: 6½–7½". Length: 8–9". Width: 5–5½".

Locality and Period
Red Wing Potteries, Inc., Red Wing, Minnesota. c. 1940–50. Similar pieces from New Jersey and Ohio. c. 1920–50.

Comment
Serving pieces in the form of various animals were popular in Europe and Asia for hundreds of years and soon became favorites in America. Redware examples were made in Pennsylvania during the 19th century. Art pottery figural pieces vary greatly, from the rabbit-shaped knife holders of the Dedham (Massachusetts) Pottery to the frog-shaped salt and pepper containers produced by a number of factories. The majority of such pieces were made after 1920.

Hints for Collectors
Figural serving pieces, such as teapots, salt and pepper shakers, cookie jars, and tureens, are popular with collectors and likely to increase in value. Since certain forms, such as roosters, swans, and cats, are relatively common, it is possible to assemble a collection of various serving pieces sharing the same motif.

Stoneware bank

Description
Bank in form of log cabin, with door at 1 end and windows on other 3 sides. Steeply slanted roof with chimney at each end. Long-tailed raccoon crouches on roof between chimneys. Embossed walls of cabin simulate logs. Shaped, rectangular base. Coin slot in roof. Incised on bottom "Thomas Haig, Philadelphia, June 3, 1852." *Variations:* Banks may have single chimney and lack animal on roof. Other decorative details vary.

Materials and Dimensions
Stoneware; exterior with salt glaze; interior unglazed. Portions of building and animal highlighted in cobalt blue. Molded; animal modeled and applied. Height: 4½–5″. Length: 4¼–4½″. Width: 3½–4″.

Locality and Period
Thomas Haig, Philadelphia. 1852. Similar pieces from New England west to Ohio, south to Virginia. c. 1840–80.

Comment
The well-known potter Thomas Haig, who made this bank, was active in Philadelphia in the middle of the 19th century. Similar banks were made in small quantities at various potteries, including some in Pennsylvania and the Strasburg area of Virginia. The log cabin form was popular during the mid-19th century, symbolizing the simple frontier virtues of political figures like Abraham Lincoln. In addition to banks, boxes and bottles came in this shape.

Hints for Collectors
Stoneware log cabin banks are less common than their redware counterparts. Examples with cobalt-blue highlights are especially desirable. Be sure to check for damage and repairs.

Hand-painted porcelain bird

Description
Ceramic composition with a robin that has slightly turned head, open beak, and tail extending beyond base. Bird rests on base with flowering daffodil plant. Snail perched on base. *Variations:* Animals depicted vary. Scenic arrangement varies.

Materials and Dimensions
Hand-painted porcelain with polychrome glaze. Hand-shaped; details separately shaped and applied. Height: 13½–14″. Width: 4¾–5″. Depth: 4¼–4½″.

Locality and Period
Edward Marshall Boehm, Inc., Trenton, New Jersey. c. 1964–66.

Comment
Porcelain birds were popular throughout Europe during the 18th and 19th centuries, and some of the finest examples were produced at German and English factories. During the past 50 years a few American makers have achieved distinction in the field. Among these is Edward Marshall Boehm, who in the 1950s began producing editions of remarkably lifelike birds and animals. Cybis Porcelains, run by Boleslaw Cybis, also manufactures realistic figures of people and animals.

Hints for Collectors
Still being made and available at prices that are reasonable considering their quality, Boehm birds represent a good investment for the collector of contemporary porcelain. As with all modern ceramics produced in limited editions, determine how many have been made and whether the model has been discontinued before you buy. Other things being equal, the smaller the edition, the greater the value of a piece.

Art pottery flower frog

Description
Crouching frog on oval, shaped base. Front legs arched and spread; back legs close to body. Mouth closed; eyes bulbous. 3 round holes in frog's back. *Variations:* Form and position vary greatly. Number of holes varies.

Materials and Dimensions
Stoneware with mottled orange and green glaze. Molded; holes hand punched. Length: 4½–6″. Width: 4–5″. Height: 2–3″.

Locality and Period
New York west to Colorado and in North Carolina. c. 1920–50.

Comment
Flower frogs are ceramic, metal, or glass objects that are placed in the bottom of vases to support the stems of cut flowers. While many are simply round or oval blocks, the most popular form produced by art potteries was that of an actual frog, probably explaining the origin of the term. Most art potteries made flower frogs, and it is possible to gather a large and varied collection. With its simplified lines, the example illustrated is especially appealing.

Hints for Collectors
Marked flower frogs are uncommon and highly desirable, but even unmarked examples find a ready market among collectors interested in figural pieces. Pottery catalogues and sales lists can be helpful in identifying unmarked flower frogs. Book dealers and those who handle paper memorabilia sometimes carry these catalogues and price lists. Another way to identify the maker is to compare the glaze, form, and construction of the piece with similar objects whose origin is known.

Redware flask

Description
Small bottle in shape of fish. Mouth of fish with plain rim. Hollow interior. Impressed eye and upper fin; body covered with embossed, stylized scales. Body terminates in bifurcated tail. *Variations:* Animals depicted vary.

Materials and Dimensions
Red earthenware with bright green glaze. Molded. Length: 4½–6″. Width: 1½–2″. Height: 2¼–3″.

Locality and Period
Salem, North Carolina. c. 1815–30.

Comment
This unusual flask was probably used to store water or whiskey. It was made in a plaster mold at the Moravian pottery in Salem, North Carolina. An 1819 inventory from that shop listed fish-shaped bottles in 4 sizes, at prices of 5, 9, and 10 cents and ½ shilling. The Moravian potters appear to have been the main suppliers of figural flasks, and the variety of forms they made includes foxes, crayfish, eagles, and squirrels. All are fairly small, usually holding a pint or less. Only a very few American potteries made these items. A few bottles in the shape of potatoes were made in Pennsylvania, and there is one known stoneware flask that is turtle-shaped.

Hints for Collectors
Flasks like the example illustrated are rare and costly. Although they are hard to find, they do sometimes come on the market. Do not confuse them with somewhat similar English 18th-century pieces, which are more elaborate in form and often composed of clays other than red earthenware.

Spongeware piggy bank

Description
Small, crude figure of a pig with egg-shaped body, 4 short, stumpy legs, tapered head terminating in blunt snout with incised nostrils, and short, triangular ears. Slot in pig's back for coins; hollow interior. *Variations:* May have more detailed features. May have embossed tail. May have embossed inscription on body.

Materials and Dimensions
Yellowware; exterior with tan and green spongework; interior unglazed. Similar pieces white earthenware. Molded; earlier examples modeled. Length: 3–4½″. Width: 1½–2½″. Height: 1¾–2½″.

Locality and Period
New Jersey, Illinois, and Ohio. c. 1890–1930.

Comment
Pigs have long been a favored form for small banks. A few early 19th-century stoneware and redware examples are known, but most American ceramic piggy banks have spongework and date from the late 19th and early 20th centuries. Some yellowware examples were made in England. In contrast to the pig shown, English examples usually have more detail. Like most other banks, these had to be broken to remove their contents, and this has obviously greatly reduced the number of examples available today.

Hints for Collectors
Pig-shaped pottery is very popular, especially piggy banks, so it may be difficult to find good spongeware examples. Look for stores that specialize in animal-shaped objects made of various materials. These banks sometimes also turn up in miniature and toy collections.

Rockingham mantel decoration

Description
Recumbent cow with head upturned, left leg outstretched, and tail curled over right hip. Large, hollow tree stump behind cow. Rectangular base with uneven surface and sprigs of coleslaw decoration. *Variations:* Position of cow varies. May lack tree stump.

Materials and Dimensions
Yellow earthenware with Rockingham glaze. Molded; ears, horns, tail, and decoration separately shaped and applied. Length: 9½–10½". Width: 4½–5". Height: 6–7½".

Locality and Period
Attributed to the United States Pottery Company, Bennington, Vermont. c. 1849–58. Similar pieces from England. c. 1840–70.

Comment
Made in matching pairs, cows like the one shown here were designed as mantel decorations or table centerpieces. A bud or small bunch of flowers could be placed in the hollow tree stump. This type of figurine was apparently produced only at the United States Pottery Company, and some of these rare pieces bear the company's "1849" mark. They are based on similar English examples, which were made of porcelain or white earthenware.

Hints for Collectors
Any piece as rare as this one should be carefully researched before you decide on an attribution. Some collectors and dealers tend to attribute all unmarked Rockingham, English or American, to the Bennington pottery, especially when a piece is rare and potentially valuable. Although unmarked, the example illustrated is identical to marked examples from the United States Pottery Company, hence the attribution.

Rockingham cow creamer

Description
Cream pitcher in form of standing cow mounted on oval, shaped base. Head tilted slightly to one side, mouth open, and tail curled across left hip. Hole in mouth and middle of cow's back leading to hollow interior. Removable lid for hole in back. *Variations:* Stance of cow, tilt of head, and position of tail vary.

Materials and Dimensions
Yellow earthenware with Rockingham glaze; similar pieces with clear alkaline glaze. Molded; ears, horns, and tail separately shaped and applied. Length: 7–7½". Width: 3–3½". Height: 5½–6".

Locality and Period
New England west to Ohio, south to Maryland. c. 1840–60.

Comment
Although cow creamers with the Rockingham glaze were made in substantial numbers, these amusing pieces are not widely found today. The prototype for such figures is the English cow creamer produced by the Staffordshire potteries. English examples are generally more skillfully modeled and more elaborately glazed. American pieces, although more primitive, have a delightful and appealing naiveté.

Hints for Collectors
These creamers were never marked, but because of their Rockingham glaze, they are often attributed to the United States Pottery Company in Bennington, Vermont. In fact, they were made at several American potteries. True Bennington cows are distinguished by the combination of open eyes, crescent-shaped nostrils, pronounced ribs, and visible neck folds.

Yellowware cow creamer

Description
Cream pitcher in form of standing cow firmly planted on oval, shaped base. Head tilted to side, mouth open, tail curled across left hip. Hole in mouth and middle of cow's back leading to hollow interior. Removable oval lid for hole in back. *Variations:* Stance of cow, tilt of head, and position of tail vary.

Materials and Dimensions
Yellow earthenware with clear alkaline glaze; similar pieces with Rockingham glaze. Molded; ears, horns, and tail separately shaped and applied. Length: 6¾–7″. Width: 3–3¼″. Height: 5¾–6″.

Locality and Period
United States Pottery Company, Bennington, Vermont. c. 1850–58.

Comment
These unusual figural creamers were made at the Bennington pottery and were inspired by similar English pieces. The great majority have a Rockingham glaze, and only a few plain yellowware examples are known to exist. Pieces like the example illustrated have been identified as Bennington products through factory records and history of ownership. No marked yellowware cow creamers have been found.

Hints for Collectors
Figural yellowware is extremely uncommon, but collectors should always be on the lookout for such pieces. Unfortunately, some of the delicate applied decoration, such as the horns and tail on the cow shown here, is apt to be damaged, so look closely for repairs and restoration. Nevertheless, these pieces are rare enough to justify purchasing them in damaged condition.

Redware figurine

Description
Small figure of a ram standing on oval base. Head upright.
Embossed features, including horns, eyes, and tail. Base has
embossed surface. *Variations:* Some figures lack base. Head may
be downturned. Legs may be closer together.

Materials and Dimensions
Red earthenware with clear lead glaze. Molded; similar pieces
modeled. Length: 2¾–3½″. Width: 1½–2″. Height: 3–4″.

Locality and Period
Pennsylvania. c. 1850–80. Similar pieces from Virginia and
North Carolina. c. 1825–85.

Comment
Small earthenware figures like the example illustrated were
generally modeled on English porcelain mantelpiece figures made
by the Staffordshire potteries, which were popular in this
country during the 19th century. It is likely that they were used
as toys as well as decorative pieces. Some were modeled by
hand, but most were cast in molds. As early as 1829 the shop
inventory of a pottery at Salem, North Carolina, listed a mold for
making rams. Because they were so fragile, few such figures
have survived.

Hints for Collectors
These small redware rams are not as common as figures of dogs,
but watch for them whenever groups of figurines are offered for
sale. Look also in collections of pottery miniatures, where they
may be mixed with much later, mass-produced European and
American figures. Pieces like the one illustrated are considered
by some collectors to approach the level of folk art. They have a
restrained simplicity that is rarely seen in pottery made in the
late 19th century.

Description
Figure of bear straddling a rock standing on oblong base. Bear's
head turned slightly to the left; mouth is open. Body and base
heavily embossed. Bottom has superimposed "M," "T," and "C"
impressed in circle. *Variations:* Deer, dogs, cats, and various
birds are more common.

Materials and Dimensions
White earthenware with black glaze. Molded. Length: 9–10".
Width: 4–4½". Height: 5–7".

Locality and Period
Mosaic Tile Company, Zanesville, Ohio. c. 1930–50.

Comment
This piece bears the logo of the Mosaic Tile Company, which was
established in Zanesville in 1894. For many years the Mosaic Tile
Company produced a variety of attractive tiles for floors, walls,
fireplaces, and even soda fountains. When construction declined
during the Depression, the firm began to make other products,
including bookends, hot plates, wall plaques, and souvenirs. The
bear illustrated may have been one of a set of bookends, although
it is larger than most known examples, and it lacks the flattened
side that is common to most bookends. The white areas on the
body of this piece result from the thin glaze, which allows the
white earthenware to show through.

Hints for Collectors
Most figural pottery like this was created in the form of
bookends, but there are also figural inkwells, paperweights,
planters, and mantel decorations. Many pieces are not marked
and can be identified only by pottery catalogues, if available, or
by reference to similar documented examples. Bears were not
particularly common pottery forms.

Art pottery bookends

Description
Pair of bookends in form of elephants mounted on oblong, shaped base with uneven surface. Front end of base flattened. Elephants in walking position with left front foot forward, head down, and trunk curled up and under. *Variations:* Form may be of other animals as well as geometric or floral designs.

Materials and Dimensions
White earthenware with celadon-green glaze. Molded. Length: 5¾–6″. Width: 3½–4″. Height: 4½–5½″.

Locality and Period
Rookwood Pottery, Cincinnati, Ohio. 1940–50.

Comment
Founded in 1880, the Rookwood Pottery was one of the most important American art potteries, and many of its wares are expensive today. However, pieces like the elephants seen here date from the period when Rookwood's importance was declining and are not in as much demand as earlier, more innovative examples. The glaze on these elephants is a type that Rookwood first used around the turn of the century.

Hints for Collectors
A matching pair of Rookwood bookends is worth more than a single example. Although not marked, the elephants illustrated are attributed to Rookwood because they are listed in the company's catalogues. Reproductions are not a common concern for these late Rookwood pieces or for most other art pottery, yet they can be a problem with the earlier Rookwood pieces. Copies were made during the 1960s of several popular Rookwood forms, and these bear the marks used by Rookwood from 1880 to 1886.

Art pottery figurine

Description
Elephant with left front foot extended, right foot back, and hind
feet squared. Head tilted slightly to side and trunk curled up and
back, touching middle of forehead. Tail curled over left hip.
Variations: Animals depicted vary.

Materials and Dimensions
White earthenware with pink matt glaze. Molded. Length: 7½–
8½". Width: 3–3½". Height: 4–4½".

Locality and Period
Van Briggle Pottery, Colorado Springs, Colorado. c. 1930–45.
Similar pieces from New Jersey and Ohio. c. 1920–50.

Comment
This elephant, although not marked, appears in a Van Briggle
catalogue dating from the 1940s. It was probably meant to be a
mantel ornament. Elephant figures were popular during the
1930s and 1940s, and examples ranged from carved ivory and
wood to commercial materials such as Bakelite and chrome.
Forms included individual figures, pairs, and groups, the latter
often consisting of several elephants in a line connected trunk to
tail. Van Briggle animals used as bookends generally had heavy,
rectangular bases.

Hints for Collectors
Van Briggle's most desirable pottery dates from the first decade
of the 20th century. Later pieces, like the elephant illustrated,
lack the innovation and quality that characterize the company's
earliest works. With its simplified lines and pink matt glaze, this
elephant is belatedly related to the Art Deco style. Although it is
not as original in concept as the earlier Van Briggle products, it
is a good example of popular art pottery and has a charm that
appeals to many collectors.

Rockingham inkwell

Description
Inkwell in shape of reclining lion with chin resting on extended front legs. Back legs and tail tucked up under body. Mouth slightly open. Embossed details. Hole in middle of lion's back. Oval base. *Variations:* Position of lion varies.

Materials and Dimensions
Stoneware with Rockingham glaze; similar pieces in yellow earthenware. Molded. Length: 4½–5½". Width: 2–2½". Height: 2½–2¾".

Locality and Period
Attributed to the United States Pottery Company, Bennington, Vermont. c. 1853–58. Similar pieces from New York west to Ohio, south to Maryland. c. 1840–70. Similar pieces from England. c. 1820–70.

Comment
Novelty inkwells were made in several different factories; in addition, more elaborately detailed examples in white earthenware were produced in England. The small ink hole, which was probably sealed with a cork, held very little fluid, so it seems likely that the lion shown here was intended more as a novelty than a working inkwell.

Hints for Collectors
Rockingham lions appear in various forms, including large mantel figures, paperweights, and inkwells. Most of the smaller figures are not marked. Although cruder, American Rockingham examples have a simple power that distinguishes them from their English prototypes. In addition, American pieces usually have a darker glaze.

Redware paperweight

Description
Recumbent lion on rectangular base with head turned to side. Mane, facial features, and claws incised. Base with chamfered corners and recessed upper edges. *Variations:* Position of lion varies.

Materials and Dimensions
Red earthenware with clear lead glaze; base with manganese-black glaze; touches of manganese black on lion. Modeled; similar pieces molded. Length: 3–4″. Width: 2½–3″. Height: 2½–3″.

Locality and Period
New England and New York. c. 1860–80. Similar pieces from Maine west to Ohio, south to Virginia. c. 1840–1900.

Comment
The lion had a great effect on the popular imagination during the 19th century. The king of beasts was not only represented in books and posters but was also featured in traveling circuses and menageries. Pottery lions ranged from large doorstops to smaller banks, paperweights, and mantel ornaments. The lion illustrated here has a crudeness to its construction that is typical of figural pottery from the second half of the 19th century.

Hints for Collectors
In collecting figural pottery it is often hard to distinguish American examples from similar ones made in Europe. American examples usually have a more simplified form and minimal decoration, while European examples are generally cast in elaborately detailed molds and made of a darker clay.

Rockingham mantel figure

Description
Large lion mounted on rectangular, shaped base. Head turned to side, with left paw resting on round ball. Curly, coleslaw-decorated mane. Tongue outstretched. Tail draped across lower back. Impressed on base "Lyman Fenton & Co./Fenton's/ENAMEL/PATENTED/1849/BENNINGTON, Vt." *Variations:* Position of lion varies. Mane may be shaped rather than coleslaw-decorated. May lack base.

Materials and Dimensions
Yellow earthenware with Rockingham glaze. Molded; coleslaw decoration separately shaped and applied. Length: 10¾–11½". Width: 5½–6". Height: 7–9".

Locality and Period
United States Pottery Company, Bennington, Vermont. c. 1849–58. Similar pieces from Ohio; also from England. c. 1840–70.

Comment
The mark on the piece illustrated is among the most common of the marks used by the United States Pottery Company and has been found on various versions of lion mantel ornaments. These ornaments were made in pairs. The company also produced pairs of deer, cows, and standing (but never sitting) poodles for mantel or table decorations.

Hints for Collectors
Extremely popular with collectors, especially in matching pairs, marked examples of Rockingham lions bring high prices. However, it may be difficult to determine if an unmarked piece came from Bennington; English examples and those made in Ohio are very similar. Compare unmarked lions with authenticated ones shown in the standard works on Bennington pottery.

53 Rockingham mantel figure

Description
Standing poodle holding fruit-filled basket in its mouth. Head turned to side; tail curls over center of back. Thick coleslaw decoration on head and front half of body as well as forming tip of tail and lining basket. *Variations:* Dog may have topknot at center of head. Head may face left or right. Many variations in basket shape and contents.

Materials and Dimensions
Yellow earthenware with Rockingham glaze; basket parian porcelain. Similar pieces in flint enamel; rarely in plain yellowware or parian porcelain. Molded; basket and coleslaw decoration separately shaped and applied. Length: 9–10″. Width: 3¾–4½″. Height: 8–9″.

Locality and Period
United States Pottery Company, Bennington, Vermont. c. 1849–58.

Comment
The standing poodle with basket in mouth was made exclusively at the United States Pottery Company in Bennington, Vermont, and is a well-known and highly desirable figurine. It should not be confused with the various sitting poodles that were made at many other American and English potteries. Note that the material used for the basket may differ from the clay in the rest of the figure.

Hints for Collectors
Bennington poodles always held a basket, but these have sometimes broken off over the years. If offered a standing poodle without a basket, examine the mouth area with great care. You will probably find traces of the clay and glaze that held the basket in place.

Rockingham paperweight

Description
Small paperweight in form of crouching spaniel with front legs extended and back legs tucked under body. Head upright and turned to side; mouth closed; tail spread behind body. Mounted on rectangular, shaped base with sides that curve in toward top. Impressed on bottom "Lyman Fenton & Co./Fenton's/ENAMEL/ PATENTED/1849/BENNINGTON, Vt." *Variations:* Base may be simple rectangular block. Dog's head may face forward.

Materials and Dimensions
Yellow earthenware with Rockingham glaze. Molded. Length: 4¾–5″. Width: 2¾–3″. Height: 3–3½″.

Locality and Period
United States Pottery Company, Bennington, Vermont. c. 1849–58. Similar pieces from New England west to Missouri, south to Maryland. c. 1850–90.

Comment
The facial details on the spaniel illustrated have been obscured by the thickness of the glaze, which often happens on Rockingham pieces. In addition to the Rockingham model, the United States Pottery Company also produced a similar paperweight in ironstone with varying details. Redware examples of spaniel paperweights were made in Pennsylvania and Virginia. Most similar examples from other American potteries are unmarked.

Hints for Collectors
Paperweights may easily be confused with larger but similar looking figures intended as mantel decorations or doorstops. In general, if the base is large in relation to the figure, the piece is a paperweight. Paperweights often show up unexpectedly in collections of miniatures and decorative figural pieces.

Description
Pair of spaniel-shaped bookends. Spaniels sit on haunches with heads slightly raised and turned to side; collar around neck. Mounted on oval base with shaped edges. *Variations:* Form and position may vary. May lack base.

Materials and Dimensions
Yellow earthenware with Rockingham glaze. Molded. Height: 5–6″. Width: 4–4½″.

Locality and Period
New England west to Ohio, south to Maryland. c. 1840–90.

Comment
Figural bookends, doorstops, and mantel decorations, notably spaniels or poodles, were popular throughout the Victorian era. They were made in many of the larger potteries and, unless marked, are hard to identify. Potters often took their molds with them when they changed jobs; as a result, the same mold might be used to make the figures at several different shops. Similar forms were produced in England, but these usually lack the dark brown glaze so typical of American examples.

Hints for Collectors
Not many Rockingham pieces bear the mark of a pottery. In the few that do, the mark was most often impressed in the soft clay with a metal stamp; hand-incised marks are very rare. Since American Rockinghamware strongly resembles that made in England, a mark can establish that a piece was made in this country, which will usually increase its value for American collectors. Rockingham pieces have been reproduced in England and the United States. These reproductions are usually made of white rather than yellow earthenware, which can easily be detected by checking the unglazed base.

Stoneware spaniel

Description
Figure of spaniel sitting on its haunches with eyes open and head erect and turned to side. Embossed leash about shoulders attached to collar. *Variations:* Many variations in position and appearance. May be mounted on square or rectangular base.

Materials and Dimensions
Stoneware glazed with brown Albany slip. Molded. Height: 7–10″. Width: 5–8″. Depth: 3–5″.

Locality and Period
New England west to Missouri, south to Maryland. c. 1850–90.

Comment
Brown-glazed stoneware spaniels were made by many different eastern and midwestern potteries, including some as far apart as the Lyons pottery in Lyons, New York, and the Underwood Pottery at Calhoun, Missouri. Used for a variety of purposes, from mantel ornaments to doorstops, most American examples are larger and far less ornate than their English prototypes. Marked American pieces are quite uncommon.

Hints for Collectors
Since they are seldom marked, it may seem difficult at first to identify an American-made spaniel. However, the English did not make large pieces with an overall brown glaze on a stoneware body, which is the typical American form. Most English examples were porcelain and white earthenware with multicolored glazes and sometimes even gilding. On some American examples the glaze may be too thick or rather dull, and it obscures the details of the piece by covering the lines of the design. Nevertheless, American stoneware spaniels are rather uncommon pieces, and their simple, bold designs have a special charm.

Redware bank

Description
Figural coin bank in form of small, sitting spaniel with head turned to side. Incised hair and facial features. Slot in upper back. Octagonal base with incised decoration about top. Date "1901" incised on base. Bottom incised "William Hinzel, Rochester, N.Y." *Variations:* Spaniels vary in form. Some banks lack base.

Materials and Dimensions
Red earthenware glazed with dark brown Albany slip. Molded. Height: 4–5″. Width: 3–4″. Depth: 1½–2″.

Locality and Period
William Hinzel, Rochester, New York. 1901. Similar pieces from New England west to Missouri, south to Virginia and the Carolinas. c. 1830–1910.

Comment
Figural redware banks were particularly popular in Pennsylvania and Virginia and include pieces shaped like dogs, various birds, such as chickens and owls, urns, and even miniature chests of drawers. Spaniel-shaped banks based on the English mantel ornaments produced by Staffordshire potteries were among the most popular. The spaniel may be found sitting or crouching and with or without a base. This bank, made in 1901, is obviously modeled after the earlier English pieces.

Hints for Collectors
Many banks, particularly figural ones, were not production items but were made specially as gifts for children. The example illustrated is probably such a piece, since it is signed and dated. Any signed and dated object is an interesting find, especially if its history can be traced.

Rockingham toby snuff jar

Description
Squat, covered storage vessel in form of man sitting cross-legged with a pitcher in his right hand and a goblet in his left. Right knee raised and coat open. Long, flowing hair. Lid consists of broad-brimmed hat that curls up at each side. Scalloped base formed by folds of coat. *Variations:* Facial features and position of hands and legs vary. Shape of base varies.

Materials and Dimensions
Yellow earthenware with Rockingham glaze; similar pieces in flint enamel. Molded. Height: 4–5″. Diameter: 3¾–4¼″.

Locality and Period
Attributed to the United States Pottery Company, Bennington, Vermont. c. 1849–58. Similar pieces from New Jersey west to Ohio, south to Maryland; also from England. c. 1850–80.

Comment
Several versions of the toby snuff jar were made at Bennington, Vermont, and they bear various Bennington marks. Similar jars were also produced at other American potteries, but they were rarely marked. English examples can usually be distinguished by their pottery marks.

Hints for Collectors
It is not uncommon to find a toby jar with a replacement for its original lid, revealed by a noticeable difference in glaze color or a loose fit. Such pieces will be less valuable. Modern versions of the toby snuff jar are currently being made in England. If not marked these can usually be distinguished by the lack of wear on the base and the absence of glaze crazing.

Description
Tall, figural bottles, each in form of man with top hat and long,
flowing cloak. Body hollow. Hole in top of hat for pouring. Man
at left holds mug in right hand. Man at right has bottle in right
hand and tassels on his cloak front. *Variations:* Details of
clothing and objects held vary. Figure may sit on barrel rather
than stand.

Materials and Dimensions
Yellow earthenware with Rockingham glaze. Molded. Height:
8½–11″. Diameter: 4–5″.

Locality and Period
Attributed to the United States Pottery Company, Bennington,
Vermont. c. 1847–58. Similar pieces made in New Jersey, Ohio,
and Maryland; also in England. c. 1840–70.

Comment
Also referred to as coachmen bottles, these tall pieces were, like
so much American Rockingham, modeled on an English
prototype. Intended to hold a fifth or quart of whiskey, the bottle
was sealed with a cork. Examples by the United States Pottery
Company often bear the firm's "1849" mark, but other marked
American examples are rare.

Hints for Collectors
Rockingham toby bottles are not especially hard to find, but they
are expensive. The bottle was also made in flint enamel, blue-
decorated, salt-glazed stoneware, and ironstone, the latter 2
types being very rare American forms. Similar stoneware and
ironstone bottles were also produced in England. They usually
are more detailed than American pieces.

Description
Matching male and female figures with large, feathered headdresses. Figures seated on rock structures that form plinthlike base. Woman holds book and has lamb at her feet. Man holds panpipe and has small dog at his feet. *Variations:* Various allegorical or mythological figures depicted.

Materials and Dimensions
Stoneware glazed with light brown Albany slip. Molded. Height: 9¼–10″. Width: 3½–4″. Depth: 2¾–3¼″.

Locality and Period
Attributed to the Lyons Pottery, Lyons, New York. c. 1870–75. Similar pieces from New England west to Ohio, south to Maryland. c. 1840–90.

Comment
These mantel figures were modeled on English and other European forms, which were widely produced during the 18th and 19th centuries at Staffordshire as well as such famous continental factories as Meissen, Sèvres, and Capodimonte. While European examples were customarily made of porcelain or white earthenware, their American counterparts might be made of anything from parian porcelain to stoneware.

Hints for Collectors
Figural pieces such as those seen here are among the rarest of all American stoneware. Surviving examples are often mistaken for European products, but the use of brown Albany slip, never found on European pieces, indicates their American origin. Few of these figurines were marked, but examples from New York and Vermont potteries are known. This set is attributed to the Lyons Pottery because of its history of ownership.

Parian porcelain statuettes

Description
Companion figures of young man and woman, each barefoot and standing against rock formation. Man, with hat and head back, holds fruit in right hand and basket of fruit in left. Woman, with hat and head tilted slightly to left, holds small bouquet of flowers in left hand and basket of flowers in right. Both pieces with shaped, circular base. *Variations:* Parian statuettes made in many forms.

Materials and Dimensions
Parian porcelain. Molded; fruit, flowers, and baskets separately shaped and applied. Height: 9–10″. Diameter: 4–4½″.

Locality and Period
Attributed to the United States Pottery Company, Bennington, Vermont. c. 1848–58. Similar pieces from the East; also from England. c. 1840–80.

Comment
Decorative figures like the examples illustrated were made in large quantities in England and in Europe. A few American factories produced them as well, often directly copying English examples. Those made at the United States Pottery Company were designed by English potters working in Bennington. Unfortunately, the figures were seldom marked, and it is usually impossible to determine a piece's origin.

Hints for Collectors
It is extremely difficult to distinguish authentic American parian figurines from imported examples. Consult the standard reference works listed in the bibliography, which often illustrate authenticated examples. Remember that while most continental and English examples will be inexpensive, those made in America are usually expensive.

Parian porcelain statuette

Description
Small statue of blacksmith with hat, shirt, and leather apron over pants. Figure has pipe in left hand raised to mouth, right hand extended above head. Anvil behind figure. Mounted on oval base with slightly sloping sides. *Variations:* Various figural representations of workers, including farmers, weavers, glassblowers, and shopkeepers.

Materials and Dimensions
Parian porcelain. Molded; details such as pipe separately shaped and applied. Height: 12–12½″. Diameter: 4½–5″.

Locality and Period
Union Porcelain Works, Greenpoint, New York. c. 1878–82.

Comment
During the nation's Centennial in 1876, and for some years after, potteries commissioned gifted ceramists and sculptors to create figural pieces in the tradition of the porcelain figurines long made in Europe. One of the more gifted sculptors to be thus employed was Karl Müller, who created the design pictured here for the Union Porcelain Works. Most of his pieces are unmarked, but a few may bear the impression or ink-stamped logo "U.P.W." accompanied by an eagle's head.

Hints for Collectors
American porcelain statuettes, especially marked ones, are relatively uncommon. Since European and American examples can often be confused, collectors of American-made pieces should seek out knowledgeable dealers who will guarantee their offerings. Most of the examples available today have traceable histories; if the provenance is unknown, the piece may be a reproduction or may have been stolen.

Parian porcelain bust

Description
Portrait bust of President James Garfield. Figure wears buttoned jacket, vest, and shirt with tie. Mounted on circular, pedestal-like base. *Variations:* May depict other presidents, including George Washington and Ulysses S. Grant.

Materials and Dimensions
Parian porcelain. Molded; base separately shaped and applied. Height: 11–13″. Width: 6–7½″. Depth: 4½–6″.

Locality and Period
Attributed to Ott & Brewer, Trenton, New Jersey. c. 1881. Similar pieces from New York and New Jersey. c. 1876–85.

Comment
Although unmarked, this piece has been attributed to Ott & Brewer, which produced very similar figures, particularly during the Centennial of 1876. Such figures were popular Victorian creations, used to decorate mantels and center tables. President Garfield was assassinated in 1881, and it is quite possible that the bust shown is a memorial piece. Other memorials to Garfield, including pressed-glass vessels and transfer-decorated plates, were produced at this time.

Hints for Collectors
Porcelain busts made in American factories are not widely collected, and they are hard to find, but any example representing an American historical figure is desirable. If you seek such pieces, advertise for them. They may still be in homes for which they were purchased 100 years ago. Since porcelain is easily damaged, all such figures should first be checked for repairs, preferably under ultraviolet light.

Art pottery perfume lamp

Description
2-piece lamp. Base circular with straight sides rising to stepped shoulder and plain rim; hollow interior contains wires, small light bulb, and repository for small perfume granules. Upper section in form of kneeling woman, probably a dancer, with arms holding full skirt and with bobbed hairdo. Small, drilled vent holes in left side of head. Torso hollow. *Variations:* May be made in 1 piece. Depiction of woman varies.

Materials and Dimensions
Porcelain; exterior partially glazed; interior unglazed; details hand-painted. Molded. Height: 7–8″. Diameter: 4¼–4½″.

Locality and Period
Attributed to the Fulper Pottery Company, Flemington, New Jersey. c. 1925–35. Similar pieces from Ohio and other New Jersey potteries. c. 1925–45.

Comment
This perfume lamp, with its electrical cord and metal socket, works by first creating a small amount of light, which shines through the thin porcelain body. The heat generated by the light melts the perfume granules, and their aroma then permeates the room through the vent holes in the figure's head. Although this piece is unmarked, identical examples are illustrated in Fulper catalogues of the period.

Hints for Collectors
Perfume lamps are not common today, for they were never made in large numbers. In lamps that were made in 2 parts, either the base or top may have been lost. Individual sections are worth purchasing, for at a later date you may be able to obtain the matching piece. As with all old lamps, be sure to check the wiring before use to avoid fire or shock.

Modern cookie jar

Description
2-piece cookie jar in form of clown's head. Jar section consists of
portions of shoulders, large embossed ruffled collar, and head
and face to just above eye level. Irregular base. Interior of
mouth with stepped rim on which lid rests. Matching lid in form
of upper portion of head with tasseled hat placed at angle.
Variations: Made in various human and animal forms, or shaped
like houses, automobiles, and other objects.

Materials and Dimensions
White earthenware with clear alkaline glaze. Details hand-
painted red, blue, black, and green. Molded. Height: 10½–12″.
Width: 7½–9″. Depth: 7–8″.

Locality and Period
McCoy Pottery Company, Roseville, Ohio. c. 1940–60. Similar
pieces from other Ohio potteries. c. 1940–60.

Comment
Cookie jars are a late but extremely popular innovation of the art
potteries, and several firms, particularly the McCoy and A. E.
Hull potteries of Crooksville, Ohio, have produced a variety of
them. Many are shaped like cartoon characters or characters
from fairy tales.

Hints for Collectors
Cookie jars are prime collectibles today and increasing in value,
even though most are of relatively recent vintage. Look for
examples in good condition with minimal paint loss. The example
illustrated here has lost most of the paint on the lid as well as a
good deal on the body; this devalues the jar by at least 50
percent.

Modern cookie jar

Description
2-piece cookie jar in form of Little Red Riding Hood. Lid consists of head and shoulders covered by red hooded cloak, and arms crossed in front. Basket under right arm. Jar consists of lower body with floral decoration on dress. Oblong base on which feet are painted. Bottom incised "Little Red Riding Hood Line/Pat. Des. No. 135889/U.S.A." *Variations:* Shapes and decoration vary.

Materials and Dimensions
White earthenware; exterior with red, yellow, tan, and violet glaze; interior with clear lead glaze. Gilding and floral transfer decoration. Molded. Height: 12–14″. Width: 8–9″. Depth: 9–10″.

Locality and Period
A. E. Hull Pottery Company, Crooksville, Ohio. c. 1930–50. Similar pieces from Ohio and New Jersey. c. 1920–50.

Comment
Hull's Little Red Riding Hood line was produced for some years and included a variety of objects, such as teapots, creamers, sugar bowls, salt and pepper shakers, and string holders. Most such pieces bear the name of the line, and some have the additional mark of the pottery, "Hull."

Hints for Collectors
Little Red Riding Hood items, especially cookie jars, are popular with today's collectors. Before purchasing one of these, however, carefully check the top and bottom for fit. Although the fit on these covered jars was rarely perfect, very poor matches will occur where a lost part has been replaced. A "married jar," as such combined pieces are sometimes termed, is both less desirable and less valuable.

Porcelain doll's head

Description

Hollow, flattened head and portion of shoulders, with drilled holes at each corner for securing cloth body. Face has embossed features, including ears, nose, and open mouth with upper teeth. Blue glass eyes open and close. Lips, eyebrows, and eyelashes hand-painted. At top of head, circular opening with plain rim. Interior has porcelain ridge; lead counterweight attached to ledge and to eyes. Superimposed "F" and "P" impressed in triangle on back of head. *Variations:* May not include shoulders.

Materials and Dimensions

Hand-painted bisque with red, brown, and black glaze highlights. Eyes blown glass. Molded. Height: 4–4½″. Width: 3½–4″. Depth: 3–3½″.

Locality and Period

Fulper Pottery Company, Flemington, New Jersey. c. 1915–25.

Comment

The Fulper doll's head seen here represents one of the few American attempts to compete with the French and German manufacturers who made fine-quality porcelain heads. Molded redware dolls and doll's heads were produced during the early 19th century at the Moravian pottery in Salem, North Carolina, and a few examples in redware and stoneware were made by Pennsylvania firms. These earlier types are extremely hard to find today, but Fulper porcelain heads are relatively common.

Hints for Collectors

American-made porcelain doll's heads can often be acquired at doll and toy auctions. Doll collectors are usually more interested in European examples, and heads like the one pictured here can sometimes be purchased quite reasonably.

List of Plates by Decoration

Porcelain
Although the most elaborate pieces of American porcelain have hand-painted and gilded decoration, others may have a simple clear glaze or may lack both decoration and glaze.

Painted or gilded
Beaker, 145; Belleek vase, 305; bird, 339; coffeepot, 135; commemorative plate, 180; commemorative vase, 306; creamer, 106; cup and saucer, 165; doll's head, 367; oyster plate, 193; pitcher, 107; presentation mug, 153; presentation pitcher, 109; salad bowl, 200; sweetmeat dish, 196; vase, 309.

Redware
In addition to the types of decoration listed here, many pieces made of red earthenware have a clear glaze or are glazed with brown slip. Some are also unglazed.

Banded
Mixing bowls, 218.

Black-glazed
Churn, 258; jar, 58; jug, 80; mug, 152; rundlet, 67; spittoon, 273; teapot, 140.

Brush-painted
Crock, 9; jars, 40, 56; miniature jug, 83.

Clear-glazed splotched with black
Butter pot, 11; deep dish, 230; flask, 74; flowerpot, 315; funnel, 256; herb pot, 33; jars, 28, 57; soup bowl, 237.

Impressed
Miniature bean pot, 38.

Incised
Bean pot, 37; butter pot, 10; jars, 3, 40.

Polychrome-glazed
Bowl, 44; creamer, 127; flowerpot, 318; herb jar, 39; inkwell, 292; jug, 86; miniature churn, 45; pitchers, 100, 102; pitcher-and-bowl set, 263; porringer, 158; rundlet, 69; spittoon, 268; sugar bowl, 41; vases, 46, 312, 314; wall holder, 311.

Sgraffito
Jar, 40; plate, 172.

Slip-trailed
Deep dish, 173; pie plates, 169, 170, 171; platters, 189, 190.

Spongeware
Sponged decoration was most often applied to stoneware and white earthenware, but examples can also be found in ironstone and yellow and red earthenware.

Baking dish, 222; bank, 286; bean pot, 32; covered bowl, 221; covered serving dish, 228; creamer, 123; crock, 25; custard cups, 247; jug, 98; mixing bowl, 214; mug, 157; piggy bank, 342; pitcher and bowl, 261; pitchers, 122; plate, 178; serving bowl, 210; serving dish, 213; slop jar, 1; soda fountain mug, 147; spittoon, 272; water cooler, 2.

Stoneware
The most important types of stoneware decoration are listed below. In addition, some stoneware pieces have a simple salt glaze or are glazed with brown or white slip.

White Earthenware and Ironstone

Although pottery made of white earthenware and ironstone was often decorated, especially with transfer printing, numerous examples with a clear glaze are also available. Some pieces also have embossed designs.

Yellowware

Yellow earthenware with a Rockingham or flint-enamel finish is extremely popular with some collectors. Others prefer simple banded decoration. Many examples are also available with a clear glaze.

Pottery and Porcelain Marks

Tracing a maker's mark can be a challenge, especially for the novice collector. Although some marks consist of the name or initials of the manufacturer, others are pictorial or simply indicate the material from which an object was made. Some companies changed their marks frequently. Others designed trademarks that could easily be confused with those of English companies. To make matters still more complicated, similar marks were often used by several firms.

Bennington, Vermont
Some marks from the famous pottery at Bennington, Vermont, help date a piece; for example, the uncommon Norton & Fenton mark was used only from 1845 to 1847. On the other hand, the 1849 Lyman, Fenton & Co. mark was used not just in 1849 by that firm, but in the 1850s by the United States Pottery Company. The U.S.P. ribbon mark, used from 1852 to 1858, contains a numerical code indicating such things as pattern.

Knowles, Taylor & Knowles
Some of the marks used by Knowles, Taylor & Knowles include the name of a specific product, such as "Lotus Ware," along with the firm's name or initials. Like many other companies, Knowles, Taylor & Knowles sometimes marked their wares with the name of the pattern or line they belonged to; the "Wyoming" mark illustrated is an example of this type.

Ott & Brewer
Ott & Brewer was just one of many companies who specifically designed marks, such as the crown, lion, and unicorn example illustrated, to resemble those used by English manufacturers. The other marks illustrated are 2 of those used on the Belleek china for which Ott & Brewer are famous.

Union Porcelain Works
Union Porcelain Works first marked their wares with an eagle's head holding the letter "S" in its beak in around 1876; in 1877 the letters "U.P.W." were sometimes added.

Rookwood Pottery
Perhaps the best-known of all the marks used by the Rookwood Pottery was adopted in 1886 and consists of the letters "RP" placed back to back. A flame was placed above the mark in 1887, and an additional flame was added every subsequent year until 1900. With its 11 flames, the mark illustrated obviously dates from 1897. Rookwood used a variety of other trademarks and often added the name of the decorator to their products as well.

Van Briggle Pottery
Although the Van Briggle Pottery has used various forms of an AA monogram since it was founded, early and valuable examples include the year of production.

Most collectors rely on standard handbooks, such as Barber's *Marks of American Potters* and Kovels' *Dictionary of Marks— Pottery and Porcelain*, to help them trace the marks they encounter. These reference books are a necessity for anyone who is seriously interested in collecting ceramics.

On the facing page we have reproduced 18 representative marks used by some major firms to illustrate many of these points.

American Pottery and Porcelain Manufacturers

This table lists the pottery and porcelain manufacturers featured in this book, as well as a representative sampling of other major establishments operating in America from the mid-18th century to the present. In addition, a number of potters who ran small shops throughout the country are included. The name of each firm or individual is followed by the approximate dates of operation, location, and principal types of wares produced. If a company changed its name during the course of operation or was known by more than one name, the alternate name is given in parentheses.

Company	Dates
A	
American Encaustic Tiling Company	1875–1935
American Pottery Manufacturing Company (American Pottery Company)	1833–92
Anchor Pottery	1894–1926
H. S. Atcheson	1841–1906
B	
Anthony W. Baecher	1868–89
Bangor Stoneware Company	1890–1916
J. A. Bauer & Company	1890–1958
John Bell	1833–80
John W. Bell	1880–95
Peter Bell	1805–24
Samuel Bell	1833–53
Samuel & Solomon Bell	1853–82
Samuel Bell & Sons	1882–1908
Solomon Bell	1837–82
Edwin Bennett	1846–1938
James Bennett & Brothers	1838–42
August Blank	1890–1900
William Boch & Brothers	1844–62
Edward Marshall Boehm, Inc.	1950–present
Gousse Bonnin & George Anthony Morris	1769–72
Daniel Brannon (Pioneer Pottery)	1856–87
Charles W. Braun	1856–96
Isaac P. Brazelton	1844–55
Brown Brothers	1863–1904
John Burger & Son	1841–90
Enoch Burnett	1853–69
Bybee Pottery	1935–40

Location	Major Products
Zanesville, OH	tiles
Jersey City, NJ	Rockingham, yellowware
Trenton, NJ	whiteware
Annapolis, IN	stoneware
Winchester, VA	redware
Bangor, ME	stoneware
Los Angeles, CA	redware, stoneware, yellowware
Waynesboro, PA	redware, stoneware
Waynesboro, PA	redware, stoneware
Hagerstown, MD	redware
Strasburg, VA	redware, stoneware
Strasburg, VA	redware, stoneware
Strasburg, VA	redware, stoneware
Strasburg, VA	redware, stoneware
Baltimore, MD	Rockingham, whiteware, yellowware
East Liverpool, OH	Rockingham, yellowware
California, MO	stoneware
Greenpoint, NY	porcelain
Trenton, NJ	figural porcelain
Philadelphia, PA	porcelain
East Oakland, CA	Rockingham, yellowware
Buffalo, NY	stoneware
Milwaukee, WI	stoneware
Huntington, NY	redware, stoneware
Rochester, NY	stoneware
Washington, DC	stoneware
Madison County, KY	art pottery, stoneware

Company	Dates
C	
John B. Caire and Company	1842–52
Cambridge Art Pottery	1895–1910
Cambridge Tile Manufacturing Company (Cambridge Art Tile Works)	1887–1929
Frederick Carpenter	1793–1810
Carrollton China Company	1901–10
Charles Cartlidge & Company	1844–56
Ceramic Art Company (now Lenox, Inc.)	1889–1903
Chelsea Keramic Art Works	1872–89
Chenango China Company	1901–10
Chesapeake Pottery (D. F. Haynes & Company)	1879–1910
Rudolph Christ	1789–1821
Nathan Clark & Company	1835–46
Nathan Clark & Company	1841–52
Clark and Fox	1829–38
Clifton Art Pottery	1905–08
Cook Pottery Company (Mellor & Company)	1894–1931
Coors Pottery Company	1910–40
John Corliss	1820–80
Cornelison Pottery	1809–present
Cowden & Wilcox (Harrisburg Stoneware Company)	1850–80
Coxon and Company	1863–84
J. Dorris Craven	1828–93
J. H. Craven & Son	1883–1900
Crescent Pottery Company	1881–1902
Clarkson Crolius	1794–1838
Clarkson Crolius, Jr.	1835–49
Crown Pottery Company	1891–1905
Paul Cushman	1807–33
Cybis Porcelains	1942–present
D	
Dedham Pottery	1896–1943
Denver China and Pottery Company	1900–05
Charles Dillon & Company	1834–39
A. P. Donaghho	1866–1908
Dorchester Pottery Works	1895–1976

Location	Major Products
Poughkeepsie, NY	stoneware
Cambridge, OH	art pottery
Covington, KY	tiles
Boston, MA	stoneware
Salineville, OH	whiteware
Greenpoint, NY	porcelain
Trenton, NJ	porcelain
Chelsea, MA	art pottery, tiles
New Castle, PA	whiteware
Baltimore, MD	majolica, porcelain, whiteware
Salem, NC	redware, stoneware, whiteware
Mount Morris, NY	stoneware
Rochester, NY	stoneware
Athens, NY	redware, stoneware
Clifton, NJ	art pottery
Trenton, NJ	porcelain, whiteware
Golden, CO	porcelain, whiteware
Woolrich, ME	redware
Bybee, KY	stoneware
Harrisburg, PA	stoneware
Trenton, NJ	whiteware
Seagrove, NC	stoneware
Mossy Creek, GA	stoneware
Trenton, NJ	whiteware, yellowware
New York, NY	stoneware
New York, NY	redware, stoneware
Evansville, IN	whiteware
Albany, NY	stoneware
Trenton, NJ	figural porcelain
East Dedham, MA	art pottery
Denver, CO	art pottery
Albany, NY	stoneware
Parkersburg, WV	stoneware
Dorchester, MA	stoneware

Company	Dates
E	
Eagle Pottery (James Hamilton)	1852–97
Eagle Pottery Company	1883–1900
East End Pottery	1800–1900
W. & O. V. Eaton (Lincoln Pottery)	1880–1903
Jacob Eberly	1880–1900
Edmands & Company	1812–1905
Elsinore Pottery Company	1900–23
F	
Faience Manufacturing Company	1880–92
William H. Farrar (Southern Porcelain Manufacturing Company)	1856–78
Frankoma Pottery	1948–present
Fulper Pottery Company	1858–1929
G	
Gardiner Stoneware Company	1874–87
Gay Head Pottery	1879–85
Geijsbeck Pottery Company	1899–1910
Glasgow Pottery (John Moses & Sons)	1863–1905
Gloucester Porcelain Company	1857–72
Goodale & Stedman	1822–25
Greenwood Pottery Company	1868–1933
John B. Gregory	1808–31
Griffen, Smith & Hill	1879–94
Grueby Faience and Tile Company	1897–1910
Grueby Pottery	1900–20
H	
Thomas Haig	1812–33
Thomas Haig, Jr.	1831–90
Hamilton and Jones	1852–97
James J. Hansen	1856–1909
Martin Happel	1890
William Hare	1857–87
Harley Pottery	1875–1900
James Hart & Son	1841–85
Samuel Hart & Sons	1832–95

Location	Major Products
Greensboro, PA	stoneware
Macomb, IL	stoneware
East Liverpool, OH	porcelain, whiteware
Lincoln, NE	redware, stoneware
Strasburg, VA	redware
Charlestown, MA	stoneware
Elsinore, CA	whiteware
Greenpoint, NY	tiles
Kaolin, SC	porcelain, whiteware
Sapulpa, OK	art pottery
Flemington, NJ	art pottery, redware, stoneware, whiteware
Gardiner, ME	stoneware
Martha's Vineyard, MA	art pottery
Golden, CO	whiteware
Trenton, NJ	Rockingham, whiteware, yellowware
Gloucester, NJ	porcelain
Hartford, CT	stoneware
Trenton, NJ	porcelain, whiteware
Clinton, NY	redware
Phoenixville, PA	majolica, whiteware, yellowware
Boston, MA	art pottery, tiles
Boston, MA	art pottery, tiles
Philadelphia, PA	redware, Rockingham, stoneware, yellowware
Philadelphia, PA	Rockingham, stoneware, yellowware
Greensboro, PA	stoneware
Hyrum, UT	redware
Hagerstown, MD	redware
Wilmington, DE	redware, stoneware
Nashville, TN	stoneware
Sherburne, NY	stoneware
Fulton, NY	stoneware

Company	Dates
D. F. Haynes & Company (Chesapeake Pottery)	1879–1910
D. & J. Henderson (Jersey City Pottery)	1829–33
Hernandez & Saley (Louisiana Porcelain Works)	1881–90
Charles E. Hubbell & Denison Chesebro	1867–87
Hudson Pottery	1868–70
Hull & Bach Company	1835–40
A. E. Hull Pottery Company	1905–present
John M. Hummel	1860–90

J

William Jackson	1811–15
J. E. Jeffers & Company	1868–1901
Jersey City Pottery (D. & J. Henderson)	1829–33
Lorenzo Johnson	1840–80
Jugtown Pottery	1923–present

K

C. & W. Kirkpatrick (Anna Pottery)	1859–94
Richard F. Kitson	1817–70
Edwin M. Knowles China Company	1854–1950
Knowles, Taylor & Knowles	1870–1926

L

Lafever Pottery	1840–1900
Homer Laughlin Company	1874–present
Lenox, Inc.	1903–present
James Long & Family	1820–1900
Lonhuda Pottery	1892–95
Low Art Tile Works	1879–1902
Lyman, Fenton & Company	1849–53
Lyons Pottery	1822–1904

M

Macomb Pottery Company	1880–1906
John Mann	1830–1900
Marblehead Pottery	1905–36
Mayer Pottery Company	1880–1900
Nelson McCoy Pottery Company	1910–67

Location	Major Products
Baltimore, MD	majolica, porcelain, whiteware
Jersey City, NJ	Rockingham, yellowware
New Orleans, LA	porcelain
Geddes (Syracuse), NY	stoneware
Hudson, NY	stoneware
Buffalo, NY	stoneware
Crooksville, OH	art pottery, whiteware
Florence, MO	stoneware
Lynn, MA	redware
Philadelphia, PA	Rockingham, yellowware
Jersey City, NJ	Rockingham, yellowware
Newstead, NY	redware
Seagrove, NC	art pottery
Anna, IL	stoneware
North Bridgton, ME	redware
Newell, WV	whiteware
East Liverpool, OH	porcelain, Rockingham, whiteware, yellowware
Baxter, TN	stoneware
East Liverpool, OH Newell, WV	porcelain, whiteware
Trenton, NJ	porcelain
Byram, GA	stoneware
Steubenville, OH	art pottery
Chelsea, MA	tiles
Bennington, VT	flint enamel, porcelain, Rockingham, whiteware, yellowware
Lyons, NY	stoneware
Macomb, IL	stoneware
Rahway, NJ	redware
Marblehead, MA	art pottery, tiles
Beaver Falls, PA	whiteware
Roseville, OH	art pottery

Company	Dates
Henry Melcher (Louisville Pottery)	1845–1922
Mellor & Company (Cook Pottery Company)	1894–1931
William Meyer & Sons	1887–1962
Minnesota Stoneware Company	1883–1906
Moravian Pottery and Tile Works	1898–1956
Morganville Pottery	1854–1900
Morrison & Carr	1858–72
Mosaic Tile Company	1894–1967
John Moses & Sons (Glasgow Pottery)	1863–1905
Muncie Clay Products Company	1922–39

N

John Nase	1830–40
Newcomb Pottery	1895–1952
New England Pottery Company	1875–1910
Niloak Pottery	1909–46
North Star Stoneware Company	1892–97
Norton Pottery	1793–1895
Norwich Pottery Works	1881–95

O

George Ohr	1883–1906
Onondaga Pottery Company (Syracuse China Company)	1871–present
Stephen Orcutt & Company	1797–1830
Ott & Brewer	1863–92
Ottman Bros. & Company	1872–92
J. B. Owens Pottery Company	1896–1906

P

Pacific Clay Manufacturing Company	1894–1910
Pacific Pottery Company	1892–1950
Peoria Pottery (Joseph Jager)	1864–89
Mauldine Perine & Company	1827–1938
Peters and Reed Pottery	1901–20
S. L. Pewtress & Company	1868–87
Phoenixville Pottery Company	1867–92
Pisgah Forest Pottery	1914–present

Location	Major Products
Louisville, KY	stoneware
Trenton, NJ	porcelain, whiteware
Atacosa, TX	redware, stoneware
Red Wing, MN	stoneware
Doylestown, PA	art pottery, tiles
Morganville, NY	redware
New York, NY	majolica, whiteware
Zanesville, OH	art pottery, tiles
Trenton, NJ	Rockingham, whiteware, yellowware
Muncie, IN	art pottery
Montgomery County, PA	redware
New Orleans, LA	art pottery
East Boston, MA	whiteware
Benton, AR	art pottery
Red Wing, MN	stoneware
Bennington, VT	redware, stoneware
Norwich, CT	stoneware
Biloxi, MS	art pottery
Syracuse, NY	porcelain, whiteware
Whately, MA	redware, stoneware
Trenton, NJ	porcelain, Rockingham, whiteware
Fort Edward, NY	stoneware
Zanesville, OH	art pottery
Riverside, CA	yellowware
Portland, OR	stoneware
Peoria, IL	stoneware, whiteware
Baltimore, MD	redware, stoneware
South Zanesville, OH	art pottery
New Haven, CT	stoneware
Phoenixville, PA	Rockingham, whiteware, yellowware
Arden, NC	art pottery

Company	Dates
R	
Red Wing Potteries, Inc.	1877–1967
Henry Remmey & Family	1810–1900
Sidney Risley & Son	1845–81
Rookwood Pottery	1880–1959
Roseville Pottery	1898–1954
A. J. & J. L. Russell	1867–75
S	
Sacramento Pottery	1855–79
John George Schweinfurt	1850–90
Israel Seymour & Company	1819–52
Shawnee Pottery	1936–61
A. E. Smith	1825–87
Washington Smith	1833–61
Samuel H. Sonner	1853–92
David Spinner	1790–1811
Adam Staats	1750–69
Star Pottery	1888–1914
Stephens, Tams & Company	1861–68
Sterling Pottery Company	1900–present
John N. Stout	1866–87
Swan Hill Pottery	1849–54
Syracuse China Company (Onondaga Pottery Company)	1871–present
Syracuse Stoneware Company	1895–1900
T	
Samuel Troxel	1820–33
William Tucker and successors (American China Manufactory)	1826–38
U	
J. A. & C. W. Underwood	1865–67
H. J. Underwood & Son	1880–91
Union Porcelain Works	1862–1908
United States Pottery Company	1849–58
V	
Van Briggle Pottery	1901–present
Vance Faience Pottery	1880–1900

Location	Major Products
Red Wing, MN	art pottery, stoneware, yellowware
Philadelphia, PA	porcelain, stoneware
Norwich, CT	Rockingham, stoneware
Cincinnati, OH	art pottery
Zanesville, OH	art pottery
West Troy, NY	stoneware
Sacramento, CA	stoneware
New Market, VA	redware
Troy, NY	redware, stoneware
Zanesville, OH	art pottery
Norwalk, CT	redware, stoneware
New York, NY	stoneware
Strasburg, VA	redware
Milford Township, PA	redware
Greenwich, CT	stoneware
Elmendorf, TX	stoneware
Trenton, NJ	whiteware
East Liverpool, OH	ironstone
Ripley, IL	Rockingham, stoneware
South Amboy, NJ	Rockingham, yellowware
Syracuse, NY	porcelain, whiteware
Syracuse, NY	stoneware
Montgomery County, PA	redware
Philadelphia, PA	porcelain
Fort Edward, NY	stoneware
Calhoun, MO	stoneware
Greenpoint, NY	porcelain
Bennington, VT	flint enamel, porcelain, Rockingham, scroddledware, whiteware, yellowware
Colorado Springs, CO	art pottery
Tiltonville, OH	Rockingham, stoneware, whiteware

Company	Dates
Vodrey Bros.	1857–1930

W

William E. Warner	1829–71
Warwick China Co.	1877–1904
S. H. Way	1863–68
Weller Pottery	1893–1948
Wellsville China Company	1902–10
West End Pottery Company	1893–1934
Western Stoneware Company	1906–present
Wheeling Pottery Company	1877–1904
Noah White & Sons (White's Pottery)	1838–1909
Albert O. Whittemore	1869–93
Alvin Wilcox	1830–59
Frank Woolsey	1882–95
Franklin T. Wright & Son	1855–68

Z

Zane Pottery	1921–41
Zanesville Stoneware Company	1887–present
D. Zittel & Company	1870–1905

Location	Major Products
East Liverpool, OH	Rockingham, whiteware, yellowware
West Troy, NY	Rockingham, stoneware, whiteware
Wheeling, WV	whiteware
Eola, OR	redware
Zanesville, OH	art pottery
Wellsville, OH	whiteware
East Liverpool, OH	whiteware
Monmouth, IL	stoneware
Wheeling, WV	whiteware
Utica, NY	stoneware
Havana (Montour Falls), NY	stoneware
West Bloomfield, NY	redware
Benton, AR	stoneware
Taunton, MA	stoneware
South Zanesville, OH	art pottery
Zanesville, OH	stoneware
Waco, KY	stoneware

Glossary

Albany slip   A lustrous brown slip formed from mixing water with a brown clay mined near Albany, New York, as well as in other parts of the United States.

Alkaline glaze   A mixture of clay, water, and wood ash that fires to a clear or a mottled dark green, yellow, or brown finish.

Applied decoration   Decoration that is separately made and then attached, using slip, to a ceramic body before firing.

Art pottery   Pottery made by hand in limited quantities by studio potters around the turn of the century; today more broadly applied to much 20th-century decorative ware.

Ash glaze   A glaze, often used in the South on stoneware, derived from wood ashes mixed with water, which produces lye; the lye is then combined with slaked lime, sand, ground glass, or clay, forming a paste that fires to a colored finish ranging from light yellow to dark brown; also called tobacco spit glaze.

Base   The lowermost part of a ceramic body.

Bisque   Ceramic ware fired without a glaze; generally refers to porcelain; also called biscuit. *See also* Parian.

Bristol slip   An opaque white slip that contains zinc oxide.

Bunghole   A small hole, usually near the base of a piece, through which liquid can be poured; usually found in rundlets and water coolers.

Ceramic   A mineral-based substance, such as earthenware or porcelain, that is fired at a high temperature to a hard state.

Clay   An earthy material that becomes malleable when wet and hard after being fired.

Cobalt oxide   A compound that forms the base of many blue glazes; primarily used to decorate salt-glazed stoneware.

Coggle wheel   A wooden or metal wheel that has a shaped edge and a handle; used to make decorative impressions in soft clay.

Coleslaw decoration   Applied decoration consisting of many tiny convoluted strands of clay or porcelain that resemble wooden shavings.

Collar   A thick, raised band that encircles the neck.

Crazing   Tiny cracks in glaze produced by the differing rates at which the body and the glaze contract and often appearing with age; also called spidering.

Drape molding   The process of shaping a ceramic body by placing unfired clay over a form, pressing the clay down, and then trimming off the excess; typically used in the production of plates and platters.

Earthenware   Slightly porous pottery that is fired at a relatively low temperature.

Embossing   Raised decoration formed as a piece is molded or shaped; not separately applied.

Extruder   A device through which clay is forced and shaped; often used to make ridged handles.

Faience   Earthenware covered with an opaque white tin glaze and then decorated with colored glazes.

Finial   A hand-shaped or molded protrusion that often serves as the handle on a lid.

Firing   Heating a ceramic body in an oven or kiln.

Flint enamel   A streaky, multicolored glaze applied to a yellow or white earthenware body and produced by dusting metallic oxides over a clear glaze before firing.

Glaze   A mixture of water, clay, and various metallic oxides or alkalies that is applied to a clay body before firing; after firing the glaze vitrifies, producing a water-resistant surface. *See also* Salt glaze.

Glaze mill   A device used to grind clay and metallic oxides or alkalies into a fine powder; consisting of 2 stones, the top one rotating against the stationary bottom one.

Greenware   Unfired pottery.

Hard paste porcelain   A translucent ceramic body composed of kaolin and feldspar or chinastone; fired at a high temperature, it is steel hard, vitreous, and nonabsorbent; also called true porcelain.

Impressed decoration   Decoration created by pressing a shaped wooden or metal stamp into the soft clay surface of a ceramic vessel before firing; may also be done with a coggle wheel.

Incised decoration   Decoration created by the use of a sharp pointed instrument to scratch designs into the soft clay surface of an unbaked ceramic vessel.

Ironstone   An extremely hard, vitrified, nonporous white earthenware; also called semi-porcelain and hotel china.

Kaolin   A fine white clay that fires to a pure white.

Kiln   A furnace or oven in which ceramic products are baked.

Lead glaze   A glaze consisting of lead oxide, water, and clay that fires to a shiny, glasslike surface.

Lug handle   A semicircular handle that is attached horizontally to the side of a ceramic body, usually found on stoneware or redware.

Lustreware   English earthenware with a deep metallic-colored glaze.

Majolica   An Italian term for earthenware covered with an opaque white tin glaze and then decorated with one or more glazes in contrasting colors.

Manganese oxide   A metallic oxide used in glazes that fires from purplish-brown to black; often used on redware.

Modeling   Shaping a clay body by hand and hand-held tools.

Molding   The process of making pottery by pouring liquid clay or pressing soft clay into a mold and allowing it to harden; once removed from the mold the piece retains its shape; also called casting.

Neck   The narrow area between the rim and shoulder.

Overglaze decoration   Decoration applied after a piece has been glazed and fired; after the decoration is applied, the piece is usually fired again at a lower temperature.

Parian   Unglazed porcelain that resembles marble.

Pierced decoration   Decoration produced by cutting areas out of a clay body; frequently seen on early Pennsylvania pieces like sugar bowls.

Porcelain   A hard, white, translucent ceramic body composed primarily of kaolin, ground flint, and feldspar mixed together and fired at a high temperature.

Potter's wheel   A device on which ceramic objects are turned; the simplest consists of 2 disks joined by a shaft and set in a frame; as the lower disk is turned, the upper one, on which the clay is formed, rotates.

Pottery   Ceramics made from clay or a mixture of clays; also the shop or factory where ceramics are manufactured.

Presentation pieces   Pottery, often quite ornate, intended to be given as a gift or to commemorate a special occasion; often one-of-a-kind and bearing the name or initials of the recipient.

Production pieces   The standard wares of a pottery, usually made in large quantities.

Redware   Pottery made from red earthenware and characterized by a porous, relatively coarse and brittle body; may be light rose-pink to dark reddish-brown.

Rim   The upper edge of a ceramic body; also called lip.

Rimmed base   A base that is inset from the sides of the body and that usually has a recessed bottom.

Rockinghamware   Yellowware covered with a mottled brown glaze; sometimes referred to as "Benningtonware."

Salt glaze   A shiny, glasslike, impermeable glaze used on stoneware pottery; produced by throwing salt into a hot kiln, where the vaporized salt combines with the silica in the ceramic body, forming a shiny finish.

Sgraffito   A decorative technique in which a potter covers an earthenware body with an opaque coat of slip and then scratches away the slip, partially exposing the clay body; used especially in Pennsylvania.

Shoulder   The portion of a ceramic body between the waist and neck.

Slip   A suspension of ceramic materials in water.

Slip cup   A small, hollow, cuplike device equipped with tubes that are often made from turkey-feather quills; slip is trailed or dribbled through the tubes in decorative patterns onto a ceramic surface.

Slip decoration   Decoration composed of slip and a coloring agent that is applied with a brush or slip cup to a ceramic surface.

Soft paste porcelain   A ceramic body composed of white clay and powdered glass or other materials; made in imitation of hard paste porcelain, soft paste porcelain fires at a lower temperature and is somewhat softer and slightly absorbent.

Sponged decoration   Slip decoration applied to a ceramic body with a sponge or piece of cloth; may be applied randomly or in a pattern.

Stenciled decoration   Slip decoration applied by brush through a cutout pattern to a ceramic body.

Stippled   Decorated with many tiny dots or depressions.

Stoneware   A high-fired ceramic body of great density and hardness that is partially vitrified; it ranges in color from a blue-gray or off-white to a dark brown; often covered with a salt glaze.

Tin glaze   A glaze that is opaque because of the presence of tin oxide.

Transfer decoration   Decoration in which a design is printed on a thin piece of paper that is then attached to a ceramic body; during firing, the design adheres to the body while the paper burns up.

Underglaze decoration   Decoration applied to bisque before the application of glaze.

Vitreous   Glasslike in appearance.

Waist   The widest part of a ceramic body.

Wheel-thrown   Shaped by hand on a potter's wheel.

White earthenware   A highly plastic, opaque, and nonvitreous white ceramic body that is fired at a high temperature.

Whiteware   White earthenware and ironstone.

Yellowware   A hard, impervious yellow earthenware body fired at a high temperature; it varies in hue from deep yellow to off-white.

Bibliography

Adamson, Jack E.
Illustrated Handbook of Ohio Sewer Pipe Folk Art
Zoar, Ohio: Privately published, 1973.

Alexander, Donald E.
Roseville Pottery for Collectors
Richmond, Indiana: Privately published, 1970.

Arnest, Barbara M.
Van Briggle Pottery, the Early Years
Colorado Springs, Colorado: Colorado Springs Fine Art Center,
1975.

Barber, Edwin A.
Marks of American Potters
Philadelphia: Patterson & White Co., 1904
Reprinted Southampton, New York: The Cracker Barrel Press,
1972.
*The Pottery and Porcelain of the United States: An Historical
Review of American Ceramic Art from the Earliest Times to the
Present Day*
New York and London: Putnam's Sons, 1893
Combined with *Marks of American Potters* and reprinted New
York: Feingold & Lewis, 1976.
Tulip Ware of the Pennsylvania-German Potters
New York: Dover Publications, Inc., 1970.

Barnes, Benjamin
The Moravian Pottery; Memories of Forty-six Years
Doylestown, Pennsylvania: Bucks County Historical Society,
1970.

Barons, Richard I.
18th and 19th Century American Folk Pottery
New Paltz, New York: State University of New York at New
Paltz, 1969.

Barret, Richard C.
Bennington Pottery and Porcelain
New York: Bonanza Books, 1958.
How to Identify Bennington Pottery
Brattleboro, Vermont: Stephen Greene Press, 1973.

Bivins, John, Jr.
The Moravian Potters in North Carolina
Chapel Hill, North Carolina: The University of North Carolina
Press, 1972.

Branin, M. Lelyn
The Early Potters and Potteries of Maine
Middletown, Connecticut: Wesleyan University Press, 1978.

Burrison, John A.
Georgia Jug Makers: A History of Southern Folk Pottery
Ann Arbor, Michigan: University Microfilms International,
1973.

Buxton, Virginia
Roseville Pottery, for Love or Money
Nashville, Tennessee: Tymbre Hill Publishing Co., 1977.

Clark, Garth, and Hughto, Margie
A Century of Ceramics in the United States 1878–1978
New York: E. P. Dutton, Inc., 1979.

Clement, Arthur W.
Our Pioneer Potters
Brooklyn, New York: Maple Press, 1947.

Conway, Bob, and Gilreath, Ed
Traditional Pottery in North Carolina
Waynesville, North Carolina: The Mountaineer, 1974.

Evans, Paul
Art Pottery of the United States: An Encyclopedia of Producers and Their Marks
New York: Charles Scribner's Sons, 1974.

Greer, Georgeanna H.
American Stonewares: The Art and Craft of Utilitarian Potters
Exton, Pennsylvania: Schiffer Publishing, Ltd., 1981.

Guilland, Harold F.
Early American Folk Pottery
Philadelphia, Chilton Book Co., 1971.

Henzke, Lucile
American Art Pottery
Camden, New Jersey: Thomas Nelson, Inc., 1970.

Hillier, Bevis
Pottery and Porcelain 1700–1914
Des Moines, Iowa, and New York: Meredith Press, 1968.

Huxford, Sharon and Bob
The Collector's Encyclopedia of Fiesta
Paducah, Kentucky: Collector Books, 1978.

Irvine, Mary E., and Ormond, Suzanne
Louisiana's Art Nouveau: The Crafts of the Newcomb Style
Gretna, Louisiana: Pelican Publishing Company, Inc., 1976.

James, Arthur E.
The Potters and Potteries of Chester County, Pennsylvania
West Chester, Pennsylvania: Chester County Historical Society, 1945.

Johnson, Deb and Gini
Beginner's Book of American Pottery
Des Moines, Iowa: Wallace-Homestead Book Co., 1974.

Ketchum, William C., Jr.
Early Potters and Potteries of New York State
New York: Funk & Wagnalls, 1970.
The Pottery and Porcelain Collector's Handbook
New York: Funk & Wagnalls, 1971.
The Pottery of the State
New York: Museum of American Folk Art, 1974.

Kovel, Ralph M. and Terry H.
Dictionary of Marks—Pottery and Porcelain
New York: Crown Publishers, Inc., 1953.
The Kovels' Collector's Guide to American Art Pottery
New York: Crown Publishers, Inc., 1983.

Lasansky, Jeannette
Central Pennsylvania Redware Pottery
Lewisburg, Pennsylvania: The Union County Oral Traditions Projects, 1979.

Loar, Peggy A.
Indiana Stoneware
Indianapolis, Indiana: Indianapolis Museum of Art, 1974.

Monmouth County Historical Association
New Jersey Stoneware
Freehold, New Jersey: Transcript Printing House, 1955.

New Jersey State Museum
Early Arts of New Jersey: The Potter's Art c. 1680–1900
Trenton, New Jersey: New Jersey State Museum, 1956.

Noel Hume, Ivor
*Pottery and Porcelain in Colonial Williamsburg's
Archaeological Collections*
Williamsburg, Virginia: Colonial Williamsburg Foundation, 1969.

Osgood, Cornelius
The Jug and Related Stoneware of Bennington
Rutland, Vermont: Charles E. Tuttle Co., 1971.

Peck, Herbert
The Book of Rookwood Pottery
New York: Bonanza Books, 1968.

Powell, Elizabeth A.
Pennsylvania Pottery, Tools and Processes
Doylestown, Pennsylvania: The Bucks County Historical Society, 1972.

Purviance, Louise, and Schneider, Norris F.
Zanesville Art Pottery in Color
Leon, Iowa: Mid-American Book Co., 1968.

Quimby, Ian M. G., ed.
Ceramics in America
Charlottesville, Virginia: The University of Virginia Press, 1973.

Ramsay, John
American Potters and Pottery
Boston: Hale, Cushman & Flint, 1939
Reprinted New York: Tudor Publishing Co., 1947.

Ray, Marcia
Collectible Ceramics
New York: Crown Publishers, Inc., 1974.

Rice, A. H., and Stoudt, John B.
The Shenandoah Pottery
Strasburg, Virginia: Shenandoah Publishing House, Inc., 1929.

Rochester Museum and Science Center
Clay in the Hands of the Potter
Rochester, New York: Rochester House of Printing, 1974.

Schaltenbrand, Phil
*Old Pots, Salt-glazed Stoneware of the Greensboro-New Geneva
Region*
Hanover, Pennsylvania: Everybody's Press, 1977.

Schwartz, Marvin D.
Collector's Guide to Antique American Ceramics
Garden City, New York: Doubleday & Co., Inc., 1969.

Schwartz, Stuart C.
North Carolina Pottery—A Bibliography
Charlotte, North Carolina: Mint Museum of History, 1978.

Smith, Elmer L.
Pottery—A Utilitarian Folk Craft
Lebanon, Pennsylvania: Applied Arts Publishers, 1972.

Smith, Joseph J., with introduction by William C. Ketchum, Jr.
Regional Aspects of American Folk Pottery
York, Pennsylvania: The Historical Society of York County,
1974.

Spargo, John
The Potters and Potteries of Bennington
Boston: Houghton Mifflin Co., 1926
Reprinted New York: Dover Publications, Inc., 1972.
Early American Pottery and China
New York: The Century Co., 1926
Reprinted Rutland, Vermont: Charles E. Tuttle Co., 1974.

Steward, Regina, and Cosentina, Geraldine
Stoneware: A Golden Book of Collectibles
New York: Golden Press, 1977.

Stiles, Helen E.
Pottery in the United States
New York: E. P. Dutton, Inc., 1921.

Sudbury, Byron
*Historic Clay Tobacco Pipe Makers in the United States of
America*
Oxford, England: BAR International Series, 1979.

Watkins, Lura W.
Early New England Potters and Their Wares
Cambridge, Massachusetts: Harvard University Press, 1950
Reprinted Hamden, Connecticut: Archon Books, 1968.

Webster, Donald B.
Decorated Stoneware Pottery of North America
Rutland, Vermont: Charles E. Tuttle Co., 1971.

Wiltshire, William E. III
Folk Pottery of the Shenandoah Valley
New York: E. P. Dutton, Inc., 1975.

Winton, Andrew L. and Kate B.
Norwalk Potteries
Canaan, New Hampshire: Phoenix Publishing, 1981.

Public Collections

Most large art museums exhibit American pottery. In addition, many of the historic houses, buildings, and restoration villages that are open to the public have fine examples. The sources listed below indicate significant permanent collections.

New England

Connecticut
Hartford: Wadsworth Atheneum. *New Haven:* Yale University Art Gallery. *Norwalk:* Lockwood-Mathews Mansion Museum.

Massachusetts
Boston: Museum of Fine Arts; The Society for the Preservation of New England Antiquities. *Deerfield:* Historic Deerfield. *Sturbridge:* Old Sturbridge Village.

New Hampshire
Manchester: The Currier Gallery of Art.

Rhode Island
Providence: Museum of Art, Rhode Island School of Design.

Vermont
Bennington: Bennington Museum. *Shelburne:* Shelburne Museum.

Mid-Atlantic Region

Delaware
Winterthur: Henry Francis du Pont Winterthur Museum.

Maryland
Baltimore: Baltimore Museum of Art; Maryland Historical Society.

New Jersey
Newark: Newark Museum. *Princeton:* The Art Museum, Princeton University. *Trenton:* New Jersey State Museum.

New York
Albany: Albany Institute of History and Art. *Cooperstown:* New York State Historical Association. *Huntington:* Huntington Historical Society. *New York City:* The Brooklyn Museum; The Metropolitan Museum of Art; Museum of American Folk Art; Museum of the City of New York; The New-York Historical Society; Richmondtown Historical Society. *Rochester:* Rochester Museum and Science Center; The Margaret Woodbury Strong Museum. *Syracuse:* Everson Museum of Art; Onondaga Historical Association. *Utica:* Munson-Williams-Proctor Institute.

Pennsylvania
Doylestown: Bucks County Historical Society; Mercer Museum of Bucks County Historical Society. *Harrisburg:* William Penn Memorial Museum. *Lancaster:* Pennsylvania Farm Museum of Landis Valley. *Philadelphia:* Philadelphia Museum of Art. *West Chester:* Chester County Historical Society.

Washington, D.C.
National Museum of American History, Smithsonian Institution.

South

Alabama
Mobile: The Fine Arts Museum of the South.

Georgia
Atlanta: The High Museum of Art; Museum of Georgia Folk Culture.

Louisiana
New Orleans: Louisiana State Museum.

Missouri
Kansas City: William Rockhill Nelson Gallery and Atkins Museum of Fine Arts. *St. Louis:* St. Louis Art Museum.

North Carolina
Asheville: Asheville Museum of Art. *Charlotte:* Mint Museum of History. *Sanford:* Potters' Museum. *Seagrove:* Seagrove Potters' Museum. *Winston-Salem:* Museum of Early Southern Decorative Arts; Old Salem, Inc.

South Carolina
Charleston: Historic Charleston.

Virginia
Norfolk: Chrysler Museum at Norfolk. *Williamsburg:* Colonial Williamsburg; The Abby Aldrich Rockefeller Collection of American Folk Art.

Midwest

Illinois
Chicago: Art Institute of Chicago; Chicago Historical Society. *Springfield:* Illinois State Museum.

Indiana
Indianapolis: Indianapolis Museum of Art.

Michigan
Dearborn: Greenfield Village and Henry Ford Museum. *Detroit:* Detroit Historical Museum; Detroit Institute of Arts.

Minnesota
Minneapolis: Minneapolis Institute of Arts.

Ohio
Cincinnati: Cincinnati Art Museum. *Cleveland:* Cleveland Museum of Art; Western Reserve Historical Society. *Columbus:* Ohio Historical Society. *East Liverpool:* East Liverpool Historical Society.

Wisconsin
Madison: Wisconsin State Historical Society.

Rockies, Southwest, and West Coast

California
Fullerton: Art Gallery, California State University at Fullerton. *Los Angeles:* Los Angeles County Museum of Art. *Oakland:* The Oakland Museum. *San Francisco:* M. H. de Young Memorial Museum.

Colorado
Denver: The Denver Art Museum.

Nebraska
Lincoln: Nebraska State Historical Society.

Texas
Dallas: Dallas Museum of Fine Arts. *Houston:* The Bayou Bend Collection.

Buying Pottery and Porcelain

Pottery and porcelain are available throughout the country at thousands of shops, shows, flea markets, house sales, and auctions. Auctions are a good source for stoneware and redware, and, occasionally, pieces of early American porcelain. The more moderately priced white earthenware, yellowware, and 20th-century ceramics are likely to be sold at shops, shows, and house and yard sales.

Shows, Sales, and Shops

Antiques shows take place regularly in most cities and give collectors a chance to meet a number of dealers at one time. Ceramics collectors can expect to find art pottery and 19th-century porcelain here; shows specializing in country objects usually include a good sampling of American stoneware and redware.

People interested in modern ceramics, including inexpensive ironstone and decorated white earthenware, will usually find what they are looking for at yard and house sales and even at the "white elephant" sales conducted by charities and churches. Pieces can sometimes be purchased here for a fraction of their true value, for sellers may not recognize what they have.

Many collectors prefer to buy from dealers. These professionals are usually glad to share their knowledge with customers. In an antiques shop or at a dealer's home you have time to examine a piece thoroughly, and you rarely need to make an immediate decision to buy. Some dealers sell by mail order through illustrated catalogues; if you know exactly what you are looking for, this approach may work for you. Since there are dealers who specialize in virtually every field, except perhaps for the most recently made ceramics, and in every price range, you are sure to find one who suits your taste and budget.

Buying at Auction

Since some of the finest and most interesting pieces of pottery and porcelain are sold at auction, it is understandable that sooner or later most collectors try their hand at bidding. Although countless inexpensive objects pass through country and city auctions, they are no longer the place to look for real bargains. Whenever a major piece is presented for sale, knowledgeable collectors and dealers usually hear about it beforehand and appear at the auction to battle over its acquisition. Yet because porcelain and pottery are so varied, and because the field is so specialized, it is likely that from time to time auctioneers will be unacquainted with unusual pieces they are selling—it is then that informed collectors can purchase bargains.

How an Auction Works

An auction is a sale of objects to the highest bidders. The seller, or the consignor, offers goods to prospective buyers through his agent, the auctioneer. The bidder offering the most money for a given item buys the "lot" (one piece or a group of pieces sold together). The auctioneer always tries to stimulate bidding and to get the highest price, since he (or his firm) generally receives a percentage of the sale as payment or commission.

The Viewing and Other Preliminaries

The first step toward informed bidding is to attend the viewing before the auction, an advertised period of a few hours or days during which the objects offered may be examined by the public.

Never bid on something unless you have checked it thoroughly beforehand. Compare what you see with the information given in the catalogue, if one is available. If you have any questions about an object, its attribution, or its condition, talk to the auctioneer or the firm's specialist in that field. If a catalogue is not available, carry a small notebook to jot down the lot number and other information about the object, particularly its condition. If you feel uncertain about the auctioneer's or your own assessment of a piece, especially an expensive one, you may wish to hire a consultant—dealers will often, for a fee, advise you or sometimes even bid for you.

The viewing is also a good time to find out what form of payment the auctioneer requires. Some will take only cash or certified checks; others will accept personal checks with proper identification, or credit cards.

The Sale

At most larger auctions, the auctioneer will provide estimated price ranges for the pieces in the sale. These are usually printed in the auction catalogue or on a separate list. Though pieces quite often sell for more or less than the estimates, these should give you some idea of what the auctioneer expects a piece to fetch. Also, many large auction houses allow a seller to set a "reserve" on a lot—the price below which it will not be sold, frequently close to the low estimate. If bidding does not reach this minimum, the lot will be withdrawn and returned to the consignor for a small handling fee.

Decide in advance the price you are willing to pay for a particular lot. The Price Guide section of this book provides general guidelines and prevailing market price ranges to help you set your own bidding limit.

The best place to sit at an auction is toward the rear, where you can see more of what is going on. There are two customary ways to bid—by raising a hand or by using the numbered paddle sometimes furnished by the auctioneer. Listen closely; bidding is often extremely rapid. When your pre-established price limit has been reached, stop. This is the key to wise auction bidding.

Patience and persistence are required, since at every auction some pieces may sell for more or for less than most people anticipate. There is almost always a "sleeper" or two, particularly just after or even just before a high-priced lot has captured the attention of the audience.

At many auction houses, someone who has attended the viewing but cannot be present at the auction itself can leave a bid. Such bids will be treated as the maximum the absentee bidder is willing to spend, so that if there is little competition when the auction house bids for you, the final price you pay may be far less than your top bid. An out-of-town collector who has seen an auction catalogue but cannot attend the viewing and auction may sometimes be allowed to place a bid by telephone, but such blind bidding is not recommended unless the bidder delegates someone to examine the object for him prior to the sale.

Collecting Your Purchases

The fall of the gavel and the cry of "sold" mark a successful bid. Now the buyer must pay for the purchase and remove it from the auction premises. Large auction houses will ship items for a fee; most auctioneers do not have such services, however, and the buyer is responsible for transporting a purchase within a stated time limit.

Price Guide

In ceramics, as in most fields, experienced collectors are much more likely to find bargains than novices are. To avoid costly mistakes and to make wise purchases, the collector must become thoroughly acquainted with ceramics and with today's marketplace. It is also advisable to understand how collecting trends change—why some varieties suddenly become popular while others experience a lightninglike decline. To keep abreast of what is often unpredictable, collectors should study auction reports and talk with dealers about price variations.

Many beginners regard auctions as the ultimate price determinant, for they do offer the most dramatic evidence of the market in action. A piece is presented; all bidders compete as equals; the highest bidder captures the prize. In reality the process is much more complex. Anyone who has observed bidders competing for the same object knows that this type of warfare can drive prices well above a reasonable figure. And because some collectors seek out objects that were once owned by the famous, prestige can warp auction records as well. On the other hand, auction prices can be unrealistically low if, for some reason, attendance at the sale is poor or doubt has been cast on the authenticity of a piece. Yet while auction results must be placed in perspective, they do reflect long-term market trends. Dealers' prices are often the most accurate guide to what is happening on the market. Their retail prices are based on the wholesale price plus a reasonable amount for overhead and profit. Because dealers must remain competitive, their prices tend to become uniform over a period of time.

This price guide is based on auction records and consultations with dealers and knowledgeable collectors. Remember that experienced collectors understand, and we agree, that a price guide is just that, a guide. No two objects are identical, and no two buying situations are the same. The prices listed are national averages, but there are factors that affect prices in specific cases. Certain types of pottery and porcelain are more popular and bring higher prices in one area of the country than another. For example, there is little interest in southern ash-glazed stoneware outside the South, and prices elsewhere may be no more than a third of those in that region. Similarly, slip-decorated redware usually brings more in New England and Pennsylvania, where it was made. Makers' marks often affect prices. Stoneware bearing the mark of an Ohio manufacturer will nearly always bring more in that state than in Maine or Georgia. Knowledge of local preferences should always be considered in evaluating the national price range.

Condition of a piece will obviously affect price. The prices given here assume that a piece is in good condition, with no major restoration, even if the example illustrated clearly shows some damage. Before you buy a repaired, altered, or damaged piece, be sure to adjust the prices given here accordingly. On the other hand, if a piece has an unusual mark or outstanding decoration, it will of course command a much higher price than an average example.

Scarcity also affects value. Rare and early pieces will, other things being equal, command a higher price. For example, since almost all 18th-century, sgraffito-decorated plates from Pennsylvania are in public collections, the few that come on the market sell for astronomical sums. As a general rule, the less often a piece or a type appears on the market the more difficult it is to predict what it will bring. If a piece is rare enough, it is almost impossible to predict what it will sell for. Thus, it is not unusual for a piece of early Bonnin & Morris porcelain to sell for triple its auction estimate simply because the estimate was based on a sale that had taken place several years earlier and under other circumstances.

Prices also rise and fall as types increase or decrease in popularity. At present, blue-and-white spongeware is in great demand, and prices continue to climb. On the other hand, except for the finest pieces, stoneware has become increasingly less expensive in the past few years. In some areas, like redware and Rockinghamware, values have remained consistent over the years, increasing with inflation and as new collectors enter a field. Changes in taste are hard to predict. Buy what you like, and buy the best. That way you are less apt to be affected by fads. Also, the ranges here reflect retail prices in both rural areas and urban communities, where asking prices tend to be higher. Finally, and most important, it should be noted that the prices given here are those for a category of objects represented by the piece illustrated, not prices of the specific object.

Art Pottery

In recent years art pottery has become extremely popular with collectors. As a general rule, the older pieces, fashioned in small studios or in such factories as Rookwood before it grew in size, are the most costly. Moreover, a piece that bears the signature of the artist who decorated it, as well as the company mark, will have a substantially higher value. Early Rookwood, for example, may command as much as $1000 to $2000, while later pieces mass-produced by the same establishment will bring no more than $100. For the novice or a collector with limited funds, there is a variety of vases, planters, and the like for prices ranging from $20 to $50, and made by such factories as Weller, Roseville, and Peters & Reed. Unmarked or unidentified pieces may cost even less, but, as most collectors seek identified examples, these are unlikely to increase greatly in value. Other factors determining price are an uncommon glaze, or the mark of a respected decorator, on an otherwise common form. To understand thoroughly this complex field, collectors should study catalogues and price lists and become familiar with the marks of the major art pottery manufacturers.

 31 Sugar bowl $5–8
 42 Sugar bowl $9–11
116 Water pitcher $30–40
120 Pitcher $90–130
133 Teapot $8–12
134 Coffeepot $65–80
148 Mug $145–165
160 Cup $28–32
166 Compote $80–125
208 Bowl $85–135
278 Tile $300–500
279 Tile $100–200
280 Tile $15–25
281 Tile $25–32
296 Ashtray $11–14
298 Vase $35–42
299 Vase $500–1000
300 Vase $30,000–50,000
301 Vase $750–1500

302 Vase $1000–2000
303 Vase $800–1500
304 Vase $2000–3000
310 Wall pocket $38–44
320 Vase $40–60
321 Hanging flower basket $65–80
322 Centerpiece $35–45
324 Planter $28–32
325 Flower bowl $45–60
327 Bowl $200–250
328 Vase and candleholders $75–100
329 Double bud vase $65–80
331 Lamp base $100–125
332 Candlesticks $45–55 (each)
333 Vase $20–30
337 Teapot $20–25
340 Flower frog $30–35
348 Bookends $100–175 (set)
349 Figurine $60–72
364 Perfume lamp $90–110

Fiestaware, Harlequinware, and Other Modern Ceramics

Most modern ceramics are machine-cast in large quantities and, like Fiestaware or Harlequinware, are produced in lines, or sets of matching pieces. Factors that determine the value of this inexpensive ware are color and pattern. For example, some Fiesta collectors favor red or blue and will pay twice as much or more to acquire pieces in these colors; others look for colors made in smaller quantities and will pay a premium for them. Generally, collectors are most interested in a set of pieces in the same line and color. Unusual or appealing accessories that match the tableware, such as cookie jars, juicers, and even banks, are also moderately priced from $7 to $22. Recently, prices have risen for Art Deco-style pieces because that style is currently fashionable. For example, Art Deco-style bowls and vases are now in the $20 to $50 range, yet with demand are likely to be priced higher. Because there is so much material available, collectors are advised to concentrate on pieces with striking glazes or handsome patterns.

43 Harlequin sugar bowl $10–14
125 Modern pitcher $12–16
131 Modern carafe $15–20
132 Fiesta coffeepot $30–45
141 Harlequin sauceboat $15–21
142 Modern gravy boat $9–13
144 Modern creamer $9–13
146 Fiesta tumbler $15–20
162 Modern cup and saucer $12–16
164 Fiesta demitasse cup and saucer $16–21
185 Fiesta plates $2–12 (each)
186 Fiesta compartment plates $12–17 (each)
187 Fiesta tray $20–30
198 Modern serving bowl $4–6
202 Fiesta deep plate and cream soup cup $12–18 (each)
203 Harlequin oval baking dish $25–35
250 Fiesta egg cup $10–12
252 Harlequin salt and pepper shakers $6–10 (each)
319 Modern vase $20–25

Flint Enamel

The pieces featured here are rare and expensive. Most American flint-enamel ware was made at the United States Pottery in Bennington, Vermont, from 1849 to 1858. Pieces with flint-enamel glaze and Rockingham glaze are often confused, especially because both glazes were used to finish the same types of pottery. Flint enamel was sometimes applied so lightly that it can easily be mistaken for a Rockingham glaze. As a general rule, the presence of flint enamel will make the piece worth from 25 to 100 percent more than it would cost in Rockingham. However, the price will vary with the quality of the flint glaze and the rarity of the example. There are even a few forms that are less common in Rockingham than in flint. The least costly flint-enamel pieces are sugar bowls, chamber pots, and toilet boxes. These can be found in the price range of $150 to $450, generally at the higher end of the scale. More expensive are such things as coffeepots, which may bring about $500, and book flasks, which will range up to $650. A flint-enamel footbath would be a real find at $850 to $1400.

Porcelain

Most porcelain examples that are popular with collectors tend to date from 1875 or later. Although porcelain was made in America before 1800, it was not a commercial success until after the Civil War, and it was too expensive for most people until the late 19th century. When rare, early examples do reach the market, they are costly. An 18th-century Bonnin & Morris sweetmeat dish may bring as much as $65,000 and a hand-painted pitcher from the 1850s often commands $1400 to $2000. Even the wide variety of unglazed, or Parian, porcelain made at the Bennington pottery and elsewhere from 1840 to 1870 regularly sells for prices ranging from $100 to $3000. Yet it is possible to find late-19th-century creamers at $35 to $65, small trinket boxes for $25 to $50, and even Parian statuettes for as little as $60 to $90. The presence of a maker's mark will greatly increase the cost of even the most ordinary piece, and it distinguishes American examples from similar English or European ones. While 19th-century porcelain has long been popular, most people still ignore the porcelain that was made from 1900 to 1940. Some transfer-decorated tableware pieces, for example, cost as little as $1 to $4. A modest investment in this area may pay off in future years. Other collectors of recent porcelain prefer figural pieces, birds and the like, produced by such artists as Boehm.

106 Creamer $35–65
107 Hand-painted pitcher $1400–2000
109 Presentation pitcher $2500–4250
114 Pitchers $200–400 (left); $150–300 (right)
115 Pitcher $125–300
135 Coffeepot $100–150
145 Beaker $75–100
153 Presentation mug $160–275
165 Cup and saucer $600–800
180 Commemorative plate $1100–1500
184 Transfer-decorated saucer $1–4
193 Oyster plate $900–1300
195 Belleek bonbon dish $165–235
196 Sweetmeat dish $55,000–65,000
200 Hand-painted salad bowl $175–220
287 Bank $300–500
294 Trinket boxes $75–100 (each)
305 Belleek vase $2500–4000
306 Commemorative vase $10,000–15,000
308 Parian vase $75–100
309 Vase $40–90
339 Hand-painted bird $600–1000
361 Parian statuettes $75–100 (each)
362 Parian statuette $5000–7000
363 Parian bust $2500–3500
367 Doll's head $85–120

Redware

Red earthenware is available in a great variety of forms and prices, from bean pots that sell for about $15 to plates that may cost more than $24,000. It is the decoration, however, not the form, that sets the price. Generally, the most elaborately decorated pieces, such as sgraffito plates and jars from Pennsylvania or slip-decorated pie plates and platters from New England and Pennsylvania, are the most expensive. On the other hand, simple jars, bowls, and miniatures can be found for very little. In the middle range are handsome crocks, pots, banks, inkwells, and the like that bring several hundred dollars. A piece is likely to cost more in the area where it was produced than elsewhere, especially if it has unusual incised or slip decoration. Other factors affecting price include the rarity of a form and whether it has an interesting history. Since most redware is unsigned, the presence of a recognized potter's mark on any piece will double or triple its value.

3 Jar $600–850
9 Crock $300–375
10 Butter pot $280–360
11 Butter pot $200–285
28 Jar $240–330
33 Herb pot $285–345
36 Bean pot $22–35
37 Bean pot $25–40
38 Miniature bean pot $12–20
39 Herb jar $275–400
40 Jar $2500–10,000
41 Sugar bowl $6500–12,000
44 Bowl $160–220
45 Miniature churn $260–350

Rockinghamware

Pottery with a Rockingham glaze has been collected for several decades, and generally prices have stabilized at rather high levels. The most desirable and thus costly examples are those with the mottled brown-yellow "tortoiseshell" glaze rather than those with the dark brown finish that was often used in later years. Made in a variety of forms, pieces such as mantel figures shaped like lions, deer, and cows may command as much as $1000 to $35,000, yet common, unmarked utilitarian objects, such as doorknobs, soap dishes, and spittoons, often cost less than $75. In the middle range, from about $75 to more than $700, collectors may acquire not only the usual pie plates and mixing bowls but also a host of less common items, such as candlesticks, cow-shaped creamers, water coolers, vases, book-shaped flasks, and even footbaths. The value of an object is increased if it bears a pottery mark; most marked pieces were made at Bennington, Vermont, although examples from Maryland, Ohio, and elsewhere may also be found. Many collectors prefer to buy Rockingham at general antiques auctions where it often brings much less than in the rather specialized shops handling these pieces.

27 Tobacco jar $250–400
30 Pipkin $350–550
110 Pitchers $200–350 (each)
111 Creamer $75–100
112 Pitcher $175–245
117 Toby pitchers $150–275 (left); $20–25 (right)
138 Teapot $60–150
156 Mug $50–90
167 Goblet $250–300
174 Pie plate $75–125
194 Relish dish $125–175
212 Mixing bowl $75–145
236 Baking dish $75–95
242 Mold $250–425
245 Soap dishes $40–75 (each)
259 Water cooler $400–700
262 Miniature pitcher and bowl $200–375
270 Spittoon $50–100
275 Foot warmer $125–225
276 Bedpan $75–150
282 Desk set $4000–5000
283 Book flask $350–500
290 Doorknobs $25–50 (each)
313 Vase or spoon holder $175–275
330 Candlesticks $350–550 (set)
343 Mantel decoration $2500–3500
344 Cow creamer $150–250
350 Inkwell $250–320
352 Mantel figure $2000–3300
353 Mantel figure $1000–2000
354 Paperweight $225–400
355 Bookends $300–450 (set)
358 Toby snuff jar $250–350
359 Bottles $400–1000 (each)

Spongeware and Spatterware

Spongeware and the earlier, rarer, and more sophisticated spatterware are much sought after by collectors, and as a result, prices have risen sharply. The origin of a piece does not appear to affect value; both types were made here and in England, and few examples are marked. The key factor in determining price is color, with blue on white the prized combination. Any form decorated with blue on white will bring 2 to 3 times the price of a similar piece in brown and white or green and yellow. Form is also important in setting price. Collectors who will pay $300 or more for a blue-on-white pitcher and bowl might give as much as $400 for a rare blue-on-white water cooler. Common, straight-sided water pitchers in brown, green, and tan will bring $75 to $150, but those in blue on white command twice the price. Some spongeware is less costly: custard cups and small creamers can be found in the $12 to $45 range, mugs for as little as $60, and small bowls and crocks for $70 to $100. However, considering that most of this ware was factory-made within the past 100 years, prices must be regarded as somewhat inflated. Collectors should seek the less costly colors rather than the expensive blue-on-white examples and keep an eye out for those with 3 colors, such as red and blue on white, which are much rarer than most collectors realize.

      1 Slop jar $135–170
      2 Water cooler $220–260
     25 Crock $75–110
     32 Bean pot $185–215
     98 Jug $110–135
    122 Pitcher $85–150
    123 Creamer $45–70
    147 Soda fountain mug $75–95
    157 Mug $60–80
    177 Plate $500–650
    178 Plate $75–125
    210 Serving bowl $70–100
    213 Serving dish $90–120
    214 Mixing bowl $125–210
    221 Covered bowl $300–375
    222 Baking dish $275–325
    228 Covered serving dish $140–175
    229 Deep dish $235–315
    247 Custard cups $12–15 (each)
    261 Pitcher and bowl $275–350
    272 Spittoon $75–95
    286 Bank $90–120
    342 Piggy bank $75–110

Stoneware

Pieces made of stoneware are available in many forms, in great quantity, and in a price range broad enough to appeal to all collectors. The most valuable examples, costing as much as $7500, are those with elaborate, finely crafted embellishments, such as incised or cobalt-blue slip decoration. Early ovoid jugs, crocks, and water coolers with skillfully rendered decoration are also priced in the thousands. On the other hand, plain crocks, mugs, jars, and pots in a brown or salt glaze can be purchased for as little as $15 to $20. Moderately priced crocks, jugs, and other forms that have simple decoration are available in the $100 to $150 range. The price is little affected by the presence of a pottery mark, because so much stoneware was marked by its maker. Nor is the value increased for a piece with an unusual form. Quite uncommon types, such as doorstops, soap dishes, flasks, and miniatures can often be found for under $100. Generally speaking, except for the finer pieces, prices remain stable and reasonable in this field.

 4 Crock $4000–5500
 5 Crock $285–365
 6 Cream pot $400–550
 7 Cream pot $250–325
 8 Cream pot $1500–3000
12 Crock $135–215
13 Butter pot $400–550
14 Butter pot $225–300
15 Butter pot $750–900
16 Butter pot $175–275
17 Butter pot $300–400
18 Butter pot $675–775
19 Crock $3800–4500
20 Crock $6000–7500
22 Crock $2–3
23 Cake pot $12–15
26 Pot $25–45
34 Bean pot $22–32
35 Bean pot $13–18
50 Preserve jar $100–125
51 Preserve jars $120–145 (each)
52 Preserve jars $80–110 (each)
53 Preserve jar $25–40
55 Fruit jar $115–135
59 Churn $55–70
60 Churn $335–425
61 Crock $125–200
62 Crock $300–600
63 Hot-water bottle $45–65
64 Chicken waterer $30–50
65 Water cooler $250–350
68 Rundlet $800–925
71 Ink bottle $25–35
72 Ginger beer bottles $15–25 (each)
75 Flask $55–70
76 Bottle $130–175
78 Corker $14–22
79 Miniature jugs $65–90 (left); $7–10 (right)
81 Jugs $65–90 (each)
84 Miniature jug $18–25
85 Jug $395–460
87 Jug $5000–6200
88 Jug $550–925
89 Jug $265–330
90 Presentation jug $300–375
91 Jug $300–425
92 Jug $60–90
94 Molasses jug $45–75
96 Jug $15–20
97 Jug $50–80
99 Pitcher $350–475

101 Pitcher $45–60
103 Miniature pitcher $90–120
104 Pitcher $750–900
113 Pitcher $165–235
119 Sewer-tile pitchers $90–130 (each)
126 Pitcher $30–45
129 Batter jar $35–55
130 Batter jar $300–450
149 Commemorative mug $160–220
150 Mug $55–80
168 Sewer-tile goblet $75–115
207 Batter bowl $75–100
215 Serving bowl $25–40
219 Mixing bowls $13–18 (each)
223 Baking dish $9–16
224 Deep dish $17–25
226 Mixing bowl $90–130
227 Cake pot $225–300
244 Miniature mold $45–60
253 Transfer-decorated spice jar $20–35
254 Rolling pin $55–85
257 Meat tenderizer $70–120
266 Chamber pot $20–28
267 Spittoon $215–265
285 Ink bottles $8–14 (each)
288 Bank $65–80
291 Sander $185–235
293 Inkwell $65–85
297 Pipes $9–15 (each)
307 Vase $35–60
316 Flowerpot $285–345
317 Flowerpot $35–50
338 Bank $3500–4200
356 Spaniel $135–200
360 Mantel figures $475–600 (set)

White Earthenware, Ironstone, Majolica, and Scroddledware

Few collectors have so far shown any great interest in American ironstone china and the less durable white earthenware. Consequently prices are low, and the field offers a real opportunity for collectors. Table settings and serving dishes are most common and least expensive. Plates at $1 to $4, cups at $2 to $3, soup bowls at $2 to $5, and platters at $10 to $15 are just some of the bargains available. Although many pieces are marked by their makers, the presence of a mark, though clearly desirable, has seldom increased prices. However, matching sets of marked ware are most likely to increase in value. While there is nothing really expensive in the field, those seeking something a bit more exotic might focus on commemorative plates priced at $60 to $250 and unusual objects such as paperweights in the form of eagles, which fetch $200 to $300. Less often seen and therefore desirable are coffeepots, covered serving bowls, and compotes; none are expensive today. Prices in this area can really only go up, so now is the time to buy.

105 Commemorative creamer $60–85
108 Presentation pitcher $150–250
121 Pitcher $25–40
143 Transfer-decorated gravy boat $4–9

154 Mug $15–23
161 Transfer-decorated cup $2–3
163 Cup and saucer $150–250
176 Pie plate $17–25
179 Plate $1–4
181 Commemorative plate $100–175
182 Transfer-decorated plate $175–250
183 Hand-painted plate $1–3
191 Platter $10–17
192 Transfer-decorated bone dish $3–5
197 Vegetable bowl $2–4
199 Serving bowl $2–3
201 Soup bowl $2–5
205 Compote $15–20
232 Deep dish $6–9
235 Decorated serving dish $200–400
251 Egg cup $3–5
260 Pitcher and bowl $700–1000
334 Paperweight $300–500

Yellowware

Except for a few rare and costly types—cow creamers at $250 to $350 and early marked coffeepots at $2000 to $3500—yellowware is appealing to new collectors with modest means. The typical yellowware collection will consist of slip-banded bowls at $25 to $40 each, molds in the $40 to $90 range, and custard cups that are a bargain at $4 to $16. "Nesting" pieces are less expensive if they are bought individually rather than as a set. Other common and reasonably priced objects are pie plates, batter bowls, serving dishes, and such humble objects as bedpans and cuspidors. However, marked pieces are at a premium, since yellowware rarely bears the mark of an American manufacturer. They will bring as much as ten times the price of a similar unmarked example. Unusual forms are apt to command higher prices too. Some collectors are willing to pay $100 or more for such items as pipkins, rolling pins, colanders, and rundlets. Although collectors continue to enter this field, yellowware is generally abundant and moderately priced.

 21 Crock $100–135
 24 Crock $70–95
 54 Preserve jar $85–135
 70 Rundlet $110–140
 95 Miniature jug $12–18
118 Figural pitcher $85–135
124 Pitcher $35–55
128 Pipkin $125–200
139 Coffeepot $2000–3500
155 Mug $65–85
175 Pie plate $35–55
188 Baking dish $55–80
204 Batter bowl $45–70
209 Bowls $25–40 (each)
216 Bowl $225–300
217 Mixing bowls $15–40 (one bowl); $240–320 (set)
220 Mixing bowl $12–26
225 Covered bowl $45–70
233 Deep dish $30–55
234 Serving bowl $55–75

238 Colanders $180–250 (each)
239 Mold $45–70
240 Mold $60–90
243 Mold $40–55
246 Custard cups $4–8 (each)
249 Custard cup $11–16
255 Rolling pin $90–130
265 Chamber pot $60–75
269 Spittoon $55–75
277 Bedpan $25–45
345 Cow creamer $250–350

Picture Credits

Photographers

All photographs were taken by Schecter Me Sun Lee with the exception of the following: 4, 8, 18, 19, 20, 40, 41, 62, 87, 90, 107, 109, 139, 140, 145, 163, 165, 173, 180, 182, 193, 195, 196, 200, 256, 258, 274, 278, 279, 299, 300, 301, 302, 303, 304, 305, 306, 307, 311, 314, 336, 338, 339, 341, 362, 363. Chun Y. Lai photographed 4, 19, and 20, and Raymond Errett photographed 274.

Collections

The following individuals and institutions kindly allowed us to reproduce objects from their collections:

Marna Anderson Gallery, New York City: 4, 19, 20.

William M. Beck, Richmond, Virginia: 61.

Ruth Bigel Antiques, New York City: 111.

The Brooklyn Museum, Brooklyn, New York: 8, Clement Collection; 40, gift of Christine V. Ness, H. Randolph Lever Fund, the Alfred T. and Caroline S. Zoebisch Fund and Others; 41, gift of Mrs. Huldah Cail Lorimer, in memory of George Burford Lorimer; 62, gift of Mrs. Ivar Paulsen and H. Randolph Lever Fund; 107, gift of Mrs. Franklin Chace and Ditk S. Ramsay Fund; 109, gift of Miss Alice Corey Robertson; 139, H. Randolph Lever Fund; 140, Dick S. Ramsay Fund; 145, anonymous gift; 163, The Emily Winthrop Miles Collection; 165, gift of Mrs. Luke Vincent Lockwood; 173; 180, gift of Mrs. Carlotta Dorflinger Atkinson, in memory of her father, Christian Dorflinger; 182, Museum Collection Fund; 193, H. Randolph Lever Fund; 195, Clement Collection; 196, Museum Collection Fund; 200, gift of Franklin Chace; 256, gift of Mrs. Huldah Cail Lorimer, in memory of George Burford Lorimer; 258, Clement Collection; 303, gift of Mrs. Carll H. DeSilver; 305, gift of Mrs. Willard C. Brinton; 306, gift of Carll and Franklin Chace, in memory of their mother, Pastora Forest Smith Chace, daughter of Thomas Carll Smith; 311, H. Randolph Lever Fund; 314, gift of Christine V. Ness, H. Randolph Lever Fund, the Alfred T. and Caroline S. Zoebisch Fund and Others; 336, 338, gift of Mrs. Huldah Cail Lorimer, in memory of George Burford Lorimer; 339, gift of Dr. and Mrs. Herman S. Alpert; 341, gift of Christine V. Ness, H. Randolph Lever Fund, the Alfred T. and Caroline S. Zoebisch Fund and Others; 362, gift of Franklin Chace; 363, H. Randolph Lever Fund.

Robert and Marie Condon: 27, 29, 30, 92, 104, 106, 108, 112, 114, 115, 117, 135, 136, 137, 153, 167, 194, 242, 259, 260, 262, 264, 275, 282, 283, 287, 290, 294, 295, 308, 309, 313, 330, 334, 343, 344, 345, 350, 353, 354, 358, 359, 361.

Fran and Douglas Faulkner: 1, 2, 5, 6, 7, 12, 13, 15, 16, 17, 25, 32, 34, 48, 50, 51, 52, 53, 59, 60, 64, 72, 79, 81, 88, 89, 91, 94, 96, 97, 98, 99, 110, 122, 123, 127, 129, 130, 154, 157, 159, 176, 188, 201, 204, 207, 212, 213, 215, 218, 219, 221, 226, 227, 228, 235, 236, 237, 238, 240, 241, 245, 246, 247, 253, 254, 257, 261, 265, 266, 267, 268, 289, 291, 315, 316, 317, 342, 356.

Osna Fenner: 31, 42, 43, 116, 120, 125, 131, 132, 133, 134, 141, 142, 144, 146, 148, 160, 162, 164, 166, 174, 185, 186, 187, 198, 202, 203, 208, 250, 252, 276, 280, 281, 296, 298, 310, 319, 320, 321, 322, 323, 324, 325, 326, 327, 328, 329, 331, 332, 333, 335, 337, 340, 347, 348, 349, 364, 365, 366.

George Hamell: 3, 9, 10, 18, 39, 45, 49, 56, 73, 102, 113, 118, 119, 158, 168, 170, 171, 181, 206, 231, 284, 351, 355, 357, 360.

Samuel Herrup, Brooklyn, New York: 11, 28, 33, 44, 57, 77, 86, 128, 151, 152, 190, 211.

Jordan-Volpe Gallery, New York City: 278 (Collection Ruth and Seymour Geringer), 279, 299, 300, 301, 302.

Kelter-Malcé Antiques, New York City: 147, 209, 210, 286.

William C. Ketchum, Jr.: 26, 47, 65, 68, 69, 74, 76, 78, 80, 82, 85, 161.

The Metropolitan Museum of Art: 304, gift of Marcia and William Goodman, 1981 (photo, courtesy Jordan-Volpe Gallery, New York).

Richard Moore: 21, 24, 54, 55, 71, 101, 105, 126, 138, 155, 156, 205, 214, 220, 223, 224, 229, 232, 233, 270, 272.

Museum of American Folk Art: 172, promised anonymous gift; 352, gift of Mrs. Gertrude Schweitzer.

Private Collections: 14, 22, 23, 35, 36, 37, 38, 58, 63, 66, 67, 70, 75, 84, 85, 87, 90, 95, 100, 103, 121, 124, 143, 149, 150, 175, 179, 183, 184, 191, 192, 197, 199, 216, 217, 225, 234, 239, 243, 244, 248, 249, 251, 255, 263, 269, 271, 273, 277, 285, 288, 293, 297, 307, 318.

George E. Schoellkopf: 46, 93, 169, 177, 178, 189, 222, 230, 292, 312, 346.

The Margaret Woodbury Strong Museum, Rochester, New York: 274, 367.

Index

Numbers refer to color plates.

Staff

Prepared and produced by Chanticleer Press, Inc.
Publisher: Paul Steiner
Editor-in-Chief: Gudrun Buettner
Managing Editor: Susan Costello
Project Editor: Mary Beth Brewer
Assistant Editor: Cathy Peck
Art Director: Carol Nehring
Art Assistants: Ayn Svoboda and Karen Wollman
Production: Helga Lose, Amy Roche, and Alex von Hoffmann
Picture Library: Edward Douglas
Drawings: Paul Singer
Design: Massimo Vignelli

The Knopf Collectors' Guides to American Antiques

Also available in this unique full-color format:

Chairs, Tables, Sofas & Beds
by Marvin D. Schwartz

Chests, Cupboards, Desks & Other Pieces
by William C. Ketchum, Jr.

Folk Art: Paintings, Sculpture & Country Objects
by Robert Bishop and Judith Reiter Weissman

Glass Tableware, Bowls & Vases
by Jane Shadel Spillman

Quilts, Coverlets, Rugs & Samplers
by Robert Bishop